PRONOUNCING

& PERSEVERING

LANGUAGE AND LEGAL DISCOURSE
A series edited by William M. O'Barr and John M. Conley

PRONOUNCING & PERSEVERING

Gender and the Discourses of Disputing in an African Islamic Court

SUSAN F. HIRSCH

THE UNIVERSITY OF CHICAGO PRESS / CHICAGO & LONDON

SUSAN F. HIRSCH is associate professor of anthropology and women's studies at Wesleyan University. She is the coeditor of *Contested States: Law, Hegemony, and Resistance.*

The University of Chicago Press, Chicago 60637
The University of Chicago Press, Ltd., London
© 1998 by The University of Chicago
All rights reserved. Published 1998
Printed in the United States of America
07 06 05 04 03 02 01 00 99 98   5 4 3 2 1

ISBN (cloth): 0-226-34463-0
ISBN (paper): 0-226-34464-9

Library of Congress Cataloging-in-Publication Data

Hirsch, Susan F.
    Pronouncing and persevering : gender and discourses in an African Islamic court / Susan F. Hirsch.
        p.   cm.
    Includes bibliographical references and index.
    ISBN 0-226-34463-0 (cloth). — ISBN 0-226-34464-9 (paper)
    1. Domestic relations (Islamic law)—Language. 2. Courts, Islamic—Kenya—Language. 3. Swahili language—Sex differences. 4. Language and languages—Sex differences. 5. Sex role.
    I. Title.
    LAW
    340.5'9—DC21   97-45178
                                                          CIP

FOR MY PARENTS
Arnold Wayne Hirsch and Rena Jean Fiedler Hirsch

Anenae kuwa pendo
si faida ni uvundo

Huyo yukatika mwendo
wa ujinga na ubaya

Mapenzi ndiyo asili
ya watu kuwa wawili

Nalau kama si hili
usingekoma ubaya.

Whoever says love
isn't worthwhile, it's rotten,

S/he is following a path
of stupidity and evil.

Being lovers is surely the base
for two people uniting

And if theirs is not like that
evil would not be prevented.

(FROM A SONG BY BHALO)

Contents

APPENDIXES

Acknowledgments

This book is about gender relations and disputing in coastal Kenya. It focuses primarily on Swahili Muslim people in the two largest coastal towns, Malindi and Mombasa. The disputes, which involve Islamic laws of marriage and divorce, provide rich and revealing perspectives on the negotiation of gender relations during domestic conflict. Yet the volume's attention to conflict perhaps risks overemphasizing the extent of marital difficulties experienced by Swahili people. Thus, at the outset, I offer the poetic epigram, from a song performed by Ahmed Kassim Juma Bhalo (coastal Kenya's Frank Sinatra figure), as a reminder of the intense love aspired to, achieved, and celebrated by many Swahili Muslim couples. As I conducted research for this book, examples of that love greatly influenced my approach, and I am grateful for the opportunity to have come to understand, as best I can, the range of emotions surrounding Swahili marriages, including the pleasure of companionship and passion and the pain of longing and rupture. In the broadest sense, this book explores the language of intense emotional connections between people and, in so doing, delineates how negotiating such connections constructs and transforms men, women, and gender relations. My ability to address this topic has depended first and foremost on the Swahili Muslim people who welcomed me, educated me, and offered me insight into their lives and their loves. *Ahsante sana*. Many thanks.

Several institutions made possible the research on which this volume is based. Conducted over several years, the research was funded by a Shell–Duke University International Studies Dissertation Research Grant and awards from the Duke University Graduate School, the Charlotte Newcombe Foundation, the Northwestern University Law and Social Science Program, and the American Bar Foundation.

In Kenya, the Office of the President granted me permission to conduct research, for which I am grateful. My affiliation with the Department of African Languages and Linguistics at the University of Nairobi led to valuable contacts with Dr. Mohammed Abdulaziz, Dr. Karega Mutahi, Dr. Lucia Omondi, and other colleagues. Former lecturer and former political prisoner Katama Mkangi afforded me a deep and lasting understanding of the political implications of academic work.

Members of the Kenyan judiciary shared with me their understandings of how law works in Kenya and thereby shaped my project. I am grateful to Chief Kadhi Nassor Nahdy for teaching me about Islamic law and offering me advice and opinions in a highly engaging manner. Kadhi Ali Mwenzagu also helped me enormously; with his calm demeanor, he never failed to impress me with the wisdom behind his judicial practice. Several other kadhis also shared their insights with me. I have tremendous respect for the knowledge, compassion, and understanding of human nature that inform the kadhis' work. Court clerks, especially Najima and Ali, were always willing to provide their valuable perspectives on conflicts and the legal system.

In Mombasa, Sheikh Ahmed Nabahany first opened my eyes to the beauty and dignity of Swahili culture. Over the years he has provided advice and assistance, and his family has been warm and welcoming. My thanks to them. Many people in Malindi welcomed me into their homes and helped me to understand their lives, and, though I thank some of them by name below, I conceal their identities in the text. I am especially grateful to the following elders and their families: Mzee Ali Mpaza, Mzee Bamkuu Athman Bamkuu, Mzee Basaini Kali Bamkuu, former kadhi Sheikh Gosso Ibrahim Gosso, Mzee Mohamed Abdallah Bulushy, and Bibi Aisha Vai. Munira Ali provided valuable assistance during my research. Shamsa Ali helped make my life in Malindi enjoyable and remains a friend who is more like a sister. Abdulrahman Mohamed Abdalla has always been ready with a quote from Bhalo or a religious text to help me appreciate the intricacies of coastal culture and the powerful message of Islam. I thank Jamal for over ten years of wise counsel, welcome diversion, and careful consideration of and correction to this manuscript.

I want to thank several people who have influenced me through their personal encouragement as well as their writings: Virginia Dominguez, Sally Merry, Susan Philips, Donald Brenneis, Judith Irvine, and John Comaroff. Naomi Quinn, whom I greatly admire, has been an especially important influence on my development as a scholar/teacher.

I could not have completed this project without the emotional support and intellectual stimulation provided by friends in and out of the academy. My thanks to Mindie Lazarus-Black, Christopher Mesnooh, Susan Shapiro, Regina Schuller, Betty Bayer, Ruth Boscov, and Betsy Spragg Geherin. Mary Porter has enriched this project with her expertise on coastal Kenya; our friendship is a treasure to me. Steven Gregory is an inspiring colleague and a dear friend.

My colleagues in Wesleyan's Department of Anthropology have been patient and supportive, especially Elizabeth Traube. Weekly writing sessions with Claire Potter contributed to the completion of this manuscript, and my friendship with Karen Bock made the process enjoyable. Sue Fisher, Cynthia Horan, and Sara Ohly encouraged me when I most needed it. I am grateful to Ashraf Rushdy for reading parts of the manuscript; his thoughtful advice and caring friendship are invaluable to me. Joanne Palmer graciously gave me a much-needed hand at critical moments. Several Wesleyan undergraduates assisted in the editing process, including Lauren Blanchard, Abby Elbow, Susannah Hand, and a class of anthropology majors who urged me to make my book both intelligent and intelligible.

I owe much to the series editors, William O'Barr and John Conley, whose work I greatly admire. John's editorial suggestions clarified and thereby improved the manuscript. Mack O'Barr's work on law and language, and his interest in East Africa, have inspired me and led to many fruitful conversations and adventures on several continents. Thanks to him and to his family for their hospitality over the years.

Two anonymous reviewers provided by the University of Chicago Press offered detailed and insightful comments that helped me to make significant improvements to the manuscript. Thanks to them and to John Tryneski and his staff, who have been enormously helpful and professional.

This book is dedicated to my parents, who have always encouraged me to pursue my interests, and my career; I thank them for their love and support. My gratitude goes as well to my brothers, my sisters-in-law, and especially my four wonderful nieces, who are stimulating reminders of the challenges of writing about gender for the next generation.

It will come as no surprise to Kenyan Swahili people that I ask forgiveness ("Samehani"), from them and everyone else, for any mistake, omission, or offense in the pages that follow.

If the law prohibits, in general, a woman from holding personal intercourse of any sort with a strange man, it makes two exceptions, in favour of the sovereign and of the judge.

EMILY RUETE (FORMERLY SALAMAH BINT SAID),
A ZANZIBARI MUSLIM, WRITING ON SWAHILI CUSTOMS
FOR EUROPEAN READERS (RUETE 1886:33).

Introduction

When I began research on gender and law in the coastal city of Mombasa, Kenya, an Islamic judge expressed his concern that my project might depict Islam as oppressing Muslim women. He cautioned me against replicating the distortions of Islam in the media coverage of the 1985 United Nations Decade for Women Conference, which was held in Nairobi. He suggested that I refrain from measuring Muslim women's status against my American ideas about women's liberation. His gentle though firm counsel—the first of many similar warnings I received from Swahili Muslims in the following months—not only challenged me to interrogate the feminist position that framed my research but also made me keenly aware of the power of the categories through which Muslim women are defined in local and global discourses.

The judge's rejection of simplistic comparisons of women's status across cultures and religions bears some similarity to Chandra Mohanty's condemnation (1991) of the tendency in feminist writing to depict "oppressed Third World Women" as subordinate, virtually invisible counterparts of their more liberated Western sisters. As Mohanty charges, such dichotomies reinforce hierarchical stereotypes that rank the West above "Third World" countries. They mask or deny the power relations connecting women across lines of religion, nation, and other allegiances, and they generally elide global and local complexities and variations in women's experiences. In so doing, they reproduce dichotomies that render those women who are designated oppressed as devoid of agency, that is, as lacking the cultural, economic, and linguistic resources to alter their lives.

At the Nairobi conference, many participants directed attention to the legal status of women across societies and depicted it as a telling diacritic of the agency, or the lack thereof, of women living under particular legal systems. Increasingly, in Euro-American scholarship, popular culture, and other media, stereotypic images of Muslim women

1

specify Islamic law as central to their "oppressed" status. For example, portrayals of "benighted" Muslim women in the mainstream media coverage of the Gulf War (see Enloe 1993), popular films like *Not without My Daughter,* and some academic writings depict Muslim women as victims of patriarchal Islamic laws that regulate them into homes and behind veils, with little claim to legal rights. Such portrayals emphasize Muslim women's silence in the face of laws that deny them the agency to transform their lives, and these laws are measured against the legal protections enjoyed by Western Liberated Woman, a.k.a. Rights-Bearing Woman. It is as if the veils in which Muslim women are frequently depicted and, similarly, the laws that are assumed to surround them prevent, preclude, or muffle any protest that Muslim women might make of their circumstances. Popular and scholarly treatments of these images suggest that Western women (liberated through law) are positioned to speak for Muslim women (silenced through law), which is precisely the impression that the judge and other coastal Muslims sought to steer me away from.

I invoke these images with the presumption that those who write or read texts about Islam and gender orient to this powerful though problematic dichotomy. The images are pervasive—"commonsense" understandings for some and debilitating stereotypes for others. Late in the nineteenth century, Emily Ruete, the daughter of a Muslim sultan, confronted a similar pernicious dichotomy. After growing up in Zanzibar, Ruete married a German nobleman, moved with him to Europe, and gave one of the first accounts of life in a harem written by a Muslim woman for a European audience (Ruete 1886). Her apologies for Islam provided a counterpoint to Europe's misperceptions of the religion. Assumptions about Muslim women's segregation occasioned Ruete's claim that women have access to sovereigns and judges (see epigraph). Yet her account vacillated between apologizing for the Islam of European stereotypes and wrestling with a deep ambivalence about life in her father's house. The multiple and, as her critics charge, contradictory perspectives in her text call into question a simplistic dichotomous portrayal of Muslim and non-Muslim women.

By examining gender, discourse, and Islamic law in the cultural area of Ruete's origin, I intend to further disrupt the simplistic dichotomy of Muslim women as the silenced Others of Western women. Moreover, I question a related dichotomy, referred to in this book's title, that depicts Muslim women as silenced in comparison to Muslim men. The images of a Muslim husband pronouncing divorce and his persevering wife silently accepting the decree are ideologically salient subject positions in Kenyan Swahili society. Husbands are authorized to make the legal pronouncement of divorce, the most appropriate means of ending marriage. Persevering wives are expected to endure marital hardships without complaint and to accept divorce in the same spirit. These gendered images are discursively constructed through Islamic law and through Swahili cultural understandings of how the legal and social positions of husband and wife entitle and require individuals to behave in gendered ways. Yet, in the postcolonial period, these images are neither rigid molds to which everyone conforms nor antiquated ideals easily ignored or dismissed. Although they configure significant subject positions through which Swahili marital relations are enacted and to which couples orient themselves in domestic disputes, husbands and wives sometimes reproduce and sometimes contest these roles. By acknowledging the cultural force of the pronouncing husband and the persevering wife and also exploring how new social relations are effected through and against these positions, I expose the limits of their hegemony in postcolonial Swahili society.

In directing attention to the process whereby gendered subject positions are negotiated in Swahili marital disputes, my project asserts that gender is made, remade, and transformed in fundamental ways through legal institutions and the discourses of disputing. The process of negotiating through and against gendered subject positions in legal arenas contributes to the construction and transformation of gender in Swahili society. The challenge of conceptualizing this process raises important questions: What are the dynamics of constituting gendered subjectivity in legal contexts? How do legal institutions and discourses define people as subjects in complex and contradictory ways? What barriers and limits do legal processes pose for the reproduction or transformation of gendered roles and relations?

Addressing these questions requires attention to discourse in its forms as interactive speech and as broader "ways of knowing" (or epistemologies) that shape understandings of social life. The law, as an institutional discourse that shapes approaches to social life, gives form to gendered subject positions and sets the parameters for who should speak, where, and when. Yet, from culturally and institutionally defined positions, speakers interact in ways that sometimes transform assumptions about their gendered status. Gender is constituted in legal contexts in ways that reproduce and also undermine dominant cultural configurations of gendered subjects and gender relations. I examine this dynamic process through the close analysis of specific disputes, showing how gender is constructed at the microlevel of interaction yet always in relation to broader discourses that define how gendered people can and should speak. The negotiation of gender through disputing can only be understood by examining the subtle dynamics of interaction in courts and other disputing contexts; however, the particular ways in which people dispute in the postcolonial period in coastal Kenya, including in Islamic courts, have had a significant effect on Swahili gender relations. Accordingly, my analysis situates disputes within the complex array of local and global power relations that configure Swahili society.

The following section introduces my approach to Swahili disputing by presenting a case from the Islamic court, or Kadhi's Court, in Mombasa, Kenya, one of the sites where I conducted anthropological research. Subsequent sections briefly describe that research and outline the plan of the book.

A Typical and Atypical Case

The kadhi (Islamic judge) who gave me wise counsel presided over Case 103 of 1985, which was heard in the Mombasa Kadhi's Court two months before I began my research. Writing up the case file by hand, he entered the following requests made by Rehema, a Swahili woman in her thirties: "a) payment of past maintenance for children and plaintiff; b) maintenance for children; c) dissolution of marriage; d) court costs." The kadhi next summarized the brief hearing in which Rehema justified these claims made against her husband, Soud. She described her marital life, which included abandonment by Soud, who did not appear in court even though he had been served with a summons. The kadhi's summary included a translated portion of Rehema's testimony: "He [Soud] neglected me and he does not maintain me and his children. He is a drunkard. I want the divorce and the custody because the marriage is irretrievably broken. The life is miserable." Other facts attributed to Rehema's testimony and that of two other witnesses filled out a picture of an abysmal home life in which Soud shirked his legal obligation to support the family, abused Rehema physically and emotionally, and finally deserted the home. The last entry in the file was a judgment in Rehema's favor that granted all her requests.

About one quarter of all cases in the Kenyan Kadhi's Courts resemble Rehema's in that they involve a wife who, having been abandoned by her husband, seeks the court's help in obtaining a divorce. Almost all of these women win judgments in their favor. Marriage laws set out the rights and duties that partially define the cultural categories of male and female. More specifically, the terms, limits, and possibilities of being male or female are constituted through subject positions that reflect both gendered and legal status, such as wife, father, "battered woman," or "virginal bride," the latter specifically relevant in Islamic communities. But these categories are simultaneously open to reinterpretation as wives and husbands experience conflict. Subject positions other than the persevering wife and the pronouncing husband emerge through disputing processes where men and women might have different access to counsel, forms of speech, or familiarity with legal discourse. Through disputing, opposing parties recreate themselves as subjects and, like Rehema, are potentially transformed as gendered beings.

Rehema, and Swahili women like her, attempt to alter their life circumstances through telling stories about domestic conflict in courts and other disputing contexts. The central role of narrated "talk about trouble" in legal proceedings has been noted by many scholars (see, e.g., Brenneis 1988; Briggs 1988b; Conley and O'Barr 1990; Mertz 1994; Yngvesson 1993). In cases and mediations, most disputants tell narrated accounts of their problems, which serve as the base for accomplishing legal tasks (e.g., blaming and mitigation) and for effecting legal and social outcomes. I will argue that stories of domestic conflict are told differently by Swahili men and women and, thus, that accounts of conflict are a critical genre through which gender is constituted in court.

On the basis of a close analysis of the language of disputing in cases and mediations in Kadhi's Courts, I demonstrate that gender is constituted in part through gender differences in the interactional speech produced by disputants. In explaining these differences and assessing their consequences for the making of gender through interaction, as well as in relation to legal outcomes, I build on theories of gender indexing (Ochs 1992). As this approach asserts, complexes of speech features (e.g., styles or genres) that are culturally associated with gendered behavior index, or point to, gender when produced by speakers. By examining how these complexes are generated in context—and how their production sometimes indexes gender in innovative or contradictory ways—this approach allows for and displays the social creativity of language. By telling her story in court, Rehema both creates herself as a wife who has persevered in the face of a bad marriage and also speaks out against her husband. Identifying such complex positionings is particularly relevant in legal contexts, where, as Mertz (1992a, 1994) has argued, social creativity can result from interactive speech that reconfigures the power relations encoded in law and legal processes.

In my first week of conducting research in the Mombasa Law Courts, I read the file for Case 103 and found it unremarkable. Several weeks into my research, this typical case reemerged, taking a bizarre turn. Rehema's ex-husband, Soud, burst into the kadhi's office and demanded to know why his marriage had been dissolved without his knowledge. The kadhi countered that Soud had neglected to appear when the case was heard. Soud explained that he had planned to come until Rehema, on the day before the hearing, told him that she was dropping her claim. When he learned that Rehema had actually come to court and obtained the divorce, he realized that she had lied to him. Soud then confronted the kadhi: "Do you know that Rehema has married someone else? Do you realize that she didn't wait until the end of *edda* before marrying again?" (Under Islamic law, *edda* is a waiting period lasting several months after which a divorced woman or widow is permitted to remarry.) Soud challenged the kadhi to explain why he had facilitated Rehema's adultery.

Clearly startled by this revelation, the kadhi ordered all the parties to court the next day. When they assembled, he castigated Rehema for lying to Soud and for contracting a new marriage before finishing *edda*. To convince her of the seriousness of her actions, he warned that she could be charged with bigamy by the Kenyan state as well as the Islamic court. Over the protests of the new husband, he dissolved Rehema's second marriage. He then set aside his judgment in Case 103, thereby reinstating the marriage between Rehema and Soud. At Rehema's insistence, he set a new date for the divorce case to be heard. All of the parties were told to stay away from each other until the rehearing of the case, which was scheduled for a week later.

My conversations with Rehema, Soud, and the kadhi revealed that they had completely different understandings of the dispute. For Soud, the marital problems primarily concerned money he owed Rehema, which he was trying to pay. He was irritated and embarrassed that the kadhi was involved and astounded that divorce might be the result. For her part, Rehema saw the dispute as the necessary means to free herself from a broken marriage. She wanted to get on with her new marriage to a wealthy man. The kadhi was most troubled about the wrongs that had been committed, possibly within the marriage but more immediately through Rehema's bigamy. He was concerned to clear up the matter before Kenyan government authorities heard about it. His concern reflected the knowledge that the Islamic courts, which operate as part of the Kenyan judicial system, were frequently the target of criticism by a secular state eager to encroach on the Muslim minority community and their legal autonomy.

On the day of the rehearing of Case 103, I watched as Rehema began her testimony confidently. She narrated scenes of turmoil experienced during her marriage with Soud, recreating them through vivid description. Her account culminated in questions blurted out almost hysterically: "What do you think of a man who would sell his own wife? 'Do you want her? For how long? A week?' "

The kadhi interrupted Rehema just as she began to elaborate on the claim that her husband had turned her into a prostitute. He proclaimed that he had heard enough descriptions of shameful behavior and now needed to sort out the issues. Turning to the defendant, who by that point was vehemently protesting Rehema's accusations, the kadhi asked a series of questions designed to get to the bottom of the controversy:

Kadhi: Prove what she said is true or not. Prove it before the court.

Soud: It's true I left the house, but she didn't want to accompany me. I got a loan. I worked. I went to help her family. After her father died, they [plaintiff's family] didn't know how to deal with money. I was paying debts and maintaining all of them. The inheritance |was

Kadhi: |Leave aside talk about the inheritance. [To woman] Did he finally pay you?

Rehema: He didn't give anything. He didn't pay. I did it all. The rent, the loan |installments.

Soud: |I paid maintenance.

Rehema: I have proof of everything.

Kadhi: Now, cruelty?

Soud: I never beat her even once. Her mother should be proof. Her mother forbade it.

Kadhi: You don't drink?

Soud: I don't drink.

Rehema: [Laughter]

Kadhi: Do you go out at night?

Soud: I don't go out at night. If I'm out, I'm just at a wedding.

Kadhi: The other issue, of selling her?

Soud: NO.

The testimony continued with each party producing witnesses who confirmed the two contrasting stories. After several attempts to ascertain what had really occurred in the home, the kadhi gave up. The proceeding ended when he ordered the parties to return to court the next week to hear his judgment.

In the second hearing of Case 103, the disputants' stories took diverse forms. Rehema told an uninterrupted narrative, while Soud's account emerged through conversation with the kadhi. Each party also interjected short narratives to refute points made by others. Given that the court is a site of interaction, where men and women speak in ways that reproduce and transform understandings about gendered speakers, such differences in the presentations of accounts of conflict can operate to index gender. In short, how parties to a dispute interact in court conveys gendered images, constituting gender and also reworking its terms.

The gendered positions that speakers play out through interaction sometimes contrast with representations of gender that emerge through other aspects of discourse. For example, the gendered images that they present of themselves and others *within* their accounts of conflict may be different from the roles they assume in courtroom interaction. In addition, instances of reported speech, such as Rehema's quoting Soud, offer other opportunities for disputants to depict gendered speech, including their own speech in other times and places. My analysis explores the contribution of each of these forms of discourse to the constitution and transformation of gender in legal processes.

Accounting for gender differences in the discourses of legal processes presents a significant challenge. Men and women bring different linguistic resources to Kadhi's Court, and they are positioned differently with respect to the law. These factors shape their speech, as does the legal institution and its personnel. For example, in Case 103, the kadhi was instrumental in directing Soud's participation in the discussion. Rules of evidence and procedure as well as other goals associated with resolving the case motivated his orchestration of the language used in disputing. At times, the kadhi directs the course of interaction through specific comments about speech, such as when he prohibits Rehema from narrating the "shameful things" that happened between her and Soud. This comment expresses an aspect of ideology about language, widely held by Swahili people, that treats narratives of familial conflict as shameful, dangerous, and best left untold. As I will describe, the production of such narratives is linked to women, particularly to those who are considered unable to persevere. How subjects are understood culturally as speakers is, thus, an aspect of gender that influences their participation in legal contexts and, moreover, defines the possibilities those contexts hold for the transformation of gender. In contrast to studies that focus solely on the role of legal institutions in shaping discourse, my analysis directs attention to the cultural understandings about language that shape legal processes.

The discourses produced by participants in legal processes constitute and transform gender in ways that are significant to Swahili social life. Although this justifies attention to the microlevel of linguistic interaction in cases and mediations, the judgments rendered in cases, and the outcomes of other forms of conflict resolution, also make dramatic statements about gender that have lasting consequences for the individuals involved and also for gender relations more broadly.

A week after Case 103 was reheard, the kadhi insisted on silence as he sternly read his judgment. Once again, he ruled in Rehema's favor, justifying his decision to terminate the marriage through a carefully worded ruling:

> Upon hearing the allegations of the parties it is clear that the marriage life is miserable, it does not serve the purpose of the marriage as envisaged by the law. The marital life is wrecked and the home is utterly broken up by misunderstanding, jealousy, cruelty and infidelity. . . . The main aims of the marriage are tranquility, mutual love and mercy and procreation. The aims are lacking in this marriage so it is better to disintegrate the family unit than to wreck the future happiness that has become odious. It is recommended that the husband should retain his wife in kindness or separate in kindness. He should not retain her to injure her. Whereas it is justice to bring about reconciliation so it is justice to terminate marriage ties if reconciliation is impossible. . . . The parties are married under Islamic law. So their marriage including the dissolution should be governed by Islamic law which regards divorce as the last social solution to the marriage crisis. . . . In the light of the situation the marriage is dissolved but that does not mean that the second marriage subsists so, the eda must be observed. Any other claim by any parties should be done with new application. You are allowed to appeal.

Everything about the day of the judgment emphasized the kadhi's authority. After telling everyone to remain silent, he justified his decision by referring to the principles of Islamic law that he was entitled to implement. He offered participants limited options for complying with or contesting his judgment. Finally, when he finished reading the ruling, he ordered Rehema and Soud to leave. Though the kadhi created a spectacle that displayed the court's authority, his authority did not go unchallenged. Opening the door to leave, Soud turned and, pointing at the kadhi, vowed to fight the decision. Rehema responded with a dismissive chuckle, but her concern was apparent.

Soud's challenge reminded all present that the authority of the Kadhi's Courts is, in reality, quite tenuous. Muslim men can wield competing authority by pronouncing some legal decisions outside court or ignoring the court's decisions. Although the kadhis know that those defeated in court rarely appeal their judgments (since the appellate process is expensive, complex, and administered through the secular Kenyan High Court), they are aware that Swahili Muslims are quite critical of Kadhi's Court, which is seen as disempowering men and allowing women to air shameful stories in public. Though judgments appear to end disputes, the discourse that follows (and sometimes continues long after) repositions the courts and their authority in unanticipated ways. Moreover, kadhis are concerned that their authority is challenged not only from below, as ordinary Muslims question the court, but also by virtue of the position of the court (and the Muslim minority community) in a secular state.

Months later, I asked the kadhi if he had heard any more from the participants in Case 103. He informed me that Soud had not returned to court. Rehema was happily remarried, though still seeking child support. But the kadhi admitted that this case continued to disturb him, partly because he felt that Rehema had duped and betrayed him. Initially, he had pitied her and had seen it as his duty to end her perseverance in a bad marriage. But, in the course of the dispute, his impression of her had changed. In addition to her lies, her self-confident comportment in court did not sit right with him. He asked me, "Do you remember how she wore perfume the day of the hearing? She put it on to spite her ex, to drive him crazy." Shaking his head and laughing softly, he asked a question for which he still lacked an answer: "What kind of woman is she?"

In contrast to the Western stereotype of the silent, veiled Muslim woman with no legal status, Swahili women actively pursue claims in court, telling eloquent stories that challenge the circumstances of their lives and their gendered, legal, and linguistic positions. Their stories, and the quite different accounts told by men, are the centerpiece of my analysis. The significance of these stories emerges as I situate the courts historically, culturally, and politically in coastal Kenya. The postcolonial period has seen an increased recognition of women's claims in Kadhi's Courts, a change that leads me to explore the question of social transformation through legal processes. In assessing what this change has meant for men and women as individuals, as well as for gender relations in postcolonial society, I emphasize the transformative possibilities and yet include attention to the limits set by the legal system, cultural understandings, and language itself.

Conducting Research in Coastal Kenya

The ethnographic research for this volume was conducted during thirteen months beginning in late 1985, and on several shorter trips over the next eight years. During the first month, I lived in Nairobi, Kenya's cosmopolitan, bustling capital in which people representing multiple ethnicities, languages, and religions interact and where the nation's extreme class divisions are most palpably evident. I examined archival materials at the University of Nairobi and the Kenya National Archives. To acquaint myself with Kenya's British-modeled civil and criminal courts, I attended several trials in and around Nairobi. Although my project would ultimately focus on the Swahili Muslim cultural context and the coastal Islamic courts, these initial observations exposed me to aspects of the expanding postcolonial Kenyan justice system—slow bureaucracy, multilingual courtrooms, state violence against defendants, and the vulnerability and tenacity of a newly professionalized judiciary.

My research, which was carried out primarily in the coastal cities of Mombasa and Malindi, focused on the urban population of Swahili Muslims, who trace their ancestry to both Africa and the Arabian Peninsula. Though for scholars Swahili ethnicity is a highly contested category, people who call themselves Swahili claim hundreds of years of residence in coastal "stone towns" and also inland "country towns," where they have engaged in fishing and trade (Middleton 1992). Divided along lines of class, status, clan, and residence, Swahili people share Islam as their religion and Kiswahili (the Swahili language, which includes a long literary tradition) as their first language. Once prominent in the economy and politics of Mombasa and the coast more generally, Swahili people have become less influential in the postcolonial era. They struggle with their status as a minority Muslim population in a nominally secular nation where Christians constitute a powerful majority.

Although Swahili people live throughout Mombasa, many, including the family with whom I resided for two months, are still concentrated in the Old Town area, where houses of several stories built early in this century are packed close together. Fortuitous building means that some apartments catch cooling sea breezes while the narrow passageways below, lined with small shops, are alternately dusty and stifling in the hot season or flowing with runoff in the rainy season. The presence of Fort Jesus, built by the Portuguese in the sixteenth century, and of numerous mosques makes both the origins of the city and its Islamic roots more evident in Old Town than in other areas of Mombasa, which cater to tourists, business interests, and international military personnel.

Mombasa is the judicial center for Kenyan Muslims, who are entitled to adjudicate matters of family law (marriage, divorce, inheritance, and personal status) in Kadhi's Courts. While living in Mombasa, I was tutored in Islamic law by the head of the Islamic judges, the Chief Kadhi. At the Mombasa Law Courts, a large, modern building erected in the 1980s to house secular and religious courts, I observed many cases and mediations involving Islamic law. I recorded some of these, and discussed them with the Chief Kadhi, other kadhis, court personnel, and disputants. Court clerks provided me with records of marriages, divorces, and court use for several Islamic courts in the Coast Province; thus, I became familiar with the region's court activity in the postcolonial era. While in Mombasa, I began to study coastal Islam and Swahili culture.

I conducted most of the research during ten months of residence in Malindi, a large town north of Mombasa. Formerly a port, Malindi sustains a declining fishing trade, several light industries, and produce markets for surrounding farms; it is a transportation hub and has hotels, restaurants, and beaches catering to tourists. A large Swahili Muslim population is concentrated primarily in the Shella and Barani sublocations of Malindi Town, which are situated at the edge of Malindi's wide beach. In Shella, the oldest Malindi neighborhood, I observed Swahili life, focusing on relations of gender, class, and religious sect among interrelated families, many of whom have lived and owned property in Shella for decades.

Much of what I learned about the enactment and transformation of gender in legal processes was through direct observation of dispute resolution in and out of court. Each weekday for about six months, I observed and tape-recorded cases and mediations heard in the Malindi Kadhi's Court. I compiled over two hundred tape-recorded "incidents" of dispute resolution, including cases, mediations, and discus-

sions among kadhis, clerks, and people engaged in disputes. I discussed
the incidents at length with court personnel and also interviewed disputants and bystanders. I reviewed records of all cases (129 in total)
filed in the Malindi Kadhi's Court over a period of twenty months in
1985–86 and many cases in other years. Studying disputes outside
court is necessarily haphazard, but, by residing with an extended family in an area populated by Swahili people, I witnessed some conflicts
as they erupted. The proximity of several young married couples put
me in the midst of problems resembling those heard in Kadhi's Courts.
Strains between spouses, relatives, and neighbors became evident even
as people attempted to hide them and others, including myself, tried
to respect privacy, a critical concern for Swahili people.

Interactions between me and the Swahili people who provided the
information on which this book is based took many forms: lectures,
courtroom consultations, conversations, solicitations of advice, formal
interviews, gossip sessions, and overhearings. Discussions were almost
always conducted in Kiswahili, which I had studied for several years
before beginning research. I participated actively in Swahili social life
by attending weddings, mosque lectures, school competitions, parties,
holiday celebrations, and festivals and, sadly enough, by witnessing
funerals, financial crises, accidents, illnesses, and painful family fights.
Through these activities, I gained a comprehensive understanding of
Swahili social practices in general, and of conflict and gender relations
in particular.

Follow-up research trips of several months each in 1988 and 1990
allowed me to confirm earlier observations and to pursue questions
unanticipated in the original project. Two additional, shorter visits in
subsequent years renewed connections and provided the opportunity
to check my analyses with Kenyans. According to some Swahili people,
these periodic returns have established me as someone who is committed to knowing things about Swahili life in an "inside" manner (cha
ndani). Paradoxically, as the return trips deepened my understanding
of "inside" information, they also illuminated the broader context in
which Swahili society is embedded. With each return my perspective
changed, and I saw more clearly how local factional allegiances, state-
level ideologies and institutions, and global discourses of religion and
gender—coming from east and west—intersect on the Kenyan coast
and shape Swahili cultural life, institutional practices, and individual
narratives.

Though being recognized as one who knows Swahili things "inside" acknowledges my persistence and purpose (in comparison with tourists and other Euro-Americans who come and go), such an acknowledgment is double-edged (see also Fuglesang 1994). As I will describe, Swahili ideologies about language question the propriety of revealing too much about oneself or one's family, especially if it involves conflict. Return trips made me increasingly aware of the awkward fit between the Swahili ideology of concealing personal matters and the goal of obtaining and writing about "inside" knowledge. To the extent that ethnographers expose the tensions underlying multiple relations of power in Swahili society, particularly by describing them ethnographically, we risk the same charge facing Swahili women who testify in Kadhi's Courts: we threaten to break community norms by narrating problems that—according to Swahili cultural ideals—are best left unremarked.

Plan of the Book

The first three chapters of the book introduce the theoretical, ethnographic, and methodological contexts, respectively, for the analysis presented in subsequent chapters. Chapter 1 delineates my approach to discourse, gender, and disputing, which draws on theories of indexing gender (the multiple ways in which language points to and thereby constitutes gender); entextualization (the processes through which speakers mark off stories from other speech); and ideologies of language (i.e., the cultural ideas about language that contribute to the meaning of speech). Chapter 2 describes the Swahili coast historically and ethnographically, focusing on gender relations in the postcolonial period. Chapter 3 presents my methods of collecting and analyzing linguistic data from Swahili disputing contexts. It includes a technical discussion of the components of spoken narrative and my methods of narrative analysis.

The next two chapters focus on disputes in Swahili society as sites where gender relations are reflected and reconfigured. These chapters identify the kinds of marital conflict common among Swahili Muslims and analyze the processes of disputing in everyday social life (chapter 4) and in Kadhi's Courts (chapter 5). Chapter 4 examines dispute processes by describing the four discourses commonly invoked in marital disputes (Islamic law, Swahili ethics, spiritual health, and state law) and by analyzing their deployment in disputes. After a brief history of Swahili women's increasing use of the Kadhi's Courts, chapter 5 argues that the postcolonial Kadhi's Courts are sites of complex political struggle where couples negotiate gender relations, men challenge the kadhis' authority, and some Swahili people—standing behind the courts as embattled symbols of Muslim law—resist interference by the secular Kenyan state.

Chapters 6 through 9 analyze speech in Kadhi's Court cases and mediations to show how gendered subject positions are constituted through the discourses of conflict resolution. Each chapter examines a different aspect of disputing from a distinct analytic perspective: the process of telling initial stories of conflict (chapter 6); the organization of interaction after the initial narrative is told (chapter 7); the reported speech embedded in narratives (chapter 8); and finally the cultural ideas about language peppered throughout cases and mediations (chapter 9). The overall goal is to demonstrate that, in court, gendered subjects emerge through speech in multiple and contradictory ways. For example, by identifying a contradiction between disputants' gendered speech in court (chapters 6 and 7) and their representations of how they speak in the story worlds of narrated conflict (chapter 8), my analysis shows the dimensions of the struggle over social relations at the microlevel of interaction. Chapter 9 directs attention to how the production of cultural ideas about discourse, gender, and speaking subjects in disputes engages and contests the gendered images produced through narratives of conflict. This analysis maps the possibilities and limitations for social creativity through the discourses of disputing. It shows that, even as Swahili women win their cases through narrations of conflict, their speech indexes gendered subject positions routinely devalued through patriarchal ideologies linking gender, discourse, and conflict. In addition to revealing this process at the microlevel of interaction, the chapter concludes with a parallel analysis of how women's use of the Kadhi's Courts is also devalued at a broader ideological level outside court.

Finally, the brief concluding chapter reflects on the Swahili case in light of global discourses about women and Muslim law in order to challenge the dichotomies through which Islam and its legal entailments for gender have been understood. As a whole, the volume argues against the idea that Islamic law and legal institutions always fail to offer Muslim women possibilities for actively reworking gender relations. Depending on legal arrangements, cultural understandings, and political and economic histories, disputes involving Muslim marital law can be important contexts for contestation and transformation.

Mwoana kwa uzuri, mwachana kwa wema.
Marry in a good way, divorce in a good way.

Legal Processes and the Discursive Construction of Gender

When they wed, when they argue, and when they separate, Swahili Muslim couples are offered the advice to "marry in a good way, divorce in a good way." The saying reflects Koranic principles and Swahili beliefs that advocate celebrating marriage and averting domestic conflict. Although divorcing—the most reprehensible of all acts permitted by Islam—can never replicate the "goodness" (in the sense of beauty or good taste) associated with marrying, couples contemplating divorce are expected to avoid acrimonious struggle and strive for "goodness" (in the sense of good will or good moral character).[1] This admonition counsels couples to handle domestic problems calmly, without malice. More pointedly, by implying that proper spousal behavior includes the appropriate production of speech, even during disputes, the saying invests the legal and social positions of husband and wife with expectations for linguistic behavior. The stereotypic images of men pronouncing divorce and women persevering in difficult circumstances signify a convergence of legal, linguistic, and gendered subject positions that embody the cultural ideal of divorcing with "goodness" and thereby establish the framework of meanings in which individuals engage in marital disputes.

Building on scholarship in gender studies, legal anthropology, and sociolinguistics, I develop in this chapter an approach to understanding how subject positions are constituted and transformed in disputes, particularly through the discourse of disputants. After describing the central features of my theoretical approach to gender, discourse, and legal processes in the following section, I discuss several sociolinguistic concepts that underpin my approach, including linguistic ideology, indexing, and metapragmatics—all of which emerge from recent theoretical work in linguistic pragmatics, a subfield of sociolinguistics that addresses the relation between language and the active construction of social life. A subsequent section, which delineates how I apply my

17

approach to disputes in the Kenyan context, explains what my analysis
of narratives in Swahili marital disputes will demonstrate about the
constitution of gendered subjects. My approach illuminates how Swahili Muslims, operating from subject positions (e.g., wives and husbands) that entail linguistic expectations, act and speak within and
against those subject positions in efforts that remake gender, for themselves as individuals and also for society more broadly.

An Approach to the Discursive Construction of Gender in Legal Processes

Debates over the methodological and ethical complexities of cross-
cultural research on gender have led some feminists to question
whether we can or should posit "women" as a category that extends
universally, across differences of culture, religion, nation, race, class,
sexual preference, etc. Framed simply, the question "Do women exist?" challenges assumptions about the universality of gender either
as an experienced phenomenon or as a category useful for theoretical
analysis or political action. More than a few feminists remark that,
in understanding gender as discursively constructed through multiple
relations of power, we have moved beyond simplistic comparisons of
women with men, or among women living in seemingly contrastive
cultural contexts. Yet, as others have charged, by conceptualizing gender as shaped by discourse, we risk failing to account for "realities"
of gendered lives and thus sacrifice the ability to marshal political responses to sexism in its many forms.[2]

Judith Butler (1993) redirects debates over gender, discourse, and
power by theorizing the gendered subject, which she depicts as an effect of discourse. In her approach, this subject is not replaced *by* discourse. That is, Butler's subject does not exist *only* discursively.
Rather, gendered subjectivity is constituted through performance. It is
pursued actively and sometimes creatively by subjects engaged in social
life.[3] Women are positioned as different kinds of subjects—sometimes
agents and sometimes abjects, in Butler's terms. To ask how gendered
subjects are constructed and performed is to explore multiple enactments of gendered subject positions in different contexts and to assess
the possibilities for, and limits of, their transformation.

Influenced by theories of the construction of gender through performed discourse, I avoid asking, "Do women exist?" but rather focus

on how power operates discursively to constitute categories of persons, often using gendered terms, and how people positioned through local and global discourses enact and (sometimes) contest their construction as gendered subjects. My approach to the reproduction and transformation of gender through the discourses of disputing relies on two assumptions about discourse and gender. First, it is *in relation to discourse* that people are constituted as and constitute themselves as gendered subjects. That is, understandings and enactments of gender incorporate cultural notions about linguistic usage. In short, being a woman or a man means being (or being taken for, or being expected to be) a certain kind of speaker. Second, gendered positions are constituted *through discourse* in specific contexts that are characterized by cultural and institutional conventions for producing speech. These two assumptions lead me to explore the construction of gender as an interactive, potentially transformative process that takes its shape and reaches its limits discursively, and with reference to discourse, in contextually specific ways.

Developing a theoretical framework to examine discourse as constitutive of social life and, more specifically, of gendered subject positions requires not only conceptualizing discourse in multiple forms but also defining the relations among those forms. Such a framework posits interactive speech as a vehicle through which social life is created; however, it also allows that speech is always shaped by and produced in relation to discourse in its sense as socially constructed, enduring frames for communication (see, e.g., Foucault 1980, 1983).[4] To illuminate the operation of power through discourse, I move beyond envisioning discourse only as an overarching formation of knowledge that configures thought and behavior and, instead, investigate the contours of its structure and influence as evidenced in its grounded manifestations, that is, in instances of interactive speech.

To be gendered is, then, to exist and act in relation to discourse (as well as to other persons). The interactive performance of gender is shaped through the discursive possibilities facing speakers in particular contexts. In speaking, subjects construct themselves with reference to these possibilities, performing and transforming gender in ways that point to, or index, gendered positions. Yet, because they always engage in displays of gender in relation to cultural ideas about gender and speech, speakers' words wield transformative potential. Produced and understood through cultural ideas about gender and discourse, the speech of gendered, speaking subjects can reproduce or transform those very ideas. Aspects of ideology that conceptualize the relation between gender and speech form part of the context of any interaction and provide the terms through and against which interaction proceeds (Silverstein 1979, 1985). Thus, my analysis identifies those understandings about gender and discourse that are relevant in Swahili coastal Kenya.

Law and legal arenas provide especially significant contexts for studying the constitution and negotiation of gender through speech. Numerous scholars have demonstrated that institutions structure social relations (including gender relations) by influencing both the production of speech and knowledge about speakers (see, e.g., Ferguson 1984; Fisher 1995; Foucault 1979, 1980; Gal 1991; Goffman 1961; Philips 1994b; Wagner-Pacifici 1994). In Bourdieu's terms, some discourses are authorized as official by those with institutional standing, and others are marginalized, silenced, or ignored.[5] Such authorizations, which are sometimes expressed through explicit ideological statements, have significant impact on speakers' abilities to constitute gender. Institutional regimes of language use combine with legal definitions of persons to construct those who enter court, shaping their discursive possibilities for indexing and reconfiguring gender.[6] Paradoxically, law "genders" individuals in ways that define their positions both in society and in legal contexts, while also affording space for contesting those positions (Hirsch and Lazarus-Black 1994; Lazarus-Black 1994). These contestations necessarily involve the law's assumptions about subjects as gendered speakers.

Legal anthropologists have long been concerned with exploring contestations of various sorts through the study of disputes.[7] The analyses of disputing that developed through the many incarnations of the dispute-processing paradigm not only charted the struggles over social relations of power mounted through disputes but also directed attention to the multiple dynamics of disputing as social practice.[8] Even though, as Moore (1986) contends, recent legal anthropology tends to examine historical processes broader than individual cases, disputing practices, or even legal systems, disputes continue to be treated as critical sites for the negotiation of social life.[9] The treatment of disputes as social actions that unfold through the efforts of disputants and third parties and that contribute to the transformation of power elevated the importance of discourse in studies of disputing (Comaroff and Roberts 1981; Mather and Yngvesson 1981).[10]

Scholarship that explicitly analyzes disputes as discursive practice generally defines discourse narrowly, as linguistic interaction (see reviews in Brenneis 1988; Conley and O'Barr 1990; Levi 1990, 1994; Mertz 1994; Tiersma 1993).[11] These studies explore, among other issues, the contrasts between "legal language" and "everyday conversation," the power relations embedded in and emergent through courtroom interaction, and the distribution of linguistic resources among participants in cases and other disputes (e.g., Atkinson and Drew 1979; Conley and O'Barr 1990; Goldman 1983; Goodwin 1990; Grimshaw 1990; Levi 1994; O'Barr 1982; Philips 1984). More than a few studies direct attention to the power of legal institutions to shape the expression of conflict by identifying, for example, the challenges facing disputants in the linguistically foreign courtroom (Atkinson and Drew 1979; Berk-Seligson 1990; Conley and O'Barr 1990; Goldman 1983; Matoesian 1993; O'Barr 1982).

Only a few studies of language in legal institutions have explored questions of gender.[12] A research team studying language in American courts used Robin Lakoff's model of "women's language" as a "jumping-off point" to investigate whether the features of "women's language" (e.g., hedging, tag questions, and empty adjectives) were produced primarily by women or whether, depending on the context, men might also produce them (O'Barr and Atkins 1980).[13] An early and critical nexus in research on law, language, and gender, their analysis demonstrated that witnesses of both genders spoke women's language.[14] They renamed the set of features "powerless language" to reflect that those who produced it generally occupied subordinate social statuses (e.g., working class, limited education). As O'Barr and Atkins argued, while gender is one dimension of powerlessness and women produce more features of powerless speech than men, gender does not determine the speech forms produced by particular individuals. The powerlessness of most witnesses in court was also linked to their unfamiliarity with the linguistic conventions of the context. The study not only demonstrates that powerless language has consequences for those who produce it but also asserts that men and women might be similarly disadvantaged in some institutional settings.[15]

In addition to demonstrating that multiple (rather than singular) categories of distinction (e.g., class, gender, race, "empowerment") are relevant to explaining the speech differences of individuals in legal contexts, the O'Barr and Atkins study recognized the inability of *most* speakers to produce effective speech in court and to assess the causes and consequences of their speech (see reviews in Brenneis 1988; Danet 1980, 1985; Levi 1982, 1994; Levi and Walker 1990; Mertz 1992a, 1994; and O'Barr 1982). More recently, scholars have moved beyond the assumption that institutions determine the form of interaction—delegitimizing some forms and some speakers—to explore the relation between individual agency and institutions (Conley and O'Barr 1990; Merry 1990; Mertz 1992a, 1994; Yngvesson 1993). Other scholarship focuses directly on the institutional and political discourses that define gendered subjects and, in so doing, delimit the discursive options available in legal processes (White 1991; Williams 1991).[16]

The organization of interaction in legal contexts, which contrasts with noninstitutional talk, presents difficulties for Swahili people that are not unlike those identified for nonprofessional speakers in most legal institutions. But these difficulties must be understood in relation to gender. Because Swahili men and women are positioned differently with respect to laws of marriage and divorce, they face contrasting, gendered options for using legal processes and legal discourse to resolve domestic conflict, and they speak from gendered participant roles once in court. Also, interaction itself is organized to privilege certain kinds of speakers, such as those familiar with the legal process or those expected to speak more readily in institutions—which, in the Swahili case, means men.

Although law configures gendered approaches to disputing, speakers in court (both laypeople and legal professionals) are constituted, influenced, and constrained as much by *cultural conceptions* of discourse as they are by legal rules and procedures. Thus, to identify the language ideologies that both configure gendered speech in court and also provide material for the creative reworking of gender, I examine not only law and legal institutions but also Swahili cultural beliefs about language and gender.

Capturing the influence of Swahili culture in disputes and legal institutions in coastal Kenya requires a broad definition of law, one that places legal processes, rather than legal institutions, at the center of the analysis. Legal processes extend beyond the walls of legal institutions, spreading out through legal discourse as it permeates social life and as it emerges in the course of disputes. Outside Islamic courts, one might hear Swahili Muslims use a legal phrase or remind listeners of a judge's decree. The porous quality of institutional walls also has another entailment: speakers do not leave behind their cultural understandings or capacities when they enter law courts. Those understandings and capacities, and how they are deployed in courts, are my focus.

Ideologies about language—be they specifically legal or more generally cultural, or a mixture of the two—include assumptions and expectations about gendered speech, which influence who engages in disputes, when they come to court, and how they speak in legal processes. Such ideologies also play more significant roles in the discourse of cases and mediations. First, in legal processes, speakers produce metalinguistic commentary on the speech of themselves and others, using ideology to endorse or challenge another's speech. Thus, interactive speech includes a metalevel of discourse that, at times, draws on and produces cultural beliefs that relate specifically to gendered speech. Such comments, which can be produced to silence a speaker *because* her/his speech is inappropriate for her/his gender, are evidence of the important role that language ideology can play in disputes. Second, speech is often an issue in marital disputes. Claims made about lies, broken promises, emotional abuse, nagging, and divorce itself are claims about language, which, given differences in the positions of men and women in Islam, relate to gender. My approach identifies points of struggle, when the negotiation of gender proceeds through reference to language. Elucidating these processes requires a technical discussion of the pragmatics and metapragmatics of language and gender, to which I turn in the next section.

Perspectives on Discourse and Gender from Linguistic Pragmatics

In critiquing studies of language and gender, Deborah Cameron (1985) argues that scholars generally adopt one of two approaches. Either they assume that gendered linguistic forms reflect the social position of those who produce them (i.e., they argue that women's speech is powerless because women are socially subordinate) or they elevate the status of devalued speech forms as a strategy for altering gender relations (e.g., they argue that women's cooperative speech forms facilitate conversation and are, thus, powerful). These options reflect not only the political strategies of feminist linguists but also distinct and long-standing epistemological positions in sociolinguistic theory.[17] Finding both approaches limited in conceptualizing the role of speech in the reproduction and transformation of gender relations, Cameron argues that they devote inadequate attention to how linguistic ideology mediates the meanings of gender differences among speakers. Thus, she advocates investigating the production of gendered speech and also the aspects of linguistic ideology that attribute meaning to gendered speech.[18]

The importance of attending to linguistic ideology is one facet of the comprehensive approach to discourse and social relations pursued in contemporary linguistic pragmatics, which, for many scholars, takes its direction from the foundational work of Michael Silverstein (1979; see also Briggs 1988a; Duranti 1994; Gal 1991; Lucy 1992; Mertz 1992a, 1994; Mertz and Parmentier 1985; Silverstein 1976, 1985, 1992a; Woolard and Schieffelin 1994).[19] Positing a dichotomy similar to Cameron's, Mertz (1992a, 1994) criticizes the theoretical inadequacy of "reflectionist" and "instrumentalist" approaches to language and advocates the need to conceptualize language as structure, usage, and ideology, always operating simultaneously. In addition, she asserts that "to understand the relationship between language and society in all its complexity, it is important to allow for a moment of linguistic creativity, a moment when language is more than a transparent window or tool expressing preexisting social divisions" (1992a:418). Theorizing language as an active force in social life requires a recognition that language is characterized by several structuring principles (Mertz 1994:439; see also Silverstein 1976, 1992b).[20] For example, all speech occurs "against a backdrop of presupposed social knowledge that can be specified ahead of time"; socially creative meanings, and new social relations, can be effected by violating these presuppositions (Mertz 1992a:421). This creativity emerges from the ways in which linguistic structure and ideology are juxtaposed in contextualized usage (Mertz 1994:238).

Emphasis on the socially creative possibilities of discourse has its roots in studies of the indexical function of language, which examine how language indexes, or points to, social context. Silverstein, who has made the important contribution to linguistic anthropology of demonstrating that indexicality is central to linguistic meaning (see, e.g., Silverstein 1976), delineates the several ways in which gender is encoded in and indexed through language (1985; see also 1979). To demonstrate the interdependence of linguistic structure, usage, and ideology, and their combined role in effecting social change, Silverstein analyzes the example of attempts to regiment the use of gendered pronouns in English. He makes the observation that feminist efforts to change pronoun use (e.g., to eliminate the so-called generic "he"), although misconstruing the operation of grammatical categories of gender, create new meaning through the indexical function of language. Specifically, a speaker's decision "to 'he' or not to 'he' " indexes him or her as either in solidarity with feminist ideology, hostile to it, or unaware of the whole debate (1985). By means of indexicality, which operates through linguistic structure (pronomial system), linguistic usage (pronouns spoken in interaction), and ideology (feminist attempts at pronoun regimentation), aspects of gender relations are altered.[21]

Ideologies that link speech and aspects of social relations, including gender, take many forms (Briggs 1992b; Cameron 1985; Gal 1991; Kramarae 1982; Kulick 1992; Philips 1992; Silverstein 1992b; Woolard and Schieffelin 1994).[22] Swahili beliefs about language and gender are routinely expressed both explicitly and implicitly in courtroom speech. Some of these expressions link men or women to particular genres of speech, such as the complaining narratives told by Rehema and other women who make claims in court. Silverstein (1992b:317) describes this type of ideological construct:

> Any reasoning that interprets a presuppositional relationship—"Such-and-suches use form '...', while so-and-sos ..."—is potentially an ideological one rationalizing the indexical value of the forms in terms of schemata of social differentiation and classification that are independent of the usages at issue.

This begs the question of whether "rationalizing explanations" (Silverstein 1992b:320) of gendered speech are more common or more relevant in contexts of gender segregation or where the politics of gender are intensified.[23]

Elinor Ochs (1992) draws on Silverstein's approach to theorize a process she calls "indexing gender."[24] Ochs argues that interactional speech indexes gender primarily through indirect and nonexclusive means.[25] Her approach advances the study of language and gender beyond equating a particular speech style or feature exclusively with one gender to explore how some discursive forms effect "stances" or "social acts" that are associated with gender.[26] By performing social acts through speech (such as praising, blaming, showing deference, asserting force, and accommodating), men and women orient to societal "norms, preferences and expectations" for gendered behavior. These norms can be understood as aspects of ideology that encode cultural understandings of gender and language (e.g., the prescribed stance for women) and thereby influence the production and interpretation of speech. As Silverstein has succinctly put it, "ideologies construe indexicality" (1992b:315). Thus, ideologies are central to the process whereby language creates gendered meaning through contextualized use.

Of central concern to my analysis are the linguistic forms that, when produced by Swahili people, point to a speaker's gender. As Ochs (1992:344) would predict, these indexes are linked to social acts that are pursued in gender-patterned ways across societies: "Several studies have noted the tendency for men to participate more in speech activities that involve formal interactions with outsiders and women to be restricted to activities within family and village contexts. In these cases, men and women display different competence in particular genres, including, of course, their grammatical and discourse structures." Given that the contribution of these genres to the construction of gender cannot be understood without reference to the language ideology, how genres index gender in legal processes is of primary concern in my project.

I use the concepts of indexing and constituting gender much as Ochs does, though taking care to emphasize that gender is transformed through speech. Because it is actively constituted in instances of speech, gender can be transformed at the same time as it is indexed. This claim relies on a conceptualization of gender not as an entity waiting to be indexed but rather as an ongoing relation performed through speech and other behaviors. To demonstrate how Swahili people index gender in disputes, I analyze the production of gender-linked genres in courtroom speech, exploring the relation between these genres as indexes of gender and the ideologies of gender and power through which the genres are understood. My approach bears the influence of studies in linguistic pragmatics that focus on the performance and poetics of genres which, when produced, dynamically constitute social life (see, e.g., Bauman 1986; Briggs 1986; Duranti 1994; Hymes 1981; Kratz 1994; Ochs 1992; Sherzer 1987; Shuman 1986; Steedly 1993; Urban 1991). For example, Charles Briggs (1986) describes how performances of verbal art display the linguistic and social competence of Mexicano people, particularly of elders, who solidify their powerful social positions through producing "competent" speech. A performed genre (depending on how it is produced) not only indexes and reconstitutes the social position of the person producing it but also engages social relations beyond the immediate speech context (e.g., relations between Mexicanos and Anglos). Briggs's example expands the notion of context and highlights the agency of speakers, allowing that their speech strategies perform the complex work of combating Anglo hegemony.

Understanding how language constitutes social relations requires attention to subtle aspects of linguistic usage—particularly the metapragmatic functions of language, which are those aspects of discourse that comment on the connection between language and contextualized usage (Briggs 1992a). Metapragmatics, which are culturally and linguistically specific, can be expressed through, for example, explicit statements about language or more implicit forms, such as reported speech or contextual cues (see also Mertz 1992b; Silverstein 1992a). An analysis of metapragmatics illuminates how speakers perceive the functions of the discourse they produce. According to Briggs (1992a: 207),

> on the one hand, metapragmatics is quintessentially linguistic. Since it is speech about speech, it appears at first glance to be doubly removed from the 'real [read non-linguistic] world.' On the other hand, metapragmatics is closely tied to history, social interaction, and political economy. We are thus left in the somewhat ironic position of needing to investigate in much greater depth the way that language reflects on language if we are to make substantial gains in understanding how language reflects—and constitutes—social life.

My own project takes up Briggs's ironic challenge by analyzing pragmatic and metapragmatic features of speech and also situating these features in a broader sociopolitical context.[27] In analyzing how gender is constituted in legal processes, I consider subtle manifestations of speech about speech in addition to more overt features, such as the production of genres, reported speech, and explicit statements of ideology.[28] Attention to these features reveals how Swahili people understand and reposition themselves as gendered speakers in disputing contexts.

Differentiating Stories in Postcolonial Contexts

My analysis of cases and mediations in Kadhi's Courts focuses primarily on narrative, which is one of the central ways in which speakers present their claims in court. Narrated stories are also a significant genre for constituting gendered subjectivity in that speakers describe and index themselves as particular kinds of people through narration. As studies of language and law demonstrate, people in diverse cultural contexts produce "narratives of trouble" (Yngvesson 1993:12) to address tasks related to disputing (see, e.g., Brenneis 1988; Conley and O'Barr 1990; Goodwin 1990).[29] Stories told in court provide evidence that can determine who's right and who's wrong, who's telling the truth and who's lying. They are also vehicles through which disputing parties vent rage at one another, and such cathartic acts, especially when performed publicly, can ameliorate the problem. As an act of speaking and as an ordering principle, narrative is significant both to the interests of the disputing parties in relating their versions of the problem and to the court's interests in evoking and organizing information. Narrative forms reflect the constraints and possibilities constructed through the conventions of courtroom discourse, and they also reflect disputants' ambivalence about whether telling their stories serves their interests.

Recent studies of narrative in disputing contexts have been less concerned with the effects of narratives on case outcomes than with exploring more profound entailments of narrating trouble. As Briggs (1988b:272) argues, "the art of connecting words to form narratives provides humans in a wide range of societies with powerful tools for creating and mediating conflict and, in doing so, constituting social reality."[30] By providing accounts of actions in the "story world" of narrated conflict, speakers effect changes in the "event world" of dispute resolution, a world that extends beyond the courtroom walls.[31] This possibility is especially significant, because those who dispute in court are frequently engaged in the explicitly performative acts—both legal and linguistic—of persuading, justifying, blaming, etc., designed to effect changes in legal and social relations.[32] Some legal speech acts are accomplished through narration, and narratives are used to enhance the performative force of those acts.

Concepts from linguistic pragmatics provide useful tools for the project of examining narrative's transformative potential (see, e.g., Bauman 1986; Bauman and Briggs 1990; Briggs 1988a). A performed narrative differs from other ways of telling a story, such as a report, which is an accounting of events with very few of the devices that enact the story (Wolfson 1978:220). For Bauman, performance is more than the production of performance features; it is "a mode of communication, a way of speaking, the essence of which resides in the assumption of responsibility to an audience for a display of communicative skill, highlighting the way in which communication is carried out, above and beyond its referential content." Performance directs attention to the story itself, to the act of storytelling, and to the teller, and it does so through the property of language that allows it to refer to itself (1986:3).

The notion that performance highlights a narrated story is delineated more specifically by Bauman and Briggs (1990), who posit the critical role of performance in processes of "entextualization" and "decontextualization."[33] Entextualization "is the process of rendering discourse extractable, of making a stretch of linguistic production into a unit—a text—that can be lifted out of its interactional setting. A text, then, from this vantage point, is discourse rendered decontextualizable" (73). Entextualization is effected through features of narration (e.g., framing devices, reported speech, poetic language, metalinguistic statements) that, when produced by narrators, distinguish the story from surrounding speech. Applying the Bauman and Briggs model, one could conclude that performing a narrative "intensifies" the entextualization of a story. This process "potentiates" decontextualization and offers the possibility for the story to be deployed in other places and times, that is, recontextualized. This model offers an important theory of narrative that retains concern for performance features and also directs attention to narrative politics: "the task is to discover empirically what means are available in a given social setting, to whom they may be available, under what circumstances, for making discourse into a text" (Bauman and Briggs 1990:74; see also Silverstein and Urban 1996:12).

Although Bauman and Briggs's "textualization" model was developed primarily with reference to analyzing performances of verbal art, it is usefully applied to analyze narratives in legal contexts (cf. Hill and Irvine 1992:23). The stories narrated by disputants in Kadhi's Courts are always potentially entextualizable by judges and clerks, who create literal texts of trouble stories in the records they keep. Relatedly, the public and institutional nature of the court means that a narrative can be reproduced as more than a private telling. To address the tasks that face them in the legal setting, speakers seek to direct the attention of the clerk or judge to their stories and to guide interpretation, quite often in the face of an opponent's equally compelling counternarrative. Thus, through performance, disputants entextualize their narratives as "evidence" critical to a claim.

My analysis of the narratives produced by Kadhi's Court disputants demonstrates that men and women turn their stories into texts in gender-patterned ways. Specifically, women entextualize their stories by embedding many features of narrative performance, while men frame their accounts through metalinguistic statements. The significance of this difference is that a particular kind of narrative—the performed story—becomes an index of gender through its production by women. Gender differences in processes like entextualization must be understood in relation to the cultural understandings that speakers and hearers use to construe gender indexing. At the level of ideology, the narrative genre is linked to Swahili women, who are thought to tell stories of various types more readily than men. The more specific form of narration that involves recounting instances of domestic conflict (i.e., telling stories that constitute complaints) is also linked to women, and this kind of story is deemed highly inappropriate. By telling stories of conflict in court, Swahili women engage in the inappropriate narration of complaints about their households and thus risk flouting cultural expectations about women's speech.

Entextualization is one of several ways in which speakers produce narratives differently with respect to gender in Kadhi's Court disputes. In addition, through narrating the behavior of themselves and others, speakers depict gender roles and relations. The "characters" of their stories play out gendered actions, assumptions, and desires. Narrations also differentiate when men and women produce them as gender-patterned contributions to interaction. For example, in Kadhi's Court, women routinely tell stories in order to attribute blame implicitly, while men narrate in order to illustrate points in an argument. Reported speech, a central feature of performed narration in Kiswahili, is also a vehicle for displaying assumptions about gender and speech.[34] Moreover, reported speech conveys information about the individual giving the report and also about the relations among the reporter, the original speaker, and others co-present in court.[35] As Bauman and Briggs (1990:70) assert, reported speech constitutes a decentering of the "narrating event and the narrator's voice" that "opens up possibilities for renegotiating meanings and social relations beyond the parameters of the performance itself." For example, Goodwin's study (1990) of reports of gossip among girls (a form called "he-said-she-said") demonstrates that reported speech not only recreates and comments on prior incidents of speech but also, in the process, reworks social relations among the participants in the narrative event.

My analysis considers the multiple ways in which an account presented in Kadhi's Court indexes gender. I include attention to the relations among those aspects of narrative through which indexing is accomplished, such as entextualization and reported speech. Rarely does the telling of a story in a dispute convey the image of a one-dimensional gendered subject. For example, women who narrate domestic conflict routinely depict themselves *in their stories* as persevering silently. However, telling a story about domestic conflict in an institutional context is an act that, for Swahili Muslims, indexes gender by directly contradicting the image of perseverance. Even if the image presented in the "story world" is of a persevering, uncomplaining wife, the act of narrating in the "event world" of the court presents a quite different image: the complaining woman. Gender is thus narrated, indexed, performed, contested, and transformed in multiple and contradictory ways, even by the same speaker and even by a speaker consciously attempting to depict herself through a particular gendered image. For their part, men also exhibit contradictions by, for example, enacting their positions as the gendered subjects authorized to pronounce on legal matters and yet also telling stories in which they depict themselves as ceding authority.

Multiple factors—legal, cultural, historical, etc.—influence speakers' representations of themselves and others in situations of conflict and its resolution. Thus, attention to the negotiation of gender becomes all the more complex, and critical, in postcolonial societies where states are inflected by competing and conflicting imperatives associated with multiple regimes of order and domination (see, e.g., Comaroff and Comaroff 1991; Cooper and Stoler 1989; Moore 1986; Philips 1994b, 1995). The microlevel interaction that is the focus of my analysis is configured through these multiple discourses (Islamic law, state law, and others), each of which encodes a particular approach to gender. The negotiation of gender through legal processes is shaped by the historical relations among discourses, and yet, at the same time, the interactive nature of disputing contributes to reshaping those discourses and thus to the possible transformation of gender relations.[36] This is particularly relevant in coastal Kenya as Swahili women's use of the courts continues to increase in the postcolonial era.

Mary Margaret Steedly's analysis of the politics of narrative in

Karoland, Indonesia, illustrates the issues at stake in postcolonial societies. As Steedly (1993) demonstrates, rather than being stories about
experiences (real or fantastical), stories told about spirit possession,
and during possession, are the means of constructing relations among
Karo people of different statuses and also among Karo people, their
former colonizers, and their current government. Steedly argues that
"narrative experience," an inherently political concept, is central to
such constructions of subjectivity.[37] Yet only some Karo narrators are
heard or believed, and estimations about the worth of their narrations
reflect gender hierarchy: "Generic standards of narrative authenticity
(what counts as a story) and style (how a story should be told) are
organized by reference to the social experience of Karo men—as patro-
nymically identified subjects occupying stable positions in a rela-
tionally constituted and flexibly hierarchical social field, and as social
actors who *do* count for something in public discourse." Karo women,
positioned differently than men, are left "doubly discounted": "first
by the literal muting of their voices, which leaves them unpracticed in
public debate and unheard in public speech; and second by the discursive limits of narrative plausibility, which require women's stories to
be cast in the borrowed phrasings of men's interests and men's experience, if they are to gain an audience." Access to authoritative narration
is thus directly related to gender (see also Tsing 1990). Assuming the
stance of storyteller is a fundamentally gendered act in Karoland and
in any context where narration is produced and evaluated in gendered
terms.

Aspects of linguistic ideology associated with institutions (i.e., institutional policies about "official" and "unofficial" discourse) can determine whose stories count—in effect, who is a valid storyteller or
who can tell what kinds of stories in institutional contexts. Thus, in
a colonial courtroom in Karoland, where women are not considered
valid speakers, "women may . . . find their own stories 'perfectly unac-
ceptable' to the official order they confront, or in which they live their
lives. They may learn that speaking for themselves requires that . . .
they speak as 'someone else' " (Steedly 1993:239). Accordingly, even
in the postcolonial period, Karo women tell their stories as accounts
of spirit possession or while possessed, which allows them to enter
into conversation with official discourse and, at the same time, to
counter it.

The situation for Swahili Muslim women is somewhat different.

In Kadhi's Court, women speak for themselves, and they tell stories that regularly subvert official (male) discourse. Through speaking as women, in ways that reinforce stereotypes of women as storytellers at the same time as they contravene linguistic prerogatives of the courts and other Swahili contexts, women challenge the cultural and institutional tendencies to silence women's stories in order to hear men's pronouncements. Thus, narration in Swahili courts produces fundamentally contradictory images. Acts of narration and the interpretations of those acts differentiate men from women, complainers from victims, gossips from those who speak properly. Not only is narrative the vehicle for resolving conflict, but it is often targeted ideologically as the *cause* of conflict. In its role as causing conflict, narrative is associated with women and their inappropriate verbal acts—their complaints, gossip, and loose speech. The notion that Swahili women's speech causes conflict reflects a fundamental gender difference that in turn reflects inequality in Swahili society. At the heart of this inequality is the Swahili cultural understanding that enjoins narrating family conflict and that suspects women to be the primary abusers of this convention. Despite court decisions favoring women, their speech in court is condemned. Understanding the link between gender, language, and conflict as it relates to Swahili social life requires a thorough discussion of cultural ideas and practices, which I begin in the next chapter.

Conclusion

In analyzing Swahili marital disputes, I direct attention to ideologies of language in order to highlight how the discourses of disputing are constitutive of gendered individuals and thus determinative of their abilities, opportunities, and tendencies with respect to narration and other speech forms. I mean to provide a counterpoint to studies that conclude that courtroom conventions, which have at their base particular language ideologies, offer women less opportunity to narrate conflict in meaningful ways. Accordingly, I explore how cultural understandings about language produced by speakers in Kadhi's Courts are integral to the telling and interpretation of narratives of trouble and to the transformations of gender that are effected through such tellings. My intention is to show how the use of language and metalanguage in dispute processes reshapes and reconstitutes Swahili disputants as gendered, legal, and discursive subjects and, as well, to chart the limits of those transformations in the postcolonial period.

Although the legal institution's practice of officializing some stories (or some forms of discourse) and ignoring others is integral to my analysis, I am ultimately concerned with ideas about language that are more broadly cultural, that is, ones that extend into and beyond the postcolonial legal institution. The idea of "institutional culture," which is often the starting point for studies of courts and other institutions, fails to capture the extent to which I incorporate a consideration of Swahili cultural beliefs into my analysis of courts and other disputing contexts. My attention to culture is meant less to accentuate cultural differences (e.g., Swahili vs. U.S.) than to avoid the simplistic conclusion that "Western" influences in postcolonial institutions are determinative either of the form of linguistic interaction or of gender relations.

Anthropologists have become increasingly skeptical of the role of "culture" in our analyses and explanations. Culture has, at its most notorious, been invoked in ways that imply or assert a hegemonic hold on individuals and has thus led to conclusions about immutable differences between collectivities. More recently, scholars have developed theories of culture that attend to historical contingency, change, and power (see, e.g., Comaroff and Comaroff 1991; Dirks, Eley, and Ortner 1994; Rosaldo 1989). Moreover, the concept has been reclaimed and reinvigorated through interdisciplinary efforts in "cultural studies" and from interest in "global" perspectives (Appadurai 1991). Lila Abu-Lughod (1991) has urged anthropologists to embrace the project of "writing against culture" in order to expose culture's false hegemony in people's lives and, perhaps, its all-too-real hegemony in the lives and writings of anthropologists! Penetrating questions about culture emerge when those who stand in marginal relations to its assumed center are brought into consideration, and when attention is directed at the widely divergent beliefs and practices of the many people supposedly living under culture's sway. The point behind Abu-Lughod's project is well taken, though I suspect that in according less privilege to culture as an explanatory category it will be increasingly important to track culture's considerable, though perhaps changed, role in social life. This is crucial in postcolonial settings, where "culture" and "traditional culture" are invoked to legitimate positions in complex struggles involving gender and other intersecting hierarchies.

In the Swahili context, the phrase "We Swahili say ..." prefaces statements that promote particular cultural practices and at the same time constitute "Swahili culture." Taking account of the continued production of statements such as "marry in a good way, divorce in a good way" and noting that their directive force comes in part from the prefacing phrase "We Swahili say ..." is critical to conceptualizing culture more processually and situating it more appropriately in anthropological analyses, including those that focus on law.

Nyumba husetiri mambo.
The house hides matters.

Representations of Swahili Society

Several days after I began observing marriage and divorce cases in his court, the Chief Kadhi of Kenya advised me to examine a legal text to which he sometimes referred. He wrote the title, *Minhaj et Talibin* (Nawawi 1914), on a small piece of paper and, handing it to me, suggested I look for the book in the law library at the old Mombasa court building.[1] The law librarian directed me to the small section on Islamic law, where I found the volume, a large book comprising numerous interpretations of Islamic laws by Muslim legal scholars. Using small notecards, I copied out the ways in which a man pronouncing divorce might negate his action—for example, through being drunk or by swearing an oath beforehand. I soon realized that my plan to make notes on the entire section on marriage and divorce was too ambitious, as the library was hot and dusty and the librarian, a Kenyan Luo man trained in Leningrad and eager to talk about American-Soviet relations, was considerably more interesting than the endless hypotheticals that seemed far removed from real-life situations. After three long afternoons in the law library, I knew that this was not the most fruitful method of studying marital conflict.

The Chief Kadhi's suggestion that I examine law in its ideological incarnation was paralleled by the advice of other Swahili people, who urged me to learn about marriage and divorce by reading locally produced pamphlets explaining Islamic family law. The concise descriptions of how, for example, revocable divorce differs from irrevocable divorce were similar to the comments of people who, upon learning of my interest in marital conflict, would recite laws of marriage and divorce. A particular favorite, told to non-Muslims for the shock value of its provocative reference to the instrumental use of sex, was the following: "We Muslims can divorce twice and still return to the same partner. After the third divorce the wife has to marry *and sleep with* someone else before she can return to the husband who divorced her."

Such statements depicted domestic relations as the consequence of rules that could be clearly articulated and applied unproblematically. It was not the case, then or now, that I was uninterested in the ideologies of marriage embodied in legal texts or recited mechanically. But a few days in court, and a few weeks in Swahili society, suggested to me that textual rules contrasted sharply with actual domestic relations, a point that one hundred years of legal anthropology had also established with certainty.

The story that I relate above is not unusual. The foreign anthropologist just arrived in a community is regularly directed toward the ideal—often toward textual sources that prescribe behavior rather than toward behavior itself. This was also the approach of the Mombasa family who graciously hosted me during the first months of my research.[2] Family members were "Swahili nationalists" in that they promoted positive images of Swahili culture, ones that sought to recapture traditions from the height of Swahili civilization in past centuries. They presented me with normative visions of an ideal Swahili society, free of discord and reverent of traditional customs. Even the two young grandsons behaved with decorum, greeting their elders by kissing their hands. More often than not, I was encouraged to spend time in the sitting room, where men discussed poetry and Islam, rather than in the bedroom, where, as I learned later, the women of the family and their female guests discussed less lofty or idealized topics.

In those first weeks, I began both to appreciate the significance of proper, "traditional" representations of Swahili life and to wonder what kind of research strategies might illuminate more mundane or contentious activities, such as those I believed were behind the presence of so many divorcing couples in Kadhi's Courts. How could I spend time in the bedroom to hear more than just snatches of conversation about runaway wives, disobedient daughters, alcoholic uncles, and abusive husbands? And a more serious problem loomed: how, once I had learned about these conflicts, could I represent the less idealized aspects of Swahili life in ways that would satisfy the Swahili nationalist sentiments of the family with whom I was staying?

Just as I was beginning to understand the complexities of my project and my position, which was no less paradoxical for being one familiar to anthropologists, a shocking event occurred in the household. And we were all plunged into the messy world of law and domestic relations and courts and kadhis and the real-life dramas that can never be anticipated in legal texts or research proposals, no matter how many hypotheticals they seek to address. As it unfolded, this event taught me a fundamental precept of Swahili culture: the necessity of hiding information about one's family.

"Jambo limekuja!" "Something's happened!"

The shocking event was the kidnapping of the two grandsons living in the household described above. Their father, who had been divorced from their mother for several years, picked them up one day promising an afternoon at the beach, and instead drove them across the border to his family home in Tanzania. When household members realized what had happened, they rushed to the Chief Kadhi's house that very evening, insisting that he verify having granted the boys' mother custody several years before. By the next morning other legal authorities, including the Children's Officer, a civil court magistrate, and the police, were also involved. The steady stream of extended family, neighbors, and friends dropping by to offer advice and support illustrated to me how people cope with serious domestic conflict. My assumptions about the hegemonic role of idealized cultural and legal principles altered considerably as we dealt with witchcraft accusations, doctored files, legal personnel who coached witnesses to lie, and threats of deportation meant to silence the boys' mother. I was aware of witnessing the operation of law behind the statutes, where tears, prayers, poems, threats, and affidavits accompanied neat legalistic assertions like "On divorce, the custody of children under seven is generally awarded to the mother."

As a result of the kidnapping, relations between me and my hosts changed. In desperate attempts to ensure the boys' safe return, members of the household abandoned the pretenses of polite behavior. The boys' mother told me about the many conflicts with her former husband that had preceded the kidnapping. Other relatives described previous court battles over the children and the couple's acrimonious divorce and urged me to write down their stories as potential evidence for future court cases. The grandfather told me that, though he was pleased I was keeping notes, he preferred that I refrain from publishing a detailed analysis of the incident. As he explained, this was a household conflict, and, as a household member, I should be discreet. We agreed that in any academic discussion I would preserve certain family secrets about the conflict, as I have done here. Moreover, I refrained from writing about the incident until well after it was resolved with the return of the boys, who had been kept away for two years.

During the ordeal, I was pleased to be treated like a family member who is trusted to "hide matters" *(setiri mambo)*.[3] Describing the terms for people who engage in gossip, Swartz and Omar (1985:241) identify the "exposer" *(mwazirifu)* as "someone who talks about or otherwise makes public, shameful things normally in his own family." Concealing knowledge about family matters is directly related to concerns over preserving social status, which have long characterized Swahili society. These concerns stem from dual tendencies in Swahili society: (1) the tendency to incorporate or "Swahilize" populations who come into contact with Swahili people; and (2) the tendency to maintain several forms of stratification. As described in the next section, cross-cutting lines of difference and power—African/Arab, underclass/elite, female/ male, among others—have long been the ordering principles of Swahili society and continue to provide the terms through which status is displayed and measured. A family's position can only be maintained if family members behave appropriately, including through their speech. By virtue of talking about family problems, exposers risk lowering their status (ibid.).

Ethnographies always expose, yet they are partial exposures, hiding some matters and emphasizing others.[4] Much of the scholarship on coastal Swahili society preserves the normative image of Swahili culture as proper, pious, and free of conflict. As scholarship has shifted from merely re-presenting the hegemonic prescriptions of elite culture, it has begun to narrate the secrets of Swahili families. This is especially true of recent academic attention to gender relations, which offers a counterpoint to descriptions of Swahili cultural ideals. Moreover, ethnographic studies of gender expose tensions in Swahili society in the very places (homes, marriages, intimate life) where hiding matters of conflict is critically important. As my analysis of gender ideologies, comportment, and marriage presented later in this chapter demonstrates, Swahili women bear a complex burden of preserving Swahili ideals in the face of social contradictions, a burden that often requires them to conceal conflict. Accordingly, I direct attention to the politics of representing Swahili life by considering what it means for anthropologists, particularly women anthropologists, to narrate the conflict associated with gender relations. In describing Swahili society, both its idealized versions and conflict-ridden everyday life, I consider the consequences of exposing the conflict underlying the ideals, be they legal statutes or everyday platitudes.

Swahili Ethnography as Partial Exposure

Historical studies of the Swahili coast are numerous and include archeological and linguistic investigations of coastal prehistory.[5] John Middleton's volume *The World of the Swahili: An African Mercantile Civilization* locates Swahili society at the nexus of trade in slaves, ivory, cloth, spices, and mangrove, among other commodities, extending into the African continent and outward to the Arabian Peninsula, the Indian subcontinent, and Europe (see also Freeman-Grenville 1988; Prins 1961; Swartz 1991).[6] Swahili people living in coastal towns and villages have served for hundreds of years as "middlemen" who prospered by forging and, sometimes, manipulating relations with conquerors and colonizers, and with local and distant partners in trade and marriage (see Le Guennec-Coppens 1989; Parkin 1989). In addition to trade, the Swahili economy has been based largely on fishing in the Indian Ocean and the waterways of the lush coastal strip.

An urban population, Swahili people live primarily in "stone towns" or "country towns," many of which are ports.[7] Each major coastal town (Mombasa, Malindi, and Lamu) recognizes a tradition of Swahili leadership through kings of mythic history, who were the ancestors of the patrician families that claim high status. Throughout colonization by Portugal in the fifteenth century, by the Omani sultanate in Zanzibar from the eighteenth century, and by Britain from the late 1900s until Kenya's independence in 1963, the history of great Swahili communities in Lamu, Pate, and Mombasa has remained in the consciousness of Swahili people and is the cornerstone of the "cultural nostalgia" of some versions of contemporary Swahili nationalism.[8]

Through their connections with Arabs from several Middle Eastern locations, Swahili people were exposed to Islam, texts written in Arabic script (which was used to write Kiswahili), and many products, including writing materials. Since the early nineteenth century, Arabs from the Hadramaut area of the Middle East have come in waves to settle at the coast and establish businesses. Those Hadrami who claim genealogical ties to the Prophet Mohammed are known as Masharifu, and they have been influential in coastal religious life. In addition, some Arab traders married the daughters of Swahili merchants.[9] In the nineteenth century, Arabs from Oman, ruling from a sultanate established in Zanzibar, achieved political and social dominion on the coast in addition to conducting an active shipping trade. This period was characterized by a significant emphasis on the Arabic elements of Swahili culture, as town-dwelling Swahili looked to Zanzibar for new fashions in clothing, religion, and governance.

The tendency for Swahili culture to "Arabize" throughout the nineteenth century set terms of social stratification that venerated practices associated with being Arab (Mazrui and Shariff 1994:28; see also Glassman 1995; Pouwels 1987). Yet these terms have always been balanced against the undeniable evidence of African origins and the recognized distinction of Swahili people from Arabs.[10] Those groups with fewer connections to patrician families or Arabs, such as the Bajuni clans of Kenya's north coast, have resisted Arab influences. Moreover, Swahili people have routinely cultivated relations with their closest neighbors (e.g., Giriama), bringing many into Swahili culture through marriage, concubinage, or conversion to Islam.[11] At the same time as Swahili culture incorporates others (largely through marriage), numerous divisions and rankings put everyone, including and most especially newcomers, into quite particular places. For much of the latter two centuries, rankings based on position within the economic system were a central feature of identity (e.g., former slave, former freeborn, former master). Over time, these rigid boundaries blurred through the use of terms of status (e.g., civilized [-staarabu], freeborn [-ungwana], uncivilized [-tumwa or -shenzi]).[12] In addition, residence has always demarcated relations among Swahili, with stone towns reflecting higher status than country towns. Residence in a particular town can correlate with "tribe" (kabila)[13] and clan (e.g., Washela, Wabakary). All of these designations carry weight in estimations of status, as do skin color and religious sect.

In the late nineteenth century, Omani influence over coastal culture was disrupted by the cessation of the slave trade and the advent of British colonization, which also brought Swahili coastal preeminence to a close. The shifting relations of power refigured internal markers of status. According to Strobel (1979:43), "colonialism altered the class and patriarchal structures of the precolonial period and further eroded the domestic and public authority of the Muslim community's leading men." Although the British initially favored the literate Swahili Muslims over other East African peoples, they vacillated over the years of colonial rule in their assistance to Swahili people.[14] Though coastal Muslims did not experience the bloodshed of colonial rule that terrorized populations in up-country areas, they were left in a narrowly defined position at Independence. Divided among themselves, Swahili people were viewed with skepticism by other Kenyans, who regarded them as opportunists, exploiters, and, when considering their Arab connections, foreigners. The Swahili community has continued to decline economically and politically in the postcolonial era.[15] Shifts in the global economy have meant that those who continue to fish or engage in trade in some commodities, such as copra or mangrove, receive steadily decreasing economic returns.

Although Swahili people have always valued literacy, they, unlike other Kenyan ethnic groups, did not enter colonial and postcolonial schools in numbers sufficient to create a large class of educated professionals (Porter 1992b). Swahili people work in the service sector (e.g., transportation, government offices) and the informal economy. Young women take jobs as secretaries and clerks, and women of all ages work out of their homes, selling cooked food or tailoring clothes. In the 1970s and early 1980s, men sought employment as laborers and clerks in the Middle East, but these jobs are no longer so readily available. Consequently, there has been a high rate of unemployment among young men since the mid-1980s. The Swahili community is not only becoming poorer but also exhibiting increased class stratification. The Mombasa port brings wealth into postcolonial Kenya, particularly the capital, but not into the hands of Swahili people (Mazrui and Shariff 1994).[16] As well as experiencing economic decline, the Swahili community lacks political clout. After failing in their efforts to retain coastal autonomy in the early 1960s (see Kindy 1972), Swahili people generally refrained from active participation in Kenyan politics. They viewed the state as potentially hostile to Muslims, while, for its part, the state questioned the loyalty of people who seemed more concerned to forge ties with wealthy Arab nations than to express loyalty as Kenyans.[17]

Some coastal people, especially Swahili nationalists, confront the community's economic decline and political marginalization by asserting a proud history of indigenous Swahili accomplishment that emphasizes Islamic elements.[18] Although Mazrui and Shariff (1994) argue, rightly, that foreign scholars have overemphasized the degree to which "Swahili identity" is a problem for Swahili people, attending to the differences and similarities of social position is a significant aspect of being Swahili.[19] As suggested below, Islam, Kiswahili, and Swahili literature operate as unifying forces in Swahili society. At the same time, they provide the vehicles for expressing differences of status, gender, religious sect, and class, which all contribute to Swahili identity.

Islam choreographs coastal life, dividing the day into periods before and after the five times for prayer and compelling believers to wash before each prayer session and to fast from sunrise to sunset during the month of Ramadhan.[20] Many Swahili Muslims also enact their beliefs by attending prayers and mosque lectures, sending their children to Koranic school, and giving charity. Although some families are known to be more observant or pious than others, most follow Islamic principles of marriage, divorce, and inheritance. With rare exceptions, Waswahili are Sunni Muslims of the Shafi sect.[21] The majority are locally oriented in their practice of Islam and engage in activities influenced by Sufism, which include saint veneration, spirit-possession cults, Islamic medicines and magic, and elaborate celebrations of the Prophet's birthday (Maulidi).[22] Varieties of Islamic practice correlate with differences of class, gender, and ethnicity (Giles 1987; Strobel 1979; Swartz 1979). Islamic practice prohibits women from serving as religious authorities or entering some mosques. Ethnicity motivates rivalries between mosques in each community, as do political differences. Some religious authorities discourage practices that constitute innovation *(bidhaa)*, in campaigns that reflect the international turn toward fundamentalism and local efforts to minimize African influences in Islam (see also Constantin 1993). Those involved portray themselves as reformers seeking to establish an Islam that fosters modernization and yet retains piety (see Fuglesang 1994:53–59).

Kiswahili, the Swahili language, is central to the identity and unity of Swahili people in multilingual postcolonial Kenya.[23] Swahili people are distinguished from other Kenyan ethnic groups in that they speak Kiswahili as their first language rather than as a second language of trade, education, or national unity. Many Swahili people assert their abilities to speak stylized versions of Kiswahili, which include word play, double entendre, and hidden meanings.[24] Among Swahili people, variations in linguistic forms, such as pronunciation or lexical items, mark diversity in birthplace, gender, and age (see Khalid 1977; Maw and Parkin 1985; Russell 1981; Shariff 1973).

The Kiswahili literature produced by coastal people is indisputably a central feature of Swahili culture, and the long history of literacy distinguishes the community from surrounding groups. However, the tendency in academic scholarship to highlight Swahili written texts while ignoring other forms of cultural expression reflects both a "modal" bias (toward literary work) and a lingering "Orientalism" that prefers the more "Arabized" aspects of Swahili society (Mazrui and Shariff 1994:96). The "high-culture" bias motivating interest in, for example, Arab-influenced epic poems entails disinterest in folktales, proverbs, and didactic stories, all orally transmitted until recently, that are produced by less elite sectors of the population (Eastman 1984a; Russell 1985).

Scholars have tended to express interest in the first element in each of the following related and parallel dichotomies that characterize Swahili social relations: freeborn/slave, Arab/African, literate/nonliterate, and male/female.[25] Although, as Mazrui and Shariff point out, foreign scholarship on Swahili literature has perpetuated a high-culture bias, a similar bias operates hegemonically within Swahili communities, promoted by the elite.[26] The tendency to cede too much power to foreign scholars must be balanced with a recognition of the agency of Swahili people, most often powerful members of society, in producing representations of themselves, including ones that circulate internationally. It is, in part, the agency of male elites that has resulted in the scholarly neglect of women's oral traditions. As a reaction, recent ethnographic accounts attend to the agency of ordinary Swahili who engage in politicized struggles over cultural practices. These accounts focus particularly on those aspects of Swahili culture that emerge from the lower strata of society, including from women, and that stand in opposition to high culture.

Historical and ethnographic scholarship on Swahili gender relations also subverts the high-culture bias of Swahili scholarship (see, e.g., Caplan 1975; Eastman 1984b; Fuglesang 1994; Le Guennec-Coppens 1983; Mirza and Strobel 1989; Porter 1992b; Romero 1988; Shepherd 1987; Strobel 1979). Relatively uninterested in whether a particular cultural practice is more Arab or more African, these scholars focus on how cultural practices facilitate the negotiation of contradictions in Swahili society stemming from the former slave economy and current inequities of class, status, and gender. For example, women's participation in ceremonies, rituals, dance, and expressive culture is treated as evidence of women's contribution to refiguring relations of power.

Margaret Strobel's history of Muslim women in Mombasa is a model for examining the shifting power dynamics of Swahili society over time and for recognizing women's central role in altering the terms of status (Strobel 1979).[27] Focusing on weddings, Strobel shows how ritual activities both symbolize Swahili culture and at the same time perpetuate internal hierarchies. For example, the movement of African elements into Swahili culture traces the historical movement of African women into coastal Muslim society through slavery and, more to the point, through concubinage and marriage. Thus, women's historical connection to African elements of Swahili culture is sustained, though greatly altered. African elements have become more prominent in expressive culture and in contexts where women's participation is critical (e.g., wedding dances and funerals), which suggests that women are vehicles for incorporating into Swahili society those elements that controvert high-culture bias.

Women's tendency to maintain African-oriented elements in Swahili social life becomes even more intriguing when another aspect of gender is considered: Swahili women are the subjects through which status is policed. As described below, through seclusion, limits on autonomy, and marriage, women's lives are shaped in ways that maintain the honor and status of individual families and of the Swahili community. It is not surprising, then, that the very figures positioned to open Swahili society to potentially destabilizing, low-culture influences are those that are closely monitored as representatives of status. Scholarship, generally feminist, that has examined how women participate in demarcating, maintaining, and transgressing the boundaries of Swahili culture has mapped most cogently the realities of Swahili social relations. Yet focusing on the contradictions and divisions that characterize contemporary coastal life risks exposing precisely those aspects of Swahili society that most Swahili people have historically tried to protect from exposure by neighbors and family members, by other Swahili people and outsiders, and by anthropologists and other foreign scholars.

Representations of Gender Ideologies

Early in this century, Mtoro bin Mwinyi Bakari, a Swahili learned man living in the coastal area of what is now Tanzania, was commissioned by Dr. Carl Velten, a German linguist, to write a treatise on Swahili customs.[28] In *Desturi za Waswahili* (Customs of the Swahili), Bakari's discussion of women's roles in Swahili society, though rather limited, reflected the explicit tension between the practices of elite, Arab-oriented patricians and the realities of most women's lives at the time.[29] Two passages about marriage depict, on the one hand, the ideal of women's seclusion and subordination to men and, on the other hand, the reality that, throughout this century, Swahili women have challenged the terms of gender:

> When a man lives with his wife, she is allowed to do nothing whatever without her husband's consent. If he forbids something that he does not like, that is the end of it, and if the woman does it she is called recalcitrant, because she does not obey her husband. A free woman may not go out by day without excuse, except for natural calls. She must be veiled if she wants to go for a talk at a friend's house, accompanied by a slave girl. If a woman disobeys her husband, it is for him to correct her; but for serious offenses he takes her to the magistrate for correction (Bakari 1981:78).

> Divorce starts when a man and his wife begin to quarrel. They quarrel because either the husband is straying or the wife. If the husband tells the wife to stay at home, she replies, "Do you want to keep me in the dark to ripen like a banana? If you want me, you must let me go out; if you do not, get yourself a stay-at-home wife." This reply annoys the husband (Bakari 1981:131).

According to Bakari, women of the patrician families depicted in the first passage spent most of their time within the walls of their large stone houses. Even when inside, they remained secluded from unrelated male visitors. When outside, these women veiled.[30] Other texts from Bakari's time and most ethnographic and historical studies produced prior to the past several decades tended to emphasize the high-culture ideals of Swahili women's proper behavior, depicting it as controlled by men (see, e.g., the famous poem written by Mwana Kupona).[31] During Bakari's time, deviations from the ideal—for example, the behavior of the woman depicted in the second passage, as well as women's participation in low-status activities such as initiation ceremonies—were most likely common for Swahili people, though rarely represented textually (see also Tanner 1962).

The cultural ideals of women's seclusion and husbands' control, as expressed in the first quote by Bakari, are much the same in the late twentieth century as they were one hundred years ago; however, only a few of the most elite patrician families achieve them (see Caplan 1989; Curtin 1984; Tanner 1964). Colonization refigured gender relations in contradictory ways, by encouraging some women to resist patriarchal oppression and yet positioning many as repositories of traditional values pitted against colonial domination (Strobel 1979). The lives of women in the urban areas where I conducted my research implicitly challenge images of gender subordination, and women from the lowest classes and statuses are least likely to approximate the patrician ideal (see also Caplan 1975, 1995). Though ideologically salient, hegemonic gender relations and the hierarchies they support face challenges from secular education, the decline of male religious authority, and shifting economic relations in postcolonial Swahili society. New ethnography on Swahili gender relations suggests that women are not just vehicles for papering over the contradictions underlying Swahili social relations. Rather, they actively confront and reshape their statuses in the face of increasing class stratification and the diminishing influence of Swahili people in Kenya.

Underlying Bakari's first quote is the assumption that men and women occupy profoundly different positions in Swahili society. Several key concepts justify the practices—sometimes interpreted as oppressive to women—undertaken in the name of this difference. One of these concepts, *heshima,* has been translated as respect, dignity, modesty, honor, and reputation (Johnson and Madan 1939; Middleton 1992; Strobel 1979). Both men and women aspire to *heshima* as a personal attribute, which they endeavor to preserve and exhibit. For men, *heshima* is acquired through "scholarship, business integrity and skill, and piety," as well as other talents and pursuits that demonstrate worldliness (Middleton 1992:138). For women, *heshima* is linked closely to another concept: *usafi* (purity). For an unmarried woman, virginity is central to her *usafi.*[32] *Heshima* and *usafi* are established and measured not only through the actions of men and women as gendered individuals but, more importantly, through their behavior in the roles of mother, father, son, and especially wife and daughter.

A local religious leader wrote the following in an advice pamphlet: "The important thing that Islamic law wants for women is respect *(heshima)* and manners *(adabu)* according to Islam when they are at home or outside of the house" (Shee 1984:36).[33] Here, *heshima* is reputation, secured through behavior that is not shameful *(aibu).* An individual has considerable control over his or her *heshima,* and, as an ideal, all interactions should be undertaken with the intention that they will reflect and augment one's own *heshima* and that of others.[34] For women, *heshima* is more directly linked to sexuality and to "uncivilized" *(ushenzi)* behavior than for men. At the same time as women are ordered not to "break *heshima*" *(-vunja heshima)* by behaving in ways that cast doubt on their sexual purity, men are urged to have *heshima* for women by refraining from actions that would violate their purity. A woman's *heshima* is called into question by any avoidable contact with a man to whom she is not related as *maharimu*, a category of persons within certain degrees of consanguinity and so forbidden to marry or have sex with each other. Men secure their claims to *heshima* as honor through the *heshima* of the women of their households. The religious leader quoted above attributes manners and *heshima* to Islamic law; however, they are linked just as closely to the patrician ideals of Swahili society (Middleton 1992:194). Because civilized behavior is associated with men and because women represent lower elements of society, the burden of maintaining *heshima* falls more squarely on women. Precisely because of Swahili women's morally and socially ambiguous position, demonstrating *heshima* is critical for women, yet especially difficult.[35]

The burdens for women of negotiating status are accentuated by the Islamic ideology that conceptualizes females as vulnerable to sexual temptation and of weak character (see Strobel 1979:55, but see also Ahmed 1992; Mernissi 1991). Moreover, religious authorities depict women as experiencing routine lapses in good sense *(akili)*. Such ideologies support men's entitlement to authority over women. Fathers or designated male guardians have the right to grant or refuse permission *(idhini)* for a woman's marriage, and, when she marries, authority passes from the father to the husband. There is remarkably little disagreement among men and women about men's entitlement to authority over women. A young girl will readily recite the requirement facing her that she obey her father and, eventually, her husband. Yet that same young girl, depending on class and status, may witness the autonomy of a mother who works outside the home or travels frequently. Fuglesang (1994:90) notes that the "incongruity" between ideal and actual roles deepens "as we move down the social ladder" (see also Strobel 1979).[36] Male control is directed toward ensuring women's propriety, although the behaviors that establish *heshima,* such as veiling, are embedded in complex systems of sociopolitical meaning that link gender with other relations of power.

Veiling and Proper Comportment

Long established among virtually all classes of Swahili women, the practice of veiling is a central means through which *heshima* is maintained. From the time they begin menstruating, women don a *buibui*—a wide, floor-length cloak with an attached veil—whenever they leave the house, even if they are going no further than to see a neighbor. Made of imported black polyester, *buibui*s are opaque, and the veil can be held or tied over the face so that only the eyes are visible. Most women pull the veil tight against their cheeks and secure the fabric under the chin, leaving their faces exposed. A woman removes her *buibui* upon entering her own house; however, when visiting, she might leave it on, just loosening the veil and allowing the cloak to drop to her shoulders or waist, depending on how comfortable she is with her hosts and whether men to whom she is not related are present. Wearing a *buibui* is an activity as much as a material marker of gendered status. Women tie and retie the veil to punctuate conversation or to reflect that a man has entered the room. When a woman walks in the street, her *buibui* can be drawn sharply across the face if the stares of loitering strangers become too penetrating.

Much Western discourse on Islamic societies betrays a horrified fascination with the veiling of Muslim women and often assumes that the veil symbolizes women's subordination.[37] Some studies of veiling interpret the practice not as marking women's low status but as hiding something, such as a woman's identity, female sexuality, or the "problem" that women represent through their capacity to destabilize society.[38] As accounts by diverse scholars, Muslim clerics, and Muslim women—some of whom veil and some of whom do not—have accumulated, they confirm that veiling in Islamic societies is a complex religious and political behavior and that its many meanings and functions reflect both local and international discourses involving gender and other relations of power (see, e.g., Abu-Lughod 1986; Ahmed 1992; Macleod 1991; Mernissi 1991; Papanek 1973). The interpretation of veiling in any one context should not, therefore, be reduced to a simplistic calculus of gender hierarchy. Like any symbols, veils become operative in political struggles involving gender, age, ethnicity, class, etc. Moreover, the meanings of veiling change over time, and veils are meaningful in different ways to those who wear them, those who compel or encourage the practice, and those who observe and analyze it.

For Swahili women, veiling is primarily a means of displaying and maintaining *heshima* outside the home. The *buibui* establishes an identity among women from all classes that conveys respectability. It marks other aspects of identity that communicate different meanings to non-Swahili people. The *buibui* as worn by Swahili women differentiates them from coastal women of other religious sects. Swahili men similarly establish their religious distinction through wearing a long white overshirt *(kanzu)* and a white embroidered cap *(kofia)*.[39] On a trip to the coast in the mid-1980s, President Daniel arap Moi was informed that many young Muslim women remained unmarried into their late twenties, most of them destined to be financial burdens on their families. Ignoring the explanation that bridewealth inflation was the recent source of the problem, he made a speech urging young women to remove their veils so that potential husbands could see their beautiful faces and marry them. Coastal Muslims were outraged, and a religious scholar who wrote a response defending the veil in the name of Islam was jailed briefly (Shee 1984). As a result, the commitment to veil was renewed; however, in contrast to other Islamic populations, Swahili people have not used veiling as the vehicle for community opposition to the secular state. Moreover, the state is ambivalent in its criticism of veiling, given that the image of the veiled Muslim woman operates as a signifier of coastal exoticism exploited by the tourist industry. This image, which appeals to international and domestic tourists, is prominently displayed on T-shirts, postcards, and posters advertising Kenyan tourism.

Within the Swahili community, the *buibui* marks differences of class and age through its style of wear and the material used. For example, married women attending a wedding let their *buibui*s fall open to show new dresses, gold necklaces, and carefully arranged makeup and hair. By contrast, women who have never been married and are thus not officially permitted to attend weddings wear their *buibui*s so that only their eyes remain visible, thereby concealing their identities as they crowd behind the invited guests.[40] In this circumstance, the *buibui* becomes a disguise behind which the young women wreak havoc by stealing food, pinching guests, and running through the streets and alleys taunting passersby.[41] Their behavior, outrageous by Swahili standards, is made possible because they are a homogenous group. Some older or extremely pious women also cover themselves completely in public. Although these women are admired for their *heshima* and for exemplifying proper or traditional veiling, Swahili Muslims condemn others who camouflage themselves in veils to avoid recognition when they are engaging in improper behavior, such as meeting a lover or going to a bar. Violations of the standard ways in which women wear the *buibui* reveal its subtle meanings. In a Kadhi's Court case, a woman was brought to court by her husband because she refused to remove her *buibui* when in their house. Her narrative in court revealed that she did not feel she was being treated as a wife by her husband, and she therefore behaved as a stranger by remaining veiled at home.

Muslim women's veiling has often been interpreted in relation to the concepts of "public" and "private." Swahili notions of what is inside the house as opposed to what is outside approximate a private/ public distinction that guides where women should veil. Porter (1992b) argues that veiling and other practices (e.g., curtaining off outdoor wedding celebrations) create private or domestic space in contexts that are seemingly public.[42] There are other parallels between the house (especially the walls of the house) and the veil, as they both operate to guard family status as embodied in its women.[43] Middleton elucidates this aspect of Swahili culture when he writes: "The distinction between public and private runs through Swahili cultural values, the private being the end of the process by which what has been in the public domain is removed to the private sphere" (1992:187).

In positing a connection between house walls and veils, I propose thinking about the veil as an *overt* means of concealing family secrets. It is explicit, partial exposure of that which is supposed to remain hidden. The veil operates through overtly indicating that something is concealed rather than, for example, concealing a woman in order to erase her. Swahili veiling displays quite publicly the very fact that there are secrets that the family actively conceals. The parallel between veiling and the overt concealment of wealth touches on a central paradox in Swahili society: the privatization of goods as a means of augmenting status only works if others are aware of, or suspect, the existence of those goods. This paradox accounts for the centrality of intrigue in Swahili social life and for the concern over keeping secrets within the family, including sources and amounts of wealth.

My interpretation of veiling as the act of openly concealing knowledge about women and family status is illustrated by the style in which most married Swahili women veil for a wedding celebration. Women dress quite elegantly to attend weddings, though they wear *buibui*s to cover their fancy dresses and gold jewelry when traveling to the event.[44] On her way to a wedding, a woman can use her veil to hide even the makeup decorating her face; however, the fact that she has primped for the celebration is not entirely concealed. Many Swahili women, having employed hair rollers, curling irons, and teasing, pile their hair high for a wedding, often adding jasmine corsages and hair combs.[45] As a result, when they put on a *buibui,* the front puffs up distinctively under the black veil, in contrast to its normal flat position. Adornments worn to a wedding are markers of class, status, and ethnicity; however, they also allude to sexuality. The implication is that a woman unveils at the wedding to show other women her finery and then, later that night, unveils again to display her beauty to her husband.[46] The puffed-head figure that women cut in the street as they go to a wedding overtly conceals women's claims to both status and sexuality.

The meaning of Swahili women's veiling is constructed not only with reference to Swahili social status but also in relation to other local and international discourses. Discourses emanating from outside the Swahili community have occasioned explicit exertions of agency by women—especially young women—who are attempting to control the act of veiling and thereby shape their familial and social positions. Since the mid-1980s, young women have increasingly adopted a form of veiling called *hijab,* rather than the *buibui.* Common in Egypt and other Middle Eastern countries, the *hijab* is a large headscarf wrapped or tied around the head and neck, leaving the face exposed. It is generally worn with a *koti,* a floor-length, wide outergarment with long sleeves that is fastened at the neck. Worn primarily outside the house, the *koti,* which is usually black, covers a dress or a robe and trousers. The *hijab* is viewed as a more pious dress than the *buibui,* in part because of its origin in countries with larger Muslim populations but also because a *buibui* can fall open to expose the dress and hair. Moreover, the *hijab* does not allow women to conceal themselves for clandestine activity as readily as does a *buibui.* The role of veiling as overt concealment is further emphasized with a *hijab,* which allows for a woman's identity (her family connection) to be displayed even as her body (the family secret) is disguised. Porter (1992a) makes the important point that this type of clothing increases the visibility of veiling in contexts such as schools, offices, stores, and other public arenas.[47] As veiling becomes more visible, it also becomes a vehicle for making fashion statements—particularly for young women, who embellish their colored headscarves with beaded designs.

Changes in women's veiling mark differences of age, class, ethnicity, and faith. The interpretation of the *hijab* as representing the educated, though religious, woman is supported by the fact that some working women, regardless of age, have adopted it. Macleod (1991) describes how working women in Egypt began to wear the *hijab* in the 1980s as a strategy of resistance in the face of contradictory gender-role expectations that required them to seek work outside the home and yet preserve their status as proper married women.[48] A similar interpretation might account for why middle-class Swahili women who are working in offices, hospitals, schools, shops, and the civil service wear the *hijab*. A contrasting tendency, one that brings together local and international interpretations, is also emerging. Because many young women have adopted the *hijab* through school or in imitation of schoolgirls, the *buibui* has become associated with mature and older women. The *buibui* may come to represent a "traditional," Swahili mode of dress in contrast to the "modern" *hijab*, associated, ironically, both with secular education and with international, reformist Islam—thus marking a split in generation and religious affiliation.

Whether wearing *buibui* or *hijab*, Swahili women are on the move. Traveling around the coast, even to Zanzibar and mainland Tanzania, they visit relatives, attend weddings and funerals, and arrange marriages. Men travel for these and other reasons (business, religious meetings, etc.), and their means of travel are subject to fewer restrictions. A woman, young or old, rarely travels alone, especially on public transportation, and groups of young women often sit clustered at the front of the bus. Of course, some women leave the house daily to travel by themselves to school or work. In some cases, family members wait at the bus stop for a woman who is expected at a particular time, in part to help her with luggage and in part to monitor her trip. Both schooling and the tendency toward later marriages provide young women with more travel opportunities, although parents intervene when they believe a trip might endanger a daughter's reputation. Divorced women, depending on their economic means, have considerable freedom of movement, and often they travel between the homes of their adult children.

Women's increased visibility in public contexts of travel, work, and education is occasioning the renegotiation of *heshima* through clothing. Fuglesang (1994:140, 198) notes the desire of young Swahili women "to see and be seen." Although I agree that the gaze is important, particularly for assessments of status, speaking and being heard are also the subject of concern. A father who has limited means cannot alter the fact that his daughter will be seen by the public as she rides a city bus to get to secretarial college. She might sit near strangers, including men. But he can insist that she comport herself properly by delineating the kinds of speech that are appropriate with those around her. The enforcement of *heshima* has shifted from the interdiction of women's presence in public areas to restrictions on women's behavior in those contexts, particularly on their speech. The *buibui* and the *hijab* continue to keep family secrets physically, even as seclusion is breaking down; however, women are still invested with the responsibility of keeping the secrets verbally, a subject taken up in the next chapter.

Marital Relations and the Preservation of Status

Historically, Swahili marriages have been arranged to join descent groups of equal status, further cementing ties between relatives and thereby preserving status.[49] How well a daughter marries, especially the eldest, signifies her family's position. Because marriages and weddings are sites for the symbolic and material negotiation of status, they are also points of vulnerability when a family can be exposed as unworthy. Situations that diminish status can arise when a betrothed daughter runs off with another man, a bridegroom is unable to consummate his marriage, or parents skimp on feeding wedding guests. In response to such crises, which relate directly to tensions involving status, class, and gender, family members try to smooth over the conflict, seeking to restore family reputation and preserve bonds with new affines.

Marriage embodies the tensions of status in Swahili society. For patricians, the ideal form of marriage is the union of patrilineal parallel cousins, which unites the children of brothers. Much rarer now than earlier in the century, these marriages emphasize patricians' interests in keeping wealth within the walls of family homes.[50] The ideal Swahili marriage calls attention to how some families endeavor to control access to their wealth and knowledge about that wealth. The concerns symbolized in ideal marriages—care in choosing a partner, the strategic union of families, and attention to preserving family status and family secrets—are also reflected in the widely varying marital practices of most Swahili people. Less elite Swahili prefer marriage between cross-cousins. A marriage that unites a man and his mother's brother's daughter is especially appreciated, as it connects men more closely to their maternal kin.[51] Although the ideal patrician marriages facilitate the retention of property by a few agnates, cross-cousin marriages maximize the access of lower-status people to wealth across multiple

descent groups. The only type of cousin marriage frowned on is between the children of two sisters.[52] In contrast to marriage as a means
of reinforcing existing kin relations, marriage ties also forge connections with business and trading partners, uniting families from different towns or from the coast and more distant places, such as the Middle East.[53] Marriages between unrelated persons also occur—a sister
can suggest that her brother marry one of her friends, or young people
find each other and declare their love. For Swahili women, marriage to
non-Swahilis is rare and to non-Muslims almost unheard-of, although
Swahili men have pursued these options.

A person's first marriage, especially an eldest daughter's first marriage, is the most likely to approximate the ideal. First marriages
should unite cousins in an official marriage *(ndoa ya rasmi),* which is
a legal agreement mandated in the Koran, and should be celebrated
by a large public wedding. Second and subsequent marriages vary considerably with respect to the relation between the people being united,
the form of the union, and the wedding itself. Second marriages generally reflect the choices of the couple rather than family concerns over
status. When a woman has been married once and then divorced, she
has more standing to refuse her family's suggestions for a subsequent
husband. A man's second marriage can occur without divorce, given
the Islamic provision allowing men to marry up to four wives. Marriages after the first, especially if they are polygamous, can join people
of differing statuses. A woman consents to a polygamous union for
her first marriage only if her chances of marrying someone else are
slim or if her financial gain would be quite significant.[54]

Legal marriages are those performed by a religious or secular official (e.g., kadhi, assistant registrar) in a mosque or a government office
and registered by that official, who issues marriage certificates to each
party. Some sources mention concubinage *(surya)* as a marital form
with roots in slave/master relations; however, few Swahili people, especially kadhis, deem this appropriate (Bakari 1981; Middleton 1992).
Secret marriages *(ndoa ya siri)* are practiced more widely, although,
not surprisingly, it is difficult to know how many exist. Some men
enter into secret marriages in order to hide a second marriage from a
first wife who will most likely disapprove and might demand compensation or divorce. Kadhis are enjoined from conducting secret marriages, although they sometimes do so unwittingly. Secret marriages
are often love matches, and couples, if they are careful and have the
assistance of family members, can manage to see each other surrepti-

tiously even in a crowded house or neighborhood. If a secret marriage lasts, it might eventually be revealed.

The extensive scholarship on Swahili weddings *(maharusi,* s. *harusi)* documents wide variation (in their length, kinds of ceremonies, number of guests, etc.) depending on whether the individuals had been married previously, the families' economic means, and the need to repay social debts or display family status (Fuglesang 1994; Le Guennec-Coppens 1983; Middleton 1992; Porter 1992b; Strobel 1975, 1979). One wedding that I attended included four main events for women, each held on a different day and involving many guests and lavish food and entertainment: beautification and purification rites performed on the bride *(kutia chooni)* and followed by dancing to drums *(vugo);* dancing in Arabic costumes; a formal ceremony where the bride in all her finery was exhibited on the stage of a crowded theater *(kupamba);* and a luncheon for all the female guests. The *kupamba* display is generally the highlight of a wedding. After waiting (sometimes for hours) to view the bride, guests were served snacks and sodas. On returning home, women shared stories about the event, answering standard questions asked by those not in attendance: "Did you see the bride? Was she beautiful?" In contrast, there were no lavish foods or dress at the wedding of a visibly pregnant young woman, who was being married by her cousin to spare her family further embarrassment over her pregnancy by a boyfriend. Only a few close friends and family attended the *kupamba,* held in the family's small sitting room; snacks consisted of a plate of cookies. As I left the house, a few girls lurking by the door asked the familiar questions sarcastically—"Did you see the bride? Was she beautiful?"—before dissolving into giggles. The next day, older women expressed disapproval that a family would exhibit their daughter in her shame.

The symbolism displayed in wedding celebrations highlights several aspects of social relations. First, weddings reflect changes in social position experienced by the husband and wife. The two are considered to have achieved their status as a married couple only after the marriage is consummated through sexual intercourse. Evidence of the bride's virginity is sometimes displayed, although couples who consider themselves modern refuse to participate. A new bride's transition to womanhood is acknowledged publicly by the position of honor accorded to her at the next wedding celebrated in the community. Second, weddings highlight new connections between the families of the bride and groom, which are symbolized through the movement of peo-

ple and goods between their houses. Several kinds of marriage ex-
changes cement affinal ties, though not all of them are made at every
wedding. The marriage payment, or bridewealth *(mahari)*, is a small
amount of money promised by the groom and his family to the bride.[55]
A larger payment (called *mahari, kitu,* or *hidaya*), given by the groom's
family to the bride's, is used to finance the wedding, to buy furniture
and gifts for the bride, and sometimes for other family needs.[56] Third,
weddings are important occasions for the celebration of Swahili Islamic culture. Because weddings provide one of the few reasons for
women to congregate outside their homes, they affirm women's connections to one another. While such performances hint at the closer
connections of *all* women to lower-status aspects of Swahili culture
and contrast their ceremonies to high culture, weddings are also occasions for displaying divisions among women (e.g., of class and status)
(see Strobel 1979). Wedding performances also make a critical link
between ethnicity and sexuality, providing evidence for the contention
that women's destabilizing influence is both expressed and controlled
through their sexuality. Condemnations of women's unbridled behavior at weddings, made routinely by religious officials as well as by husbands, reaffirm high-culture views of propriety, setting boundaries that
women sometimes accept and sometimes transgress.[57]

The popularity of weddings, the centrality of marriage to adult
status, and the assumption that everyone will marry eventually are all
aspects of the hegemonic role of marriage in Swahili culture. Veneration of heterosexuality in the specific form of marriage is typically
found in gender-segregated societies where men and women spend
considerable time in the company of their own sex. The hegemony of
Swahili heterosexual marriage does not, however, preclude homosexual relations. Weddings are an important context for male homosexu-
als *(mashoga)* to gain public recognition through drumming and sing-
ing performances. *Mashoga* are reputed to serve as the passive partners
of *basha,* another category of men who engage in same-sex sexual relations yet who, unlike *mashoga,* tend to conceal their sexual interests
in men. Shepherd (1987) describes strong bonds between Swahili
women that sometimes include long-term sexual relations, although
her evidence is limited (cf. Porter 1995). Men and women who are
known or thought to be homosexual are sometimes marginalized or
brutalized.[58] More often they are treated by heterosexuals with be-
musement, or their behavior is simply ignored.

In Swahili society, marriage faces a crisis of legitimacy in the postcolonial period, given the increasing numbers of people of marriageable age who remain unmarried and the frequency of divorce. Economic difficulties facing the coastal population account for the inability of young men to meet inflated bridewealth payments and for the tenacity of parents to hold out for high-status marriages for their daughters. Activities previously undertaken by married people are increasingly pursued by unmarried women (e.g., child fosterage). Young women plan events such as school outings, birthday parties, and picnics to entertain themselves, since their attendance at "adult" activities (such as weddings) is restricted. Other scholars have pointed to the high divorce rate—at least two-thirds among the nonpatrician classes—as evidence that marriage is not even a "key institution" in Swahili society (Prins 1961:xv; cf. Porter 1992b). However, getting married and being married, or having been married, are perhaps more important as aspects of status than the relations between a particular husband and wife. Remarriage is routine for both men and women, and divorced people face little stigma unless they have divorced many times.[59] But marital relations are problematic as they are the point at which a family's vulnerability can be exposed: status is diminished when tales of a married couple's conflict leak out. The maintenance of family honor thus turns on whether a person who has married into the family can be trusted to "hide matters." Unlike a family's wealth, which others are meant to suspect, these secrets are best left unspoken.

Women's Narratives and the Gendered Representation of Swahili Culture

The next chapter expands on the point that Swahili men and women are restricted from speaking about family conflict. For women, this means that they have few sanctioned contexts for narrating the difficulties they experience in married life. Women's life histories, a recent addition to Swahili scholarship, narrate some of these tensions and also add a new dimension to the problems of exposure and representation. A unique volume published in both English and Kiswahili (Mirza and Strobel 1989) compiles life histories told by three Swahili women. Each woman describes her childhood, her multiple marriages, and changes in Swahili culture over her lifetime. The difficulties of marital life recounted in each narrative offer personalized insight into domestic conflict. For example, Mishi wa Abdalla's account describes the relationship between her parents and also her own marriages:

My father bought the farm . . . that belonged to an Arab for twelve rupees, with coconut, mango, and orange trees—every kind of tree. When he divorced my mother he left everything for her. Then he got angry and came and sold everything, took the money, and went away (Mirza and Strobel 1989:75).

He [Mbaruk Msalim] divorced me and I married another man, another husband who was good natured. He was an Arab, a Mazrui, Lamini. He came from Takaungu. He was kind and he raised all my children. I didn't have any by him. Even up to now the children cry when they remember him. He was a very good man. Mbaruk Msalim divorced me and married another wife, but Lamini remained my husband until he died (Mirza and Strobel 1989:78).

To the extent that the accounts of Mishi and the other two women document tragic life experiences (e.g., divorce), they resemble stories of personal misfortunes told by Muslim Paxtun women living in northern Pakistan (see Grima 1992). In analyzing the Paxtun stories of loves lost, the deaths of loved ones, and financial disasters, Grima depicts the genre as both reflecting the centrality of tragedy in the lives of Paxtun people and, when produced in gatherings of women, asserting a uniquely women's culture. By contrast, telling stories about the problems of one's life is a more problematic undertaking for Swahili women. There is no cultural aesthetic that, parallel to Paxtun understandings, values personal tragedy as the emotional key in which to articulate a story. Rather, revealing the conflicts in one's life is generally disapproved in that it threatens family status.

The disjuncture between life stories that recount personal experiences of conflict and the norms of speech generally recognized in Swahili society makes the published life histories a fascinating document. As Mirza and Strobel suggest, the collection is a product of its academic time—that is, of a moment when feminist scholars sought to include the voices of "real" women in their texts and, at the same time, to question their own positions as "objective" observers.[60] By depicting conflicts that each woman experienced, as well as the ways in which she confronted those conflicts, the narratives reveal how women are embroiled in the central tensions—of gender, ethnicity, class, and status—in Swahili society. The narrative genre that results from this collaboration allows the Swahili narrators and the scholars to reveal the details of women's lives in ways that profoundly challenge Swahili culture and its scholarly representations. Yet, in exposing personal, familial, and community conflict, these narratives risk conferring "exposer" on all of the women involved in telling, editing, lishing these stories. Experimental genres offer possibilities for women to make observations about their lives that they might not articulate in everyday contexts. So, too—as I argue in this volume—new institutional arrangements, such as postcolonial courts, make it possible for Swahili women to narrate their lives against the strictures on speech that limit the exposure of personal experiences.

... be of good behavior,
With a discreet tongue,
That you be as one beloved,
  Wheresoe'er you shall enter

Let you make yourself entertaining,
By words that have not guile.
But do not make impertinent jokes,
  Which people dislike.

Talk with them cheerfully
Of things which give them pleasure,
But when words might give offence,
  It is better to hold oneself silent.

(MWANA KUPONA, AS QUOTED IN WERNER 1934:41–43)

Analyzing Talk about Trouble

In this chapter I describe the research context, appraise the influence of that context on my methods of research and analysis, and delineate those methods. Conley and O'Barr (1990) describe how, in developing research methods to investigate small-claims courts, they had to "learn to listen" so as to hear the particularities of discourse in that ethnographic context. Their description of the learning process highlights the crucial role of cultural understandings about language in the process whereby people, including researchers, learn how to listen and how to speak. The fact that such cultural ideas vary with context reaffirms the interdependence of linguistic and ethnographic research (see also Duranti 1994; Moerman 1988) as well as the importance of considering the cultural particularities of speech in any ethnographic endeavor (see, e.g., Briggs 1986). Moreover, as has been recently argued, research on language should consider the linguistic analyses made by those whose speech is studied (Briggs 1992b; Mertz 1992b).

The following section describes Swahili ideas about language, focusing on those that concern gender and conflict. Swahili linguistic prescriptions, that is, ideas about how language *should* be used, shaped my access to and experiences with speech during ethnographic research. In its early phases, my research experience was interwoven with the process of learning about appropriate forms of talk in courts and in every other context in which I interacted. How I modulated my speech and conformed my interactions to comply with Swahili expectations was a critical factor in my research methods.

My methodological discussion is influenced by Duranti's approach to methods "as forms of life," which recognizes that linguistic data are subject to the politics of the contexts where they are collected and analyzed and that those who study language should address those politics in their texts. The lessons I learned about listening and speaking as a participant-observer reflected my status as a white American, a researcher, an (initially) inarticulate Kiswahili speaker, a non-Muslim,

and a young woman. Through conforming to prescriptions for gendered speech, as well as violating some, I attained new perspectives
on the content and deployment of Swahili understandings about language and gender and on how they related to conflict that I myself
might generate. My interest in learning about the relation of language
to gender was subject to my own participation in linguistic interaction,
which was halting by some standards and bizarre by others, and my
deployment of methods (e.g., repeated questions, searches for "the real
story") that were, in some instances, inimical to cultural ideals or conventions.

The following section describes how Swahili people analyze speech
and its relation to social roles and proper behavior. Their metalinguistic analyses guided my research methods and led me to define narrative
as my central analytic focus. Later sections describe those methods,
including the techniques of narrative analysis on which I relied.

Swahili Analyses of Language

I heard many linguistic prescriptions, and other comments about language, while conducting research, as have other scholars of the region
(see Bakari 1981; Eastman 1984a; Foster 1984; Maw and Parkin
1985; Russell 1981, 1985; Swartz 1982; Swartz and Omar 1985).[1]
Linguistic prescriptions demand that Swahili women's speech maintain *heshima*. Not only must they speak in the right place, at the right
time, and to the right persons, but also they must use the proper genre
and register. Enshrined in poems and proverbs, linguistic prescriptions
counsel women to speak softly, politely, and deferentially in order to
show respect, especially in the presence of elders. The epigraph for this
chapter quotes Mwana Kupona, the well-known nineteenth-century
poet whose long poem written to her daughter advises women to be
especially conscious of correct linguistic usage. This ideal persists
among Swahili women and men, who use phrases like "that one's reserved" *(mpole huyo)* or "she doesn't have many words" *(yeye hana
maneno mengi)* to compliment young women. Knappert (1970:133)
notes that a highly praised virtue for a Swahili person is to be quiet.

Linguistic prescriptions can be wielded against a speaker to compel
or control behavior. The accusation that someone has "broken respect" *(alivunja heshima)* through speech is used more often against
women than men. Explicit valuations of women's speech result in linguistic deference on the part of many women, who accuse each other
of inappropriate speech at least as often as they are accused by men.

Lower-status people are assumed to violate *heshima* more routinely. A range of persons possess the authority to comment on the speech of young women (parents, teachers, elder brothers, etc.). The speech of elderly women is subject to fewer restrictions. Welcome in some mixed-gender settings, on rare occasions it can be coarse or vulgar. Prohibitions on women's speech especially emphasize the preservation of *heshima* in situations that offer the temptation for improper behavior.

As aspects of linguistic ideology, the above prescriptions delineate proper linguistic behavior. Other aspects attribute certain types of speech to men or to women and (sometimes) provide reasons for the gender difference. Swahili men's speech, even when produced among themselves, is said to concern "serious" matters, such as religion and politics; women's speech is described as trivial, focused on weddings, luxury goods, or entertainment (Swartz 1982). These attitudes correspond to differences in the speech genres that are associated with men and women. The association of the mosque lecture almost exclusively with men reinforces expectations that men interpret Islam and, in the process, make authoritative pronouncements on proper behavior. Many Swahili people believe that these lectures, peppered with Arabic phrases and Islamic references, are good examples of the Islamic "high culture" considered to be men's province (Abdulaziz 1979; cf. Mazrui and Shariff 1994). Although women do not initiate lectures, either in mosques or in other contexts, they do recount lectures that they have heard (Russell 1985:206).[2] Women are associated with telling two types of fictional stories: *ngano* (short tales involving animals, spirits, or nonreal beings) and *hekaya* (stories based on actual characters living at another time), although they find fewer occasions to tell stories for entertainment than in the past (see Russell 1985). Men and a few women tell the more didactic *kisa* (short moral tales) and *hadithi* (short moral tales about the Prophet Mohammed). As Eastman (1988) has argued, folklinguistic valuations of expressive culture—and until recently the valuations of foreign and indigenous researchers—favor the written over the oral, the epic over the folktale, and the public lecture over the private story, thus reflecting status distinctions involving class and ethnicity as well as gender (cf. Middleton 1992; see also Mazrui and Shariff 1994).

In accounting for the lower value accorded women's speech in many societies, some feminist scholars argue that the casual exchange of information can strengthen oppressed groups and at the same time threaten oppressors. This instrumentalist approach to language would assert that some information passed along through casual storytelling or "gossip" can expose unfair or inappropriate behavior.[3] Gatherings of Swahili women, at weddings or routine late-afternoon visits to friends and family, are a time for sharing stories and expressing good will. Fictional and nonfictional stories told in this setting provide information about the details of life, and many have explicit morals that guide future behavior.

The valuations of gendered genres assess the form and content of speech as well as the propriety of its production in a particular context. Thus, the speech, the context, and the speaker are all considered in evaluations that delineate who is a legitimate speaker. The trivialized conversation associated with Swahili women amusing themselves is quite readily recast as talebearing that calls into question a woman speaker's status and that of her family. The dismissal of idle gossip is accompanied by other comments warning against the dangers of Swahili women's speech. The disapproval of women's talebearing is broad, with far-reaching implications for interdicting speech. Since narration and storytelling are associated with women, the condemnation of talebearing falls squarely on them.[4] While talebearing is generally condemned in Swahili culture, the particular way in which women share stories with each other is said to cause irreparable damage.

Swahili men and women express the opinion that women routinely engage in speech that creates conflict.[5] Through words to each other, women can "put trouble in the house" *(tia dhiki nyumbani)*. The stereotypic pattern is that one woman will "bring words" *(leta maneno)* to another. The two might be close friends or archenemies, but the words—most often about an errant husband's behavior—set off domestic conflict. "Words" *(maneno)* can mean gossip, criticism, information, or worthless information. Many men, including some Islamic judges, agree with the assessment that the meddling of female friends through "bringing words" causes marital conflict and divorce, and, during mediations in Kadhi's Court, judges advise women not to listen to friends' tales when they concern the activities of an allegedly unfaithful husband.

The specific denunciation of women who "bring words" has roots in the general disapproval of talebearing in Swahili culture. Swartz and Omar (1985) describe a complex ideological system of honor and insult in which Swahili individuals are vulnerable to verbal attacks on their reputations (see also Swartz 1982:31–32). Several Swahili "characters" participate in these attacks, and their behavior is condemned. One of these, the *sabasi*, is described as "a person who causes quarrels between people by telling one bad things the other is saying about him and telling the other equally bad things the first person is saying about him" (Swartz and Omar 1985:242). More generally, *sabasi* means a talebearer.[6] The *sabasi*'s partner in crime is the *mdaku*, a person who seeks out embarrassing information about others. The threat of being called *sabasi* or *mdaku* discourages speech that might lead to conflict. "Bringing words" also has the broader meaning of making accusations, which range from general complaining *(kushtakia)* to making specific claims *(kushtaki)*. Arguing *(-gombana, -nenea)* is a related form of speech that is also suspect. Quarrels, even when conducted in private, are antithetical to a Swahili linguistic prescription that limits argumentative and complaining speech, holding that bad words make everyone emotionally, spiritually, and physically vulnerable. The Swahili notion of "inviting devils" *(-shiriki shetwani)* captures the idea that people face spiritual peril when evil matters are discussed in their presence or household. Disapproved kinds of speech, which include making accusations, repeating accusations heard elsewhere, or insulting others *(-tukana, -sema matusi)*, cause bad feelings by unsettling everyone involved, including the audience, and rendering them vulnerable to further harm. The notion that argumentative words cause harm is one factor in the prescription that wives persevere rather than confront their husbands. As wives are routinely reminded, silent perseverance ensures that no one is subjected to bad words that would make them vulnerable to evil spirits.

The beliefs about speech described above suggest that the prototype devalued speaker in Swahili culture is a woman, specifically a woman who tells tales. The several negative ideologies about one linguistic form—narrated stories—converge and bolster each other. Emphasis on the trivial and potentially fictional quality of women's speech merges with emphasis on its dangerous and disruptive qualities to create the impression that women's speech is suspect, not to be counted on, and to be suppressed when it gets too close to home, literally. Related to this estimation is the notion attributed to Islamic sources that women's words are unreliable. This idea underpins the legal stipulation that the testimony of two women witnesses equals that of one man (see chapter 5).

My analysis has highlighted cultural ideas that are widely shared and produced. By contrast, Briggs urges scholars not to treat the ideological level of language "simply as part of the linguistic background shared by the members of a speech community" (1992b:398).[7] Rather, he argues for examining how dominant ideologies are contested and deployed situationally as ways of exercising power through speech. As

I will describe in later chapters, subordinate people in many instances produce aspects of dominant ideologies yet speak in ways that violate or challenge them—for example, through gossiping or complaining. By describing aspects of dominant ideologies, I emphasize their normative force on Swahili people more cogently than I do through subsequent situational descriptions that suggest their manipulability. Although Briggs has argued for emphasis on the latter, presenting these ideologies as overarching beliefs that silence some speakers is partly an artifact of my experience as a young woman conducting research in Swahili society, where I was conscious of my own conformity and where I sometimes spoke in ways that were more effective in satisfying the imperative of preserving *heshima* than in eliciting data.

Accumulating Talk about Trouble

The cultural ideas about language described above shaped my research from my first days in Mombasa, when I was conscious of learning to speak appropriately, in ways that would display my modesty and preserve *heshima*. Mimicking the unmarried Swahili women closest to my age, I spoke demurely in most settings, especially in the presence of men. Reserved behavior resonated with my personality and gained accolades from the families with whom I interacted; however, behaving as an ideal young Swahili woman restricted my speech and movement in ways that impeded my research. Moreover, I became disturbed at the thought that I was trying to reflect an ideal of proper Swahili behavior that few young Swahili women cared to achieve. Was I trying to be more pious than everyone else? As I described in the previous chapter, the events of conflict in the household in which I was staying disrupted my initiation into Swahili society and made concerns over ideals less immediate. As the months went on, instead of acting out an ideal, I sought to emulate young educated women who worked as clerks or teachers. Their struggles to preserve *heshima* in public settings and in conversations with unrelated men instructed me with respect to not only my own behavior but also gender relations outside the household. As young women we were all subject to criticisms, including linguistic prescriptions when our speech came close to violating *heshima*.

An incident that occurred two months into my research in Malindi made me keenly aware of the contradiction between my efforts to speak in ways that, on the one hand, preserved my good name and, on the other hand, furthered my research. On a holiday afternoon when people were visiting in each other's homes, taking tea and sweets or watching song-and-dance groups outdoors, I was summoned outside to speak with a young man my own age who wanted some advice about his camera. After I answered his question, we began to talk about law and domestic conflict. As we spoke, I realized that my previous efforts to maintain *heshima* had meant that I had little access to young men's perspectives. My interest in our animated conversation clouded my awareness that we had drawn the attention of many people, including family members peeking out of the house windows behind us and children who stared as they walked by. I finally realized that we were violating *heshima* when an elderly man asked us point-blank what we had been talking about for the past "half hour." Embarrassed, I described my research and said a hasty good-bye to my interlocutor. On entering the house, I was confronted by an older sister who lectured me about speaking openly to a man, particularly to a cross-cousin (a potential marriage partner given my position in my host family). My reaction was a complex mixture of triumph at being treated as a family member (I had heard the same lecture delivered to other young women), remorse at having let people down, and trepidation from the knowledge that I would probably disappoint them again. The incident convinced me that I needed access to young men as informants outside court. I accomplished this by further distinguishing my position from that of the family's daughters, suggesting—to some disapproval—that I would need to talk to young men on some occasions and would try to do so in appropriate ways. I also adopted some duplicitous behaviors engaged in by women who preserved *heshima* outwardly and yet found ways to converse with men. Both of these strategies allowed me to accumulate the talk about trouble that is the data for this study while minimizing the talk about trouble that positioned me as its subject.

Although my research methods included diverse interactions with many different people, my gender, age, foreign status, and interests meant that young women and, eventually, young couples provided much of my data on conflict talk. Contrary to Middleton's contention (1992) that older Swahili people tend to hide information from young scholars, I learned a good deal from interactions with male and female elders. The two richest sources of talk about trouble were relaxed conversations with the families with whom I lived and visited and the cases and mediations that I witnessed in Kadhi's Court. Each source posed different methodological problems for studying discourse, law, and gender, yet through each I came to focus on narrated accounts of conflict.

Stories about conflict arose spontaneously when small, generally single-sex groups gathered to visit in bedrooms or living rooms. The stories often included descriptions of problems that others (not the teller) had experienced. From these sessions I learned the mechanics of relating stories and heard details about specific conflicts that involved people in Malindi, including some who had claims in court. After initial attempts to question narrators about ambiguity in a story or about incidents that seemed implausible, I came to realize that presenting "the facts" was less important than telling an engaging account. Asking whether something "really" happened was treated as a metalinguistic violation. I was especially confused by stories of fantastical events that were replete with throwaway lines of "I would not lie" or "Haki ya Mungu!" (God's truth!), meaning "Truly!" In some instances, close friends took it upon themselves to debrief me, so that I got the facts behind any story related to my work. The range of metapragmatic frames for storytelling revealed to me the complexity of narration as a form for talking about trouble. For me, learning to listen to stories about trouble meant quietly accepting even those stories that exaggerated my own behavior.[8]

People who show inordinate concern with the problems of others risk being placed in the category of *mdaku* (one who encourages others to tell compromising tales), a label I tried desperately to avoid. Although I reassured all of my interlocutors that I would never expose their stories of trouble in ways that would alter their status, I called attention to this role by taking notes after (and sometimes during) sessions where stories about conflict were told or instances of actual conflict erupted. I rarely tape-recorded spontaneous sessions of gossip and stories, though responses to my requests to tape were generally positive. I tried to avoid complex issues of taping and secrecy by limiting my recordings to events in which "texts" such as poems, lectures, or prayers were publicly presented.

The status of courtroom interaction as a public record meant that I had little difficulty tape-recording many instances of talk about trouble in Kadhi's Courts. I tape-recorded about two hundred cases, mediations, and less formal incidents of disputing over a period of one year in Mombasa and Malindi courts. I was present at all tapings and made the tapes myself, using a small recorder and an attached microphone. I also took notes with which to clarify gaps in the tape or inaudible sections. In all instances, I attempted to record the dispute from the time that disputants began to interact with each other or with legal personnel until the proceeding was concluded. Mediations, which were less formally initiated, sometimes went on after the clerk or kadhi had decided they were over, as parties continued to battle with one another. I endeavored as much as possible to capture these "unofficial" disputings, in addition to recording any disputes involving parties who returned subsequently.

My concerns over violating Swahili understandings of privacy motivated my careful attention to changing the names of all parties involved in courtroom matters as well as to hiding the identities of those from whom I received information in other circumstances. Conversations with one kadhi suggested that my concerns over collecting this information contrasted with his: he worried that someone of my young age could become spiritually vulnerable as a result of so much exposure to talk about conflict. More pointedly, he lamented that after my year or so of listening to domestic conflict, I would never agree to be married to anyone.

Transcribing Talk about Trouble

Thus far in this chapter, I have endeavored to link the metalinguistic analyses offered by Swahili speakers to the analyses ultimately produced through my research. Linde makes the important point that the methods appropriate to studying any particular linguistic form depend on the questions that one intends to ask about it (1993:51; see also Cameron et al. 1992). As my questions came to focus increasingly on gender differences in narration and the forms and functions of narration in talk about trouble, I found the need to isolate narratives as texts to be analyzed and compared.

About thirty-five cases and mediations were transcribed for this study. Transcripts were made of cases that appeared "representative" by virtue of sharing the same organization as many others. In addition, I also transcribed cases with unusual issues or outcomes. The transcripts were produced in Kiswahili with the assistance of Kenyan speakers of Kiswahili who also assisted me as I interpreted and translated them. The features of transcription used to create the texts are provided in appendix B.

Most excerpts of transcribed data are presented in English. Kiswahili versions are included in appendix D. When features such as word order or word choice are integral to my argument, I offer phrase-by-phrase Kiswahili and English versions in the body of the chapter to facilitate a direct examination of the Kiswahili example. In a few examples, complex features such as linguistic poetics are demonstrated through morpheme-by-morpheme transcription and translation. Following Russell (1981), I divide some narrated accounts into clauses and number each clause separately at the far left for easy reference (see Ochs 1979 on how transcripts reflect theoretical concerns). The numbered lines in the appended Kiswahili versions of the texts correspond as closely as possible to the English versions.

I have endeavored to produce transcripts that will be useful for those interested in technical, linguistic analysis and yet readable for those with less linguistically oriented concerns. Duranti has written eloquently of the contradiction facing linguistic anthropologists. On the one hand, the notion that transcripts are reflections of the analysts' interests and the circumstances of the research process has become an important corrective to viewing any transcript as capturing the "truth" of an interaction. On the other hand, analysts insist on employing systematic, highly labor-intensive methods of collection and analysis that produce transcripts intended to be useful to the broader scholarly community (see Duranti 1994:40).

I follow the trend, encouraged by Duranti, Goldman, and others, of providing transcripts of whole disputes or lengthy segments to encourage alternative analyses. Yet I approach with skepticism the assumption that inclusion of these texts affords other scholars complete access to the data. The transcription process fails to capture so much of what made these narratives meaningful to participants at the time and, later on, to me as analyst. Tiny yet meaningful details fall out: unusual turns of phrase, the relation between the judge's speech in two disputes adjacent in time but not in the chapter's narrative, and virtually imperceptible (not to mention untranscribable) metapragmatic framing devices. Rather than simply encouraging others to interpret at their own risk, I make two seemingly contradictory interventions. First, I provide as full a context as possible for interpreting the linguistic data through describing Swahili society and the Kadhi's Courts in which these interactions occurred. Moreover, I include my analyses of case files and other court records and descriptions of informal interviews with the parties and legal personnel. I also provide summaries of transcribed and untranscribed disputes in appendix C. Goldman has harshly criticized the ways in which case summaries "are specifically designed in accordance with the prior interests of the ethnographer, and his or her evaluations of what is important about any stream of events" (1983:2).[9] While I agree in principle with Goldman's claim, and his call for including transcripts as a corrective, I am concerned to provide scholars enough background to facilitate interpretation of transcripts. Case summaries contribute to such contextual background.

Second, even though I present lengthy transcripts of disputes, I seek to question the authority of these texts as accurate or complete representations of disputes. Thus, I include transcripts in several forms to emphasize that our understanding of them is often superficial. Several texts of entire disputes are appended. (By "entire," I mean from the moment the parties enter court until they leave.) Shorter excerpts are presented and analyzed in the text of later chapters. Moreover, bits of the transcribed material appear as epigraphs to some chapters or simply pepper the text. These bits of data convey important points made by Swahili speakers about discourse, gender, and conflict. Such bits are often the only linguistic evidence those unfamiliar with a context will carry away from the transcripts of others. The pithy phrases that leap out from other ethnographers' texts, and of which I have only limited comprehension, shape my understanding of law and society. By presenting transcribed texts in various forms, I take the now routine postmodern turn to create a text that in its admittedly limited innovation comments on itself as text and on the process of entextualizing others' words.

The Analysis of Narrative Features in English

Interest in charting how narrative constitutes "social action" and thereby reconfigures social relations has led scholars to abandon traditional reverence for divisions that have made conversation analysis, ethnography of speaking, and pragmatics separate analytic and theoretical pursuits (Briggs 1988a; Conley and O'Barr 1990; Goodwin 1990; Shuman 1986; Steedly 1993). Similarly, my analysis of language and social transformation in Kadhi's Court cases relies on a combination of approaches to narrative: (1) as a form of speech characterized by features of structure and performance; (2) as a vehicle for performing legal tasks and other functions in court; and (3) as a genre whose gendered production and interpretation are influenced by and in turn influence attitudes about language commonly expressed in Swahili society and with specific instantiations in Kadhi's Courts.

Even for those scholars who are most concerned with the study of narration as a discursive practice that leads to social transformation, investigating narration processually entails attending to its structural and functional features and situating the production of these features in real contexts (for reviews, see, e.g., Gulich and Quasthoff 1985; Linde 1993; Polanyi 1989; see also Goodwin 1990; Briggs 1988b). Defining narrative through its structural features is a useful tactic of analysis that facilitates comparison. The following points, drawn from the work of linguists reviewing the study of narrative, provide a definitional base:

> 1. A narrative refers to a series of real or fictional actions or events that take place in the past relative to the time of the narration (or are told as if occurring in the past). In more succinct terms, a narrative is a story. . . .
> 2. . . . the story of action or events that makes up the story contains some kind of transformation or change. . . .
> 3. The participants involved in the actions and events related are animate, usually humans. . . .
> 4. Narratives are specified by certain formal characteristics. (Gulich and Quasthoff 1985:170–72)

Each of these points was anticipated in the work of Labov (1972) and Labov and Waletzky (1967), who are generally credited with having developed the most detailed descriptions of the structural features of oral narrative in English. For Labov, the central feature of narration is its "event line," or "spine," those descriptive statements that advance the story's action. According to Polanyi (1989:189), "[t]he narrative line in English language stories is built up through simple past-time event clauses. These are main clauses that encode instantaneous, noniterative, positive, completive occurrences in the past." A narrative taken from Polanyi's study reflects these features:

> S: We . . . we called the cops immediately and they came and they already had the guys and so they took us in his car to where we had to identify them, you see. (Polanyi 1989:82)

This narrative is composed of past-tense clauses that recount the action that transpires following a robbery. Most narratives also include utterances that describe states of being, in addition to actions or events. The clause "they already had the guys" portrays the state of being at a moment in the unfolding action. Although state-of-being clauses set the scene for the story, the event line is generally the primary focus of the discursive act of narration, as listeners wait in anticipation for the speaker to advance the story.

As reflected in point 2 above, things happen in narratives. Changes and transformations are reflected in the structure of narrative. For instance, there is a strong narrative presupposition in English that events or actions described first in a narrative are those that occurred first in the actual incident (see Labov 1972). Put simply, the events of a story are told in the order they happened, as far as is possible given the vagaries of human memory. Violations of this presupposition are questioned by listeners if they become confused, and narrators are generally careful to correct themselves when they realize they have described something out of sequence. Much of the change in the action of the narrative is carried out by animate agents, as point 3 indicates. To some extent, causality is embedded in the narrative structure, a point that is critical when narratives are told for legal purposes.

The organization of narrative—that is, the ordering of its structural features—has also been well documented (Labov 1972; Labov and Waletzky 1967; see also Bauman 1986; Linde 1993; Polanyi 1989). Narratives told in conversation generally begin with an announcement by the potential narrator that a story will follow.[10] Some announcements are routinized: "I've got a great story . . ." Announcements can also summarize the narration to follow or give an indication of what the story will contribute to the conversation. People sometimes "sell" their story in order to gain a place on the conversational floor (see Watts 1991:34). Following the announcement, orientation clauses set the scene for the subsequent narration by locating it in time and space (e.g., "It was a very cold night . . ."). The past-tense clauses that constitute narrative in its narrowest sense—in effect, the narrative clauses—follow. In describing the action of the story, these clauses might reach a high point, climax, or resolution, depending on the semantic content being conveyed (Labov 1972; Watts 1991). Finally, a narrative is often closed with a coda, a short statement that signals the end of the narration and on occasion asserts a moral.

The four ordered parts of narrative (announcement, orientation, event line, and coda) need not all be present. In particular, whether the announcement or the coda occurs depends on a narrative's conversational context. For example, a question soliciting a narrative often substitutes for an announcement by the potential narrator, and, similarly, a coda is more likely when listeners indicate that they have not understood the story. Jefferson (1978) argues that stories are "locally occasioned" in talk, an approach that does not entirely discount the presence of the structural features, such as those identified by Labov, but insists that they emerge from the dynamics of conversation (see also Watts 1991).[11]

The fifth component of narrative—evaluation—can appear in any part of the narration and takes many linguistic forms, ranging from phonological to discursive (Labov 1972; Labov and Waletzky 1967; Polanyi 1989). For example, emphasis on a word can constitute evaluation in that it draws the listeners' attention to that word as important to the story. Announcements and codas frequently include "explicit evaluatives" that convey the narrator's opinion of the story. Because there are so many ways in which speakers evaluate stories, evaluation is a rather vague analytic category; however, it plays a critical role in making narratives meaningful for listeners and in processes of entextualization.

The Analysis of Narrative Features in Kiswahili

The few studies of Kiswahili oral narrative identify narrative features similar to those described above for English (see, e.g., Maw 1992; Russell 1981). In her analysis of personal narratives and folktales gathered through interviews of Kiswahili speakers in Mombasa, Russell (1981) relies extensively on the approach to narrative developed by Labov (1972) and Labov and Waletzky (1967).[12] The narrative presuppositions that hold that action is almost invariably described chronologically and that, with some exceptions, causality is implied by sequential organization are present in Kiswahili narration.[13] Most narrative clauses are positive, completive, and expressed in the past tense *(-li)*, although it is possible in Kiswahili, as in English, to produce the conversational historical present (*-na* or no tense marker).

The verb tense used most commonly in Kiswahili narration has no English counterpart. This is the *-ka* tense, which indicates that the action or state described is subsequent to the action or state expressed through the previous verb.[14] When the first verb is framed in the past tense *(-li)* and each succeeding verb in the *-ka* tense, all of the actions are interpreted as occurring subsequent to one another and in the past, as is evident in the following example:

Nilirudi nyumbani, na nikapika chakula.
I returned home, and I [then] cooked food.

Narrators typically produce multiple repetitions of the *-ka* tense in telling a story. I would argue that these repetitions definitively signal the presence of narration and are thus central to the process of a speaker's entextualizing a story (see also Maw 1992; Russell 1981).

The following narrative told in Kadhi's Court illustrates narrative features. In this example, Munira, a woman who previously obtained a divorce from her husband through the Kadhi's Court, returns to complain about being beaten by her ex-husband (see "The Beating," appendix C). She had met separately with the kadhi the day before to urge him to confront Atwas, the former spouse, and on this occasion has returned with him.

1	Kadhi:	You, what do you say? Explain that news of yours.
2	Kadhi:	Wewe, wasemaje? Eleza ile habari yako.
3	Munira:	My news I (1.4) it's that one I told you, that I want
4		to be divorced.
5	Munira:	Habari yangu mimi (1.4) ni ile nilikuambia, kama mimi
6		nataka kuatwa.
7	Kadhi:	Uh huh (2.8) That's it. (2.5)
8	Kadhi:	Uh huh (2.8) Bas. (2.5)
9		That's your news, that one, you don't have anything
10		else?
11		Ndiyo habari yako lile jambo huna lingine?
12	Munira:	I do have. Isn't it that the other day when he came to:
13		hit me
14	Munira:	Ninayo. Sivo jeuzi alipokuja ku:nipiga
15		even I went to the police I was given a P-3 [form]
16		hata nikaenda polisi nilipawa P-3
17		I filled [it] yesterday I returned to the police.
18		(1.6)
19		nikajaza jana nikaregesha polisi. (1.6)
20		He hurt me. It's ( ) sides and kidney. ( ) He's
21		been hurting me a lot.
22		Akaniumiza. Ni ( ) mbavu na figo.
23		( ) Ameniumiza sana.

In this excerpt from the beginning of the mediation, the kadhi requests an account of the conflict (line 1). Munira's attempt to avoid recounting the most recent incident of violence by referring to a conversation that she and the kadhi had earlier in the week is initially treated as an announcement (line 3). This is evident from the kadhi's response of the discourse marker ("uh huh") that signals her to continue (line 7). When she fails to, the kadhi, in irritation, questions whether the reference to the prior conversation is Munira's only point (lines 9–10). The interchange, which leads to a second announcement (line 12) followed by a brief story, exemplifies how narration is negotiated in interaction (lines 12–19). Munira sets the scene for her narrative by citing both the day and the relevant event—the beating—that marks the day as worthy of narration. Her subsequent narrative recounts what happened after she was beaten: she went to the police to file a P-3 form charging her former husband with assault. The coda to this short narrative emphasizes the harm Atwas caused her and thereby serves to justify her trip to the police (lines 20–23). More implicitly, her final comment appears to explain her presence in the court, yet she does not refer specifically to any actions that the kadhi should take now that he has heard her story.

The narrative above is an excellent example of the basic structure of Kiswahili narration, especially with respect to the technical issue of verb tenses and the syntax of the narrative sequence. Lines 14–19 describe the action using both the -*li* and -*ka* verb tenses. These clauses, and their ordering, typify Kiswahili narration and thus create the narrated "text." In her final utterance, Munira breaks the pattern of -*li* and -*ka* verbs by producing the -*me* tense, which is used to describe actions that have already been completed at the time of the statement and which is rarely present in Kiswahili narrative clauses.[15] The usage resituates the narrator in the narrative event rather than in the narrated story. This clause operates as a coda to the story.[16] In Kiswahili, changes in verb tense indicate when people are narrating and when they are commenting on their narration, which, as later chapters will assert, is integral to entextualizing a story and to accomplishing legal tasks.

Kiswahili narratives tend to be agent-centered, and, depending on the context, the narrator may perform the parts of the animate characters through reported speech. Reported speech in Kiswahili takes direct and indirect forms that resemble those in English:

Nikamwambia "Nakungojea."
I told her "I am waiting for you."

Nikamwambia namngojea.
I told her I was waiting for her.

Reporting clauses introduce reported speech through verbs such as say (-*sema*), tell (-*ambia*), think (-*fikiri*), and explain (-*eleza*) (Russell 1981: 240).[17]

Joan Russell's extensive study of Kiswahili narration reveals differences in the features of narrative associated with several commonly produced genres: fictional tales, religious stories *(hadith)*, and conversational narratives (1981). Speakers are more likely to produce variations on the structural features of narrative in telling stories of personal experience as opposed to fictional tales.[18] Across the narrative genres, the core of narrative clauses is produced with similar syntax; however, there are differences in evaluative and performance features, such as expressive phonology, augmentatives and diminutives, "marked" syntax, direct expression of feelings, sound effects, and gestures. For example, sound effects and gestures are most often associated with the telling of fictional stories. Russell finds that certain types of fictional narrative are more likely to be told using "traditional" phonology, that is, a variety of Mombasan Kiswahili associated with older speakers who did not receive government education. Thus, the telling of fictional tales indexes a way of speaking associated with earlier times, and with women. Though Russell is intrigued with the possibility that other gender patterning might occur in narration, she was admittedly unable to investigate this question, given that her data were elicited through interviews.

Conclusion

My methods of analyzing narrative draw on the wide range of approaches mentioned above. Specifically, I focused first on narrative structure, then function, and finally ideology. After identifying the initial narratives of conflict and distinguishing between narrative and non-narrative statements, I identified the various evaluative devices produced by narrators and assessed the degree to which the narrative was performed. My interest then turned to how the stories contributed to the dispute and the court proceeding. This sometimes led me to attend to clauses outside the narrative that characterized why the story had been told or why it had been told at that particular juncture in the case or mediation. Finally, I examined how the initial narratives fit into the larger structure of discourse in the court and ideas about language in Swahili Muslim society.

The next two chapters return to the ethnography of Swahili coastal Kenya to describe the problems and disputes in which people are embroiled and to emphasize that they are positioned in gendered ways with respect to those problems. As I will show, gendered positioning influences their production of speech in Kadhi's Courts, as do understandings about what it means for men and women to tell a story, both inside and outside of court.

SHAABAN: . . . And I saw that I had to return to the house to see my wife and the way that she was living, you see. So I left that work. I went to the house. When I came to the house I saw my wife, the life that she was living. It wasn't like a person who has a husband. She lived really just like that. Like a person who doesn't have a man nor small children. Really I was truly shocked|truly

CLERK: |Now how does she live?

SHAABAN: She lives like a person who doesn't have a man.

CLERK: In what way hasn't she? What does she do?

SHAABAN: Really she does whatever she wants.

CLERK: Like . . .

SHAABAN: Like she's a person without a husband.

CLERK: *In what way?*

SHAABAN: She does whatever she wants like (   )|that woman.

CLERK: |An example, tell us *what* does she do? What does she do? You have to say everything.

SHAABAN: It's so, bwana. (I am telling you) you see. I tried to bring my wife words. To agree with her. We stayed we stayed now she then she then she- So when I arrive my wife does not cook me food. She doesn't wash for me, you see bwana?

(FROM A KADHI'S COURT MEDIATION)

Discourses of Marital Disputing

One woman whom I came to know personified the cultural ideal of *heshima*. Halima was in her fifties, and her radiantly calm and pious demeanor ensured that she was respected and beloved in a household I frequented. She also spent time there, staying for several months every other year at the behest of the head of the family, a cousin of hers who had raised one of her children as his foster daughter. Like her cousin, Halima was born into a patrician family from an island off Kenya's northern coast. She was married in her teens to a cousin, and they had seven children before divorcing in the late 1970s. During the marriage, Halima's husband provided her a well-appointed house and enough domestic help to ensure that she had little reason to venture out. Much of her life was lived in the seclusion of her home, where she raised her children, entertained guests, and pursued her own deep religious commitments. I had warmed to Halima immediately upon meeting her and was moved by her grace and her unselfish commitment to family. She dedicated herself to living a religious life, particularly to preserving *heshima,* and even her most mundane actions displayed attention to modesty. She kept a cloth *(leso)* permanently draped over her head and pulled it close when any man came near to the bedroom or kitchen, where she spent most of her time. Since it was in these rooms that I often engaged in conversations about Swahili society, I became aware of Halima's reticence to participate in discussing the problems of other people. As I came to appreciate that gossiping about conflict, or witnessing that gossip, could be interpreted as behavior without *heshima*, I sometimes felt guilty when, in her presence, I encouraged young women less concerned with *heshima* to expand on a juicy story.

One day during a conversation in which I had responded to Halima's inquiries about my family and whether I missed them, I asked her about her own life. Expecting her to graciously decline to discuss herself, an approach she had taken when I had posed a similar question months before, I listened in surprise along with the young women of the household as she related her story. Predictably, Halima's narration was brief and unembellished as to her divorce: "I lived with my husband for many years. When my youngest child was still in school, my husband told me that he wanted to divorce me so that he could marry another woman. So he divorced me. I left his house to live at a cousin's so that I could be close to my children. Now I stay with my grown children, my relatives at my birthplace, and here. What can I do?" This last question was asked rhetorically, with no hint of self-pity or resentment. I inquired, "What did you say to him when he divorced you?" "I didn't say anything. What could I say? It was his right *(haki)*. Others told him that he was not being fair. Even the children begged him to stay with me. But I had to accept his decision."

The young women swiftly condemned the divorce as shameful. From their perspective, the husband's behavior had no justice *(haki)*, an opinion they expressed using the same term as Halima, though with the very different meaning described below. As we lapsed into silence, saddened by how divorce had forced this lovely person to rely on her extended family, a bold young woman asserted that Halima was now free and could visit her children. "She could even go to Europe if she wanted to. There's no husband to stop her!" We laughed with Halima at the outlandish idea of her traveling to another continent when she generally avoided going anywhere, especially unaccompanied. For her, divorce had not meant freedom from her husband's authority, but, because it compelled her to travel, maintaining *heshima* was more difficult. Another lapse into silence allowed me to ponder whether the passage of time had altered Halima's memory of her divorce, which might in reality have been a more protracted event. But more reflection on Halima's quiet demeanor led me to think that she had indeed remained silent in the face of the lawful but unjust act of her husband. Almost involuntarily, one of my standard research questions popped out: "After your husband divorced you, did he maintain you during *edda*?"[1] "No," she responded. "Did you think about going to court to ask for it? Wasn't it your right *(haki)*?" She laughed, "In those days we did not go to court for such things. We stayed at home. It's different now. In those days we would have felt shame to go to court." It was her turn to laugh at how things had changed and perhaps at the insignificance of three months of maintenance money in light of the changes in her life caused by the divorce.

Halima's reluctance to protest her husband's behavior can be interpreted in several ways. As she suggests, she was personally reticent to expose herself and her family to public scrutiny and thus sought to avoid the shame of recounting family problems. Or belief that her husband would control the outcome may have led her to forgo objecting. Finally, she may simply have felt no entitlement to engage in marital conflict, because, as she stated, the law of divorce was on her husband's side. Accounts from other societies claim that, for these and other reasons connected to their subordinate status, Muslim women are disinclined to address conflict through Islamic legal institutions.[2] Yet some questions remain: Was Halima's approach to the divorce shaped by the hegemony of patriarchal legal discourse or a wish to "hide matters," or both? If the strictures of Islamic law determined her approach, what accounts for the young women's angry reactions to the injustice done by Halima's husband? Has the connection between men and Islamic legal discourse weakened over time in Swahili society? And what options besides Islamic law are used to contest divorce?

This chapter addresses these questions by examining how Swahili Muslims use the discourse of Islamic law, and other discourses, to resolve marital conflict. The following section describes four discourses of marital disputing: Islamic law, Swahili ethics, spiritual health, and state law. Drawing on Merry's approach (1990) to discourses in U.S. lower courts, I treat each discourse as a frame of reference that structures the expression of conflict. Specifically, each discourse positions men and women as gendered subjects who possess different (gendered) relations to legal (or moral) claims. Each discourse also offers different (gendered) access to the various disputing contexts and to the forms of speech produced in those contexts. Accordingly, how a disputant makes a claim (or responds to one) is determined in part by the discursive options that configure his or her legal standing in gendered ways and, as well, by cultural ideas about speech and conflict, which were articulated in chapter 3.

Along with depicting how discourses shape gendered approaches to conflict, this chapter directs attention to the agency of those who participate in disputes. Swahili men and women produce all four discourses, and they do so in gendered ways. These gender differences are evident when specific conflicts (e.g., lack of maintenance, jealousy) are examined over time, as demonstrated in later sections of the chapter. As disputants make claims, as events push the dispute beyond the original issues, and as third parties offer interpretations, the framing of a problem shifts in patterned ways from one discourse to another. These "discursive shifts" are related to the nature of the conflict as well as to the strategies of the disputants and third parties within the frameworks provided by the discourses and the disputing contexts. This chapter's analysis of the types of marital conflict routinely experienced by Swahili people identifies the patterns of men's and women's deployments of the four discourses and the discursive shifts that characterize common marital disputes.

On the one hand, discourses determine disputants' subject positions and their access to disputing contexts and forms of speech. On the other hand, discourses provide the terms through and against which subjects refigure their positions. Merry (1990) argues that in U.S. courts neither court personnel nor disputants fully control the three discourses (moral, legal, and therapeutic) that frame their discussions of conflict (see also Conley and O'Barr 1990; Lazarus-Black and Hirsch 1994). Thus, she depicts legal processes as sites of contestation over power where disputants are guided by legal discourse and yet wield all three discourses to resist the court and confront other parties. Such negotiations offer critical possibilities for social transformation.[3] The terms of discourse shape the abilities of disputants to reconfigure their interpersonal relations. More pointedly, what is at stake, as well as what is being created through the operation of discourses, are the very subjects who participate in disputes (see also Yngvesson 1993). Given the transformative possibilities facing individuals, the process of disputing also has the potential of altering the relations among social groups. This chapter and the one that follows reveal how gender relations are negotiated and transformed through the discourses of Swahili marital disputing.

This chapter also has the ethnographically oriented goal of describing the kinds of marital conflict in which Swahili Muslims are embroiled and the options for resolution. As Comaroff and Roberts (1981) have argued, the processes through which disputes emerge and occasion the application of rules and resolution procedures reveal the structural contradictions in a sociocultural order. The multiple discursive framings of marital conflict highlight tensions in Swahili society, displaying the effects of an increasingly class-stratified postcolonial society on households and individuals who must adjust to shifting status markers and strained economic circumstances. At the same time, these disputes expose the expression of patriarchy in Swahili social life and the efforts by some to contest it.

Four Discourses of Swahili Marital Disputing

In Kenya, the array of discourses available for conflict resolution reflects the history of British colonization, which included the imposition of discourses that contrasted markedly with precolonial ways of knowing. In postcolonial Kenya, deployments of these discourses through institutions or by individual speakers continue to reflect complex negotiations of hierarchies. Institutions are important in these struggles as they can attribute legitimacy to discourses that have, at their roots, distinct ways of being and knowing. My observations of contemporary and remembered court cases, public and private discussions of spousal problems, and domestic arguments all confirmed that Swahili Muslims frame marital conflict through multiple discourses. Although some discourses (e.g., legal) have historical associations with institutional contexts, one of Foucault's insights is that discourses radiate out of institutions to organize social life. Therein lies the power of discourses as barely perceptible ways of ordering contexts where they are least expected.

Islamic Law

Underlying the discourses of Islamic law and Swahili ethics is the concept of *haki,* which is central to understandings about order in Muslim societies. Clifford Geertz (1983:188) describes the Arabic term *haqq,* from which the Swahili term *haki* derives, as having three sets of interrelated meanings. The first—reality, truth, actuality, fact, God—refers to what is really real and what should exist. The second—right, duty, claim, obligation—corresponds to Western conceptions of laws, rules, and rights. The third—fair, valid, proper—can be roughly defined as justice. For Geertz, the inseparability of these three senses in Muslim ideology implies a conflation of reality and law that contrasts with the epistemologies of other belief systems. These senses of *haki* figure in Swahili disputants' discussions of marital conflict, as evidenced by the frequency with which statements such as the following are made in disputes: "I want my rights." "Nataka haki zangu." (From a man claiming his right to sleep with a wife who has been refusing him.) "What kind of justice is this?" "Hii ni haki gani?" (From a woman who has discovered that her husband, from whom she has received inadequate maintenance, intends to marry another woman.) When disputants use *haki,* they produce distinct senses of the term that presuppose identifiably different discourses—one of specific, actionable laws and one of ethics or just behavior. Although these correspond to two of Geertz's definitions, I am less concerned with his assertion of their connection than with identifying their separability in Swahili marital disputing, where distinct discourses of Islamic law and of Swahili ethics coexist.[4] In the abstract, *haki* can embody all three senses, but, in Swahili disputes, most deployments tend either toward rights or justice, each of which is linked to a discursive frame.

In disputes I witnessed, *haki* was generally invoked to refer to specific marital rights and duties facing husbands and wives. A Muslim man's obligations include providing maintenance for his spouse(s) and children and engaging regularly in sexual relations with each spouse. He can marry up to four wives; however, he must provide for each of them equally. The stipulation that a wife has the right to sex can be suspended for reasons of health or separation related to employment or a family emergency. By contrast, financial obligations are non-negotiable. Under Islamic law, a legally married man must support his wife and children by providing accommodation, food, clothing, and funds for medical treatment.[5] In addition to regular maintenance, a husband must offer extra compensation to a wife who is nursing his infant. The contractual nature of Islamic marriage is evident both at its inception, when the man must pay bridewealth *(mahari)*, and at its dissolution, when he must, in most circumstances, support his ex-wife for three months (the period of *edda*). Correspondingly, wives have commonly acknowledged obligations articulated through Islamic legal discourse. As one kadhi, and many men, insist, a woman's primary marital duty is to "get up on the bed" *(panda kitanda)*—that is, a wife must provide sexual access to her husband. She is relieved of this responsibility at the end of a pregnancy, during the early weeks of nursing an infant, and during menstruation and illness. In the three-month *edda* period after a man divorces his wife, he may return to her and reinstate the marriage by engaging in sexual intercourse, even if she protests.[6] A wife is obligated to reside with her husband unless she has good reason to live elsewhere (e.g., employment, presence of a co-wife).[7] The provision that a woman must obey her husband's reasonable requests also has legal force.

Although kadhis and religious leaders are familiar with the sources of Islamic law (the Koran, stories of the Prophet Mohammed's life *(hadith)*, and the exegesis of Muslim legal scholars), most Swahili people learn the basic obligations of marriage from family elders, Islamic schooling, mosque sermons and lectures, and simply written pamphlets. Men, who attend religious lectures more regularly than women, have greater access to such information; however, legal consciousness of marriage is widespread. Islamic legal discourse includes terms such as "rules" *(kanuni)* that "must" *(lazima)* be followed. Behaviors are either "permitted" *(halali)* or "not permitted" *(haramu)*, and the latter are forbidden through statements that begin "Islamic law says ..." (Sheria kiislamu inasema ...). People refer to their rights possessively when they make claims on each other or when they explain their behavior. A man can invoke *haki* to divorce his wife with no explanation. Given that some aspects of *haki* resemble those of Western legal discourse (e.g., legal terminology), I want to reiterate Geertz's broader point that the force of Islamic law derives from its connection to the divine. Laws, though framed as the rights of individuals, are conceptualized as creations of Allah, not of humans. This sense of *haki* is always present in its deployments and thus distinguishes the discourse of Islamic law from other legal discourses.

Swahili Ethics

Haki in the sense of ethics is central to a second discourse of domestic disputing. A spouse's behavior can be evaluated as to whether it conforms to divinely inspired assumptions about ethical behavior, including the idea that couples should treat each other with fairness, kindness, patience, and, above all, *heshima* in order to foster a "good life." For example, treating one's wife with kindness is an example of ethical behavior deemed commendable *(sunna)* (rather than obligatory) and which achieves this designation through its link to the Prophet Mohammed's behavior. The domestic atmosphere should be free from cruelty, and wives should not live in fear that they will be divorced without reason. Criticisms of behavior within marriage refer to a person's failure to embody justice *(haki)*, fairness *(sawasawa)*, or righteousness *(maadili)*. To say that something "is of no use" *(haifai)* is one way to indicate its impropriety or unacceptability.

The discourse described above warrants the designation of Swahili ethics, because, in justifying the appropriateness of behavior, Swahili people often refer to beliefs about how one *should* act. In some instances they are referring to Swahili customs *(mila)*, which encompass local norms. Caplan (1995) has noted that Swahili *mila*, treated as principles of "customary law" in some areas of Tanzania, contrast with Islamic laws on some issues, such as inheritance and land tenure (see also Moore 1986, 1989). In urban Kenyan Swahili populations, *mila* are not referred to or deployed in this jural sense. Judgments about behavior are invested with authority by the insistence that "We Swahili say . . ." (Sisi Waswahili tunasema . . .). This phrase indexes the ethical force of what follows, which generally emphasizes behaviors appropriate to living a good Swahili life or to participating ethically in marriage.

The versions of ethical life espoused by patricians are often close approximations of the letter of Islamic law, while people with less status and fewer resources appeal to local ethical principles that would, for example, forgive a debt or request cooperation through hard times. My point is not that upper-status people use one discourse and lower-status people another. Rather, the two discourses tend to reflect the broad division in Swahili society that has historically connected those of upper statuses to textual Islam. For most Swahili people, the distinction between Islamic law and Swahili ethics emerges primarily in disputes as opposed to abstract discussions. By contrast, distinguishing between legal rules and ethical principles has become a political project for Muslims in other countries, particularly for Muslim feminists (see, e.g., Ahmed 1992; Mernissi 1991).[8] From my observation, this evolving scholarly and political approach is not influential in motivating the discourses used by Swahili people; however, the relation between ethical discourse and women's strategies is described in a subsequent section.

Spiritual Health

Swahili cosmology includes beliefs about an active spirit world in which several kinds of nonmaterial beings intervene in human affairs (Giles 1987; Middleton 1992). Possession by one of these beings, a *jini* (pl. *majini*), causes a person to be disruptive, including in marital life. People believed to be predisposed to possession, such as those who are physically or emotionally vulnerable, must take precautions.[9] Otherwise-healthy people are targeted for attack either by a *jini* or by a human acting through a *jini*. Though Islamic ideology posits an active spirit realm, such beliefs gain force only in some Muslim societies or subgroups. Giles (1987) argues against the notion that only persons who are socially "peripheral" concern themselves with beliefs in *majini* by demonstrating that Swahili possession cults include people of all statuses. My research indicates that a minority of Swahili people from all statuses express the view that it is "superstitious" to believe too strongly in *majini* or to allow them too much explanatory power in one's life. Yet specialized practitioners *(waganga, walimu)* skilled in making medicine *(dawa)* to induce and counteract possession do an active trade and frequently assist when someone exhibits the erratic behavior of one possessed (Giles 1987; Middleton 1992).

In Swahili marriage, the discourse of spiritual health is sometimes invoked to explain why one partner violates the legal and ethical principles of marriage. Accounting for behavior as the work of spirits is especially constructive when there has been little prior conflict between the spouses or when there is no other "explanation" for why a spouse would behave with cruelty, withhold sex, or fail to maintain the family. Such a diagnosis includes assessing who caused the possession and procuring treatment. It is frequently alleged that marital problems are caused by people who, out of jealousy or malice, send bad spirits to disrupt stable unions (such as a co-wife). Even if a husband or wife has behaved unlawfully, unethically, or reprehensibly (e.g., using violence or breaking *heshima*) while possessed, he or she is excused for not being in control. Blame is placed on the *jini* or the person responsible for sending the *jini*.

The practitioners who exorcise *majini* also prepare "love" medicines *(dawa),* which clients procure to improve marital life or to woo a romantic interest. Many people with difficulties at home seek out *dawa* practitioners for remedies, which can take many forms (medicinal drinks, charms, ceremonies, prayer) and generally include therapeutic discussions.[10] A spouse might obtain medicine for a partner and dispense it surreptitiously to stimulate sex, counteract jealousy, or ensure domestic harmony. Such acts require secrecy, as knowledge that a partner is commissioning *dawa* introduces distrust. Although trying to influence someone through *dawa* differs from arranging for their possession by a *jini,* both are aspects of the realm of spiritual health. Even a medicine designed to produce only good effects can render a person vulnerable to possessions or other problems.

Kenyan Law
A final discourse, the law of the Kenyan state, is invoked rarely in Swahili marital disputes and only in relation to domestic violence, child custody, and contempt of Kadhi's Court. The discourse of state law involves rules of British-modeled civil and criminal law, secular judicial personnel (e.g., magistrates, Children's Officers, and police), legal forms, hearings, and other official, institutional trappings of the Kenyan legal system.[11] Evidence and proof are central to how knowledge of a conflict is presented, and judgments of guilt or innocence are primary outcomes. Only a small minority of Swahili people are conversant with their rights and duties under Kenyan law, and thus

few are capable of manipulating legal discourse in police precincts, magistrate's courts, or social welfare offices.

By its association with the secular state, Kenyan legal discourse has historically been viewed by Swahili people as remote from their experiences. Opposition to the secular legal apparatus, once framed as a religiously based rejection of the colonizing process, is refigured in the postcolonial period as opposition to a state that has excluded and subordinated the interests—economic and social as well as religious—of coastal people. Legal discourse is viewed as a secularizing and subordinating intrusion. The contrast that Swahili people make between state law and more familiar discourses (i.e., Islamic law, Swahili ethics, and spiritual health) reflects the hierarchies of religion and ethnicity that Muslims have had to endure in a postcolonial state that insists on adjudicating most matters in secular courts.

Writing of law in Tonga, Susan Philips (1994b) criticizes the notion that postcolonial states impose a unitary ideology throughout the legal system that necessarily undercuts customary law. Rather, she describes postcolonial legal systems as typically inflected with multiple ideologies, even though one ideology might be presented (by legal practitioners or laypeople) as characterizing the system.[12] Her approach to ideology in postcolonial settings offers a model for understanding the role of discourse. Though the Kenyan legal system is overwhelmingly oriented to a discourse of secular state law, the discourses of Islamic law and spiritual health are recognized in various sites. Yet the nondominant discourses are "known" authoritatively through Kenyan state law. For example, the discourse of spiritual health operates in relation to state law as a subjugated discourse (in Foucault's terms), given the history of restrictions on the mention of witchcraft in Kenyan courts (see, e.g., Mutungi 1977 and the critique by Mutunga 1994). Less subjugated than circumscribed or subordinated within the state-level Kenyan legal system, Islamic law occupies a well-defined place: it applies only to certain substantive matters and only in the form permitted by the encompassing institution. Moreover, the discourse of Islamic law derives part of its authoritative force precisely from its connection to the state and its similarities to Kenyan law with respect to legal concepts (e.g., the rule of law, proof, and rights) and symbols that embody the authority of hegemonic state institutions.

Gendered Discourses and Disputing Contexts

In contrast to secular state law, Islam not only provides an authoritative base for the other discourses of marital disputing but also reproduces long-standing hierarchical divisions of status and religious sect. The ethnic hierarchy that links Arabs to the elite versions of Islam also subordinates African-oriented discourses of Swahili ethics and spiritual health. The struggle waged in these terms, a pervasive though muted concern in the postcolonial period, positions certain discourses and disputing contexts as subordinate to others. Moreover, to the extent that status differences have gender entailments, the relations among the several discourses of disputing can be understood in gendered terms. At a symbolic level, the discourse of Islamic law is understood culturally as masculine in comparison to subordinated discourses. To designate the discourses of Swahili ethics and spiritual health "feminine" is to mark their subjugated position in relation to other discourses. From this perspective, which broadens what it means to identify a discourse as gendered, discourses stand in gendered relation to one another over and above how they are produced by people in gendered categories.

The images of the pronouncing husband and the persevering wife emphasize the structural hierarchy of Muslim marital and gender relations, which privileges husbands to control the resolution of marital conflict and connects them more closely to Islamic legal discourse. In court, kadhis remind men of the provisions for conflict resolution elaborated by Islamic commentators: first, a man should talk with his wife. If no agreement results, he should refuse to have sex with her until she consents to work toward a resolution. If, after a short, specified period of time, this approach fails to lead to reconciliation, then the husband is permitted to use mild physical force. In local practice, beating one's wife is condemned, and the Koranic reference is interpreted as meaning "symbolic beating." [13] If this produces no result, the husband can take a formal oath of sexual continence lasting up to four months. If after the period of sexual abstinence the couple has still failed to reconcile, they should approach a third party for assistance. These procedures are understood as measures taken *before* one invokes legal discourse (see Antoun 1990:43). Finally, if all efforts fail, men are permitted to wield Islamic law to pronounce divorce.[14]

Far from being invested with the authority to use Islamic legal language, women are counseled to persevere when they encounter domestic problems. A wife is said to be more loved when her husband knows that she is keeping quiet about a problem. Informants counsel that persevering silently when a husband takes a second wife ensures that a woman will avoid greater problems (e.g., abandonment). Yet, even as women's silent perseverance is generally valued, any woman who puts up with severe abuse from her husband is thought of as a "stupid person" *(mjinga)* or a "martyr" *(mnyonge)*.

When disputing spouses choose—either jointly or separately—to take problems to a third party, their choices reflect not only their gendered status under the law but also their different understandings of the availability, affordability, and approachability of various disputing options. Moreover, as demonstrated in dispute-processing studies, cultural ideas about where a problem can be voiced also play a role in disputants' choices. Most often Swahili couples approach family members, and older relatives frequently intervene. Women seek out the woman, called a *somo* (teacher), who counseled them at the time of puberty or marriage about sex and married life (see Mirza and Strobel 1989). A *somo* who also helped arrange the marriage has additional authority. Similarly, family elders have more influence over marriages that they themselves arranged. An elder's advice should be sought in an appropriate manner so as to conceal problems behind family walls.[15]

Marital disputes are sites for negotiating consanguineal and affinal relations. The degree to which parents or other relatives influence marital disputes depends on several factors, including how the marriage was arranged, the marriage payments and agreements as to property, and the proximity of families to the disputing couple. Swahili couples whose marriages most closely resemble the patrician ideal of cousin marriage experience extensive involvement of their families in creating and resolving disputes. Generalizing about the role of extended families in disputes is difficult. Relatives who might be called on to help a divorcing man meet his bridewealth payments or to maintain a divorcing woman find it in their interests to intervene.[16] The influence of families on the couple tends to decrease over the course of a marriage. Moreover, as the nuclear family becomes increasingly central to Swahili kinship, the degree to which marital conflicts are attributable to or controlled by extended family members has declined (see also Caplan 1995; cf. Antoun 1990:37).[17]

When family elders fail to resolve a conflict, couples are sent to people whose skills in dispute resolution are recognized in the community. Women are especially likely to relate their domestic problems to practitioners of spiritual medicine; however, "talking about the problem" is not encouraged as a resolution strategy. Rather, quieting evil spirits or learning to persevere is the most usual counsel. Medicines prepared by practitioners allow the recipients to surmount problems by no longer noticing them. In Malindi, men and women also turn to local religious leaders (e.g., heads of mosques or Islamic organizations), subchiefs, and assistant registrars, who draw on Islamic law and Swahili ethics to resolve conflict.[18] In addition to managing paperwork concerning legal matters, assistant registrars are permitted to mediate conflicts, but their advice is not legally binding. Finally, others take their problems to the Kadhi's Court, where they speak with the kadhi or his clerk. Kadhis and mosque officials are linked to law; certain elders are skilled in spiritual medicine. Any one practitioner might draw on several discourses.[19]

In disputes in urban Ghana, even men who realized that they would "win big" (i.e., be awarded money) in the state court began the disputing process with the less lucrative local council of elders (afiesem) (Lowy 1978). Going "straight" to court was considered "immoral," and most people chose to conduct disputes morally in order to preserve their "good name." In Swahili society, the morality of choosing one disputing option over another turns in part on the degree to which a disputant risks exposing family matters to public scrutiny. Depending on the topic, the more distant the third party, the greater the risk of inappropriate exposure. In addition, if a person must see the third party in a public office, the risk of violating heshima is more salient. Going to Kadhi's Court, even for a consultation, is less appropriate than visiting a therapeutic practitioner in his or her home, though more likely to preserve heshima than proceeding to the police. Yet, as Lowy also found for Ghana, men and women have different approaches to airing family conflict.[20] Swahili women express embarrassment at speaking about certain problems (e.g., those involving sex or abuse) to male elders or in-laws. Some insist that the more impersonal atmosphere of the kadhi's office allows them to speak more openly about intimate matters. Also, women become less concerned with the problem of revealing family secrets once a conflict escalates beyond a couple's ability to repair the problems.

Cultural understandings, particularly of heshima, guide people to minimize discussions of conflict in order to hide matters, a burden that women are counseled to bear through silence and men through legal speech. The choice to speak in legal discourse is separate from, yet related to, the choice of taking one's claim to Kadhi's Court. Both acts are linked to the law's gendered quality, given that legal discourse and the courts are controlled by men (see also Philips 1994b).[21] But the ties connecting men to law and women to silence are less than hegemonic. The legal standings of Muslim men and women, along with prescriptions for culturally appropriate speech, shape disputants' approaches to disputing and, depending on the nature of the conflict, lead to the discursive shifts described below.

Discursive Shifts in Marital Disputes

Marital disputes evolve through escalations, capitulations, silences, escapes, and interventions. In exploring these acts, and others with labels that reflect the more standard categories of lumping it, staking a claim, naming, etc., studies of dispute transformation have moved away from earlier approaches that explained disputing through the choices of rational actors (Yngvesson 1993:8–9). By contrast, dispute transformation now attends to how disputes shift in relation to actions taken by disputants, by third parties, or by the audiences to a dispute, whether those actions are intended or successful. Even as the perspective of dispute transformation retains a concern for the choices of agentive, though unpredictable, individuals, it understands those choices as the acts of persons situated in complex power relations that serve as structural and discursive frames for the conflict.

In describing typical patterns of disputing, my goal is to emphasize that the discourses, institutions, and cultural understandings associated with disputing structure how trouble is articulated; they give voice to the tensions of familial life.[22] One source of tension is the competition for resources—both financial and emotional—in a situation where those resources are scarce and other real and potential competitors exist. Another source involves divergent approaches to domestic control and personal autonomy, both of which are central to the maintenance of *heshima* and the preservation of status. Disputes are routinely framed in ways that reflect gendered strategies; however, it is not the case that men produce one discourse and women another. Rather, gender differences emerge through disputing processes, as disputants shift among the several discourses. By directing attention to the points at which men and women shift from one discourse to another, my analysis exposes both the role of discourses in shaping gendered approaches to conflict and the agency of disputants in addressing conflict and transforming gender relations.

"Good Cases" and the Invocation of Islamic Law
One day, as I passed by her mother's house in Shella, Binti called me over to ask whether it was true that I was studying divorce. When I answered affirmatively, she related her experience of divorcing from her husband, Kassim, several years before. Binti had faced a young

wife's worst nightmare. After four years of marriage and the birth of two children, Kassim had abandoned her. During their marriage, they had had many disagreements involving complaints made by her mother, with whom they lived. Binti's mother claimed that Kassim contributed inadequately to the household budget and that he was not trying hard enough to find separate accommodations for his growing family. Even though Kassim and Binti cared for each other, in her family's estimation, he had worn out his welcome. When Kassim went to Mombasa, ostensibly to pursue a job, and failed to return after several weeks, Binti became suspicious. With no money for maintenance, she was forced to begin selling cooked food from her home and to rely on her mother and sister. When word reached her that Kassim had taken a job in western Kenya, she decided to seek a divorce. Her decision was influenced by her mother and uncles, who believed that if she divorced, she could remarry. Binti filed a case in Kadhi's Court requesting a divorce and maintenance for her children. She admitted to me that she had been afraid to approach the kadhi, yet in the end she was pleased that she was able to tell her story simply and to win. Kassim never responded to court summonses nor did he attend the ruling. For several years, Kassim provided nothing for the children.

Instances of abandonment display a husband's failure to meet the primary obligations of marriage. Depending on their class, age, and status, a few abandoned women have the means to subsist, although most seek support from the husband's family or from their natal family. In general, abandonment is a claim easily proven by a husband's absence; however, a husband can contest it by showing that he is absent with good reason or has maintained his wife and family. Identifying the problem of abandonment in legal terms did not require going to court, but Binti, like many women, needed the support, encouragement, or threats of older relatives to convince her to take the claim to court. Given that Kassim's absence could hardly be concealed from the neighbors in an area where houses are close together, concerns over hiding family secrets were minimal. Binti found it relatively easy to pursue her claims in court, because she faced no direct opposition from her husband. Telling her story was only minimally burdensome, given that she spoke with the kadhi in relative privacy about a matter of absence rather than about the twists and turns of an ongoing conflict. Kassim's absence—from the house and the court—and the absence of countering frames that he might have offered made this a good case for Binti to articulate through legal discourse, even in court.

For Love or Money, "Feelings or Funds"

The most common problem identified by parties to Kadhi's Court cases is the failure of husbands to provide adequate support for wives and children.[23] Over time, Binti came to frame her problem as one involving rights in the legal sense of *haki*. However, Swahili couples avoid talking about maintenance as a legal obligation until conflict is severe. Men's duty to provide is well established in Islamic law and Swahili practice; however, demands for maintenance are made obliquely, generally framed as claims for a husband's love. Shifting from the language of love to that of money signals an escalation of a dispute, one that marks a discursive shift from ethical to legal discourse (cf. Nader 1990).[24]

Although couples are aware of husbands' maintenance obligations, they often disagree as to what constitutes adequate support (see also Lazarus-Black 1991).[25] A wife expects to receive at least the level of maintenance that she enjoyed as an unmarried daughter in her father's house. The perception of appropriate maintenance is sensitive to factors such as the family's size, the number of nonfamilial household laborers, and fluctuations in the prices of subsistence goods.[26] Many couples make an agreement as to how much maintenance is required, and this amount is turned over regularly. Husbands out at work send home meat, fish, or other staples for the main meal; divorced men sometimes convey maintenance via their children. Polygamists are required to provide equally for each of their children, even if they have divorced a child's mother. A disparity between the woman's expectations and the man's ability to fulfill those expectations results in disagreement over maintenance, particularly when a couple is fighting, estranged, or divorced. Even when a woman marries into a family of equivalent means, she may find that her new husband has yet to establish himself financially and thus falls short in maintaining her.

In Malindi neighborhoods, the majority of Swahili men find it difficult to obtain employment that yields enough funds to support a family adequately. The following testimony of a husband accused of nonsupport in Kadhi's Court sums up the position of many men: "About clothing, whenever I'm financially good, I give her money to buy clothes, and when I'm not good financially, that's the time I don't give her clothes." Financial strains within a family are directly related to class, and most men who head households experience persistent conflicts over material support.[27] Households headed by women face even more severe difficulties unless they are among the few whose absent husbands or ex-husbands hold high-paying jobs outside the country and remit maintenance. Even men with salaried positions can fail to provide adequately when prices rise suddenly or misfortune occurs. Maintenance becomes a burden at holidays and before events such as weddings and funerals as women stretch the budget to clothe children properly and prepare food for guests.

The financial difficulties facing families mean that some wives receive barely enough money for food, clothing, and shelter. Yet, to a large extent, transactions over maintenance, including those that involve inadequate amounts, are conducted with minimal discussion. Even when a husband fails to remit the agreed-on amount, a wife generally holds back from inquiring as to the problem. She might borrow from a family member or use her own money, expecting that she will be compensated later. Perseverance through times of inadequate maintenance demands that wives rely on a variety of self-help measures.[28] Increasingly, women hold waged or salaried positions, and, though Islamic law contends that they need not contribute to the household budget, they use this income to support the family. When major expenses arise suddenly, couples appeal to wealthier relatives for assistance; however, keeping up the appearance of financial stability is critically important to arranging and cementing affinal ties that might place a daughter or son into a wealthy family and thus provide parents with future resources.

Women persevere, sometimes for many years, without protesting to their husbands or anyone else about their unfulfilled desires for maintenance. Many Swahili women address the problem of inadequate maintenance by manipulating household finances to meet subsistence requirements, purchase extra clothes for holidays, host guests at weddings and funerals, and maintain access to cash for emergencies.[29] For many women, such perseverance is not an intolerable condition to be condemned but a reflection of the family's class position and the difficulties of the Kenyan economy. Their contributions to the family finances, as well as their perseverance, stand as evidence of their commitment to, and love for, their husbands. Many families continue a pattern of daily existence—without severe conflict—even though maintenance levels are low.

My emphasis on the persevering Swahili wife who manages money carefully contrasts with Swartz's depiction of Swahili women as skilled manipulators who strategize to obtain money from their husbands in order to purchase luxury items (e.g., fancy dresses, jewelry) and the commodities needed to host elaborate events (Swartz 1982, 1983, 1991; see also Fuglesang 1994:128). Swartz points out that most Swahili women are keen to obtain the latest fashions as displays of their wealth and status. Through such behavior, they both amuse themselves and evoke the jealousy of peers. Swartz reports that Swahili men routinely agree to these expenses, though grudgingly, in order to keep their wives emotionally supportive. Wives play on men's fears of emotional loss by describing the "funds" requested for luxury items as evidence of husbands' "feelings" for them. The argument turns on Swartz's assertion that, because Swahili men have few other avenues for obtaining emotional connection outside the nuclear family, they will pay wives' price (1982). This argument demands acceptance of Swartz's assertion that men require emotional support and that other forms of support are unsatisfying. Although idle trafficking in luxury goods may be common for some wealthy families, most Swahili women are engaged in more than pursuing the admiration or envy of their peers. Finery worn to a wedding is a critical signifier through which a woman negotiates her family's status. The role of status in contracting marriages calls into question Swartz's assertion that women's displays of status are unimportant to men. Status is, after all, constructed through appearances, especially given that a family's real worth is hidden from outsiders. By exerting control over how a husband allocates money, women's demands for luxury goods achieve broader influence for their projects. This dynamic underlies men's blustering condemnations of their wives' interests in luxury goods even as they fork over the cash.[30] I observed men demonstrating that their financial support should not be taken for granted through refusing to pay for luxury goods, providing less than the requested amounts, and protesting when confronted with requests.

Although misconstruing the aims and consequences of women's status competitions, Swartz (1982) makes the important point that Swahili couples negotiate conflict over household resources through references to love *(mapenzi).*[31] A wife's demand for money is expressed as a request for a husband to show his "love" by providing above and beyond regular maintenance. Wives' ability to procure extra money demonstrates to others that they are in "good standing" with their husbands. As Swartz points out, women who cannot dress well for weddings are pitied as being unloved. Marital squabbles are frequently articulated in the idiom of "feelings" rather than "funds," and the notion that the latter is evidence of the former is routinely mentioned. Women make good use of the language of "love" in their ethical claims to money, but men are also adept at wielding the idiom of love to manipulate household finances. When a woman makes a request for money, a man cushions his refusal by asking her to persevere as a demonstration of love.

The language of love is also invoked by third parties who assist in resolving disputes. For example, family elders might calm an accusing wife by suggesting she draw on love for her husband to sustain her through lean times. During mediations, kadhis also attempt to persuade women to persevere until finances are less strained, even as they urge husbands to work harder at making money. Most kadhis prefer not to dissolve marriages because of poverty. Thus, the language of love expressed in the discourse of ethics can work against women, particularly in court, as they are pressured into avoiding demands for *haki* as rights. Moving from the language of feelings to assertions of rights to funds marks a fundamental discursive shift in a dispute and often in the marital relation itself.

Rights to Work

In comparison to women, Swahili men assert legal claims earlier on in disputes. Men's assertions of rights to women's labor (e.g., cooking, cleaning, laundry, and childcare) exemplify this tendency to make legal claims. Women, who are expected to perform household work without assistance from husbands, generally shoulder this burden without question. In all but the poorest homes, women avail themselves of the abundance of cheap domestic labor, particularly to accomplish difficult chores such as laundry. Wives who work outside the home and thus have limited time either arrange for other female household members to perform domestic tasks or hire help with their salaries. Both men and women characterize household duties as women's contribution to marriage, depicting this labor as balancing men's financial contributions. Nevertheless, household work is frequently the subject of marital quarrels. Complaints about lack of culinary skill or limited attention to the children's cleanliness or manners are standard means of suggesting that a woman is shirking her duties. Men readily frame these claims in terms of their rights to a wife's work. Elders make this assumption as well, and if disputes over chores arise, they generally support men's claims.

Kadhis listen carefully to such claims when aired in court. They affirm that a good marriage includes contributions by both parties and that women contribute through housework. But they rephrase men's claims to rights, counseling in the language of ethics that both parties must contribute to harmonious marital life. When asked directly, kadhis admit that Islamic law does not require women to perform any work other than childcare for their own children. Yet in disputes, they pragmatically suggest that, if a woman wants a trouble-free marriage, housework is evidence of her good faith.[32] Most men are surprised to learn that their assumptions about housework have no legal teeth. Even when prompted by the kadhi, these men do not shift to the discourse of ethics but rather offer muted versions of the discourse of rights.

For their part, women are well aware of the crucial role their labor plays in the household. Even women who, because of age, infirmity, or inclination to take it easy, have delegated most household tasks to others perform special tasks such as drawing a husband's bath or cooking a dish that he associates with her culinary skills. Food preparation is a critical source of women's power. One young wife who worked for a local merchant and found it virtually impossible to prepare the noon meal each day asked her husband's sister for assistance. When the husband quarreled with his sister to the point that she refused to help any longer, the young wife found the burden too great. Seeking her husband's recognition of her difficulties, she dealt with the problem by cooking stew in the morning and then, instead of boiling rice to complete the lunch, served the stew with a loaf of commercially produced bread. In a society where rice and food are virtually synonymous, her action was deemed curious on the first day and downright hostile when continued for a week. With limited prodding, the husband apologized to his sister and begged her to cook again. The point of this story is that, although household chores are women's burden, they can be negotiated to secure women's claims.

Disputes about children and childcare are also a frequent source of conflict that leads some men to invoke their marital "rights." Spouses can disagree over the number of children that they desire and whether or not they should use birth control.[33] Aspects of childrearing such as how much education is necessary for each child, whether children should reside with parents or other relatives, and whether stepchildren should be raised with the children of the matrimonial couple are also issues of contention. Husbands and fathers have authority in such matters, though decisions about childrearing come to a head in custody battles after divorce. In custody cases, parents' conduct is scrutinized to assess who best meets the standards of "mother" or "father" (see chapter 5 for further discussion of custody).

Labors of Love

The discourse of rights is invoked more readily in the case of insufficient attention to household duties, where it is *not* legally applicable, than in the case of sexual access, where legal action to request conjugal rights is permitted. Husbands and wives can both claim rights to sex, although identifying sexual problems risks exposing the household's shame. Although the Koran provides that spouses should engage regularly in sexual intercourse, it makes no recommendation as to frequency of encounters, and either party can refuse for health reasons.[34] For monogamous couples, conflict over sex can occur when a man is impotent or when either spouse refuses sex for an extended period of time. In polygamous marriages, conflict can arise when a husband does not take equal turns with each wife. Sexual problems change over the course of a marriage.

Immediately after a wedding, problems involving impotence or refusal to have sex are the concerns of not only the married couple but also their respective families, who made the marriage possible through bridewealth and wedding expenses. Quite commonly, young couples are unable to consummate their marriage for several weeks after the wedding due to the pressure. In a marriage arranged within the family, the young man and woman may also be struggling to reorient their feelings for one another from what was a relationship of cousins to one of sexual partnership. In the past, and doubtless in some contemporary situations, a bride's refusal to engage in sex led her relatives to assist the man by holding her down on the matrimonial bed so that he could consummate the marriage.[35] The shadow of potential male impotence hangs over the wedding-night dinner, during which grooms are prepared for the task ahead by being given foods thought to enhance sexual vigor.[36]

If a newly married couple's sexual problems persist, they come to be explained as involving spiritual health. Afflicted parties are taken to practitioners, who prepare medicines to relax them and ward off evil spirits who make sex impossible. In some cases, spirits are thought to be jealous of the new husband or wife. In other cases, spirits act at the behest of humans who, out of jealousy, deny a couple happiness. The prominence of explanations of sexual dysfunction that refer to spiritual health means that spouses do not have the opportunity to frame their refusals as strategic actions. Although discussions of sex are highly circumscribed, the number of people seeking spiritual assistance for their sexual difficulties suggests that such problems are widespread.[37]

Finding a forum to dispute over sex without violating *heshima* is particularly difficult when problems involve abusive or abnormal sexual activities.[38] When the kadhi ascertained that a woman who came to Kadhi's Court to beg for a divorce had no grounds with respect to maintenance or physical abuse, he encouraged her to tell him the real story. Before she would answer, she insisted that he clear the courtroom. Once they were alone, she held her veil in front of her face as she whispered to him that her husband wanted her to use drugs that would enhance their sex life and would cause her to agree to perform oral sex, something that she had refused. Such a claim, which is not uncommon, implicates the *heshima* of the accused man. Yet, in uttering it, a woman necessarily calls into question her own *heshima*.

Young women have an especially hard time articulating their perspectives on sex. Following her first child's birth, which was so medically complicated that she nearly died, Rehema refused to end the customary forty days of postpartum convalescence at her mother's house to return to her husband's apartment and bed. Although she explained that her refusal reflected her uncertainty over whether she could care for her infant while recovering, the fact that she refused her parents' offer of a private room in their home suggested that she wanted to sleep apart from her husband. Rehema handled her husband's unspoken questions by treating him pleasantly yet speaking to him only in the company of others. Older relatives questioned Rehema, but she insisted that she was too embarrassed to speak with them. Though the elders were concerned that the husband's prominent Mombasa family might denounce their family for the recalcitrance of one of its daughters, they were also reticent to insist on a conversation with Rehema about such an embarrassing topic. After several more weeks, two married female cousins of Rehema's who were her own age pulled her into the bedroom for a private talk in which they joked about the pleasures of sex. The giggles stopped as Rehema said soberly that she disliked sex, had not experienced it many times before becoming pregnant and being confined to bed, and was terrified of giving birth again. The cousins were sympathetic yet offered her no solutions except to say that her behavior was inappropriate, in both ethical and legal terms.

Only in rare cases do disputants invoke the discourse of rights when making claims about sex. When men ask third parties to assist them in compelling a wife to return to the matrimonial home, they are more likely to discuss tasks such as cooking and laundry, rather than sex, as the chief duties that wives shirk by staying away. Those who intervene generally downplay the discourse of rights in relation to sexual problems. Elders and judges tend to frame sexual problems as ones that require coddling, trips to the doctor, lots of sympathy, and sweet talk. This is the case even though Koranic law insists that husbands and wives provide sexual access. On rare occasions, when provoked, kadhis use the discourse of law to address sexual problems.

The End of Love and the Beginning of Law

Women who have persevered without adequate maintenance for years, as well as those who have suffered only a short time, regularly adopt the discourse of law and rights at the moment they become aware of a husband's intention to marry again. Sadly enough, marriage to an additional wife is interpreted as evidence that a couple's love has faded (see also Fuglesang 1994:260), yet love is not the language through which protest is articulated. Rather, rights to maintenance and money are central to how women frame their disapproval of the lawful, though unethical, choice of polygamy. Feelings of betrayal and embarrassment, as well as fears of economic decline, lead some wives to make claims that have the force of law; only a few women bear this situation calmly or silently. For their part, men stress their legal right to multiple wives, though kadhis, some elders, and young men seeking to be "modern" insist that only special circumstances warrant marrying more than one woman.[39] On taking an additional wife, a man customarily appeases his current wife by giving her a gift, such as a watch or money.

Jamal married Kauthir, his first wife, in a match arranged by their parents, who were related and lived near each other in Shella. When they married, the cousins were very young and, by all accounts, very much in love. They had three children during ten years of relatively peaceful coexistence. Then Jamal became infatuated with Sauda, a young, attractive woman from Mombasa who worked in Malindi and had befriended his sisters. After seeing her in his parents' home, he proposed marriage and began to arrange a wedding in Mombasa. When several wedding guests coming by bus from Malindi arrived at the Mombasa bus station, they encountered, quite by chance, the brother of Jamal's first wife. Thinking that, as the cousin of the groom, he was planning to attend the wedding, the guests mentioned their expectation that the celebration would be grand. Kauthir's brother boarded the next bus for Malindi in order to assist his male siblings in responding to the perceived insult to their sister and their family. When Jamal returned to Malindi after his wedding, he was confronted by his father-in-law and cousins. They insisted that he immediately divorce his new bride or, failing that, divorce Kauthir. When Jamal refused to pronounce divorce, Kauthir announced that she would take him to Kadhi's Court to claim for maintenance. She planned to ask for five hundred shillings per day in maintenance, an astronomical figure, and to tell the kadhi that Jamal had failed to support her adequately during their marriage. Concerned that he might be hauled into court and made to pay, Jamal divorced Kauthir. However, he was not convinced that Kauthir wanted a divorce but rather believed that her family had used her to scare him into divorcing Sauda.

After a month of marriage to Sauda, Jamal returned to Kauthir surreptitiously. At first, only the women in her family knew, and they helped to arrange the couple's romantic meetings. They kept the revoked divorce a secret to allow Jamal to break the news gently to his new wife. When Sauda found out that he was "eating" at his former wife's house, she flew into a rage and demanded that he divorce one of them. The ensuing crisis alerted the men of Kauthir's family, who insisted that Jamal resolve the issue more definitively. Once again, he divorced Kauthir in order to preserve his marriage with Sauda, to whom he owed a good deal of bridewealth. This time, Kauthir asked for the divorce and "forgave" any monetary compensation, thus making the divorce irrevocable under Islamic law.[40]

The situation between Jamal and Kauthir was traumatic for the interrelated families. The elders were well respected in the community and known for helping others to repair their marriages. Unable to resolve the conflict without resort to official discourse and ultimately divorce, the elders of the family were mortified at their own failure to solve problems "in the house." The two families ignored each other in the neighborhood and at social events. Even the younger cousins, who attended school together, were enjoined from interacting. In one house, the names of those in the other family were never mentioned; in the other, when mentioned, they were routinely denounced. It was not until three years later, at the sudden death of Jamal's younger sister, that Kauthir's sisters spoke to their aunt, uncle, and cousins, when they came to the house to express their grief.

As I sat with Jamal in his living room one evening several years after the divorce, he spoke with great regret about losing Kauthir. He believed that the threats to take him to the kadhi would never have materialized and that ultimately he was pressured into divorce. He believed that, had he been given the opportunity to spend time with Kauthir, he could have convinced her that his decision to take a second wife had nothing to do with his love for her and his commitment to their marriage and children. Saddened at his loss, he ended his story by explaining his decision to divorce as an enactment of the proverb "Marry in a good way, divorce in a good way." In response to overhearing our conversation, Sauda teased Jamal about wanting to return to his cousin. She and I were both shocked by his heartfelt and candid response: "You never forget the person with whom you first learn love. We were young, and we taught each other how to love." Love, framed as *mapenzi*, continued to be Jamal's most salient memory of his first marriage. The tenderness of that conversation did not prepare me for the rancorous fights that led to his subsequent divorce from Sauda nor for his later exploits, which garnered him the label of a man who "likes to marry."[41]

Many women who divorce while still young remarry almost immediately. Kauthir, however, bitterly refused all marriage proposals for many years, staying in her father's house and raising her children. If she had not been so well loved by her family, she might have been considered a burden. One day when I was visiting her father, she called me into the sitting room to show me something privately. When she pulled out a photo album, I thought that we would engage in the familiar Swahili ritual of looking at family photos. However, Kauthir was most intent on showing me the photos of her wedding to Jamal. I asked the appropriate questions about how many days the wedding lasted and who attended. I could not interpret her expression as she closed the album. Gingerly, I asked whether she was sad or angry about the divorce. She told me firmly that once the love was gone she could no longer live as Jamal's wife; however, I was not convinced that the love had disappeared. Several years later, she beamed as she told me about her recent marriage to an older man from Mombasa. Her sisters teased her about the chores of being a new bride after spending most of her thirties alone. Perhaps remembering our previous conversation, she said to me, "Those other days are over."

Assessing Commitment and Expressing Jealousy

The number of nights spouses spend together, the amount of attention they give to adorning themselves, and the expenditures of money or time they offer each other are all interpreted as evidence of the depth of their love and commitment. When the signs indicate that commitment is waning, the charge can be made that the disinterested spouse is more concerned with expending his or her attentions on someone else. Assessments of commitment are commonly framed as expressions of *wivu* (jealousy), which refers to the complex feelings of anger and hurt that accompany suspicion that a partner is interested in someone else or is the object of another's affection. From women's perspectives, the possibility of polygyny builds jealousy into the structure of marriage. From men's perspective, the importance of *heshima* and family honor mean that jealousy is a critical aspect of policing a wife's behavior. Doubts about commitment, framed as jealousy, are commonly expressed in marital arguments, especially between young couples.[42]

Swahili proverbs, songs, and poems, in addition to reality-based stories, depict polygamous marriages as ridden with the jealousy of co-wives. Speculation by a wife that her husband gives more emotional attention to another wife leads to serious conflict.[43] Co-wives routinely refuse to acknowledge one other, even at weddings, where they strategically position themselves on opposite sides of the room. Much rarer are stories of co-wives who cohabit peacefully.[44] As some women in polygynous marriages suggest, they mute feelings of jealousy with the knowledge that, in comparison with the other wife or wives, they receive better shares of love, sex, and money. But most women claim that one necessarily feels antagonism over a second wife.

Conceptualized as an individual sentiment expressed as a situational response, jealousy is the expected reaction to a second marriage, reports that a spouse was seen speaking to a potential lover, or the knowledge that a spouse once loved someone else. Some couples make claims about jealousy in playful and teasing ways that are part of the erotics of their marriage; however, such games turn dangerous if played carelessly. A few individuals are thought to be jealous by nature, given their excessive reactions to situations that would not occasion jealousy in others. Some people experience jealous phases attributed to immaturity.

Claims that emerge from the sentiments of jealousy are difficult to articulate in disputing contexts, as they threaten the *heshima* of the accused and the accuser. The potential connection to adulterous behavior means that many accusations are made privately. Many women seek to counter their jealousy through Swahili medicines that practitioners prepare to alleviate jealousy or avert its expression. Medicines are thought to dull the response of the treated party to situations that might arouse a jealous temperament. However, jealousy can also be instigated through spiritual medicines that cause one to read a spouse's every action as evidence of infidelity.

In Kadhi's Court, judges rely on the discourse of ethics rather than spiritual therapy to address jealous tendencies, and they are generally reticent to explore the charges made by jealous parties. On a few occa-

sions, when they have ample evidence to suggest that jealousy is motivated by a spouse's improper behavior, kadhis confront the accused,
often ignoring accusations of jealousy. For instance, a young couple,
Rashid and Zulecha, entered the kadhi's office and began to talk with
him about their difficulties. They had come to see him previously, and
he was familiar with the deterioration of their three-year marriage.
The two were terribly angry at each other, and their discussion before
the kadhi quickly became acrimonious. The accusations made by Zulecha, the wife, shifted from claims of nonmaintenance to the specific
point that Rashid was in the habit of paying frequent visits to his
former wife, spending more time with her than with his own family.
Rashid countered that Zulecha should avoid the subject of infidelity
because she had a boyfriend. Zulecha, by this time in tears, cried out
that Rashid was sleeping with his ex-wife and other women. My reaction to the scene was shock. Claims of adultery had never been made
with such rancor in other marriage disputes and cases that I had witnessed. Moreover, the daily conduct of Swahili people rarely includes
references to improper sexual behavior. The kadhi took the situation
in hand. Speaking sharply to Rashid and Zulecha, he insisted that they
refrain from accusations of adultery. In reprimanding the couple, the
kadhi neglected to pursue the truth of their accusations. Rather, he
forced them to return to the issue of maintenance. When they were
calmer, he suggested divorce as the best solution given the severe strain
in their relationship, and they agreed to separate.

Accusations of sexual impropriety are a potent register for disputing about troubled marriages, one indicative of a severe problem. The
invocation of such grave issues calls attention to the rupture in a marriage without mentioning other causes, which, in the case of Rashid
and Zulecha, involved long-standing disagreements over his financial
obligations. Earlier in their marriage, the couple had spoken about the
conflict between them through other terms. They talked about love,
about lack of money, and about the morality of treating one another
with cruelty. The deterioration of their marriage, and their inability
to resolve the conflict, led Rashid and Zulecha to articulate their claims
against each other in the most severe terms. Public accusations of adultery, which bore little relation to their conflict, were the only means
left for expressing the deep desire to end their marriage.

Public accusations of adultery achieve their powerful effects in part
through their association with the discourse of Islamic law and its prohibition of extramarital sex. Making an accusation of adultery not
only invokes the law but also defies the Swahili cultural preference for

"hiding matters." By directly impugning the accused party's *heshima,* public accusations make subsequent reconciliation highly unlikely.

Controlling Conduct

For some men, the fear of a wife's lack of commitment can be so strong, and their feelings of jealousy so intense, that they forbid their spouse to leave the house without permission. Such behavior shows the link between jealousy and the controlling actions with which jealous men respond in order to preserve *heshima.* Restrictions on a wife's movements are within a husband's rights, although kadhis counter unreasonable assertions of rights with the discourse of ethics, emphasizing trust between partners rather than restrictions.[45] In rare cases, a man's desire to control leads him to abuse his wife physically. Isabel Marcus's model (1994) of "terrorism in the home" links abuse to assertions of power and control that reflect patriarchal relations. Not surprisingly, Swahili men physically abuse women more frequently than the other way around. Informants describe physical abuse of many forms, including slapping, punching, kicking, and pinching. Among Swahili people there is very little tolerance of physical abuse, and people will intervene to stop it. Strict seclusion and extensive abuse can go hand in hand. A few stories of women living at the mercy of husbands they cannot escape are thought to depict very rare exceptions, although the hidden nature of the problem makes this difficult to substantiate.

One evening at a home I routinely visited, I witnessed an argument between the young couple who lived there with several children and a domestic servant. Initially similar to other quarrels between them, the argument concerned the wife's claim that her husband went out too often at night, leaving her to watch his child from a previous marriage. In an act of great cruelty, she insisted, in front of the child, that she had no interest in caring for him. When her husband ordered her to be quiet, she abused him verbally, using a severe insult. The husband flew into a rage and lunged at her, telling her to stop speaking that way in front of the child. Ducking his clutches, the wife continued yelling insults, and her husband threatened to silence her with physical violence. At this moment the servant, who had worked for the man for many years, stepped between the couple. He stated that it was not seemly for Muslims to fight and refused to move. The husband and wife backed away, moving into different parts of the house. The servant went back to the kitchen, apologizing for his intervention yet saying that, as a Muslim himself, he had to intervene.

In cases of severe or recurrent physical abuse, kadhis urge victims to file claims of assault with the police. The shift from covering up incidents of violence to seeking the state's assistance reflects a shift from the discourse of ethics to that of Kenyan state law. Swahili women rarely make the discursive shift to threaten an abusive husband with a police charge. Trying to convince an unrepentant husband that beating his wife was gravely wrong, a Kadhi's Court clerk said: "Beating your wife is not permitted. Even the Kenyan government does not allow you to beat your wife."

Disputing Patterns, Gendered Discourse, and Agency

Swahili people orient to and produce the four discourses of marital disputing in gender-patterned ways. The options for disputing are significant factors in determining how disputes are processed and transformed, as are cultural understandings about language. Through the legal role of husband, men have unquestioned access to the rules, personnel, and authority of Islamic legal discourse. Swahili men's connection to law means that they possess the authority to speak in legal contexts and to produce the discourse of Islamic law. However, wives also have significant legal standing. Their entitlements to maintenance are well established in Islamic texts and widely publicized. Though Swahili women readily produce the discourses of Swahili ethics and spiritual health to counter difficult domestic situations, they are sometimes reticent to speak about their entitlements, let alone to claim them, through Islamic legal discourse. Just as Halima's case demonstrated at the outset of this chapter, a woman might remain silent in the face of both the ambivalence of her legal position and the threat to *heshima* posed by bringing a claim. Yet, when disputes escalate, women are adept at shifting to articulate their legal rights. Their acts of agency belie the scholarly and popular assumption that women have no access to Islamic law and that law is solely the province of men and male-dominated institutions.

The discursive shifts described above are much more than skillful strategic moves made by disputants who want to win. The agency of disputants is critical to their production of discourse, but it is circumscribed as well. Yngvesson (1993:10) recognizes structure and agency—as well as power—in the disputing process:

The analysis of disputes is always an analysis of power relations, as these structure the definition and interpretation of trouble in fam-

ilies, neighborhoods, courts, and in other 'private' and 'public' settings. Disputing needs to be theorized, but not as an activity distinct
from these relations of power. Rather, disputing can be theorized
as a form of action-in-the-world in which the connection of the
'personal' to the 'structural' is both given and emergent, and in
which disputes both affirm asymmetries of gender, class, and ethnicity and may challenge these, revealing their openness to contestation.

In Yngvesson's approach, actors' choices are conceptualized neither
as narrow strategies nor as determined by an overarching explanatory
model (e.g., rational choice) but rather as acts of persons operating
on interests that are not always fully understood by them, not always
relevant to their projects, and not always congruent with the interests
of others, including those in similar social roles. Yngvesson attends
not only to the power relations that structure the conflicts underlying
disputes but also to the processes through which they are resolved. At
the same time, she recognizes that actors embedded in changing power
relations affect the course of disputing and thereby, in some instances,
reconfigure power relations.

The goal of this chapter has been to illuminate how gender asymmetries are structured through the available discourses of marital conflict and how they are both reinforced and contested in disputes.
Through the action-in-the-world of disputing, gendered subjects engage in disputes within the structural constraints of the discursive
frameworks for conflict resolution and the broader social fields in
which marital problems arise. Disputants' deployments of the terms of
the four discourses reflect their gendered orientations to the discourses
themselves and to cultural understandings about what kinds of speech
are appropriately produced by what kinds of people. When those involved in disputing shift from one discursive realm to another—either
strategically or less consciously—they necessarily reposition themselves within the set of cultural understandings about gender and
speech. These shifts across discourses offer sites for investigating the
connection between "the personal and the structural" and thereby for
assessing the possibilities for transformation through disputes.

Each instance of disputing occasions change in a dispute, the relations between disputing parties, and potentially between categories of
people (e.g., changes in gender relations). For example, when a woman
shifts to legal discourse in a dispute, she reconfigures her own status
as a particular kind of legal and gendered subject. For an individual,

this can mean significant change, including relief from an oppressive relationship or condemnation for exposing family problems. But do these acts of agency have broader effects? For example, do they transform the culturally recognized connection between men and Islamic law, which is a source of male social power? At the level of cultural understandings, the connection between Swahili Muslim men and Islamic law remains firm. As the examples have shown, women produce legal discourse only at particular moments of a dispute and generally after having persevered and tried other discourses. Moreover, a woman's invocation of Islamic law is more credible and respectable if she has attempted other forms of resolution and found no relief. Thus, women are not the proprietors of Islamic law in the way that men are, only potential users in appropriate circumstances.

That the discourse of Islamic law remains "masculine" suggests that discourses of disputing can retain their gendered quality—in the sense of hierarchical positioning or who has authoritative connection to them—even though members of both genders produce them. And yet, women's recent increased use of Kenyan Islamic courts for disputing, which has resulted from a structural change in the postcolonial legal system, means that they are producing all four discourses in a "new" context, that is, one in which they had previously ventured only rarely. Chapter 5 explores what brought about the structural change and assesses the effects on gender relations.

WOMAN: What if he's just tired of me?

KADHI: It's his right, but he has to maintain you.

WOMAN: What if I say I'm just tired of him?

KADHI: Don't say that. Your duty is to work at it.

WOMAN: What if love is gone?

KADHI: You still have the children.

(FROM A KADHI'S COURT CONSULTATION)

Marital Disputing in Kadhi's Courts

Early each weekday morning, for about eight months, I left my house in Malindi and passed along narrow dirt paths winding among modest stone houses into an area of small shops and offices perched on a hill overlooking the sea. On the way I warmly greeted neighbors, exchanged nods with the men congregated near a mosque, and, after a few weeks of attracting children's stares, eventually proceeded with little notice past the primary school to my destination: the Malindi Kadhi's Court. The court is housed in the same building as the secular Kenyan government courts. The complex is a one-story square; offices and courtrooms form the perimeter, and the center is a small courtyard with grass and a tree. The courtyard is lively with the sounds of typing and testimony from the surrounding offices and courtrooms. Witnesses sometimes stretch out for a nap on the grass, and attorneys consult with their clients and with each other. Some days the courtyard serves as a temporary storage area for evidence—clothes found at a crime scene, goats at issue in a theft, or part of an engine. One sunny afternoon, police used the courtyard to burn a cache of marijuana, evidence that had served to convict one of Malindi's organized-crime bosses. The burning was halted when several of us remarked that the smoke was making everyone high.

The Kadhi's Court offices occupy less than half of one side of the square. A set of windows in the clerk's office faces into the courtyard and another out toward the tree-lined road that passes beside the court, leading down to the beach. Muslims with business in the Kadhi's Court enter at the corner of the square, make an immediate left, and proceed the short distance to the office of the Kadhi's Court clerk. Some might later emerge from the clerk's office and walk the few steps to the kadhi. In past years, those with cases continued further, to a large room at the corner of the building. Previously a formal courtroom, it is now a storage area for files and broken furniture, and consequently the kadhi hears cases in his tiny office.

On entering the courtyard, Muslim women pull their veils closer and walk quickly, treating the Magistrate's courts and offices as public space in which they might be exposed inappropriately. Once in the office of the Kadhi's Court clerk, they take seats on benches along the walls or in chairs by the clerk's desk. Muslim men are less concerned about getting a seat. Instead, they stand by the office door or wait outside. Some congregate near the open window to hear the clerk conduct business, while others move into the courtyard, especially if an interesting case is being argued in the large Magistrate's Court across the way. When the clerk's office is crowded and people must wait outside, women stand in small groups with their backs to the courtyard. They appear less interested than the men in the business of the surrounding secular courts and rarely acknowledge the non-Muslims around them, including police and court personnel.

The image of women sitting inside and men standing outside displays spatially two relations of power operating in the postcolonial Kadhi's Courts. The first is gender segregation, an ongoing challenge for Swahili Muslims in public settings. Men and women automatically divide the courtroom space, with women predictably seeking and creating seclusion through walls or their own bodies.[1] The spatial arrangement also highlights a second relation of power: the marginality of Islam in the Kenyan state as symbolized through the location of the Kadhi's Court in a building controlled by the secular legal apparatus. These relations intersect as Muslim men, assumed to be more familiar with and less threatened by dealings with the state, position themselves at the blurry borders where secular and Islamic commingle. To preserve *heshima,* women remove themselves from the secular as much as possible. This gendered behavior is ironic in that women accomplish *heshima* by occupying the Kadhi's Court, that is, the site of Islamic law. Thus, they challenge the assumption that Muslim legal contexts are men's domain. A more subtle irony, one that emerges through this chapter, is that men's position on the border between the Islamic and secular courts, far from illustrating that they are authorized to occupy either site, reflects their alienation from both.

This chapter describes how the Kadhi's Courts have come to serve as an increasingly important forum for Swahili women in troubled domestic situations. It documents the success of women's claims and assesses the consequences for women who seek assistance and for men who are alienated from the courts. Because the Kadhi's Courts operate as complex sites for contesting power along several interrelated dimensions, explaining how and why they recognize and support women's claims requires consideration of the courts' role in power struggles involving local communities and the state. The position of these courts within multiple "webs of power" (Abu-Lughod 1990) facilitates women's making claims yet also renders their success tenuous. Individual women who win claims in Kadhi's Court experience changes in their personal situations that might alleviate their oppression by specific men. However, women's use of these courts—even in increasing numbers—constitutes an ambiguous form of resistance to male domination in Swahili society. Indeed, as this chapter argues, the complexity of the political field in which these courts operate—specifically, the crosscutting power relations of gender, class, ethnicity, and religious sect—calls into question any simple application of the concept of resistance in this or other legal arenas.

In recounting the development of the Kenyan Kadhi's Courts, the following section identifies the several political and religious interests that shaped them historically. I then analyze the courts' operation in the postcolonial period and specify their role in handling marital claims. My discussion suggests that women's success has multiple causes and consequences that are related to the antagonistic relationship between kadhis and many men in the community. This antagonism, which has deep historical roots, is exacerbated by women's success in court. Later sections address the relation between the Kadhi's Courts and the state, concluding that Swahili men and women, pitted against each other in legal cases, come together to defend the courts' autonomy in the face of the secular state's intervention. As the conclusion asserts, curious and paradoxical realignments of interests and individuals have resulted from the multiple negotiations of power that take place in courts and from the operation of courts both as sites for disputing and as community symbols.

Although this chapter emphasizes the historical roots and reach of the Kadhi's Courts, it also devotes attention to the individuals who are central to the courts' activities. Court personnel play pivotal roles in negotiating power in legal contexts (see, e.g., Conley and O'Barr 1990; Fallers 1969; Gulliver 1977; Yngvesson 1988, 1993). By skillfully manipulating the discourses described in the previous chapter to resolve disputes and, at the same time, preserve their own compromised authority, kadhis and their clerks negotiate the courts' roles as community symbols and as sites for constituting gender relations.

The Historical Indeterminacy of Coastal Islamic Courts

When I asked government officials in Nairobi about the role of Islamic law in Kenya, they cited the Kadhi's Courts as proof of the government's tolerance of religious difference even if it means legal diversity. These non-Muslim officials viewed the Kadhi's Courts as the authorities on Islamic law for the Kenyan Muslim community. But, as described below, the standing of the courts and their personnel as Islamic legal authorities in the coastal area has shifted over time and is contested in the postcolonial period.

Muslims held power in Mombasa from before 1500 through the decline of the ruling Shirazi dynasty in 1590, and they most likely enforced Islamic law through a system of Kadhi's Courts.[2] Reliance on Islamic law continued even throughout the period of Portuguese rule in the sixteenth and seventeenth centuries, although the Portuguese acted on some matters in accordance with their own laws.[3] Following the expulsion of the Portuguese from Mombasa, Omani Muslims controlling the coast further institutionalized Islamic law by establishing courts in many areas (Swartz 1979:33). In 1735, members of the powerful Mazrui family, acting as agents of Omani rulers, assumed positions as kadhis. Mazruis were associated with the class of notables from influential Southern Arabian immigrant clans, who, in contrast to indigenous Swahili, possessed the knowledge in Islamic law *(fiqh)* and Koranic exegesis *(tafsir)*, as well as the status as learned holy people *(mashaikh)*, to justify assuming judicial power (Pouwels 1987:40).

After capturing Mombasa in 1837, the sultan of Oman, from the Busaidi clan, took control of most of the coast, eventually governing from Zanzibar.[4] Relations between the Omani sultans and coastal people varied over the course of the century, as some sultans interfered with local practices more than others and some regions were targeted for intervention more directly than others.[5] The sultanate appointed district governors *(maliwali, s. liwali)* to handle local administration in the coastal communities. Most district governors were members of the Busaidi family; however, they relied on *ulama*, local elders learned in both Islam and local practice, to accomplish administrative tasks and on indigenous kadhis to administer Koranic law and provide religious advice (Salim 1973:73, 76, 141). The jurisdiction of district governors and kadhis overlapped, though for the most part the former dealt with criminal matters and the latter handled civil and religious claims. Busaidi rule on the coast, though diffuse early in the nineteenth century, increasingly impinged on the indigenous population as the dynasty gained power (Pouwels 1987).[6]

The impact of Busaidi rule varied across coastal communities, and scholars offer different interpretations of its consequences for law. Swartz (1979:33) describes the period from 1837 to 1895 as a time of judicial autonomy for the coastal Islamic courts when kadhis of Swahili ethnicity gained prominence.[7] The indigenous kadhis, generally elders *(wazee)* in the towns, were more knowledgeable about customary legal interpretations than strict textual interpretations. Presumably, their brand of local law was popular. The political power of the indigenous Swahili community, at least in Mombasa, grew substantially during the period (Swartz 1979:33). However, Pouwels (1987) describes the increasing control of the Busaidis over some local communities. By the latter years of the nineteenth century, the autonomy of the kadhis deteriorated to the extent that they were merely "creatures" of the Busaidi (Pouwels 1987:136). District governors and sultans (especially Barghash) routinely interfered in cases heard by kadhis. In sum, the autonomy of kadhis and their relation to the sultanate varied by community, especially depending on the community's distance from Zanzibar.

With European imperialist expansion, the sultanate's control over the coast began to break down. From 1888 to 1895, the Imperial British East Africa Company (IBEA) paid annual rent of eleven thousand pounds to the sultan for the concessionary rights to a ten-mile-wide strip of coastal land stretching through Kenya and Tanzania. During the concessionary period, the sultanate began to relinquish control of the legal system. An 1887 act by the British permitted the sultan to appoint IBEA officials as judges, but changes in the act two years later reduced the sultan's role to "consultation" alone (see Mungeam 1978: 29; Pouwels 1987:175). During the IBEA's dominion, the company clarified legal jurisdiction by ordering that newly appointed European magistrates would hear criminal cases, leaving civil cases to the kadhis. This decision hardened a division of labor that had previously been flexible.

In 1895, the IBEA relinquished the concession to Britain to be administered as the East Africa Protectorate, and the coastal Kadhi's

Courts became part of the colonial administration.[8] An 1897 order in council established two classes of Native Courts to adjudicate matters between non-Europeans. Courts of the first class were presided over by kadhis, district governors, and chiefs. Europeans sat as judges in the second class of courts, which included Provincial Courts, a Chief Native Court, and a High Court (Salim 1973:81). Each of the eleven districts *(wilayet)* had a Kadhi's Court.[9] The kadhis heard claims between Muslims involving personal status, inheritance, and family law and also advised colonial officials on questions of Islam. The British rounded out the "native" political administration by creating the post of chief *(mudir),* intended as an assistant to the district governor and empowered to hear minor civil and criminal cases. Preference for native positions was given to Arabs, who had gained British respect.[10]

The 1897 order in council also created the position of Chief Kadhi, or Sheikh-ul-Islam.[11] The Chief Kadhi's Court served as the appellate court for the lower Kadhi's Courts. The place of Muslims in the colonial structure was further established in a 1901 decision to grant Muslim attorneys *(wakil)* permission to represent Muslim clients in court (Salim 1973:86). The 1906 Mohammedan Marriage and Divorce Registration Ordinance solidified Islam's position in the expanding colonial administration.[12]

In the early years of colonial rule, the British were concerned with preserving Islamic practice, but not without some modification. The colonial government established the Courts Commissioners of Kenya, which regulated the Native Courts, including by altering laws. The British justified interference in "native" affairs by citing rumors of corruption, especially customary practices such as claimants' offering "gifts" to kadhis (Pouwels 1987:81). The commission sought to convince kadhis of the impropriety of considering witnesses' status or wealth in assessing credibility. In theory, kadhis were appointed with the sultan's consent until 1907, but, in fact, the British controlled the process early on. British interference in Kadhi's Courts—based on misunderstandings of customary practice and on racial discrimination— further alienated a population already skeptical of the courts and resentful of the colonial government (Pouwels 1987:162, 174–75).

Opposition to the kadhis also came from non-Muslims, particularly British residents of Kenya who opposed including kadhis in the colonial regime. Two letters written in 1928 offer differing views on the advisability of retaining the kadhis. One, written by a "Tax Payer" and published in a national newspaper, counsels eliminating the positions, citing the expense of maintaining a dual legal system and the availability of young, educated personnel to replace the "overpaid" kadhis.[13] The other letter, written by the chief justice to the governor, supports retaining the kadhis, given their leadership function in the community.[14] The letters illustrate the dependence of the kadhis on the British for their positions and thus their vulnerability as authorities in the colonial regime.

In the early colonial period, both men and women were suspicious of the kadhis, though for different reasons. According to Strobel (1979:46–48, 58–62), several Mombasa women who were dissatisfied with their treatment by kadhis appealed to colonial government officials to consider their claims.[15] In bypassing a patriarchal system supported by the kadhis, these women expressed a lack of faith in the authority of the religious courts. Anderson's review (1955) of coastal Muslim law includes the observation that women fared poorly in court.[16] At the same time, men also questioned the authority and legitimacy of the Kadhi's Courts; however, their reservations stemmed from a rejection of collaboration with the colonial government.

By the end of the colonial period, the Kadhi's Courts had been the site of contestation within and among ethnic groups, religious factions, and men and women. Though weakened by these divisions, the Kadhi's Courts were recognized by the national government at Independence. With the adoption of the Kenyan constitution on December 12, 1962, the government guaranteed the position of the Kadhi's Courts in the judiciary of the post-Independence state. Since the late 1960s, the Kadhi's Courts have operated separately from the District and Resident Magistrate's Courts, which handle most civil and criminal claims (Judicature Act of 1967, S. 66, subs. 5; see Jackson 1970). The Kadhi's Courts Act (No. 14 of 1967) held that Muslim law be applied in matters of personal status, marriage, divorce, or inheritance when "all the parties profess the Muslim religion" (Jackson 1970:20).[17] Thus, the kadhis, who had previously served as advisors to the district governors, became the Muslims designated to serve in the post-Independence government and to hold the only nonsecular judicial authority.

Whether kadhis are viewed as local leaders or as state agents has always reflected political struggles at local, national, and global levels.[18] Swartz (1979) makes the bold claim that the Kadhi's Courts have come to mark ethnicity among coastal Muslims. He argues that use of the Kadhi's Courts by Mazrui and Busaidi Arabs binds these clans with Swahili people as against the primarily South Asian Shia Muslims, who avoid the courts. By claiming that the kadhis' positions as judicial leaders serve as an ethnic marker, Swartz depicts the courts as integrative for the community, rather than divisive. This interpretation is intriguing and warranted to some extent by ethnic patterns of court use; however, clan affiliation and degree of religious orthodoxy divide the Swahili, Mazrui, and Busaidi in their loyalty to the kadhis as well as in their extracourt relations. These divisions, which originated in the nineteenth century, continue into the postcolonial period (see also Pouwels 1987:201). Moreover, the role of the courts as a symbol for the union of some Muslim ethnic groups has to be evaluated in light of the gender divisions evident in court use, an issue Swartz fails to consider.

The position of one of the postcolonial Chief Kadhis exemplifies how kadhis and their courts can both encourage unity and foment contestation. Sheikh Abdallah Swaleh Al-Farsy, the most popular Chief Kadhi (for biographical information, see Bakari 1995; Swartz 1982; and Farsy's later writings), wrote over fifty books and numerous popular pamphlets on Islamic law. Many Muslim families in East Africa own a copy of his 1969 Kiswahili translation of the Koran. Farsy preached an orthodox version of Islam that criticized many local practices as *bidhaa*, innovations grafted onto Islam after the death of the Prophet Mohammed and therefore not permitted under Islam.[19] Farsy published several popular handbooks that outline his position on *bidhaa* (e.g., Farsy 1977, 1981).[20] He and other scholars (such as Al-Amin Mazrui) were revered even if their rather strident exhortations were politely ignored by some sectors of the coastal community and actively opposed by others.[21]

Against the historical backdrop of questionable and shifting authority, the post-Independence Kadhi's Courts accommodate increasing numbers of claims by women. The tension over portraying kadhis as revered local leaders or detested collaborators is part of the discourse of Swahili people as they evaluate the courts, including kadhis' decisions. As described below, the postcolonial kadhis actively negotiate their position in relation to the state and also their relationships to others who handle disputes in local communities, some of whom compete for political or judicial authority.

Kadhis and Clerks in the Postcolonial Kadhi's Courts

When I reach the Malindi court one morning, a few men and women are already gathered at the clerk's office. The clerk arrives at eight-thirty. After greeting us and settling behind his desk, he invites a sad-looking woman to pull her chair closer and tell him her reason for coming. Speaking in low tones, she says that her husband left the house the night before, declaring that he would divorce her. She says she is confused and begins to cry. The clerk calms her with assurances that he will determine the husband's intentions. He writes a note summoning the husband to court. Handing it to the woman, he counsels her to deliver the note and to return, with her husband, in the afternoon. As she leaves, a man at the window leans in over the desk and asks whether his ex-wife has come to claim the maintenance money he was supposed to deposit with the court. Perturbed, the clerk warns him that paying the money is a legal obligation that he has to meet as soon as possible. The man offers reasons for his inability to pay and promises that he will bring the money the next day. The clerk asks two other women if they have come to complain about problems at home. They both nod in assent. One of the two has been to court numerous times. As she approaches the clerk, they banter with each other; the clerk quips that she might save her marriage by coming to court less often. Becoming more serious, he urges her to make peace with her husband. Another man at the window echoes this advice, and the clerk invites me to agree with him, which I politely refuse to do. Intent on getting the clerk's undivided attention, the woman departs, saying that she will return later when the office is less busy.

After a phone call, the clerk goes across the courtyard to retrieve some files, telling all of us he'll be right back. The women waiting on the bench begin talking quietly with each other, vaguely alluding to their difficulties. When the kadhi arrives at nine o'clock, passing by the window, most of us follow him to his office. He sees each party separately; others wait in the courtyard. Curtains ensure that no one interferes through the windows, and there is an aura of formality that contrasts with the clerk's office. First, the kadhi performs a marriage, chanting the blessings melodically and joining hands with each party as they repeat their vows. The couple, along with several male relatives who have accompanied them, proceed to the clerk's office to obtain marriage certificates. Telling the next parties to wait, the kadhi calls the Chief Kadhi to discuss a controversial case involving the use of police to enforce a custody order. Upon hanging up, the kadhi tells me that the Chief Kadhi has advised that, if non-Muslim police are asked to assist, they must be ordered not to violate the *heshima* of any Muslims. Next, a woman comes in to report that her husband has not complied with the kadhi's order to provide her with a place to live.

He speaks to her about perseverance yet tells her to return if there is no change in a week. When she leaves, eight people enter, and the kadhi remembers that their case is scheduled for that morning. Glancing at the file, and his watch, he tells those assembled to return in the afternoon, when there will be more time to hear the case. I walk out with them and stop by the clerk's office. He teases me that I have missed the real action by sitting with the kadhi rather than him. We talk over the morning's events, which were not as exciting as he had suggested. I head home for lunch and a quick nap before returning for the afternoon session.[22]

The events described above represent a typical morning's activities in the Malindi Kadhi's Court at the time of my research. Complaints are screened by clerks, who mediate disputes when the kadhi is occupied or absent. Much of the court's activity does not involve disputes: kadhis perform marriages and notarize documents; clerks process marriage and divorce certificates, maintain files and records, and handle other bureaucratic tasks. In addition, kadhis and clerks negotiate the many administrative and physical relations between the Islamic court and the secular state.[23] All court personnel are employed in the Kenyan civil service. Any Kenyan is eligible for clerical positions, though most Kadhi's Court clerks are Muslims.[24] Requirements for becoming a civil servant include secular education and fluency in English. Until the 1970s, kadhis were generally older (sometimes elderly) men. Their standing as community elders was the primary criterion of appointment, along with knowledge of Islamic law. In the postcolonial period, increasing emphasis on English literacy as a qualification for the position of kadhi has resulted in younger individuals' assuming office, as is the case throughout the Kenyan judiciary.[25] Though they trace their origins to different coastal towns, the kadhis are, for the most part, ethnically Swahili. In contrast to past kadhis, they are less likely to be from the oldest and most respected families. Pressure on the government and the Chief Kadhi to appoint kadhis from non-Swahili ethnic groups has been partly successful.[26] Kadhis are generally assigned to courts outside their communities of origin. Frequent transfers mean that kadhis are relatively unable to establish strong ties in their town of appointment and are uninterested in doing so. That kadhis and their clerks move between the secular and religious legal systems has always strained their relationships to local communities, where their influence is tenuous, especially among men.

The requirements for the position of Chief Kadhi, also a civil service position, include extensive knowledge of Islam and Islamic law (though not necessarily formal legal training); ability to mediate disputes and judge cases; and leadership in the Muslim community. Having studied Islamic law in the Middle East is not necessarily a better credential than having worked with a learned teacher on the East African coast (see Bakari 1995:175). The Chief Kadhi acts as a liaison between the Kenyan government and the Muslim community; he is a member of the Supreme Council of Kenyan Muslims (SUPKEM), a political organization that, among other activities, monitors the government's treatment of Muslims. He also represents Muslims at national and international events requiring the presence of religious leaders. Sheikh Mohammed Nassor Nahdy, the Chief Kadhi at the time of my research, assumed office when Sheikh Farsy retired and has held it into the 1990s.[27]

The Chief Kadhi monitors the decisions and practices of the kadhis who serve under him. Newly appointed kadhis go through a probationary period during which the Chief Kadhi reviews their work and provides guidance. For the most part, kadhis perform their duties independently of one another; however, they meet periodically at the Chief Kadhi's request to discuss court practice, especially compliance with procedural rules. Occasionally, kadhis consult about substantive issues or specific cases. More often, they discuss such issues with their clerks, who also provide information about the local politics behind a case. The Chief Kadhi has the power to monitor how kadhis conduct themselves in and out of court and to advise them if needed.

Kadhis must negotiate their legal authority with the clerks who serve under them and who sometimes claim expertise in religious law or dispute settlement. This negotiation can be contentious, as some clerks, depending on experience and personal predilection, seek to expand their authority. To a certain extent, clerks perform the "watchdog" function attributed by Yngvesson (1993:45) to the New England court clerk who alternates between "gatekeeping" in the court and "watching" in the community. Clerks, who are often appointed to the court in their town of origin and residence, are more familiar with the local inhabitants than are kadhis. Kadhis seek advice from clerks not only in local matters but also with respect to the Kenyan state (e.g., court procedures and government forms), as most clerks are career civil servants with experience handling secular government practices. In their roles as recordkeepers, mediators, and kadhis' consultants, clerks wield considerable power to negotiate relations among the court, the state, and the local community. Court clerks shape the discourses people use by deciding which claims are appropriately sent to the kadhi, which should be resolved by elders, and which waste everyone's time. Through discussions that range from teasing banter to formal inquisition, clerks screen out the "meaningless" cases, which resemble the "garbage cases" identified by Yngvesson (1993). This process eases the court's burden by dismissing claims and, more significantly, determining the appropriate "subjects" of conflict resolution. Even though they occupy roles more circumscribed than those of Yngvesson's clerks, Kadhi's Court clerks are positioned to structure conflict in innovative ways, applying discursive frames unanticipated by disputants.[28] Yet the clerks' marginality sets limits on their "capacity for governance" in that their framings are vulnerable to challenge by kadhis and disputing parties (see Yngvesson 1993:58). A clerk's influence also depends on his or her experience and personal demeanor.[29]

The power of the clerks has grown as the state has limited the semiofficial and quasi-legal roles previously occupied by local elders. Until the late 1960s, *wakil*s (lawyers, or men knowledgeable about Muslim law) appeared on behalf of clients in secular and religious courts and were recognized as legal professionals. The Kenyan government abolished the position of *wakil* and thus weakened the Muslim legal apparatus. There are conflicting explanations for their removal, including the *wakil*s' corruption and inefficiency, disagreement among *wakil*s over some laws, and the Kenyan government's desire to create a "modern," secularly educated judiciary. Also eliminated in the 1960s was the *baraza* (literally, porch) of elders, who decided cases referred to them by a kadhi when he was very busy or desired a more locally tailored solution. Assistant registrars, who are empowered to prepare marriage and divorce certificates and perform other legal functions (e.g., serve summonses), have been increasingly marginalized in relation to the Kadhi's Court. This is further evidence of the attempt to professionalize the judiciary and minimize interference by elders.[30] In the past, kadhis often sent mediations to the elders, but the newer kadhis vary in their willingness to do so.[31] Moreover, previous kadhis and clerks were more like these elders with respect to social position, level of education, and family and community ties. The postcolonial kadhis and clerks are less publicly prominent than local religious leaders *(ulama)*, particularly those who control mosques.[32]

Even though kadhis and clerks compete with other Muslim men

for authority over dispute resolution and Islamic law, they encourage some people to seek the advice of elders. Yet, in making these referrals, kadhis actually emphasize their own official capacity. Thus, some couples who are discouraged from filing a case before consulting with elders are also informed that, should either party be dissatisfied with the elders' disposition of the matter, they can return to court. Through these procedures, kadhis and clerks diminish and subordinate their competitors' authority. The increasing disjuncture between court officials and elders allows women to pursue disputes outside the influence of local, powerful Muslim men.

Conflict Resolution in Kadhi's Court

The number of cases filed and decided in the Malindi Kadhi's Court has increased steadily since the 1970s (see table 5.1).[33] There is a similar trend in the Mombasa Kadhi's Court. Moreover, in Malindi, the number of divorces registered for 1985 and 1986 exceeded the number of marriages (see also Brown 1987).[34] The majority of claims are brought by women; their increased use of the courts is beyond dispute. In court, most parties to a dispute participate in mediations rather than cases, which are filed only after the clerk or kadhi has attempted settlement. For example, the two women mentioned earlier in this chapter

Table 5.1 Cases and Decisions in Malindi Kadhi's Court

Year	Cases filed	Decisions
1974	46	43
1975	34	39
1976	29	26
1977	40	35
1978	54	46
1979	68	66
1980	62	68
1981	71	72
1982	48	46
1983	75	68
1984	71 (through Oct.)	76 (through Oct.)
1985	80	66
1986	62	53

came to Kadhi's Court with problems they considered serious. One was encouraged to seek resolution outside court, even though she had sought the court's intervention in the past; the other was told to return for mediation. Even after serious conflict, couples are encouraged to reconcile.

This section analyzes the 129 legal claims filed in the Malindi Kadhi's Court over twenty months in 1985–86. With respect to the numbers, kinds, and dispositions of claims, these court statistics and those for several previous and subsequent years are quite similar. Disputants' problems, though initially framed through multiple discourses and subject to the complex transformations outlined in the previous chapter, are defined through a narrow set of categories when filed as claims. Both men and women can claim for restitution of conjugal rights, return of property (e.g., clothes, furniture), child custody, court costs, and "any other relief." Women can claim for dissolution of marriage (for reasons such as physical or emotional cruelty, inability to provide conjugal rights, etc.), maintenance for self, maintenance for children, past maintenance, bridewealth, *edda* payments, accommodation, or a divorce certificate. Men can claim for a wife to return to the matrimonial home. Generally, one party files a case in which several claims are made. The other party then responds to the claims and can make counterclaims.

All but four of the 129 cases involve the gender-related issues identified above. Of these, men brought 17 cases and women 108. Failure to provide economic support of one kind or another is the central claim in 93 of the 129 cases in the data set, or about 72 percent. In most cases, the issue of support is one among several claims that a wife makes against her husband. Claims of physical or mental abuse (25.6 percent) and for child custody (5.4 percent) occur less frequently. Women who have already been divorced come to the court to make claims when their ex-husbands have failed to fulfill obligations. Nine of the cases involve claims made by divorced women for *edda* maintenance. Divorced women claim for bridewealth in nine cases. Lack of "attention" is at issue in ten cases. The outcomes of these cases are summarized in table 5.2. Cases are classified by the clerks as "no resolution" when couples file a claim and never return. The end result in the eighteen instances of no resolution could be divorce or reconciliation, but the court is not informed. After a year or so with no further communication, the clerk closes the Kadhi's Court file, and the case is officially designated "no resolution."[35]

Table 5.2 Outcomes of Kadhi's Court Cases by Gender of Plaintiff

	N	Win (%)	Lose (%)	No res. (%)	Settle (%)
Male	17	23.5	29.4	11.8	35.3
Female	108	42.5	1.9	14.8	39.8
Total	125				

The most striking fact is that women lose very few cases. The two cases lost by women in 1985 are a maintenance case denied because the woman had been disobedient to her husband[36] and a claim for maintenance and bridewealth by a divorced woman whose ex-husband had made initial efforts to pay and then became ill. In deciding against her, the kadhi urged the woman to be patient until the man recovered. Men lose more cases than they win, even when they are the plaintiffs. Binti's case of abandonment in the previous chapter depicted the common occurrence of a wife's winning her claim through an ex parte trial. About half of the cases filed and argued successfully by women were heard ex parte, as the husband or ex-husband could not be located or refused to come. If he does not appear, his absence is used as evidence of a wife's claim of abandonment.[37]

Most of the forty-six cases won by women resulted in awards of maintenance and/or dissolution of marriage. The standard amount awarded for the *edda* period or for back maintenance is a modest sum calculated at a daily rate and an additional amount for clothing.[38] Claims for maintenance for the children of an ongoing marriage are calculated as part of household maintenance. Court personnel suggest that men will agree to only small child-support payments after a divorce, as they want to ensure that the ex-wife receives nothing for herself.[39] Claims for child custody are filed separately from claims for maintenance or divorce. Yet women assert that men routinely seek custody only after they have been ordered to pay maintenance.

In many cases, women are awarded the amounts that they request for maintenance; however, enforcement of the awards is a different matter. Particularly in ex parte cases, monetary awards are rarely paid. If a woman complains to the court that her husband or ex-husband has failed to comply with a maintenance agreement, the court becomes the collector. But the court's ability to elicit payment is limited, and the clerk and kadhi rely on shaming men who refuse to comply by

Table 5.3 Outcomes of Settled Cases by Gender of Plaintiff

	N	Granted	Denied	Mixed
Male	6	3	1	2
Female	43	35	2	6
Total	49			

summoning them to court repeatedly.[40] Because maintenance awards are generally low, Kadhi's Court cases rarely offer women significant gain unless remarriage is considered as a strategy for upward mobility.

Many cases are settled during mediation or by agreement between the parties outside court. Even in court, kadhis encourage disputants to reach a solution before the judgment. The outcomes suggest that women attain what they are claiming for, even when the case is settled rather than adjudicated (see table 5.3). Cases in the "mixed" category are those in which some claims were awarded and some denied. Typical mixed settlements involve cases in which the husband grants a divorce on condition that his wife "forgive" his debts to her.[41]

Court personnel screen out or reframe many problems, turning both men and women away. Men are particularly discouraged from bringing claims of adultery against women. Women who bring problems not easily subsumed under the standard claims recognized in Islamic law are steered toward mediation or perseverance. For example, in the epigraph to this chapter, the kadhi deftly reframes a wife's attempt to assert rights to a happy marriage by reminding her that she is being maintained. Later in the consultation, she complains that she has been made to feel that she has no rights to liberation from an unwanted marriage. The kadhi's suggestion that she treat the conflict as a "test," almost like a religious trial, provided little comfort.

Offering advice rather than facilitating legal action is also the kadhis' approach to claims of emotional cruelty or "lack of attention." By contrast, court personnel treat women's claims of physical abuse very seriously and frame them through the discourses of Islamic law and state law. The accused is immediately summoned and sternly admonished. Claims of abuse do not, however, automatically result in a divorce. Very often no case is filed, and the couple is simply given advice on how to live more peacefully. Even so, the court emphasizes the severity of the claim by encouraging women to file assault charges with the police.

Most women who file cases are successful. Even if men fail to comply with case decisions or settlement agreements, the decisions themselves and the authority they represent are important tools that women use to change their positions within troubled domestic circumstances (see also Landberg 1986). Those women who return to difficult marriages do so with the crucial knowledge that the court provides a context in which they might seek further remedies.

But why do women win in Kadhi's Court? First, most women tend to bring good claims to court, having taken their problems to other disputing contexts as well as having persevered, collecting evidence of marital strife over time. Perhaps more importantly, kadhis take women's claims seriously. By recognizing women's perseverance, kadhis minimize the power that men assert through pronouncements, even about Islamic law. Taking women seriously constitutes a direct reaction to men's attempts to dismiss the claims of women or to contest the court's role. Kadhis thus assert their authority over these men and, in so doing, support women and their claims. One might imagine a converse scenario in which kadhis augment their own authority by identifying with or appealing to the men they encounter in their court, rather than supporting women. This is certainly how informants describe the alliances of kadhis in the past. Moreover, many elders who decide disputes outside court are seen in this light. My observations suggest that most kadhis and clerks are struggling to establish their authoritative positions *relative* to Muslim men in the community, including elders. The newer kadhis are less likely to make decisions that have the appeasement of men as their central goal. Accordingly, kadhis face the hostility of those men who lose in court and of other men who criticize their lack of solidarity. Certainly, the record of favorable decisions for women fuels this hostility and, in a circular way, forces kadhis to further establish their authority by refusing to be pressured by local elders or by other Muslim men. In short, women win cases in part because kadhis are in conflict with other men for authority.

Kadhi's Courts and the Postcolonial State

Through statutes and directives, the postcolonial Kenyan government has institutionalized more rigorously the historical relationship subordinating the Kadhi's Courts to the central government. For example, the government regulates Kadhi's Court staff. Moreover, it has narrowed the courts' jurisdiction by designating Children's Officers, pub-

lic trustees, and juvenile courts as forums for some claims previously
heard by kadhis.

For example, the Kenyan Guardianship of Infants Act provides for
Children's Officers to appear before magistrates on behalf of children
in disputes involving maintenance, custody, and child abuse.[42] In increasing numbers, Swahili women take claims to Children's Officers,
at the recommendation of kadhis, the police, or family members.
Women claim that their preference for Children's Officers does not
represent a rejection of kadhis or Muslim law, since their primary concern is their children's welfare. They see the Children's Officers as a
form of social service, rather than as a legal body, and point out that
these officers, in conjunction with Magistrate's Courts, are better able
to enforce decisions than kadhis. Turning to Children's Officers, however, has the potential of competing with Islamic legal practice. Several
aspects of the Guardianship of Infants Act and the Juvenile Protection
Act differ from the principles of Islam followed in Kadhi's Courts. For
example, Children's Officers routinely grant custody of children under
sixteen to the mother. Kadhi's Courts, in contrast, frequently support
the claims of fathers who request custody of children (especially boys)
age seven or older. In general, Kadhi's Courts award mothers custody
of girls to age fourteen. In both forums, custody decisions rest on subjective estimations of who is a fit parent, yet a decision by the kadhi
to award custody to either parent can be justified under Muslim law.
Even though Children's Officers ground their decisions in secular law,
women accept them as an alternative to the Kadhi's Court, where their
chances of winning custody are less certain.[43] Kadhis have been able
to do little to stop the use of Children's Officers, and, when they have
trusted the individual officers, they have in fact encouraged women to
seek them out. Yet it is just this type of intrusion by the state into
domestic legal matters that Muslim men have condemned.

The following subsections examine the consequences of attempts
by the state to alter Kadhi's Court practices with respect to procedural
law, the appellate process, and substantive law. These attempts, which
have encountered resistance from the kadhis and, in some instances,
the broader Muslim community, have called into question the kadhis'
authority in the secular state.[44]

Procedural Rules

The application of Muslim principles of evidence in Kadhi's Courts has
fluctuated since colonial times, when Muslim evidence law applied.[45]

Subsequently, kadhis were encouraged to apply British-modeled rules of evidence and procedure (Pouwels 1987:180). Later case decisions insisted on the application of the Indian Evidence Act, which was being used in Magistrate's Courts throughout Kenya.[46] Muslim jurists were not immediately responsive to colonial Court of Appeal decisions demanding that they put aside Islamic evidentiary principles. Their unfamiliarity with the Evidence Act (and secular law generally) partially explains their reluctance; however, Anderson (1955) argues that they were unwilling for reasons of faith to apply any principle besides Muslim law. Kadhis continued to follow some Muslim evidentiary practices regarding oathing, the belief that the number of witnesses determines the strength of the evidence, and the prohibition on certain persons (e.g., non-Muslims and women) serving as witnesses; however, they acceded to other demands, such as dispensing with the orthodox screening of witnesses in favor of questioning before the court.[47] Anderson (1955:100) reports that kadhis "chuckle[d] at" the Evidence Act in the mid-1950s and concludes that "[t]he state of affairs is obviously unsatisfactory, as it makes a farce of the law."

The Kadhi's Courts Bill of 1967 resolved the ambiguity of conflicting case decisions by decreeing that Muslim evidentiary principles would apply in Kadhi's Courts with three provisos (Morris 1968:16). The first demands that "all witnesses be heard without discrimination on grounds of religion, sex or otherwise." Second, facts must be determined on the credibility of the evidence rather than the number of witnesses. Third, the application of Evidence Act principles is not subject to reversal on appeal. The demand that kadhis follow secular guidelines is presumably intended to standardize proceedings; however, the consequence for kadhis is serious, as they must adjudicate using principles contrary to Islamic law. The first proviso stands in direct opposition to certain tenets of Islamic evidentiary law that provide that the testimony of one male witness is equal to that of two female witnesses (see Schacht 1964:193).[48] Kadhis contend that they treat the testimony of all witnesses equally. Kadhis speak directly to women, even if they have come with male representatives (which was more common in the colonial era).[49] The stereotype that Muslims devalue women's speech, however, has left kadhis open to criticism from the Kenyan government. Although they follow secular laws of evidence, they admit to being more comfortable when more than one woman testifies on a matter, and they sometimes seek out additional witnesses for corroboration. Kadhis do not permit disputants to impugn the testimony of a female witness on the grounds that women provide unreliable information. Although kadhis refer to Muslim doctrine citing gender differences to justify some decisions, they never officially characterize women's speech as less reliable. Admitting that women are silenced in many contexts, several kadhis told me that they make special efforts to ensure that women's voices are heard in Kadhi's Court.

Even though the strict Muslim provisions concerning testimony no longer apply in Kadhi's Court, they are known to many coastal Muslims. The inadequacy of women's evidence relative to men's is frequently cited *outside* Kadhi's Court as a tenet of Muslim law. The surprise expressed by men who, on coming to court, find themselves unable to impugn a woman's testimony outright suggests a lack of awareness that certain Islamic legal principles are not applicable in Kadhi's Court.

Another area of procedural law reflects a different dynamic of relations between religion and state. Kadhis sometimes seek the assistance of Kenyan police to enforce rulings, subpoena witnesses, and make arrests for contempt of court. Each year, the Malindi kadhi jails a few people for failing to comply with rulings, such as a young woman who refused to live with her husband after losing a "return of wife" case. The kadhi suspected that her father, who had married her off to an elderly husband, was coercing her refusal because he wanted to collect another bridewealth. By jailing her, the kadhi expected to encourage the father to abandon the matter. Instead, her family refused to deal with the court, or with her. Intervening on her behalf, the attorney general argued that, at sixteen, she was too young to be jailed.[50] On her release, she immediately returned to her parents, and they left the area. The kadhi was furious, as she and her family owed the costs of the civil jail in which she had been kept. Another example, told to me by a former kadhi, confirmed that jail has long been used by kadhis as a coercive tool.[51] To be jailed in a Kenyan civil or criminal jail seriously compromises *heshima*.[52]

The Appellate Process

As the appellate court for Kadhi's Court decisions, the Kenyan High Court differs from the Kadhi's Courts in ways that make disregard for Muslim legal principles likely. In the High Court, parties to an appeal must be represented by counsel; however, advocates, even if they are Muslims, are not often trained in Islamic law.[53] Consequently, memoranda of appeal routinely cite principles of secular rather than Islamic law. Appeals are reviewed by a High Court judge and at least one assessor from among the kadhis.[54] Kadhis claim that secular judges pay little attention to the complexity of Islamic law or its correct application. When Islamic legal principles are turned aside, the appellate process itself poses a challenge to the autonomy of the Kadhi's Courts and to the authority of Islamic law.

My analysis of all the appeals from Kadhi's Courts to the High Court of the Coast Province from 1974 to early 1986 confirms that the appellate process is lengthy, and many appeals go unheard or undecided. At the time of the research, forty-two of the sixty-three appeals had been withdrawn, had stagnated, or were still pending. Court personnel claim that, after filing before the High Court, some disputants abandon the appellate process because of the expense of hiring an advocate, their unfamiliarity with and distrust of the secular system, loss of interest, or extracourt resolution of the matter. Of the twenty-one appeals heard by the High Court, nine were allowed, thus overturning the Kadhi's Court judgments. Most memoranda of appeal argue that the presiding kadhi failed to follow secular, rather than Islamic, rules of procedure, jurisdiction, or evidence.[55] The High Court overturned two Kadhi's Court cases on grounds of substantive law.[56] At issue in one was whether a wife is entitled to furniture as well as household utensils upon divorce.[57]

Secular and religious authorities have clashed over the issue of legitimate paternity since the early colonial period (see Anderson 1955: 101 for earlier decisions; see also Mwangi 1995). In 1984, an appellant petitioned the High Court to overturn a Kadhi's Court decision that established that her ex-husband was not the father of her child.[58] The appellant argued the same case that she had presented in Kadhi's Court: since the child was born within two years of her divorce, Islamic law attributed paternity to her ex-husband. She disputed the father's pronouncement of a customary oath *(lian)* denying his paternity by pointing out that the oathing occurred many months *after* the birth.[59] Under some interpretations of Muslim law, the intervening months would have rendered the oath invalid. The memorandum of appeal asks the court to adhere more closely to the principles of Islamic justice concerning oaths by rejecting the husband's denial of paternity. Two appellate judges offered different justifications for the decision to set aside the Kadhi's Court ruling. The appellate kadhi reversed on the grounds that the child was indeed that of the ex-husband for the reason cited by the appellant (i.e., the faulty oathing). The secular appellate judge called for a rehearing to establish the facts. He counseled application of the following portion of the Evidence Act (Cap. 80 at 60(1)): "The courts shall take judicial notice of the following facts—'the ordinary course of nature.'" In calling for a rehearing of the evidence, the secular appellate judge rejected Islamic practices regarding attribution of paternity.

Even though appeals are rare and appellate decisions even rarer, the appeals process challenges the autonomy of the Kadhi's Courts. Claimants in the lower court realize that they can go beyond the kadhis, even the Chief Kadhi, in pursuing a claim, and some declare their intention to do so after losing a case. In theory, any court of appeal poses such a threat. In coastal Kenya, however, appeals challenge the authority of an entire legal tradition, as they move from Islamic courts into the realm of secular law and thus from the discourse of Islam to that of state law.

Substantive Law

Statutes proposed in the Kenyan Parliament that would reform the laws of marriage, divorce, and inheritance constitute blatant attempts to alter Muslim substantive law, as well as the religious laws applicable to Hindus and the customary laws of diverse ethnic groups. Most versions of the Marriage and Divorce Act, proposed first in 1968 and several times subsequently without being adopted, contain provisions that contravene Muslim law.[60] A more serious challenge to Muslim legal autonomy is posed by the Kenyan Parliament's adoption of the Succession Act in 1972 (see Hirsch 1994).

Proposed in 1968, the Succession Act calls for rules of succession "applicable to all the inhabitants of Kenya, without regard for the religious or customary laws by which they had previously been bound" (Commission on the Law of Succession 1968:18). Its proposal, like that of the Marriage Act, was one of numerous attempts in the early years of independence to standardize and "modernize" law.[61] The act provides that, in the event of intestate succession (i.e., succession without a will), children inherit equally regardless of gender or legitimacy. Muslim law, in contrast, calls for sons to inherit larger shares than daughters and disallows inheritance in the case of illegitimacy. Another contrast is that Islamic law designates a specific set of heirs (e.g., spouse, children, siblings) who inherit regardless of whether a will has been written, while the act provides that a spouse inherits the entire estate in the case of intestate succession (see Anderson 1976:204–5).[62]

When the act became law in 1972, Muslims, including the kadhis, vowed to ignore it and to continue to apply Muslim laws of succession. The Kenyan Muslim community protested through newspaper editorials, petitions, and a violent public demonstration in Mombasa in the early 1980s. Irate Muslims raised the specter of coastal secession in order to guarantee their religious freedom. Several organizations prominently opposed the act, including the Women's Islamic Association, which commissioned several members to write a report summarizing their oppositional stance.

Since its passage, a few Muslims have tried to invoke the act in inheritance cases, but kadhis have dismissed their claims as contrary to Islam. For their part, the kadhis continue to rely on Islamic law to determine successors, calculate the division of shares, and supervise the disposition of inherited property. In decisions, kadhis never refer to the Succession Act, and they refuse to recognize any will that contravenes Islamic law. Daughters and wives, who would gain considerably under the act, decline to invoke it, preferring to rely on Islamic law.

Kadhis' opposition to the act, which has been mounted through case decisions and political action, stems from the belief that it encourages Muslims to ignore or violate Islamic law.[63] In the early 1980s, a committee of kadhis and other Muslim scholars and elders began monitoring the act's implementation and proposed modifications, including an amendment exempting Muslims. The Chief Kadhi, a committee member, was especially active in opposing the act. He insisted that any amendment had to contain a provision barring Muslims from writing wills that contravene Islam. The Kenyan government dismissed this request, arguing that the state should not be in a position of forcing adherence to religious law.[64] The act was amended to exclude application to Muslims in the early 1990s.

By turning opposition to the Succession Act into a political project for coastal Muslims, the Chief Kadhi also transforms the Kadhi's Courts into a rallying symbol for the community. I have argued elsewhere that the Chief Kadhi's bold and brave action is also ironic in that "he sought a secular legal means of compelling Muslims to apply Islamic law." By attempting to transform the hegemony of the Kenyan government in order to accommodate the interests of Muslims struggling to retain autonomy, "the Chief Kadhi bolstered the legitimacy of the courts as sites that represent the Muslim community in a hostile secular state. . . . Perhaps he also used this strategy to remind the community, especially Swahili men, that the courts, far from being the weak remnants of past Islamic authority, could still serve as focal points for Swahili identification" (Hirsch 1994:223). Though the Chief Kadhi has been a prominent opponent of the Succession Act, the political project to contest and amend it has been pursued by many Muslims and thus has brought together people who find themselves in opposition on other issues.

Kadhi's Courts as Complex Sites of Resistance

The Kadhi's Courts are a symbol of both Muslim governance and its vulnerability in the postcolonial era. Even though Muslim men have been harsh critics of kadhis, who have historically been viewed as collaborators with the state, they join with kadhis to oppose the state in order to protect and promote Islamic legal practice. The behavior of these men is contradictory given their criticism of the kadhis for allowing women to use the courts successfully and in greater numbers. Condemning the Kadhi's Courts as "women's courts," some men express concern that kadhis, in their efforts to favor women, hardly apply Islamic law at all, a reference to the secular state's role in the courts.[65]

In reflecting on their influence, kadhis admit that they are criticized by local populations. They characterize the criticisms as the gossip of disgruntled disputants and refuse to treat them as a serious threat to their authority. However, their sensitivity to the tenuous nature of their position comes through in court decisions. They are especially angered by individuals who question their authority by, for example, refusing to follow a decision. Such interactions are vivid demonstrations of the tension between kadhis and local men who routinely question, resist, and flout their authority.

Swahili women's use of Kadhi's Courts enhances the complexity of the courts as sites of resistance. In part, the state's role in monitoring Kadhi's Courts has facilitated women's success in their attempts to alter domestic relations through law. But should women's use of the Kadhi's Courts be considered a form of resistance to male domination? The concept of resistance, particularly in relation to law, is the subject of extensive scholarly scrutiny (see Hirsch 1994; Hirsch and Lazarus-Black 1994; see also, e.g., Abu-Lughod 1990; Comaroff and Comaroff 1991; Scott 1990; Yngvesson 1993). Some definitions imply that an act must be pursued consciously to be considered resistance. Women who make claims in Kadhi's Courts are generally well aware of contesting the terms of their personal circumstances, and this might, in some instances, constitute opposing or resisting individual men (e.g., husband, ex-husband, or father). Yet there is no larger political discourse among women that positions the Kadhi's Courts as sites for resisting unequal gender relations or patriarchy. In other words, resistance by these women is ideologically unelaborated—treated by the women themselves as individual acts rather than a politicized trend. Even the kadhis speak about women's success in the courts as resulting from individual actions and discrete case decisions. They do not describe their role as innovators expanding women's rights but rather speak of deciding each case on its merits and being faced with Muslim women who bring strong cases of long-term abuse or inadequate maintenance.[66] Kadhis depict these women as needing assistance, and they adamantly defend breaking up bad marriages. In delivering a judgment, a kadhi writes: "Divorce is the medicine for sickness" (Talaka ni dawa ya magonjwa) (Shee 1984:34).

The lack of ideological elaboration of the courts as sites for women's resistance does not diminish the significance of women's actions and decisions, both for individuals and, as the decisions mount, for women and gender relations more generally. The growing consciousness, expressed most explicitly by men, that the courts are partial to women influences subsequent disputes and perhaps indirectly empowers women. From another perspective, whether or not the act of a Swahili woman's filing a case in Kadhi's Court is called resistance (by the women themselves or by me), it confronts cultural expectations for female behavior by positioning a woman outside the domestic realm and in a public, official context in which she seeks to alter her circumstances. Turning to Kadhi's Court affirms her connection to Islam, even as it calls her piety into question and, simultaneously, constitutes her as a supplicant to the state. Perhaps most importantly, as the following chapters suggest, Kadhi's Courts provide the context for women to narrate problems.

KADHI: Yes, what do you want to explain?

WOMAN: Now I've come, we've split up, me and my husband. The week it ha::ppened was the end of [the month of] Ramadhan. There was one week left. (2.5) Now, we fought. Someone came to reconcile us. We fought and I went to my parents' house. From then until now. He hasn't come. (1.8) I have been tormen:::ted by him. (1.5) Meaning he provides nothing, soap, oil, he doesn't give me clothes the children's clothes are torn. And my illness, also I was sick up till I went to my parents'. I was to::ld, he told me: "If you go to live there, give me back my bridewealth." So, I came to my parents' place came- called my father, he came to get me and took me there. I went to my parents. When I went there, they asked me, "Now what will you do?" I told them, "I will wait and see if he comes, that's all." And so he hasn't come and I'm just there with nothing. And he's got three wives. And I say to him "now how's this going to work?" And he says "Are you going to make trouble? You can all stay together. If you want a house, build it yourself." Okay. (1) I told him "Now I am not a person who doesn't care about [her husband's] taking another wife. I went to my husband and there wasn't anyone else no no anyone-" I can't deal with what's happened. That's the way it is.

(FROM A DISCUSSION PRIOR TO A FILING
OF A KADHI'S COURT CLAIM)

Indexing Gender:
Initial Courtroom Narratives

At the outset of mediations and cases in Kadhi's Court, clerks and kadhis initiate interaction with requests for accounts of conflict: "Una shida gani?" (What's your problem?) "Eleza taabu" (Explain the trouble). "Lete 'stori'" (Give the "story"). These requests offer little guidance as to the form an account of trouble should take, and most disputants are uncertain about how to respond. Should they talk about the early days of the marriage or only the most recent troubling event? Should they describe what they said or thought during a fight? Disputants' initial hesitations and false starts reflect not only their unfamiliarity with court procedures but also their confusion over whether an account told in court resembles tellings outside court. Yet most disputants quickly surmount their uncertainty and produce long, relatively uninterrupted accounts of the problems preceding their courtroom appearance. By documenting the history of conflict between the parties, and incorporating disputants' perspectives on that history, these initial narratives are instrumental in effecting the outcomes of Kadhi's Court disputes. Moreover, they reflect gender differences in the discourse of conflict resolution. Thus, disputants, through their stories, begin to present themselves as gendered speakers.

Referring to disputes in Samoa, Duranti (1994:5) observes that "there is no storytelling for the sake of storytelling. There are accusations to be made or avoided, there is blame or mitigation, there are willful agents or ignorant victims." In court, how a story is told can determine whether or not a narrator proves a point, makes an effective accusation, or justifies an action in a convincing manner. As Hayden (1987) reminds us, the "tasks at hand" (e.g., blaming, proving, mitigating responsibility) bear a direct relation to the forms of disputants' speech and the organization of interaction in court.[1] Providing a satisfactory initial account is one way disputants address the tasks of presenting themselves and their issues in court.

139

This chapter analyzes the initial stories of conflict that disputants tell in Kadhi's Court cases and mediations. Initial narratives are told in different ways by men and women. Swahili women perform experiences of conflict as animated stories, using many conventions of narrative common to storytelling outside court. Men tell stories less frequently, and their stories include fewer features of storytelling performances. Some features of narrative performance, such as sound effects and reported speech, contribute to acting out a story; some, such as lexical repetition and reported speech, are used by narrators to evaluate their stories by including their own perspectives. These features contribute to the process of entextualizing stories, which turns stories into texts. The entextualization of initial narratives plays a key role in addressing legal and linguistic tasks (e.g., blaming), and it is accomplished in Kadhi's Courts in gendered ways.

The first section of this chapter analyzes an initial narrative told in a Kadhi's Court dispute. The analysis identifies performance features that contribute to entextualization and asserts that such features are produced in gendered ways. A subsequent section focuses on the features of evaluation included in disputants' accounts and shows how these engage the legal "tasks at hand." Two types of evaluation—features of narrative performance and commentary on narrative—highlight the events described as well as the narrator's perspective. In much the same ways as narratives are performed differently by men and women, evaluatives are produced differently. Women tend to evaluate through features of narrative performance. By contrast, men produce metalinguistic evaluation or commentary on their accounts.

Who people are as gendered, legal, and linguistic subjects shapes how they produce gendered speech in court. Studies of participant roles and participation frameworks have been centrally concerned with the positions of speaking subjects in contextualized interaction and how these relate to particular linguistic features and acts (see, e.g., Goffman 1981; Goodwin 1984; Goodwin 1990; Hill and Irvine 1992; Irvine 1996; Schiffrin 1990; Silverstein and Urban 1996).[2] Attention to participation frameworks is crucial in accounting for the production of a genre, the tasks accomplished by a speech act, or the course of interaction. In the context of a case or mediation, initial accounts are offered by speakers sequentially. With rare exceptions, legal position determines the sequencing. The claimant produces the first account, which is followed by the respondent's account. As chapter 5 demonstrated, most claimants in Kadhi's Courts are women and most respondents are men. Thus, the participant roles in mediations and cases reflect the legal positions of disputants, which at the same time are, to a significant extent, gendered positions.

As the concluding sections of this chapter assert, explaining gender differences in initial accounts of conflict in Kadhi's Courts requires attention to several related factors: the interactional context of the dispute, the legal position of each speaker, and the linguistic resources available to each, both in and out of court. The proposed explanation considers how speakers are positioned as gendered, legal, and linguistic subjects in Swahili society as well as in court. Although the chapter concludes by accounting for the gender-patterned speech of initial accounts, the examples provided throughout contribute to this volume's broader examination of how gender is constituted and transformed through the discourses of disputing. By producing gendered speech in their initial accounts, men and women index culturally salient images of themselves as gendered speakers in Swahili society—women as storytellers and men as commentators. Yet these and other gendered images also appear in the course of interaction (chapter 7) and in the reported speech of the participants (chapter 8) in ways that reveal deep contradictions in the construction of gendered subjects. Moreover, the production of these multiple and contradictory images in court, which has increased in the postcolonial period, affirms that disputing contexts provide space for social creativity in gender relations and links transformations in gender to the production of speech.

Narrative Performances in Kadhi's Court

Disputants narrate vivid, sometimes action-packed incidents of fighting and pleading portrayed through compelling delivery. Many women, appearing alone in court after being abandoned by a husband, describe marital life, its breakdown, the husband's departure, and futile attempts to convince him to return. Some disputants "perform" their narratives of trouble, acting out incidents through features of narrative performance. In performing stories, disputants highlight events that they want their listeners to find significant and dramatically reveal their own perspectives.[3]

The following narrative from a Kadhi's Court mediation illustrates a Swahili woman's production of performance features. Mariamu first came to Kadhi's Court to request the kadhi's assistance in compelling her husband either to provide maintenance for their son or to take custody of him (see "Abandoned," appendix C). Several days later she returned with her husband, who had received a court summons. The following narrative is the first speech to be produced as Mariamu, her husband, and the kadhi begin mediation:

Text 6.1

1	Mariamu:	My problem re::ally is that he left me pregnant. I went
2		to our place. I went through my pregnancy, up till I
3		gave birth. Before I gave birth I got a letter from- that
4		he was divorcing me. I wai:::ted until I had given birth,
5		then I went to Shariff Abdallah. Went. Explained. I
6		told him since he left me and now I am- me [he said]
7		"until you give birth yes you will finish edda after
8		being left. You will wait. When you finished edda from
9		when you gave birth." Then (finished) my edda. I went.
10		I explained (.) about the certificate. He told me "OK I
11		will write him a letter." He wrote him two letters, Sha
12		faa Shariff Abdallah. "I have already written his letter.
13		He answered me that he is coming." I wai:::ted. Finally
14		he told me I better go to Mombasa. Meaning he's in
15		Mombasa and me and a small child and every day
16		getting on the buses and if I get off. I went my way, all
17		the way there. When I- when I went there I wrote him
18		a letter. If I call him, he doesn't come. That day that he
19		arrived there, Tuesday. Tuesday, me I was waiting. I
20		waited for him. He did not come. I told him. "OK you
21		go another day you arrive each after every week you
22		come you will know him." Now it's like me, my daily
23		work, every day, is to go to see if he's there. ( )
24		He's not there. I went the last time. I told him "OK it's
25		best if I go to Malindi." It's so, I came here.

In form and content, Mariamu's narrative is typical of narratives told by women in Kadhi's Court. Her first sentence announces the problem. She then narrates her attempts to deal with the difficulties of living without child support. Use of the *-ka* tense throughout indicates that she is narrating the entire time (as opposed to commenting on her narration). Mariamu's narrative includes performance devices, for example, the lengthened vowels in lines 1 and 4. Vowel lengthening creates performative tension, though it can sometimes reflect hesitation as a speaker searches for words. Her narrative also includes instances of reported speech, another component of performance. She acts out the speech of Shariff Abdallah, a local elder, by varying her pattern of intonation. Her lack of production of the verbs of speaking, a tendency in Kiswahili narration, indicates that she is performing the speech, rather than merely reporting it. Her performance of the narrative is also evident through the production of poetic sequences. For example, she produces two syntactically simple sentences in which the first clause (consisting of one word) describes an action on her part and the second clause (also consisting of one word) indicates her husband's failure to take any action:

Text 6.2

1	Mariamu:	When I- when I went to my place
2		I wrote him a letter.
3		If I call him,
4		he doesn't come.
5		That day that he arrived there, Tuesday.
6		Tuesday, me I was waiting.
7		I waited for him.
8		He did not come.
9		I told him . . .

The proximity of the repetitions of syntactic structure lends a poetic quality to her narration, an effect often produced by other speakers.

In Kadhi's Court cases and mediations, women produce the performance features described above to a greater extent than do men. They deploy a wider range of performance features, such as poetics, and their performed segments are longer and comprise more of their speech. In part, this is because men surround their narrations in nonnarrative speech. Men produce a wider range of types of speech in court, including, among others, lectures about what is appropriate behavior in a marriage, questions asked of the kadhi, and attempts to discuss issues in legalistic terms. Narrative is generally the central form of speech that women produce in Kadhi's Court and is thus most prominent in their accounts. Given that many features contribute to performance, measuring the amount of "performed speech" is a difficult calculation. My assertion that women perform more narrative than men is based on an analysis that identifies blocks of performed speech rather than counting instances of particular features. There are variations in the degree to which narration is performed and in the amount of narrative produced by any individual, but the gender difference in narrative performance is evident when the accounts are considered overall.

Several studies of Kiswahili narration outside court are useful in accounting for why narration is produced in court in gender-patterned ways. Russell's analysis (1981) of Swahili narration in Mombasa demonstrates that speakers are more likely to produce performance features when narrating fictional stories (e.g., folktales) as compared with personal experiences. Maw (1992) concurs with Russell, however, in indicating that personal narratives are frequently performed in "relaxed" conversational groups, which, in Swahili culture, generally means speakers of the same gender or of exceptional intimacy. To explain why Swahili women perform narrative, Russell draws on Wolfson's finding (1978) that narrative performance is most likely when speakers are conversing with relative equals in terms of gender, age, ethnicity, and occupation.[4] If Wolfson's conclusion is correct, it is hard to explain why women perform narratives in Kadhi's Courts, given that this is an unfamiliar context in which they are not equal to their male interlocutors.[5] Perhaps narrative performance in Kadhi's Courts has less to do with being "comfortable" than with the resources that speakers have for the combined task of presenting a believable, convincing story and demonstrating personal worth. In Swahili society, telling a narrative dramatically, in any context, denotes linguistic skill, maturity, and "competence," a linguistic ideology that applies to both men and women (Russell 1981; see also Briggs 1988a). Narration is one of the few linguistic skills to which women can lay claim. While men have the ability and ideological authorization to produce lectures and religious exegesis (and other public speech), women have few options other than narrated stories to account for their behavior and impugn that of their husbands.

The tendency of all disputants to perform at least some of their accounts in Kadhi's Courts suggests that narrative performance in Kiswahili is a widely shared resource for speaking in a convincing manner. Narrative conventions in Swahili society, which link storytelling to women, combine with the conventions of courtroom discourse, which offer women a limited range of linguistic forms, with the result that women present themselves as storytellers even as they address the tasks of disputing (e.g., blaming, explaining, justifying).

Evaluating Stories and the Tasks at Hand

Accusing, refuting, denying, mitigating, and allocating responsibility are important components of courtroom interaction. Blaming and blame avoidance are perhaps the most extensively studied tasks of courtroom speech, and much of this scholarship focuses on the conversational organization of blaming (Atkinson and Drew 1979; Berk-Seligson 1990; Pomerantz 1978).[6] Narratives play multiple roles in blaming. For example, in response to questions posed in trial courts, witnesses tell narratives in order to mitigate the blame that they assume an attorney's question attributes. Thus, narratives that provide justification for potentially blameworthy actions are produced to deflect blame, sometimes even before accusations are made. Narratives also allocate blame by telling about others' blameworthy actions. Moreover, a speaker can refute a prior account by offering an alternative story.

Features of narrative performance contribute to the way in which narratives blame, mitigate, or explain; and, more importantly, evaluative devices, by offering the narrator's perspective, also address the tasks at hand. Two kinds of evaluatives produced in performed narration are relevant in Kadhi's Court: (1) evaluatives embedded within narrative performances and (2) explicit evaluatives, that is, metalinguistic statements that comment on the story. Explicit evaluatives convey what narrators intend for a narrative to accomplish or how they believe it should be interpreted. Such commentary can occur during a narrative performance, even though it is produced outside the clauses that narrate the story.

Evaluatives embedded within narrative are particularly important for Swahili women presenting claims in Kadhi's Courts, as women are more dependent on evaluations produced within narrative to convey their perspectives. Men evaluate their narratives in court primarily through metalinguistic statements. For example, one disputant ended his initial account by saying, "And that's a true story." In Kiswahili narratives, metalinguistic statements can set the scene for, clarify, or interpret narrative, and, at the same time, they function evaluatively (Russell 1981).[7] Explicit evaluatives often occur at a narrative's beginning or end, although they are also found internally. Evaluatives are critical to the disputing process, as they constitute attempts to pull the kadhi, the audience, and the other disputing party toward a particular interpretation. In court, highlighting the moral of the story or reasons for its telling can address legally relevant tasks.

For women in court, the organization of blaming reflects Pomerantz's finding (1978) of how, in conversation, speakers routinely make announcements prior to blaming that tend to hide who is really at fault. Swahili women avoid blaming through this tactic and also by appealing to the court to alter their situation, as does Mariamu (see Text 6.1). Even though women are usually positioned to blame first, they rarely announce the problems they have endured. Men are more likely to produce agent-centered blaming, even though their participant role in the dispute positions them to mitigate their own bad acts.

Although both men and women blame through their narratives, the pattern of blaming is different in part because men's assessments relate more explicitly to their narrations. Men narrate incidents of conflict to illustrate claims made primarily through explicit evaluatives. Women produce fewer non-narrative statements generally. A more important difference lies in the organization of blaming statements in relation to stories. Specifically, women are less likely than men to draw connections between narrative and non-narrative sequences. They make "points" as they speak; however, these are not ones that they address directly through subsequent stories. Rather, women's focus is on narrating experiences of conflict in which they draw attention to key points primarily through evaluatives internal to the narrative. It is the vivid entextualization of the performed story that conveys the point, rather than an explicit iteration of what the story means.

Examples of Evaluatives in Performed Narration

Evaluatives in performed narration contribute to the sense that a disputant is telling an engaging story, one that is relevant to the tasks at hand in court. When produced by narrators, several kinds of evaluatives—namely, expressive phonology, lexical repetition, and poetically structured sequences—intensify narrative performance as well as further the speaker's goals. In court, disputants produce evaluatives at critical moments in their testimony, such as when they describe events or actions that are central to their perspectives on the conflict.

In Kadhi's Court accounts, both women and men produce expressive phonology, such as vowel lengthening and raised pitch.[8] The following example from the narrative presented previously demonstrates that vowel lengthening conveys the narrator's perspective at a critical moment, when Mariamu is describing her attempts to obtain the maintenance owed to her by Ali, her husband (see "Abandoned," appendix C).

Text 6.3

1 Mariamu: I wai:::ted. Finally
2   he told me I better go to Mombasa.

The lengthened vowel (line 1) emphasizes the duration of time, which is central to Mariamu's complaints against her husband. It draws attention to the amount of time that she has spent attempting to get maintenance from Ali, an issue to which she refers frequently. According to Russell (1981:221–22), vowel lengthening can convey length in terms of distance or time and is often applied directly to quantifiers. The following example, from the beginning of another account, illustrates a similar usage of a lengthened vowel to highlight a critical issue (see "Words," appendix C). Zulecha, asked by the kadhi about her problems with her husband, responds:

Text 6.4

1   Zulecha: And I have persevered a lot a lo:t with him a *who*:lot
2   *ma*:ny days[9]
3   Kadhi: Why up to now don't you persevere?
4   Zulecha: until it's gotten to thi:s

In this segment, Zulecha emphasizes the length of time that she has persevered in her relationship with Saidi by the vowel lengthening in "a whole lot" (sa:na) and "many days" (siku nyi:ngi).[10] Raised pitch often accompanies vowel lengthening. A man is more likely to exhibit raised pitch and other expressive phonology when he reports the speech of others than when he narrates in his own voice.[11]

Lexical repetition is a common evaluative in Kiswahili narration in courts. According to Russell, it intensifies meaning or conveys aspect. The prototypical performance use of lexical repetition advances the action of the story through the repetition of verbs or whole clauses such as "we went and went and went . . ." Three or more repetitions give the sense of time passing or the continuation of an action.

Russell (1981) claims that multiple modifications of noun phrases or time designations call attention to the characters or to particular events. At the same time, they provide extra information to help listeners keep the characters straight or remember something significant to the story. In court, multiple modification contributes to a narrator's ability to perform legal tasks by clarifying details central to an argument. Maw (1992) makes the important point that multiple modification of the subject can also circumvent the confusion that routinely results from the use of pronouns, which are gender-neutral in Kiswahili. Repetition using noun phrases in addition to a pronoun disambiguates the gender of the character being discussed. Noun phrases may be preposed or postposed in relation to the verb (Maw 1992:34). A postposed subject is syntactically marked and thus carries an evaluative function that calls attention to that character in the story.[12] What "attention" means, of course, depends on the content of the narration.

In the following example, Munira has just finished narrating the events of the night on which she was beaten by her husband, Atwas (see "The Beating," appendix C). In response to a question from the kadhi, which interrupts her narration, she produces multiple modifications of the date of the beating.

Text 6.5

1	Munira:	(3.3) When he finished hitting me |I felt ( ) hot
2	Kadhi:	|when? when? when?
3	Munira:	it was the day of:: Iddi[13] fourth (4.2)
4		meaning isn't it::
5		people began ( ) the day of, which day, the day of
6		Idd meaning it the day of Wednesday
7		I went to Mombasa.
8		Went to Chief Kadhi.
9		When I returned [from] Mombasa that evening it was so
10		he came to beat me, the day of Wednesday, the day that
11		people began work, the day of Idd.

In this example, the kadhi attempts to establish the date of the beating (line 2). Munira produces several multiple modifications (lines 6–7 and 10–11), a tactic used when people want to be precise or when precision is requested, as in this instance. Yet two other factors might also have influenced Munira's repetition. The first is the habitual confusion and contention surrounding the date of Idd, the Islamic holiday. Because people sometimes celebrate on different days, Munira might want to make clear her understanding of the timing of Idd (see chapter 5 for a fuller discussion of this issue). But, more likely, the modifications function evaluatively to call attention to the fact that Munira's husband beat her *on Idd,* a usually joyful occasion for families that is a highly inappropriate time for violence.

Repetitions of syntax and lexical items are common in Swahili narrative performance. Many narratives include at least several instances of lexical linking, whereby the narrator repeats the previous clause as the first clause of the next sentence. Although lexical linking has limited evaluative function, it, like other kinds of poetic language, calls attention to the act of narration, which is critical to entextualizing a story. The following example is from a mediation involving a husband, Shaaban, and his wife, Rukia, who have come to Kadhi's Court seeking reconciliation after a violent fight (see "The Knife," appendix C).

Shaaban has been asked to explain their problems, and the following excerpt is taken from the middle of his narrative:

Text 6.6

1	Shaaban:	And I left that work
2		I came to the house
3		When I came to the house
4		I saw my wife . . .

Another example demonstrates lexical linking as exact repetition and shows as well that several clauses can be linked (see "Abandoned," appendix C):

Text 6.7

1	Mariamu:	If I call him,
2		he doesn't come.
3		That day that he arrived there, Tuesday.
4		Tuesday, me I was waiting.
5		I waited for him.
6		He did not come.

Lexical linking occurs twice in this small segment from Mariamu's long account (lines 3–4 and 4–5). In addition, line 3 could be considered a multiple modification, similar to the ones produced by the speaker in Text 6.5. Repetitions of lexical items, syntax, and clauses constitute poetic language, which is critical to the entextualization of narrative through performance and contributes to the accomplishment of legal tasks.

Two other features of Kiswahili narrative performance "comment on" or draw attention to the message being conveyed yet are themselves devoid of referential content. The first is the high-pitched exclamation produced after the narration of a significant incident.[14] An evaluative with a different form but similar function has been described as the "pregnant" or "dramatic" pause (Maw 1992; Maw and Kelly 1975:45). This evaluative manipulates intonation by effecting a nonneutral tonal pattern, one that rises at a point in the clause when it would—if neutral—go down. This "high-level tonic"[15] is "almost always followed by what seems to be a deliberate break—for dramatic effect, perhaps" (Maw and Kelly 1975:45; see also Maw 1992:41). The last word in the unusual tone may also have a glottal stop. The subsequent pause is not a turn-taking opportunity but rather an "institutionalized break" during which a narrator continues to hold the floor. For Maw, the drama created through the manipulation of tone and silence has an iconic quality.[16]

Whether or not the dramatic pause or the other evaluative devices described above have iconic entailments—both sound effects and poetic structuring are possible iconic vehicles—is less important as a way of understanding how evaluation creates meaning than is the well-established view of evaluation as operating through contrasts (phonological, lexical, etc.) that draw attention to the message.[17] Polanyi (1985:196) argues that "there are no absolute evaluative devices. Evaluation operates on the principle of 'difference is salient', and therefore it is possible to use any normal encoding device as a mark of salience by using it unexpectedly. . . . It is also possible to use any normally distinctive encoding devices . . . nonevaluatively by using them as the norm in a given part of a given text." Polanyi urges an analysis that interprets potential evaluative devices as they are produced processually. As Maw (1992) points out, skillful Kiswahili narrators manipulate both conventional and unconventional speech in imaginative ways to draw attention to important points in their stories.

Identifying devices as evaluative need not imply that a particular meaning or emphasis has been communicated successfully. The assumption that performed narratives constitute more vivid tellings is based on similarly problematic reasoning. Some linguists would argue that "vivid" is in the eye of the beholder (or the ear of the hearer) rather than in the form of the utterance. The debate over the "power" of certain linguistic forms in political language provides another example of a flawed approach to the function of language (see, e.g., Bloch 1975; Brenneis and Myers 1984; Kedar 1987; Kramarae, Schulz, and O'Barr 1984; Paine 1978). At issue is the degree to which power, vividness, or evaluative interpretation can be assumed from a linguistic form. The conclusion appears to be that the degree to which a linguistic form effects its function for the listener can never be determined precisely, particularly without reference to specific potential hearers. And even then, such information is perhaps always elusive.[18] I examine evaluative devices not for their contribution to an assumed vividness but rather as evidence of other functions of narrators' speech in court. First, the presence of evaluatives indicates that narrators are skilled in manipulating the performance features through which they entextualize their stories. Second, through these features they embed their own perspectives on the stories and thereby attempt to influence listeners' interpretations and legal outcomes.

Examples of Explicit Evaluatives

Narration, including the most stylized versions, is, then, a more important resource for Swahili women in court than for men. Women are
less likely than men to respond to the request for a narrative with a
non-narrative statement, especially one that articulates the legal task
they intend for their story to accomplish. The non-narrative statements
that they *do* produce are oriented to tasks different from the ones that
their narrations address. An example of this disjuncture can be seen
in a previously presented excerpt. Munira, who had been to court previously, responds to the kadhi's prompting with a non-narrative statement that is neither a declaration of the task she intends to accomplish
nor a summary of the story she then narrates:

Text 6.8

1	Kadhi:	You what do you say? Explain that news of yours.
2	Munira:	My news me (1.4) it's that one I told you, that I want
3		to be divorced.
4	Kadhi:	Uh huh (2.8) That's it (2.5) That is your news, that one,
5		you don't have anything else?
6	Munira:	I do have. Isn't it that the other day when he came to: hit
7		me even I went to the police I was given a P Three. I filled
8		[it] yesterday I returned to the police. (1.6) He hurt me.
9		It's ( ) sides and kidney. ( ). He's been hurting me
10		a lot.

Munira's initial response is not phrased as an explicit statement of
blame. Her last statement comes closer to attributing responsibility for
the beating and thus begins to respond to the kadhi's request for insight into the conflict, yet it does not constitute a summary of the narrative or an assertion of its point. The disjuncture between the non-
narrative framing of her story, which directs attention to her desire
for a divorce and to the beating, and the story, which describes her
own actions after the beating, is a typical manifestation of women's
tendency to avoid declaring the meaning of their stories.

In a previously presented example (Text 6.1), Mariamu begins her
initial account by making the point that her husband left her while
she was carrying their child. The narrative that follows this accusation
does not explain the claim but rather tells the story of seeking maintenance after her husband's departure. While Mariamu's narrative demonstrates that Ali has not responded to her or to the elder assisting

her, it does not specifically summarize his inaction. Mariamu brings the account to a close in the last line by locating herself back at her home, having run out of options. The organization of blame within her narrative suggests that she is more concerned with the initial act of his divorcing her, which is not a legally actionable claim, than with the problems she has experienced. Mariamu situates her own actions as appropriate and deserving of reward while obliquely suggesting culpability on her husband's part. Her veiled accusations rely on legal and ethical discourses. At first she highlights her attempts to obtain the maintenance legally due to her. In reporting her actions, she carefully emphasizes her reliance on the elder (i.e., someone more knowledgeable in law) and her diligence in following his advice, which demonstrate her ability to act in accordance with legal procedure. By narrating the problems of transportation and childcare that make her compliance burdensome, she invokes a discourse of ethics.

When a disputant is positioned to offer the second narrative of trouble, rather than the first, he or she (though it is usually he) can respond by taking up the tasks at hand presented by the first account. Often, an initial account given by a woman is treated as having allocated blame, even when the narrator fails to produce a non-narrative blaming statement. In response, some men attempt to mitigate their actions. Others turn the situation around by blaming the wife or ex-wife explicitly. The narrative offered by Munira's husband, Atwas, responds to both the kadhi's formulation of blame and the blame implicitly encoded in Munira's narrative with a narration of the events that led to the beating. He describes several incidents indicative of a troubled domestic life before beginning an extended account of how and why he beat Munira. Justifying his behavior is a central point of his narration; he builds a case that depicts his behavior as appropriate and, at the same time, cites acts for which Munira can be blamed.

Text 6.9

1	Kadhi:	She says, this woman, that you hit her.
2	Atwas:	It's true but for a reason. And it's not my intent to want
3		to hit her that day, but when I returned from a trip, when
4		I came I- she had moved from that house that she'd been
5		in. She moved. She was in another house there, above,
6		near to there. I had been doing, me, work, it was me I
7		moved from there, that house, above.
8		Now after there, I moved from that house,

9	above that house, above the one I had been going like that.
10	Taking money, taking [it] to her, there to her room.
11	There was even time times, and she abused me filthy filthy filthy
12	abuses, so it was that we were estranged. [Me] going
13	to call her grandmother sometimes to give her money.
14	Until she herself says "this isn't possible. It will not be possible,
15	meaning, you here at the house, it's a person, and your child
16	necessarily you come, you hear?" OK, so me, I started
17	going. It was her bad words, she had stopped.
18	And I stayed I explained "if you have stopped those
19	filthy words." I went to her. I went I went
20	I went I went until she moved again in that
21	house where she was now again. She returned to me in
22	that house over there, the place where we lived. That
23	house of her mother from her uncle. She returned again to
24	that house. Now when she returned there, I was- I went
25	there to the house like usual, you hear,
26	to take money like usual.

Atwas's initial utterance accepts the blame implied by the kadhi's prompting statements (lines 2–3). He then produces a justification for his actions. Though the first lines after the initial justification indicate acceptance of some blame, they also operate to blame Munira. Atwas sets the scene for his narration through an announcement alleging that Munira had moved while he was away, an implicit means of blaming her, given Swahili cultural understandings that a woman should not leave the house without her husband's permission (lines 4–5). He also describes other blameworthy behavior on her part that caused their separation (e.g., lines 11–12). His description of attempts to give Munira money, even when he had to use her grandmother as a go-between, displays his behavior as a good husband, which even her family recognized as exemplary (lines 14–16). Atwas reiterates the problem of Munira's bad behavior as he reports a discussion of her reformed language, after he had returned home.

As evidenced by the initial scene-setting utterances, the next part of Atwas's narrative begins to describe the night of the beating:

Text 6.10

1	Atwas:	Now that day I was going on a trip I came
2		at night. Like about eight o'clock or so.
3		When I came from the trip, I went to my place.

4	Me, I entered I didn't hear (husband) first I heard the husband of
5	my sister-in-law Mariamu. I waited there. And my in-law.
6	I ate dinner I finished. When I finished about the time
7	nine-thirty, ten a relative came. And
8	I knew that relative is her friend. When he knocked
9	at the house. I didn't answer him. I told him/her "you"
10	my in-law. I told him/her "( ) and you go open for
11	him that one's (who)." You hear.
12	When he went that relative to open for him that door,
13	my in-law, he asked "Munira here?" That in-law
14	of mine, that in-law of mine, told him
15	"Her husband is here." He left, that relative, but
16	it was that I had already known that, you hear. I told that
17	one "I already knew that. Me, I knew that he, you relative
18	that he was tight with that Munira" but I ( ).
19	I stayed quiet.

In this text, Atwas recounts the events prior to the beating using conventions of performed narration, such as reported speech. In addition, several postposed subjects draw attention to the illicit visitor (e.g., line 12). The negative in line 9 operates evaluatively by showing Atwas's craftiness in not addressing the visitor but rather waiting to trap him in the compromising situation of requesting to see Munira, a married woman who should not be receiving male guests, especially at night. Line 17 asserts that Atwas was already aware that Munira received visits from this alleged lover and that her siblings facilitated such visits. Atwas repeats this claim as reported speech and thereby demonstrates his knowledge of the situation as well as confirms Munira's infidelity.

The next part of Atwas's narration brings him into direct confrontation with Munira in both the story world and the event world. His justification that he was going to her bedroom simply to give her the money deflects speculation that he had ulterior motives. When he describes Munira's extremely blameworthy behavior, Munira interrupts:

Text 6.11

1	Atwas:	Left, I went to that 'room' of hers and
2		( ) I went to her 'room' like I went
3		to give her money but when I reached there I asked her
4		"Munira?" "Eh." "Do you remember that I've not
5		yet divorced you?" "Ah I don't want your (stupid)
6		words stuff like dogs." "Ah I'm a dog?

7		I ask you good word, with patience, taking a

7   I ask you good word, with patience, taking a
8   careful road." She abused me. You told me I am a dog,
9   it's nothing. Tell me anything but when she began to
10   (leaving) from my room. "Me, I didn't call you into my
11   room get out get out, until your end." When she started
12   to abuse my mother "your mother's cunt"
13 Munira: Don't you tell a lie.
14 Atwas: Be quiet. I am not speaking to you I am speaking to the
15   kadhi.
16 Munira: I will take an oath that I didn't abuse your mother.
17   Okay why is he quiet?
18 Kadhi: Leave it, leave it.
19 Atwas: Don't you speak to me. Have you heard, bwana? When
20   she dared to abuse my mother "your mother's cunt" that
21   moment right then a slap came from me this moment I
22   slapped her one time. I didn't increase it (on her). If I hit
23   her even. She hit me with a board. Blood started coming
24   from me. Me if I had known had known that war I
25   didn't know it. You hear? Then indeed first she said her
26   that I hit her. True, there I hit her meaning' when she
27   was (   ) to abuse me my mother that very time a slap
28   [was] ready.

The utterance of abuses against his mother drives Atwas to hit Munira. His reduplication in line 21 ("that moment right then" "saa hiyo hiyo") is a standard deictic that indexes a time simultaneous with the previously mentioned event and emphasizes the link between her utterance of the words and his blameworthy act. In accepting responsibility for hitting Munira, Atwas describes the blow using a verb construction that distances him from the action itself and thus attempts to mitigate responsibility (lines 21–23).[19] His use of the negative is an evaluative means of showing that his behavior could have been otherwise but for the fact that he controlled himself. At the end of the narrative he reiterates his story, demonstrating that there was ample reason for hitting Munira. He positions her behavior, specifically her tendency to use abusive language, as the reason for their fighting, their separation, and his violence. He closes his account by reiterating the non-narrative statements that he is to blame, just as Munira has said, which of course makes more of her accusation than she articulated. The conclusion of Atwas's narrative summarizes his own claims, and Munira's claims, and then justifies his behavior as reasonable. This elaborate closing is typical of men's narratives, which often end by articulating the tasks they sought to accomplish through their narration. Their final utterances emphasize the point of the story, which generally relates to blaming and justification.

According to Polanyi (1985:193), the "final remarks of the tellers can be thought of as a coda to the story as a whole (Labov 1972). They join storyworld time to the ongoing time of the interaction." In other words, the coda "puts the spin" on a story. This act, at the juncture between the story world and the event world, is relevant to disputants' struggle for recognition that their stories provide evidence for claims expressed in court. Getting the proverbial Labovian "So what?" in response to an account told in court has enormous consequences. Women risk this possibility, given that their non-narrative statements do not direct listeners to specific interpretations. Women's codas often direct attention back to themselves through statements like "I can't do this anymore" (Siwezi tena) or "I have persevered a lot" (Nimestahimili sana), which emphasize their isolation and vulnerability. By commenting on the story and also constituting it, non-narratives accomplish meaningful acts in the legal context, acts most often engaged in by men.

In identifying a gender difference in the production of explicit evaluatives, I am not suggesting that women are less able to undertake the tasks associated with disputing in Kadhi's Courts. Rather, by showing how women entextualize their stories through devices that contribute to both performance and evaluation, I suggest that they are quite skilled. When incidents of conflict, especially confrontation, are told one after another, using similar syntactic structure, women create the powerful image that marital conflict itself was repetitive. Their narratives suggest that the "same story" happened over and over again, even though some of the details might change. In short, the teller's repetitive, poetic speech operates as an icon of the repetitive difficulties endured in the marriage. To those for whom persevering in a bad marriage is the central issue requiring demonstration, this form of narrative iconicity displays repeated efforts to persevere.

There is no easy way to measure the impact of a woman's vivid story told in a dispute as against a man's explicit statement of blame. The point in providing examples of each is to suggest that much of courtroom interaction results not only in legal tasks' being addressed in different, gendered ways, but also in reproductions through speech of familiar gendered images: with some exceptions, women tell stories; men comment and pronounce.

Interpreting Gender Differences in Narratives

The gender differences depicted in the previous sections present contrasting ways in which disputants entextualize their stories. By directing attention to entextualization as a process in which speakers actively engage, the entextualization model proposed by Bauman and Briggs (see chapter 1) emphasizes speakers' agency to produce speech and to construct themselves. In narrating, speakers are not just reproducing stories in patterned ways that reflect their gender (or some other social factor), but rather they are constituting themselves as particular kinds of speakers, and persons. By focusing on speakers' agency, though, the model leaves open the question of how to account for the different ways in which people accomplish entextualization. Agency is a tricky concept in social theory, threatening to impute intentionality and consciousness to agents' actions even when they are the product of limited motivation. Attention to agency always risks overemphasizing the production of speech as a strategic act. Moreover, to claim that men and women speak strategically in order to succeed in court is not necessarily to explain the forms that their speech takes.

Speakers' strategies account in part for the speech presented in Kadhi's Courts. But the differences must also be explained with reference to the participation frameworks operating in the courtroom context and, specifically, two related factors: the speaker's legal position and his or her linguistic options in Swahili society. Swahili women narrate because their legal position upon entering court as claimants requires them to show that there has been a problem for which they seek redress. The literature on Kiswahili narration suggests that telling stories is the way in which women manage the task of discussing conflict in other places. But the association of Swahili women with narrative does not address why they fail to frame their narratives with reference to legal tasks and why they produce so little non-narrative speech. There are two possibilities. First, by virtue of being women, they have little authority to wield legal language in court. Relatedly, they are unable to speak to the judge as a peer by producing the language associated with men in a context like the court. Second, legal pronouncements are generally inadequate for articulating the problems women bring to court. For example, most claim that marital life is unlivable. Demonstrating this rather vague claim requires depicting the circumstances of life rather than making assertions of dubious legal validity. Swahili men produce more non-narrative statements of blame and mitigation in part because they produce a broader repertoire of speech across the range of institutional contexts and in public generally. Men's legal position in disputes also accounts for their tendency to frame the stories they tell through statements of blame and justification. For the most part, they enter court as respondents and thus must defend against accusations. But they go beyond merely answering accusing stories with refuting statements. Rather, they take the opportunity to make accusations at the same time as they mitigate their own responsibility or explain their actions. Men possess an authority in relation to the law; as Muslim men, they are supposed to understand legal language and produce it when necessary. Accordingly, they engage directly with the kadhi in the conversation world of the court, rather than relying on stories. This is not to say, however, that statements outside narrative afford them strategic advantage but rather to suggest that their legal positioning and linguistic options furnish this possibility.

I offer these explanations tentatively, hoping to emphasize the primary importance of identifying the forms of speech themselves and assessing their consequences when they are produced in gendered ways. To delineate further the dimensions of this admittedly multifaceted and indeterminate explanation, I turn to two studies of disputing that report findings similar to what I have described for the Kadhi's Courts.

Using techniques of conversation analysis, Laurence Goldman demonstrates that Huli women's initial narratives in New Guinea courts contrast with men's. Women's stories focus on establishing coherence (see Halliday and Hasan 1976) by justifying the speaker's actions as reasonable responses to unreasonable acts. Huli men link narrated events through adverbs that mark chronology, thus creating a different textual density. The rather disjunctive presentations of male litigants force interlocutors to draw their own conclusions about the speakers' behavior, while women provide more of a road map of the inferences that motivated them. Huli women's presentational style in court contrasts with their speech in other contexts, and Goldman interprets the courtroom speech as a response by women to what they perceive as "system imbalances" in the disputing context (Goldman 1986: 233). Goldman's explanation assumes that women hold two presuppositions about court: (1) it is male dominated;[20] and (2) displaying the reasoned inferences behind actions makes those actions more acceptable in court. Goldman argues that Huli women believe they gain power in court by making explicit why they engaged in certain behaviors.

Comparing the Swahili examples with those presented by Goldman, Swahili women are less explicitly concerned with guiding the interpretation of their narratives than Huli women appear to be. This suggests that Swahili and Huli women address their subordinate positions in court very differently. Swahili women's subordinate position in court leads them to tell their stories with limited external interpretation, choosing instead to let the story stand on its own. Although I am swayed by Goldman's claim that gender differences in narration are a strategic response, I question whether this adequately explains the differences that he found. For example, he does not address women's legal position in terms of substantive law.[21] Perhaps, as the example from Kadhi's Courts suggests, gendered disparity in how people stand as legal subjects motivates the organization of narratives of trouble. Swahili women's narratives are organized in relation to the claims that they are able to advance (e.g., desire for maintenance or divorce), which differ from the claims available to men. Many Swahili women tell stories that provide evidence of a life full not of legalistic violations, but of difficult circumstances that must be endured. Their entextualized narration of that endurance contrasts with the stories men tell of specific violations or of circumstances justifying or mitigating blameworthy actions. Focusing on strategy, even as a response to institutional bias, is too narrow an approach to explaining gender differences in court narratives, which also emerge from gendered legal relationships.

An adequate explanation of gender differences in courtroom speech must also include attention to the linguistic resources available to litigants. In comparison to men, Swahili women are less familiar with the discourse of Islamic law. This may account for why they avoid commentary on the "meaning" of their narratives, which they may assume requires reference to legal discourse. Although the storytelling genre is a resource for both men and women, speakers produce it in different, gendered ways that accord with cultural understandings of their roles as narrators. I am not suggesting that men and women, by virtue of either gender or experiences narrating outside court, are

locked into types of storytelling from which they do not deviate; however, a consideration of the genres produced outside court helps explain the forms of speech produced in court.

In her study of gender and disputing in Tenejapan, Mexico, Penelope Brown (1993) argues that the direct and confrontational speech
produced by women in court can only be explained in relation to the
genres they typically produce outside court. In research on politeness,
Brown finds that women's tendency toward deference and social distance is characterized by complexes of conventionalized features such
as high-pitched speech and constrained demeanor, which are routinely
produced by Tenejapan women in public. Other politeness markers
(e.g., rhetorical questions and ironies) are generally produced among
female intimates. Although women "can be seen to be more polite than
men," Brown makes the point that they are polite in a variety of ways.
That is, depending on the interactional contexts, they make different
use of linguistic features.

Brown argues that gender is indirectly indexed through such features. She analyzes a dispute between two women as "a paradigm example of verbal interaction in one social context (a court case) being
played out in opposition to the norms for verbal interaction in another
social context (everyday public interaction), in order (partially) to reinforce those first-context norms (appropriate gender behavior) and . . .
where face is threatened, in order to restore face" (1993:156). The
women profiled fight angrily, using features of speech (e.g., rhetorical
questions) generally reserved for polite conversation among intimates.
When produced in court, sarcastically and in the heat of pseudoargu-
ment, these features play out an irony that "[reworks] face by face
being thrown to the winds." Her point is that "in terms of gender
women are being given license to do what they never do in order to
clear the air" (158). Brown's analysis draws on women's habitual uses
of linguistic constructions and their resultant association with particular stances and social acts.

Through their production of performed narratives in court, which
resemble the fictional narratives they are associated with telling outside
court, Swahili women demonstrate their competence as speakers. Men
also produce narrative; however, their managed and interpreted accounts meet the kadhi, also controlled in his speech, on his own terms.
Thereby, men index their collective right, as men, to produce authoritative discourse. Yet Brown's study leads me to ask, What is the significance of the gendered role that women index in constituting them-

selves as storytellers in court? Swahili women's public narration of conflict indexes a linguistic and social act that is culturally discouraged, especially for women. Telling stories in court that iconically exhibit the shameful activities going on at home has the effect not of clearing the air by throwing face to the winds (as for the Tenejapan women), but rather of throwing face to the winds in a public act of desperation for which women are ultimately condemned.

Conclusion

Identifying the consequences of gendered speech is almost as difficult as explaining why the different forms are produced. Goldman admits that "assigning a relative weight and importance to the many contributing factors to any dispute outcome is inevitably a problematic venture" (1986:237). Huli women's tactics are largely ineffective with respect to case decisions. For Brown, who recognizes a range of pragmatic effects of gendered speech, courtroom drama has multiple consequences for a dispute and for social relations, consequences that stand as evidence of the creative force of language in and out of court. Even though Swahili women win their claims and thus experience changes in their individual lives, case outcome is only one among several consequences of the gendered speech produced in disputes.

Examples of conflict narratives provide information about the possibilities and limitations of creative reworkings of social relations in different cultural contexts. For example, Tenejapan avoidance of public exposure of problems resembles Swahili preferences for keeping one's problems in the family (see chapter 2). However, Kadhi's Court disputes are not sites for "clearing the air" by violating this linguistic ideology. Rather, the effects of such speech uttered in public linger on, tainting storytellers with cultural disapproval. Through narrating in court, Swahili women push against the boundaries—legal, customary, and linguistic—to construct who they are and who they have been in marriage. Because their stories are told in the context of the official Kadhi's Court, women have the potential to shift the boundaries that delineate appropriate gender relations. This is certainly happening as the number of cases increases in Kadhi's Courts, an issue to which I return in chapter 9. But as storytellers, women narrate things that are better left unsaid, a situation that reinforces gender differences.

Huko kwenu huko na huko huko.

There at your place you aren't there and there you aren't there.

(FROM A KADHI'S COURT DISPUTE)

Constructing Audience: Interaction in Cases and Mediations

One day in mid-July of 1986, Ahmed and Amina, a Swahili couple, traveled from the small town where they lived not far from Malindi to appear before the Malindi kadhi. Both looked tired and distressed, perhaps because they had been waiting all morning to see the kadhi, who had dealt with six other matters before theirs. The couple, in their thirties and married for about fifteen years, was accompanied by five relatives, including Ahmed's sister and Amina's father. The group filed somberly into the kadhi's office.

Each party presented initial narratives that addressed the same central issue: whether Amina stayed longer at a relative's wake than she said she would. As in most mediations, this act of alleged disobedience was only one among a number of issues raised. Ahmed's manner was matter-of-fact as he related the reason for their appearance in court. Much of his account involved narrating specific events: Amina's departure for the wake and her tardy return, their confrontation when he accused her of disobedience, and his discovery that she had left him. Ahmed performed parts of these narratives, interspersing stories with pointed commentary. Amina's initial account was longer than Ahmed's, and she told it with more emotion, speed, and intensity. For the most part, her story consisted of descriptions of participating in the wake and her return home, offered as counternarratives that justified her behavior. But she also managed, at the beginning and end of her narration, to accuse Ahmed of serious breaches of his duties as a husband. After the initial accounts, the kadhi shifted the focus of discussion from the specific incidents described by the disputants to the issue of how to handle marital problems without destroying the marriage. The mediation continued with Ahmed and the kadhi as the primary participants. When an agreement was close at hand, the kadhi called on Amina's father to offer his opinion. Although he tried to prolong the argument, the couple agreed to reconcile, return home, and seek help, rather than separate, if and when new conflicts arose.

Even though the kadhi turned attention away from the accounts, telling stories about what had transpired was important to each disputant. Yet their initial accounts differ in significant ways that reflect the gender differences in entextualization described in the previous chapter: Ahmed relies heavily on statements and questions to frame his narrated stories; Amina constructs her narrative with the poetic language and repetition characteristic of a performance. By presenting the initial narratives of Ahmed and Amina in their entirety and then examining subsequent interaction, this chapter not only demonstrates previous claims about entextualization but also, more importantly, establishes that participants position themselves, and are positioned, in gendered roles as speakers in courtroom interaction.

By telling an account, a speaker positions everyone present in relation to one another as participants in the interaction (Goffman 1981; see also Goodwin 1984; Goodwin 1990; Hill and Irvine 1992; Irvine 1996; Schiffrin 1990). In Kadhi's Court, male and female disputants each occupy the position of "speaker" at certain moments. In addition, through the features of speech produced, they constitute themselves as "interlocutors" or "storytellers," depending on gender. The features of narration produced by men and women also serve as gambits to position other participants in interactional roles. For example, in response to the gendered tactics of disputants, kadhis routinely find themselves in the role of "ally" to a man or "witness" to a woman. These positions are constituted through gender-patterned speech, which is shaped not only by the constraints of court interaction but also by cultural conventions of speech.

The following section examines theoretical literature that suggests that a study of participation frameworks contributes to understanding the interactional constitution of gender. Then, the mediation involving Ahmed and Amina is analyzed to reveal gendered approaches to interaction. Subsequent sections focus on the gendered interactional roles that male and female disputants exhibit through narrative and their attempts to position the kadhi in specific interactional roles. As the conclusion asserts, these participatory roles are one aspect of the complex gendered subject positions that are displayed and challenged through the interaction of disputing.

Shifting Worlds, Repositioning Subjects

In Kadhi's Court, narrators routinely position themselves outside their narratives—in the event world of interaction—in order to manage interpretations of their behavior as presented in the narrated stories. As the literature on participation frameworks suggests, by switching among speaking roles, a speaker reframes the interactional "footing" and repositions the other participants (see, e.g., Goffman 1981; Goodwin 1981, 1986; Goodwin 1990; Schiffrin 1990).[1] For example, the roles that a narrator can assume include author (the composer of the speech), animator (the vehicle for conveying the speech), figure (the self presented through the story), and principal (the individual whose beliefs are articulated by the speech) (Schiffrin 1990:241).[2] By shifting among these roles—sometimes describing one's own actions or convictions, sometimes commenting on misspeech as an animator—a narrator changes the participation framework. Moreover, through shifting across complex participation structures, speakers can deflect the allocation of responsibility (for bad actions or abusive speech) away from themselves, a feature of particular import in disputes (Hill and Irvine 1992; Irvine 1992).

The frequency of Swahili men's metanarrative commentary suggests their ease in moving between the story world and the event world and among the various speaking roles associated with narrating. Commenting on one's role in the story can serve to distance a speaker from the character who performed the action. In stories told during arguments, a narrator's shifts among positionings "create a widened base of support for the speaker's position, they free the author from sole responsibility for the truth of a position, and allow the principal to share responsibility for commitment to a position with the audience" (Schiffrin 1990:255).[3] As they produce narrative and commentary, men effect the role of interlocutor, one who can engage with the kadhi. For Swahili women, long stories mean that there are fewer instances of this kind of shift in the participation framework. Thus, they establish themselves as storytellers focused on producing narratives to be interpreted by others. In her analysis of children's disputes, Marjorie Goodwin (1990:239) shows how the telling of stories, by expanding participation frameworks, "makes it possible for parties not initially involved in the argument to align themselves with particular positions within it."[4] Based on research with adolescents, Amy Shuman argues that the telling of a story of a fight that occurred in the past occasions an escalation of an ongoing dispute among participants in the storytelling event, especially among those who were also participants in the narrated event (Shuman 1986:25). When these adolescents referred to their "rights" to hear or to tell a narrative, they abruptly shifted the focus of the speech event away from the events narrated to the ongoing situation, which, in turn, shifted the relationships among the participants and altered the dispute.

In Kadhi's Court, disputants generally listen intently to one another, even when they are not the direct addressees. Listeners can be more or less engaged in a storytelling event; however, speech events such as court trials and course lectures involve participants in "binding talk" (Goffman 1981), which implies responsibilities that extend beyond merely hearing the words and commit listeners to subsequent action.[5] Even though kadhis and clerks control how interaction proceeds—making available to narrators the very possibility of speaking in court—they are frequently repositioned as disputants narrate conflict and in subsequent speech. As a disputant shifts the participant framework, the kadhi is moved among several roles: a spectator to the performance, a "witness" on the sidelines of the narrated events, a commentator on the behavior of characters in the story, an empathetic "ally" taking the narrator's perspective, an active participant in the dispute, and a responsible party in any future conflict, among others (see also Shuman 1986). Narrators deploy a variety of devices to pull the kadhi back and forth between the worlds of the story and the storytelling event, and among the participant roles; for their part, the kadhis and clerks embrace some such shifts and resist others.

Kadhis (and clerks) frequently find themselves drawn into two complex and problematic positions. The first involves the kadhi as an "ally" of the speaker, one who agrees with the speaker's position and supports him or her. This can occur when the narrator shifts out of narration to interpret the event being described and thus forces the listener to "see it from his or her perspective."[6] When this reframing is accomplished through direct address or a question, the kadhi has the opportunity to become the narrator's empathetic ally. The second role is the kadhi's positioning as a "witness" to the disputant's story. "Witness" in this usage refers neither to the technical legal term nor to the fact of presence at the storytelling. Rather, a listener is established as a witness by hearing a narrative entextualized with performance features. If the story told is so dramatically rich that the hearer is encouraged to feel as if he or she has actually "been there," or if numerous repetitions replay events, the kadhi comes to be a "witness" of the incidents described.

Before turning to Ahmed and Amina's initial narratives, I offer a caveat about the decision to examine one example in detail. An analysis based on one "case" is common in studies of both language and law. The utility of such an analysis in linguistics is articulated by conversation analysts, who believe that the detailed study of one example of interaction can reveal insights about how speakers organize interaction—which illuminates the construction of social life through talk and need not be replicated to be convincing (see Levinson 1983; Moerman 1988). In law, cases are critical units defined by legal discourse. Some scholars expand what constitutes a case, recognizing that a contextualized, in-depth study of one instance allows analysts to appreciate its logic (see, e.g., Brenneis 1988; Epstein 1967). Legal scholars are more likely than most linguists to apologize for an example that deviates from generalized trends. As a practical matter, it is extremely difficult to present more than one set of initial narratives in their entirety. By giving space below to two narratives and some subsequent mediation, I provide an example of how disputes transpire and the roles that stories play in the process. Given that talk itself becomes part of the context for subsequent talk, readers are afforded a fuller context for the analysis of this example and thus can draw their own conclusions about how gendered participation frameworks contribute to the constitution of gender in Kadhi's Court.

Ahmed's Claims

Ahmed had come to Kadhi's Court the previous week to speak with the clerk about bringing Amina to discuss their long-standing conflict, which involved claims of inadequate maintenance, jealousy, and strained relations between the extended families (see "The Wake," appendix C).[7] The couple had already sought intervention from their elders and the local subchief. Also, they had separated several times. Upon entering the kadhi's office, Ahmed and Amina sat down in front of his desk. In response to the kadhi's inquiring "Yes?" Ahmed began his account of the recent incidents of conflict:

Text 7.1

1	Ahmed:	The point is:: (1.4) her manner is:: defiant. (3.0)
2		The reason for saying this is tha::t (2.3)
3		is the time which it's not ve:ry long ago
4		she lo:st her grandmother.
5		Now then: she wanted to go to the burial.
6		I gave her money for going (2.2) to the funeral
7		even though that was all I had.
8		Now she ha:d gone.=
9		Before she went
10		I asked her (.)
11		"you'll return when?"
12		She said
13		"I'll return whenever."
14		I told her
15		"since you will return *whenever* (.)
16		I won't give you [the money]."
17		(It seemed) tha:t she wouldn't do this.
18		If it will be whenever like that
19		a person s/he will go then' (.)
20		I, it's my understanding, that s/he comes that very day
21		then returns. (1.5)
22		And she didn't do that.=
23		She *went* (1.5)
24		when she went there
25		she stayed
26		until the wake had finished.
27	Kadhi:	Hmm
28	Ahmed:	When she came that day
29		she came in at night.
30		And she knows that she left me with my children.
31		Children need to go to school.
32		And she didn't care about things like that
33		when she came a::t *night* (1)
34		I that time I told her
35		"Now indeed you ful*fill*ed that promise of yours that (.)
36		you will co::me whenever. Meaning, we did no:t say that
37		you would go to stay at the wake. How is it that you
38		today you have- you have gone and you have *stayed* (1)
39		at the wake and you come in here in the evening, it's

40		even Monday evening and the children were here, they
41		didn't go to school since morning there weren't any
42		[school] uniforms."
43		Now
44		and I am a person who's not able to (.) stay with them,
45		kids in order to take care of them like the way she does.
46	Kadhi:	Hmm. (1.5)
47	Ahmed:	Okay. (1.4)
48		She the thing that I told her (.) that time (.) at night I
49		said "Okay let's sleep. In the morning (1.2) I will' (.) I
50		will go to the kadhi. I will ask if there's a law a person
51		can make herself and make her own decision herself
52		without umm (agreeing on it) with her husband. We will
53		go to find out."
54		I went out.
55		When I went out at that time at night
56		I had my work sometimes business business
57		my ( ).
58		Shop (which I took)
59		there's money which I took to the farm.
60		I didn't tell her (.) that I would go.
61		When I returned in the morning
62		because I went
63		I' (.) I slept [there].
64		When I returned in the morning
65		then (.) she wasn't around
66		she had left the key and
67		she went out
68		she went to (1.5) her place [her parent's home] (2.0)
69		Okay.
70		I saw that now this one went to her place
71		leaving me what kind of message?[8]

Ahmed treats the stories he tells as evidence to prove his initial statement (line 1), which identifies Amina's defiant manner as the root of their conflict and the reason for their court appearance. He claims that Amina defied him by staying at the wake too long. He narrates her defiant words and deeds, announcing and commenting on the narrated incidents with non-narrative statements. For example, after initial blaming and scene-setting statements (lines 1–3), Ahmed offers the first narrated example of Amina's defiance: her refusal to agree to return from the wake at an appropriate time (lines 10–16). He then describes how she stayed at the wake until it ended, her main act of defiant behavior (lines 23–26). His emphatic "she *went*" (line 23) and the subsequent pausing for emphasis suggest that this is critical evidence of her impropriety. The non-narrative statements that introduce Ahmed's narration of Amina's blameworthy behavior (lines 23–26) refer to abstract rules about expected behavior (lines 18–21). He uses a negative phrase to state her violation (line 22), which, because negatives are unusual in narration, highlights her inappropriate behavior and suggests that the subsequent narrative reveals her culpability.[9] By interpreting the events through non-narrative statements, Ahmed emphasizes the similarity between his role and that of the kadhi, who also possesses the authority to judge Amina.

Later in his account, Ahmed describes other examples of Amina's defiant behavior (lines 28–33 and 35–42), including her return home and their confrontation. These narratives reiterate the original point that Amina disobeys him (see also Goodwin 1990). Reported speech, a central feature of these brief narratives, positions Ahmed as principal, animator, and figure and thus highlights his centrality in the events. He also emphasizes his control over the conflict by reporting his accusations. More pointedly, he turns to legal discourse when he quotes his threat to ask the kadhi about her behavior, suggesting that he, in concert with the law, would expose her defiance (lines 49–53). By establishing a connection between his concern with law as a participant in the mediation and his concern with law as a character in the dispute, Ahmed reinforces his claims to closer connection with the kadhi and opens the possibility of positioning the kadhi as a supportive ally.

In addition to establishing Amina's tendency toward defiant behavior, Ahmed's account, specifically his assessments of narrated incidents, also suggests that she has more serious character defects. Two sets of non-narrative statements direct attention to her improper treatment of their children (lines 30–32 and 43–45). Ahmed implies that Amina is not a good mother, because she uncaringly leaves her children with him, a man who, by his own admission, is an inferior caretaker. Her absence is inappropriate because, in leaving the home, she defies her husband's authority, abandons her duties to the children, and leaves a man to manage the household. Thus, his final story of returning home to find her gone follows the same logic that defines her behavior as morally flawed. However, reporting her final act of defiance—that she left home without leaving word for him (lines 70–71)—puts Ahmed in an awkward position. He has presented himself as controlling the action in the story, and yet he is unable to control his wife, a serious deficiency for a Swahili husband. By keeping his distance from her in the narration, he protects himself from culpability in the problem. He provides no motive for Amina's pattern of defiant actions, except to characterize it as uncaring. Amina, a nonpresence, passes out of his authoritative reach. Ahmed turns to law and the kadhi for support in his attempt to bring her back.

Similar to most narratives of trouble told by men in Kadhi's Court, Ahmed's account contains justifications for his own actions as well as accusations. Ahmed responds to an accusation that has not yet been made concerning why he stayed out all night after their fight. His unprovoked explanation counters the image painted of Amina as leaving home with no reason. By insisting that his absence was related to business (lines 55–59), he reinforces his image as a man who acts properly, mindful of his family's interests. His persistent attempts to manage his own impression, as well as the interpretation of his account, demonstrate his close resemblance to the kadhi. Ahmed depicts himself as possessing the double authority of one who knows the law and thus behaves correctly and one who tries diligently to guide others. The effort to position himself as possessing the knowledge to be taken seriously in a legal context becomes even more apparent as mediation continues and Ahmed directly solicits the kadhi as an ally.

Amina's Response

After Ahmed finishes his account, the kadhi prompts Amina to respond:

Text 7.2

1	Kadhi:	Mama[10] you heard what he said.
2	Amina:	I heard but
3		everything he said is untrue
4	Kadhi:	Yeah.
5	Amina:	This man the first thing (.) the first conflict
6		did not come over this wake stuff.
7		This man doesn't buy me new clothes.
8		The second thing, nice words he has none.

9	The third thing at home, yes, he doesn't sleep [there] at
10	all
11	When he goes out in the morning at eleven o'clock
12	until the next day at eleven o'clock.
13	When he goes out at eight o'clock
14	until eight o'clock the next day.
15	When he comes early it's two o'clock three o'clock it's so,
16	that he sleeps.
17	When you question him
18	he's furious.
19	He did this the first time
20	he did again a second time
21	he did a third time.
22	The fourth time he came that day at 3 o'clock.
23	I came
24	I asked him.
25	He told me
26	"I can't speak to you (.) take off.
27	You if you have a home [parent's home] ( ) you go.
28	Every day I throw you out 'you go to your place' you're
29	just here."
30	I told him
31	"okay you wait" for his father.
32	He told me
33	"even if you call" his father
34	"he won't do anything for us."
35	So I just left all that.

The double burden faced by respondents—they must defend themselves and also put forward their own accusations—is evident in Amina's account. She repeats the kadhi's words (line 1) in denouncing Ahmed's claims against her (lines 2–3). Narrators routinely incorporate phrases from the request for a narrative in their announcements. But she does not at that point begin to narrate the story that, in countering Ahmed's, justifies her actions. Rather, she suggests that they are not even addressing the right issue in that the conflict over the wake was preceded by other problems. She then offers three precise and legally potent reasons why she considers Ahmed responsible for the problems (lines 5–10). What is most interesting about Amina's subsequent account is that she never refers explicitly to these accusations.

The first and third accusations are entirely ignored; the accusation that Ahmed has no "nice words" for her is indirectly addressed when she recreates scenes of his abusive behavior. Similar to the examples presented in chapter 6, Amina's narrated stories bear little connection to legal tasks; they provide no narrated evidence of the problems she cites as most critical to the conflict.

Text 7.3

1	Amina:	Then I was brought some news around late afternoon.
2		This woman said that it's true
3		it's my grandmother. It's the mother of my mothers. (.)
4		I told him
5		"okay that grandmother who was sick. She died."
6		"She'll be buried what time?"
7		I told him
8		"She'll be buried maybe ten o'clock given that she died
9		early." (1)
10		We slept.
11		In the morning I waited
12		until he gave me carfare
13		I went.
14		When I went
15		when I arrived the:re
16		the ticket that he gave me is for twenty shillings.
17		When I got there
18		the ticket is five shillings
19		from there [the first stop] to there [the wake].
20		When I got there [the wake]
21		there's a wake fee.
22		The wake is our family's.
23		'First' five shillings from twenty how much remained?
24	Kadhi:	Fifteen.
25	Amina:	Ten shillings remained.
26		A five shilling ticket from there to there.
27		On arrival there's a wake fee it's five shillings.
28	Kadhi:	'Yes' ten shillings.
29	Amina:	Then ten shillings.
30		That's what's left.
31		And to go from there by foot in the evening
32		I can't go all the way here.

33   I stayed over.
34   The next morning I couldn't get someone to come with
35   and to take the road by myself I can't.
36   The road is scary.
37   I stayed over.
38   The next day the wake was finishing.
39   I thought that it would be best for me to finish it
40   then I go
41   because it's not the first time.
42   (This has happened [before])
43   we were mourning
44   and I went
45   and I stayed
46   until the wake was finished
47   I have yet to hear any of this fuss.
48   I came now.
49   When I came to my [parents'] place
50   I stopped by my mother's house by foot
51   from Kakayuni until Ganda which is our place.
52   I stopped by my father's house.
53   I went
54   I explai:ned to him
55   he told me
56   "okay now you stay because the *buses* don't pass *this*
57   way. In the late afternoon I'll take you."
58   We waited until five o'clock
59   we went with dad
60   we came all together to Bakshweni's [a shop in town].
61   (When we got) to Bakshweni's
62   it was evening.
63   He told me
64   "now I've got friends who will return home with me by
65   foot. You go."
66   I took the road
67   I went to my place to the house.
68   When I arrived home
69   this man [Ahmed] had locked the door.
70   He's not around.
71   I asked my friend who lives near me
72   "He left me a key?"

73	She told me
74	"heh." [affirmative]
75	"He went out at what time?"
76	This one she said
77	"he went out a little while ago."
78	I waited.
79	I waited then
80	I left
81	I went to the neighbors.
82	I stayed at the neighbors
83	then when I came' (.7)
84	and he was coming in.
85	When he arrived
86	he was- he was told
87	"Mama has come."
88	Okay, even though he was told that I had come
89	he had a fit right there at the door
90	before he came inside.
91	He came inside
92	and I was behind
93	I came in.
94	Even as I took hold of the door
95	wanting to enter the room
96	he told me (1)
97	"why did you shut the door like a thief? You were late
98	tonight on purpose in order to
99	spy what are you snooping for?"
100	I objected
101	I was shocked at first.
102	I said
103	"how did this start?"
104	Then I entered inside
105	I entered inside
106	I sat down.
107	He asked me
108	"How come since day before yesterday you haven't
109	come?" I started to explain to him
110	"that money that I went with had finished. Now to go
111	from there by foot to here I can't by
112	myself. The road is scary. On Sunday

113   the wake it really was finished. It was finished
114   late afternoon. I thought it would be better
115   that I sleep. Then in the morning I'll get the friends
116   who I had come with there to the burial
117   to the wake. We'll come together. We'll go with
118   each other all together those friends up to Ganda
119   where we parted. I went to my father's."
120   "Now you have been brought by whom?"
121   I told him
122   "I came with dad."
123   "That's a lie you since the day before yesterday, even
124   you, there at the wake, you weren't there.
125   You were here, right here in Malindi. There
126   at your place you aren't there, and there
127   you aren't there. (1.2) You're right here in Malindi."
128   Here in Malindi *what* house? (2.5)

Most of Amina's account consists of long, sequentially ordered narrations that address issues raised by Ahmed (e.g., lines 11–127). In describing and at the same time justifying her decision to stay at the wake, Amina provides reasons for her behavior (e.g., she did not want to travel alone; she ran out of money) that counter Ahmed's accusations of her defiance or moral laxity. She disrupts her narration only rarely with comments that explain her reasoning at the time and offer interpretation based on law. Essentially, she defends herself using ethical discourse, insisting that she made hard decisions in good faith. One of her justifications refers to a previous experience of attending a wake (lines 42–47). The experiential grounding of her example contrasts with Ahmed's abstract reasoning about the same issue (Text 7.1, lines 18–21). This gendered contrast is typical across mediations. Women tend to refer to real-life events, while men justify their actions and beliefs on the basis of rules. Amina also provides narrative evidence of her willingness to comply with the wishes of authority figures, for example, her father. She thereby provides a counter, albeit an oblique one, to Ahmed's claims that she defies authority. Her narratives blame Ahmed as well as justify and mitigate her own actions. In all these tasks, Amina rarely steps outside her narrative to offer commentary, legal or otherwise, on the story or its interpretation. Thus, unlike Ahmed, she does not position herself as someone who claims legal knowledge that entitles her to speak on a par with the kadhi.

Amina's narrations are vivid and intense, full of performance devices that entextualize her story (e.g., raised pitch, word emphasis, reported speech, and narrative poetics, such as lexical linking and syntactic repetition). Her account contains several examples of evaluation through vowel lengthening (e.g., Text 7.3, line 15). The lengthened vowel in *ku:le* (there) emphasizes the distance that she had to travel to the wake, a critical justification for staying longer. Her depiction of this central issue is made all the more vivid by the fact that she repeats it twice. First, she describes how she decided to stay, carefully indicating that the circumstances made it the only option. She then renarrates the incident by quoting her effort to explain the decision to Ahmed once she returned home and faced his accusations. As principal and then as figure, she draws attention to her behavior, depicting it as appropriate.

Amina describes several occasions on which Ahmed confronted her with requests and accusations. In recreating these through reported speech that closely mimics the anger in which it was presumably uttered, she illustrates being bombarded with unreasonable accusations. Her production of multiple examples highlights the abusive nature of this verbal confrontation (Text 7.2, lines 25–29; Text 7.3, lines 96–127). Her reaction during one of these confrontations—"how did this start?" (Text 7.3, line 103)—expresses bewilderment over her husband's accusatory statements. By presenting these confrontations with little information about why Ahmed engages in verbal abuse, she allows the third party to come close to feeling bewildered, too. There is then an iconic portrayal of the conflict that has occurred between them. She positions herself as a character caught in her husband's unanticipated, abusive behavior and provides enough entextualizing devices to attempt to capture her audience, especially the kadhi, as a witness to those experiences.

The slight pause in Amina's narrative, perhaps to allow her to catch her breath or to let her narrations sink in, offers the kadhi the opportunity to begin mediation:

Text 7.4

1	Kadhi:	Listen Ma Amina. You all have kids.
2	Amina:	We have kids.
3	Kadhi:	How many?
4	Amina:	Five.
5	Kadhi:	Five kids.

6	Amina:	Mmm [affirmative].
7		And it's not the first time.
8		EVERY TIME HE'S WITH A WOMAN OUTSIDE
9		HIS DEAL IS *THIS THIS THIS*.
10		|It's not the first time at all-
11	Kadhi:	|Up to now you've got five kids and
12		you all are still crazy like this?
13	Amina:	I'm not at fault.
14		The fault lies with him
15		because of outside women.
16		*These* so- his problems if they- if they begin problems it's
17		an outside woman.
18		Right now he has one.
19		See how at the house he doesn't sleep. (3.5)
20		He doesn't sleep *at all* at home.
21		He has told lies.

Amina's accusations are delivered with striking vehemence. Speaking with raised volume and pitch, she accentuates the seriousness of her claim (lines 8–9). Women rarely mention the topic of men's adultery in court, because men's adulterous behavior is not treated as a serious offense in legal and most other contexts. But Amina leaves the claim unexplored; she offers no narrated evidence.

Amina's claims against Ahmed are remarkably similar in one respect to his accusations against her, *as reported by her*. Her allegation that he has another woman comes out of the blue in the same way that his accusations, particularly the charge that she did not attend the funeral but rather stayed in Malindi (Text 7.3, lines 123–27), repeatedly emerge as surprises. The similarity between her blaming and his is that both Amina (in her account) and Ahmed (in her report of his speech) come up with accusatory "zingers" that have little grounding in previous speech. The reconstruction of *his* words demonstrates how *women's* narrative and non-narrative statements generally fail to connect topically, which often results because women find it difficult to provide stories in court of the issues that concern them (e.g., polygamy, adultery). Amina is focused on entextualizing her experience of one aspect of the dismal existence that has become her marital life, namely, being subject to Ahmed's unfounded and insulting accusations. At the same time, she describes her attempts to accomplish what was expected of her: she attended the funeral, she did not travel the highways alone, she sought her father's supervision. Her narrative shows her victimization and compliance, though she rarely steps outside the story. She endeavors to make the kadhi a witness to her life, not an ally with whom she converses or trades interpretations.

At the end of her account, Amina makes the damning though ambiguous statement "He has told lies." In following the accusation that Ahmed is involved with another woman, this statement could be interpreted as referring to Ahmed's tendency to lie when Amina confronts him about sleeping away from home. But the utterance could also be understood as her contention that he has not been truthful in court. By casting doubt on his narrative, Amina directs attention to her own story as providing a more accurate account of their problems.

Narrative Poetics and the Pervasive Story World

Amina's account is structured to highlight the events in the story world; by contrast, Ahmed's account brings audience members back and forth between the story world and the storytelling world. Amina's extensive reliance on features of narrative performance contributes to entextualizing the "facts" of the story-world incidents. Moreover, narration is so prominent in her account that its form, particularly its poetic construction, also structures the non-narrative portions of her account, such as blamings. Her extensive use of narrative features is evidence of the centrality of narration in her account and, as well, the prominence of the story world in her courtroom appearance. More importantly, Amina's reliance on narrative poetics displays her attempts to construct audience members as witnesses to her conflict. Typical of narratives produced by many Swahili women, Amina's narration includes several types of narrative poetics.

Poetic language includes the constant repetition and density of linguistic forms, rhythmic and measured syntagmatic units, and phonological parallelisms (see Silverstein 1979; Hymes 1981). Bauman and Briggs (1990:63) cite studies that demonstrate "the way parallelistic constructions at both micro and macro levels can signal illocutionary force." This signaling involves metapragmatic and metasemantic functions that Silverstein, following Jakobson, argues are *explicit* in poetic language. That is, the poetic function of language is a means of directing attention to the message itself as against surrounding talk.[11] Moreover, poetic language indexes who has the right to use what kind of speech in what circumstances and thus reflects aspects of linguistic ideology particular to institutional and cultural contexts. Narration with a high degree of poetic structuring can operate to call attention to itself as entextualized speech. In producing poetic language, Swahili women index the fact that they are playing out the events of conflict. Moreover, the repetitive and parallelistic forms through which narratives are told in Kadhi's Court, especially by women, call attention to similarity and recurrence as characteristics of speech and by extension as dimensions of social life. Poetic language thereby indexes repetition in women's stories and in their lives.

As Amina moves toward describing her final confrontation with Ahmed, the most serious conflict between them, her speech becomes more rapid and intense. She produces features of performed narration, including narrative poetics. There are repetitions of lexical items and syntax as she quotes how she told Ahmed about her trip home in response to his question, as reported by her:

Text 7.5

1	Amina:	"How come since day before yesterday you haven't
2		come?" I started to explain to him
3		"that money that I went with had finished. Now to go
4		from there by foot to here I can't by myself.
5		The road is scary. On Sunday the wake it really was
6		finished. It was finished late afternoon. I thought it would
7		be better that I sleep. Then in the morning I'll get
8		the friends who I had come with there to the burial to the
9		wake. We'll come together. We'll go with each other all
10		together those friends up to Ganda where we left each
11		other. I went to my place at my father's."
12		"Now you have been brought by whom?"
13		I told him
14		"I came with dad."

In this example, lexical linking moves the action of the story as Amina prepares to leave the wake (lines 5–6). Another poetic construction is produced through her repetition of syntax (lines 11–14). Repeating the statement that she was brought home by her father both reinforces her contention that she is generally obedient to authority and, at the same time, adds a poetic dimension. In addition to repeating nearly exact words in these utterances, she also replicates the intonation. She ends on a high tone, which in Kiswahili is interpreted as plaintive or "wheedling" (see Maw 1992).

The reported story sets the scene for a confrontation between Ahmed and Amina. In quoting the most serious accusation made by Ahmed against her, Amina produces a high degree of phonological and lexical repetition and also syntactic parallelism. In acting out his speech, she speaks loudly and quickly, with raised pitch:

Text 7.6

1	Amina:	". . . since the other day even you there at the wake you
2		weren't there
3		you were right here in Malindi
4		there at your place you aren't there and
5		there [at the wake] you aren't there. (1.2)
6		You're right here in Malindi."
7		Here in Malindi, *wha:t* house?

The first line establishes a syntactic organization that is replicated (lines 4–5). The syntax is marked in that the deictic locative "there," meaning "at the wake," is produced prior to the subject, verb, and repetition of the locative. These accusatory utterances are answered (line 6) by a syntactically standard statement that locates Amina in Malindi, rather than at the wake. Thus, Amina reproduces Ahmed's speech as syntactically parallel accusations and responses. The lexical and syntactic repetitions contribute to the high degree of phonological similarity, which draws attention to an accusation that is quite serious when made by a husband against his wife:

"Huko kwenu huko na huko huko."
"There at your place you aren't there and there you aren't there."

Huko	*kw-*	*enu*
place (dem.)	place belonging to	you all
hu-	*ko*	*na*
you (neg.)	(to be in a) place	and
huko	*hu-*	*ko.*
place (dem.)	you (neg.)	(to be in a) place.

This sequence is filled with phonological repetition, a much prized feat in Kiswahili verbal art (see Hinton, Nichols, and Ohala 1994). The morphological breakdown shows that two homonyms *(huko)* create repetitive sound. The heightened emphasis through Amina's report of Ahmed's speech builds to a critically important though ambiguous statement: "Here in Malindi, what house?" This question could be interpreted as Ahmed's speech reported by Amina, Amina's report of her own speech to Ahmed, or a question that she asks to the open court. The inability of the listener to determine which of these is the appropriate interpretation is another example of how Amina's stories blur the lines between the story world and the ongoing narration in court.

As the example above demonstrates, poetic constructions appear at some of the most critical moments in narratives. When a narrator moves from a poetically structured story to poetically structured non-narrative speech, performance features are extended into acts such as blaming. The beginning of Amina's account demonstrates this point:

Text 7.7

1	Amina:	This man the first thing (.) the first conflict
2		did not come over this wake stuff.
3		This man doesn't buy me new clothes.
4		The second thing, nice words he has none.
5		The third thing at home, yes, he doesn't sleep [there] at
6		all.
7		When he goes out in the morning at eleven o'clock
8		until the next day at eleven o'clock.
9		When he goes out at eight o'clock
10		until eight o'clock the next day.
11		When he comes early it's two o'clock three o'clock it's so,
12		that he sleeps.
13		When you question him
14		he's furious.
15		He did this the first time
16		he did again a second time
17		he did a third time.
18		The fourth time he came that day at 3 o'clock.

Amina makes three numbered accusations against Ahmed (lines 1–6). Her subsequent elaboration (lines 7–12) of the third reason for their conflict (that Ahmed stays out overnight) is a good example of poetic blaming in women's accounts, whereby the syntax repeats with paradigmatic substitutions. The non-narrative poetic lines are followed by poetically structured, albeit abstract, narration (lines 15–17). These statements are technically narrative; they do not, however, tell a detailed story of a specific instance of rule violation.[12] The entire sequence is highly poetic in that Amina produces three sets of syntactically similar triplets. Her narrative style—her tendency to perform non-narrative statements using features of performance and poetics associated with Kiswahili narrative—is also similar to the speech of other women who produce what sounds like a narrated performance, even when they are not narrating. This tendency increases the amount of performed speech and perhaps increases the possibility that non-narrative statements resembling performed narrative might be received by listeners in the same way as they receive narration.

Haviland's interpretation (1988) of poetic language in marital disputes in Zinacantan, Mexico, offers an intriguing comparison case (see also Briggs 1988b). For Haviland, the "disorder" of marital conflict, including the uncontrolled language of fights and gossip about disputes, contrasts with the ordered language of marriage rituals. Ritual language is typified by poetic couplets uttered by authority figures to instruct the Zinacanteco bride and groom in proper marital behavior. In disputes, marital disorder is "redomesticated," or brought under control, through similar poetic couplets uttered by authorities or disputants. Using poetic couplets to mediate marital discord reinforces authoritative order and the conservatism that upholds it. The connection between the poetic structuring of ritual language and the creation of order is potentially applicable to other cultural contexts; however, Haviland does not make this general claim. Rather, his argument focuses on the specific role that poetic couplets (as reflective of a ritual genre) play in Zinacanteco marriage.

In Swahili disputing, poetic language provides order by structuring performed narratives and also other forms of disputing discourse. Poetically framed blaming statements are not brought into disputants' language from an external context (e.g., a ritual) but rather are directly related to the poetics of narration, which for women is the primary form of speech in disputes. By using poetic language, Swahili women are not indexing the authoritative, ordered speech produced by authority figures. Rather, they revisit and repeat the order that they themselves establish through performing their stories of marital conflict. In that sense their production of poetic features, even in the non-narrative parts of their accounts, indexes the story itself and the fact that women have ordered tales to tell. The Swahili example leads me to question Haviland's assumption that disputing language depicts "disorder." In most narratives in court, Swahili women do not depict their lives as characterized by disorder that needs to be controlled. By narrating stories that illustrate the pattern of abusive behavior that they have been subjected to in their marriage and that they can no longer endure, women display an order in their lives, albeit one involving inappropriate behavior that has become routine, repetitive, and even commonplace. By narrating these incidents in ways that emphasize their recurrence, they are not bringing chaos under control but, rather, iconically displaying repetitive abuse. Moreover, they compel the audience to "experience" the logic of "ordered" lives, a logic that plays out through repetition. The iconic quality of these narratives turns audience members into witnesses by bringing them through the story, several times, and with attention to the repetitive quality of endured abuse iconically reproduced.

Surrounded by a story dramatized through dialogue and emotional description, the kadhi is turned into a "witness." The kadhi can never be a witness to the actual events of conflict underlying disputants' claims, as those have already occurred. But in recreating events, disputants endeavor to surround the kadhi with the story world and to make it difficult for him to deny that he has "witnessed" the conflict. Women's unbroken narrations address and perhaps accomplish this goal.

Kadhis as Reluctant Witnesses and Allies

During mediations, kadhis' interactional roles shift radically. While disputants tell their initial accounts, kadhis generally remain silent though attentive, ceding the interactional "floor" for disputants' accounts.[13] Even when they produce minimal feedback (e.g., "umhmm" or "yes") that indicates receipt of the story and encourages the speaker to continue, kadhis make little effort to participate beyond the role of audience member. The kadhi's initial detachment contrasts markedly with the control he exercises over the interaction after the disputants conclude their narratives. Bauman and Briggs (1990:70) point out: "Even when audience members say or do practically nothing at the time of the performance, their role becomes active when they serve as speakers in subsequent entextualizations of the topic at hand (e.g., in reports, challenges, refutations, enactments of consequences, and the like)."[14] Following the initial accounts, the kadhi situates himself as an active participant in the event world of the ongoing dispute.

After Amina asks the cryptic question "Here in Malindi, what house?" she stops speaking, perhaps to collect her thoughts or catch her breath. In the short gap or pause, the kadhi reminds Amina that she and Ahmed have had children together. Because his statement diverges topically from the points Amina has just made, it ignores and displaces her account. Although this discursive move appears to echo Ahmed's charge that Amina is an uncaring mother, its more critical function is to deflect attention away from the incidents of conflict depicted by the disputants. The kadhi's reference to Amina's parental burden is the first of many efforts to shift the focus of mediation away from the incidents of conflict. He is the primary speaker for most of the rest of the mediation, which continues for thirty minutes. At the conclusion of Amina's initial turn, the three principal speakers engage in a brief, heated discussion characterized by simultaneous speech and interruptions, which culminates in the following exchange:

Text 7.8

1	Kadhi:	She knows the way to think about it. You all do things
2		like children.
3	Ahmed:	Okay, it's her just like she told me, bwana.
4	Amina:	What for? He causes trouble. And you sleep outside every
5		day.
6	Kadhi:	Now you all in front of God who has given five children.
7		You will answer what to God? I think, or what you'll
8		hear at your place, if trouble comes, who will it harm?
9		Isn't it the children?
10	Ahmed:	It's the children.

In a voice full of anger and pleading, the kadhi invokes the specter of God's wrath to persuade Ahmed and Amina that their children are more important than their claims against each other. The exchange displays concisely the concerns that each participant raises in the subsequent mediation. Ahmed places blame on Amina for her behavior as described in his account. Amina reproduces her accusation that Ahmed never sleeps at home. The kadhi turns attention away from both concerns by suggesting that dwelling on them will further harm the children. Although Ahmed appears to agree that the children might be hurt by the dispute, he raises his concern again a minute later, just as the kadhi uses a hypothetical example to explain how misunderstandings might emerge. Ahmed refuses to speak in hypotheticals, preferring to assert that Amina has no reason to believe that he behaves inappropriately by staying out. In this manner, he draws attention back to the story for the next few minutes, until the kadhi tells him firmly to leave those concerns behind.

After the interchange described above, the kadhi retains control of the interaction through long turns in which he urges Ahmed and Amina to learn to get along. His examples of what causes problems in marriage and how to deal with them are framed as hypothetical situations or as future stories. Through phrases such as "for example" or "let's just say" followed by an account that refers neither to specific individuals nor to events that actually occurred, the kadhi refuses to acknowledge connections between his examples and those of the disputants. Thus, any evaluative remarks on his part, including any denunciations of behavior, cannot be treated as recontextualizations of the disputants' stories. By eliding the "theories" put forward by each party (see Ochs et al. 1992), the kadhi holds no one accountable.

Some mediators point to the destructive effects of strategies that encourage resolution without requiring disputants to elucidate their conflict.[15] The kadhi's tendency to avoid discussing the issues is accomplished interactionally and is subject to challenge, primarily by Ahmed. Upon gaining the floor for his first long turn, the kadhi bemoans the effects of disputing on children. He then insists that husbands and wives must develop a good rapport to avoid misunderstandings. Just as the kadhi suggests that he has offered a resolution to the dispute— one that condemns neither Amina nor Ahmed—he is interrupted by Ahmed, who points out another blameworthy act by Amina. He responds to Ahmed by directing attention to marital problems generally. By depicting marriage as an "institute," using the English term, he insists that couples learn to get along. This interchange does not encourage discussion of their claims against each other.

The kadhi also refuses to engage Amina's attempts to revisit the issues. When the kadhi appears to conclude his advice to Amina, he is interrupted:

Text 7.9

1	Kadhi:	Bear with him if he messes up. Bear with his, mother,
2		mother, and that one, his friend, if he messes up, your
3		father. ( ). Go outside if it's defeated, to the side of
4		the kadhi or something. You put your house together.
5		You take good care of your children.
6	Amina:	This one, he isn't at work. Those words that he said were
7		untrue, this one.

8	Kadhi:	Ah, yes but now I have not yet said, meaning, that [thing]
9		he is unable to prove if it's true or a lie. But now, let's
10		say. If he says "I'm going to work" you will tell a person
11		he isn't going to work? You will say something like that?
12		And even if it's so. You, isn't it on you to stay each time
13		causing misunderstanding like that? Meaning, it will ruin
14		you.

Initially, the kadhi agrees with Amina's accusation that Ahmed lied when he said he went to work at night (Text 7.1, lines 54–59). The kadhi sympathizes with her position;[16] however, by insisting that it is impossible to know whether Ahmed has told the truth, he refuses to use his knowledge as a "witness" to the narrated incident to determine the credibility of either story. The kadhi admonishes Amina to resolve their problems by being a good wife and ignoring relatives who cause problems. Although in this exchange the kadhi willfully disregards Amina's most acute concerns, much of his discussion explains and supports her position on this matter as well as the incident of staying at the wake. He emphasizes the point, albeit hypothetical, that a woman whose husband sleeps at home only irregularly can be expected to complain. This argument is phrased in terms of how "everywoman" might act; thus, he avoids commenting directly on Amina's behavior and thereby antagonizing Ahmed.

The kadhi's support of Amina is evident when, late in the mediation, he reframes her return, and the subsequent disputing, as a "misunderstanding."[17] Responding to discourse markers that signal closure of the discussion, as well as the kadhi's suggestion that he forgive Amina, Ahmed interrupts for a final challenge to the kadhi's refusal to blame Amina:

Text 7.10

1	Kadhi:	Now you, your reason you have stayed extra days eh she
2		stayed extra days but she went abruptly poor thing. It's a
3		humble act going to their place and you, her husband.
4		You should turn your cheek.
5	Ahmed:	Meaning she did a bad thing. She didn't say the thing she
6		started to say at the house that "Me, I don't know, any
7		day I will stay it's so [until] I want to come."
8	Kadhi:	It's like that meaning
9	Ahmed:	She completed that answer, she will stay.
10	Kadhi:	I'm telling you go ( ) it's so and you you didn't insist

11		"No I have told you to return tomorrow." Did you tell
12		her? (2). You would have finished right there. Done.
13	Ahmed:	There she answered like that I saw you said that it's: she
14		will do it, it's just words. And she completed [the wake]
15		this woman.
16	Kadhi:	Now she completed [the wake] but (you had already) not
17		yet finished (to tell) her she goes there she will return any
18		day but you did not tell her "you return tomorrow."
19		You did not tell her. You understand? Now then.
20	Ahmed:	It shows openly that even if I would have told her she
21		would not have come.
22	Kadhi:	Uh uh but 'at least' wouldn't there have been a rea:son?
23		It's so, to tell her, if a person like that (says) "I'm going
24		to a place. I don't know when I will return." And you
25		agreed with her. Okay. Hasn't she been 'permitted'? And
26		you can't put her in the wrong.

Ahmed displays striking persistence in his attempts to discuss the issues and to force the kadhi to reproach Amina. Exasperated by yet another interruption, the kadhi addresses the issue of the wake directly, clarifying that he is not allied with Ahmed in condemning Amina. His confrontation with Ahmed leaves him no escape from the point that Amina has been wrongly accused. The kadhi's censure follows from Ahmed's endeavor to index and exploit his ability to engage the kadhi in conversation. Such interchanges are a struggle over authority in which only men participate. Unable to gain the kadhi's agreement as an ally, Ahmed tries to engage with him to reinforce his standing as one who can assert authority in the legal institution.

The kadhi's strategy of counseling, combined with his refusal to act as a trier of facts, has several consequences for the participation framework. In effect, the kadhi denies that he was a "witness" to the events recounted by the disputants. As a consequence, Amina is silenced; the narrative she told initially is ignored, and the kadhi requests no further evidence. This silencing is paradoxical in that it follows the kadhi's insistence that wives who are mistreated can be expected to complain. With respect to Ahmed's attempts to position him as an ally, the kadhi first avoids the issue of blame and then refutes Ahmed's interpretation. His control of the conversation systematically ignores or reframes the "context" created by the initial narratives. Changes in the participation structure are thus directly related to how the kadhi addresses the disputants' accounts. By distancing himself from the stories, he effects a participation framework that limits the disputants' abilities to call on him as either witness or ally. Consequently, the disputants find it hard to challenge his interpretations or each other. In the end, however, he manages to interact more with Ahmed than with Amina, and it is possible that Ahmed, though he encounters direct censure, has had more influence. The next section briefly discusses questions as an important discursive strategy through which men seek interaction with kadhis.

Questioning Kadhis

Questions can alter the participation framework by effecting direct engagement between the questioner and other participants. In legal contexts, questions are produced more frequently by judges, attorneys, and clerks than by disputants. In Kadhi's Courts, disputants question and cross-examine witnesses using the question-and-answer format that typifies courtroom interaction (Atkinson and Drew 1979). In addition, in mediations, disputants can question the kadhi or clerk in order to clear up mishearings or misunderstandings.[18] Questions are rare in disputants' initial accounts; though more plentiful in the ensuing mediation, they are nonetheless restricted to particular types. How disputants ask questions reflects gendered strategies for altering the participation framework that emerge from disputants' positions as gendered, legal subjects. In Kadhi's Court, men produce most questions, and their questions tend to solicit the clerk's or kadhi's agreement with their opinions.[19] Men's questions also demand responses that index the kadhi's position as an ally. Ahmed's several questions request the kadhi's agreement with his views. Moreover, the questions attempt to engage the kadhi in conversational interaction—that is, to establish him as a peer or an ally, which, as indicated above, Ahmed carries out through other linguistic forms as well. Women only rarely attempt to draw attention to their position through questions. Their questions tend to check the listeners' attention or engage them in telling the story (Text 7.3, line 23).

Through questions, disputants solicit agreement with their evaluation of the story. Several examples from a mediation involving Rukia, a woman who has accused her husband, Shaaban, of beating her, dem-

onstrate how questions seek confirmation (see "The Knife," appendix
C). Shaaban describes his version of the incident:

Text 7.11

1	Shaaban:	I went back to my place.
2		When I returned
3		I saw that she stayed right there at the house.
4		Doesn't it mean, if you have a disagreement with your
5		wife,
6		isn't [it] necessary that she stays there?
7		If you reconcile,
8		you'll reconcile while apart?

Shaaban's unanswered questions, which interrupt his narrative (lines
6–8), appeal to the kadhi for agreement with his assessment that his
wife should stay nearby after a fight to facilitate reconciliation. His
reference to "your wife" assumes a male interlocuter, which among
other factors indexes solidarity with the kadhi.

Combining a question with an assessment is a powerful means
of requesting the kadhi's participation. Below, Shaaban describes
his opposition to Rukia's desire for mediation. As he reports, after
first refusing to meet with the kadhi, he insists that they speak with
elders:

Text 7.12

1	Shaaban:	I stayed again like seven days or so
2		I said
3		"No"
4		(coming)
5		I called a family member
6		I said
7		"My wife has no reason for us to go to the kadhi
8		you see.
9		Let's go to our place,
10		that we come to an understanding again."
11		We stayed,
12		meaning, this will be a problem we ( ) problem
13		(stay) far [away from] the family there.
14		Life truly it has been wrecked,
15		isn't it, bwana?

16   Kadhi: Hmm.
17   Shaaban: I said
18   "there's no need."

Shaaban offers his opinion of the difficulties of repairing their relationship while living apart. A tag question requests the kadhi's agreement
(line 15). As a term of address, *bwana* implies equality between interlocutors.[20]

Similar to tags in English, Kiswahili tags can be either invariant
(e.g., "truly?" "kweli?") or variant (e.g., "is it not so?" "siyo?").[21]
Tags appear in the ordinary conversation of both men and women,
but in court only men produce them. The extensive literature on tag
questions, which includes considerations of gender differences, tends
to focus on the frequency of tags rather than their functions (cf.
Holmes 1982; for reviews, see Cameron 1985; Coates and Cameron
1988).[22] Holmes's study (1982) of English tags suggests that the modal
function of tags is less common than the affective function, a pattern
that is also reflected in Kadhi's Court.[23] Affective functions can include
expressing solidarity, appealing to solidarity, and protecting solidarity.
Holmes's use of the term *solidarity* resonates with the idea of creating
allies. Appealing to solidarity accounts for most of the tags produced
by disputants (see also Hirsch 1987, 1990).

In producing questions, Swahili men assume shared experience
with kadhis and thereby index solidarity with the authority figure.
Women tend to produce questions that affirm the kadhi's authority
over them. When men solicit agreement on the substance of an assessment through questions, they also index their relation to the third
party as male authorities, thus making a connection of socially recognized solidarity unavailable to women. Yet it is not the case that men's
attempts to effect relationships are always welcomed. Through rebuke
or silence, kadhis routinely refuse to be relocated in the participation
structure, particularly when questions request their solidarity or agreement.

Conclusion

Showing how speakers reorder interactional roles in disputes in court
demonstrates that legal processes contribute to social change. When
a male speaker assumes the role of interlocutor, he indexes and en-

hances his connection with legal authority. Like the authorities, he can assume the role of interpreting how a narrative allocates responsibility (see also Hill and Irvine 1992). By interpreting their stories, men locate themselves as insiders, as individuals with claims to authority. By contrast, the storytelling genre fails to offer women institutionally recognized authority. When women disputants focus on telling stories, they remain on the outside of the conversation. In addition, the Kiswahili example shows that there are cross-cultural differences in the degree to which women facilitate interaction and also differences across institutional contexts.[24]

Litigants constitute themselves in gendered roles not only through the ways in which they tell and then orient to their stories but also in relation to their efforts to position the kadhi as an ally or a witness. Yet the kadhi's position as the controller of courtroom interaction affords him the authority to regulate shifts in the participation framework more coercively than either disputant. Kadhis (and clerks) can avoid becoming allies of male disputants by rejecting attempts at repositioning. Moreover, as the examples suggested, when kadhis draw attention away from the story, they defeat women's efforts to create witnesses. Even though kadhis and clerks reject some reframings of their roles, the gambits made by disputants leave lasting effects. One is that male litigants can and do challenge authorities; they constitute themselves as positioned to confront the kadhi or to appeal to him. Another effect is that the telling of the stories, by men and by women, makes everyone in the context into witnesses. That all present have heard the stories of conflict is an important factor in any subsequent interaction (see Goodwin 1990; Shuman 1986). This is the broadest change brought about through the disputing process in Kadhi's Court, a point that draws on Duranti and Goodwin's notion (1992) that speech itself becomes the context in which subsequent speech is produced. The act of narration, of having told the story, becomes part of the new event world.

Toward the end of the mediation between Amina and Ahmed, the kadhi counsels each party to try harder to cooperate, offering gender-specific advice about being a good husband or a good wife. He also takes the opportunity to blame their families for the ongoing conflict. As well, he defines the role that he will play in future conflict resolution, suggesting that he should be approached only after family members have failed to reach a solution. Perhaps the kadhi is guarding against excessive use of his office; however, his counsel ensures that he will likely be a party to future disputes. And yet the couple may find it difficult to appear before the kadhi again, if they have ignored his advice. Thus, the participant structures of future disputing events have been preconstructed by the kadhi, and subsequent actions by either party will be undertaken with awareness of his ambivalent presence. The "future world" of real-life conversation will necessarily reflect what has transpired in court.

NASIRA: Now indeed he began to be angry
and to abuse me
He told me
I should get out (.)
I should give him his house keys.
I told him first
"I will not get out."
He told me
"Get out. And anything at all that I bought for you I want it myself."
I told him
"The first thing like your TV take [it]."
He told me
"Starting today, this TV, don't you turn it on."
I told him
"If you have told me to get out and to give you the keys -here, we will leave. I will not turn on the TV, me."
"Ah, okay and my kid I want (him/her). And my money, I want it, you will produce it."
I told him
"You didn't give the money to me. The money you took to our place, so go after your money at our place."
He left.

(FROM A KADHI'S COURT MEDIATION)

Portraying Gendered Speakers: Reported Conversations

In giving accounts of domestic conflict, Ahmed and Amina—the couple profiled in the previous chapter—relied extensively on reports of the speech they and others produced during their many altercations. Through reported speech, they advanced the narrated action and provided insight into their own perceptions of and reactions to the conflict. In court, speakers act out dialogues in which they yell at their spouses, accept orders from their parents, plead forgiveness, and pronounce divorce. Reported speech can add excitement to a narrative, audibly displaying the perpetrators of blameworthy or mitigating acts, and thus contributes to disputants' attempts to address the tasks of disputing. As studies of reported speech have shown, quoting the words of others is a means of "sharing" onerous linguistic tasks, that is, making others take responsibility for insults, accusations, or interpretations of a situation. The more complex the participation frames in which reporting is accomplished, the more opportunities for shifting responsibility for speech that includes controversial messages or consequences (Hill and Irvine 1992; Hill and Zepeda 1992; Irvine 1992, 1996). In Kadhi's Court disputes, speakers are frequently operating within multiple participation frameworks, and, as I argue in this chapter, they engage in gendered strategies of producing reported speech and of moving across participant frameworks.

Courtroom reports of conversations depict Swahili people enacting gender-appropriate roles—the pronouncing husband and the persevering wife—in conversations outside court. The content and sequencing of reported speech portray men as initiating and controlling most interactions and women as responding to men and complying with their direction. The fact that this asymmetrical division of agency and patiency is represented in the reports of *both men and women* is intriguing in light of the contrast between these depictions and the actual participation structures of disputing in court, where Swahili women do, in effect, challenge men. By examining reported speech in Kadhi's Court cases and mediations, this chapter exposes the contradictory images of men and women as speakers that are produced linguistically and metalinguistically. In Kadhi's Court, the production of reported speech contributes to the constitution of gender by displaying ideologically saturated perspectives on the speaker giving the report, on the relationships between the reporter, the original speaker, and others co-present in court, and on other aspects of linguistic ideology that concern gender and speech.

The following section demonstrates that disputants' productions of reported speech in Kadhi's Court accounts not only emphasize critical moments of conflict (as would be predicted by the literature on reported speech in U.S. courts) but also reflect understandings about speech particular to the Swahili context. Subsequent sections examine how gender is portrayed and constructed in Kadhi's Court accounts through reports of conversations outside court. The final section examines instances when reported speech is avoided, discouraged, or disallowed and provides evidence of the aspects of linguistic ideology that operate in court to restrict abusive and obscene speech. Using the example of reported speech, the chapter concludes with the broader point that speech about conflict, particularly speech by women that threatens the *heshima* of those who hear it, is condemned in Swahili cultural understandings about language. These understandings play a significant role in structuring the possibilities for transforming gender relations through disputes.

Reported Speech in Accounts of Conflict

Although kadhis are charged to follow Kenyan rules of evidence and thus exclude hearsay, testimony in Kadhi's Courts generally includes considerable amounts of reported speech.[1] Kadhis do not admonish witnesses to limit reported speech in their accounts, nor do they advise them as to whether such speech will be evaluated as less reliable than other testimony. Kadhis' records of the evidence presented in cases do not generally reflect that something was related as a report of speech rather than as fact.

Russell asserts that the most engaging Kiswahili stories are told at least partly through dialogue, and other scholars conclude similarly that reported speech has dramatic force (Briggs 1988b; Hymes 1981; Russell 1981; Wolfson 1978).[2] As I have argued previously, the claim that a speech feature escalates drama is not necessarily the most important point to make about why it is produced or what function(s) it serves in court.

Reported speech is central to several tasks addressed by disputants. For example, in describing incidents of conflict, the person testifying often feels the need to report what was said as well as what was done (Conley and O'Barr 1990). Surveying research on reported speech in legal contexts, Conley and O'Barr (1990:8) summarize hypotheses about variations in reported speech:

> (1) using direct quotations displaces responsibility because the authority of reported speech resides with the attributed source; (2) direct quotations, especially when performed, are more dramatic and engaging; (3) using direct quotations demonstrates that the reporter was present at the reported event; and (4) direct quotations identify those aspects of an account that the reporter seeks to present as more reliable.

Based on an analysis of trials in U.S. courts, Philips (1986) identifies several forms of reported speech.[3] Quoted speech (direct quotation of words presumably uttered at a prior time) is often reserved for evidence about "critical events." By contrast, reports of substance (speech reported indirectly or merely described) and topic naming are used when providing background information rather than evidence central to claims (see also Hickmann 1992; Lucy 1992). Philips's point that quoted speech is used to convey "critical events" holds for Kadhi's Court, where disputants animate the most serious claims through performed dialogue. Yet, in the Swahili context, the distinction between narrating critical as opposed to background events appears less relevant than Philips found for the United States, as Swahili speakers produce quoted speech to recreate many incidents, even banal ones. Most likely, reported speech is a more central feature of Kiswahili narration in comparison with English.

Whether reported speech constitutes a valid representation of exact words is a central issue in the evaluation of court testimony, which justifies the hearsay rule in many legal contexts. The quoting device itself serves to give quoted speech "more credibility as 'exact words' than other forms of reported speech are given" (Philips 1986:154–55). However, the truth value assigned to reported speech through culturally and linguistically specific ideologies of language varies widely (Coulmas 1986).[4] In coastal Kenya, stories told outside court routinely incorporate embellishments—to evoke surprise or humor—that bear little relation to the actual words spoken in the original event. Rarely is a narrator challenged as to whether the statements were actually uttered (cf. Besnier 1992). For Swahili people, whether speech is quoted depends not only on its relation to critical events but also on the type of speech. For example, some critical events are unspeakable—that is, to repeat the words uttered at the time would be blasphemous, obscene, or extremely embarrassing.

The following excerpt from a Malindi Kadhi's Court mediation demonstrates the use of directly quoted speech to report a critical event. This example involves a mediation in which Atwas is accused of beating Munira, his wife (see "The Beating," appendix C). Atwas first explains how and why he beat Munira. In her account of the conflict, Munira merely reiterates the facts already specified. She then describes the subsequent events, which are critical to her claim that she is entitled to a divorce:

Text 8.1

1	Munira:	Now he when he when he when he finished (.) beating
2		me he said
3		"Oh, I'm not leaving you until you gi:ve me my kid.
4		Isn't you- if you give me the kids, I will leave you."
5		One o'clock the other day, the day of Tuesday
6		indeed it wa::s-
7		I came with them, all those children.
8		I came.
9		I waited with them
10		and he didn't come.

Munira is most concerned to describe the critical speech event, which she interprets as a bargain. The terms of the bargain required her to give him custody of their children in order to secure a divorce. As she describes, her attempts to comply with the bargain failed. In a subsequent description of another instance of violence, Munira again refers to the bargain and her hopes that Atwas will finally honor it and divorce her. Several authors have interpreted double reporting as emphasizing the incident reported (Philips 1986; see also Hickmann 1992). Moreover, double reporting contributes to the repetition that characterizes reports of enduring domestic conflict.

Inasmuch as opposing parties tell different stories about "what happened," so they differ in reporting "what was said." The following excerpt is from a mediation in which Shaaban is accused of beating his wife, Rukia (see "The Knife," appendix C). They are in their twenties and have had a short, stormy marriage marked by much conflict and many attempts at reconciliation before elders. Speaking in front of the Malindi kadhi, Shaaban tells a long narrative that becomes animated when he recounts the incident that has brought them to court. As he describes, he was left with their baby when, unbeknownst to him, Rukia went out. When she returned, he confronted her:

Text 8.2

1	Shaaban:	I asked her
2		"Where are you coming from?"
3		She said
4		"I'm coming from the toilet."
5		"You're coming from the toilet, and I am at the hotel
6		here. Why didn't you take the kid to the toilet? Why
7		should he cry? You didn't enter here?"
8		There, to the toilet, you see, she started to go back
9		again
10		(I followed her).
11		I tried to hit her three times (.)
12		you see, bwana?
13		I went back to my place.

Rukia's nightly trips to the toilet have been a source of conflict in this marriage, as Shaaban has previously accused her of visiting a lover during the outings. In this instance, he focuses on her disregard for their baby as the blameworthy act that leads him to hit her. His account continues for some time before Rukia has the opportunity to offer a counterdepiction.

Rukia's description of the beating occurs well into her long narrative of their many problems. Her version differs somewhat from Shaaban's:

Text 8.3

1	Rukia:	I went out
2		I went to my place, to the toilet.
3		Right then I returned.
4		When I returned
5		he was sitting
6		"Where are you coming from?"
7		"The toilet."
8		"Where are you coming from?"
9		"I'm coming from the toilet."
10		I kept quiet.
11		He hit me, the first time here and here

A comparison of his account and hers further demonstrates that quoted speech is rarely an exact repetition of what was said at the time. The differences themselves indicate more than the fact that at least one party is lying or misremembering. The accounts share the report of the first critical question-and-answer sequence through which Rukia claims she has been out at the toilet. By following this sequence with his own repetition of her answer and a series of questions, Shaaban depicts Rukia as guilty of abandoning the baby and thereby blameworthy. By contrast, Rukia merely repeats the question-and-answer sequence, which tends not only to emphasize its importance but also to suggest harassing behavior by the questioner.

By topic-naming her act of "keeping quiet," Rukia offers no reason for the beating. Thus, she depicts Shaaban as irrational and guilty, while she appears to be a "blameless victim." As Philips (1995) demonstrates, women's reports of escalating violence tend to portray the female victim as having performed no action that could be construed as provoking the accused to commit violence.[5] In part, this stems from the fact that speech reported in sequential relation to action is a critical means through which the image of the blameless victim is created. Philips demonstrates that this applies across cultures and offers several explanations that, at their root, posit universals of gender, power, or language.[6] Based on examples from the Swahili data, in which women routinely depict themselves as refraining from speech or action that would suggest they occasioned the violence against them, I agree with Philips that this tactic is pervasive and also that it contributes to the portrayal of women as passive victims.

Several aspects of Shaaban's account bolster the interpretation that he provides justifications for his actions and thus attempts to mitigate blame. In the following excerpt, which comes directly after his account above, Shaaban engages the issue of Rukia's staying at her family's restaurant rather than at the couple's matrimonial home:

Text 8.4

1	Shaaban:	When I returned, me
2		I saw that she stayed right there at the house.
3		Doesn't it mean,
4		if you have a disagreement with your wife,
5		isn't [it] necessary that she stays there?
6		If you reconcile,
7		you'll reconcile while apart?
8		She moved, this one.

9	She shouldn't go over there to the restaurant
10	you see.
11	And now I have already known
12	she stays there
13	stays at the restaurant
14	you see.
15	I stayed the first day, the second day, the third day
16	I went to call her mother, bwana.
17	( ) I, that we hear each other and my wife
18	meaning, I don't feel bad
19	meaning, that this didn't originate with me, bwana
20	every person has to do this to his wife ( )
21	there, I did to my wife my work.
22	She already knows.

In describing what happened after the beating, Shaaban criticizes Rukia's decision to move away from him. He also asserts what generally happens when people fight. Although he seems to be making a universally applicable point, he actually sets out what a *man* would generally do to reconcile. In referring to every man's actions toward a wife, Shaaban also uses the second person singular to draw the kadhi into expressing agreement. In his final assessment, Shaaban suggests that by hitting Rukia he was only doing what others do to their wives. His use of "person" *(mtu)* lends a generalizing quality to the statement, although it clearly applies only to men. The use of "my work" as a reference to beating Rukia suggests that this activity is, like work, routinely and perhaps necessarily performed, even if odious.

My extended analysis of Shaaban's account provides an example that dovetails with the claim made in previous chapters that, by seeking to ally with the kadhi, men rely on tag questions and assertions about the universality of their approaches to conflict. These features contribute to men's presenting themselves as authoritative speakers in court. Moreover, as the next section demonstrates, reported speech allows men to establish themselves authoritatively at an even more subtle level, and it also affords both men and women the opportunity to sculpt images of themselves and others as gendered speakers.

Reported Speech and the Construction of Disputing Subjects

Reporting dialogue presumably spoken in a conflict is a significant way in which disputants not only embed their own perspectives on a claim (why something happened, their role or responsibility, etc.) but also influence how the narrators themselves are evaluated for their behavior in both the narrated conflict and the courtroom.

Besnier identifies subtle ways in which reporting speech indicates a speaker's social standing. Examples from the South Pacific island of Nukulaelae demonstrate that reported speech is a vehicle through which speakers manage impressions of themselves as they participate in gossip sessions where incidents of conflict are discussed. Besnier (1990) profiles a speaker who, in narrating an instance of conflict, reports his own speech in ways that associate "his role in the reported conversation with the social attributes of the most responsible and powerful members of the community." The speaker establishes himself as authoritative and credible by self-reporting his speech as "calm, thoughtful, and level-headed." Moreover, by producing assessments through these reports, the speaker makes subtle comments on the behavior of others, which position others as deficient and, at the same time, invest the narrator with the knowledge and authority to judge others (306–8).[7] Through depicting himself as offering the opening lines of reported conversations, the speaker emphasizes his own superior standing relative to his interlocutors (314). The narrator displays his self-control, credibility, and authority by controlling asymmetrical interactions. Control over interaction is depicted through turn sequencing, types of turns, and the communication of affect. These features are also found by Philips (1995) in female victims' reports of asymmetrical conversations in which they are threatened with violence (see above). Male perpetrators are depicted as initiating turns, and female victims are presented as contributing little in response. The type of control manifest through such asymmetrical conversation differs markedly from that exhibited by Besnier's authoritative narrator; however, in each example, speakers report asymmetrical conversations that, by positioning them in the narrated action, influence the narrative event and the status of the participants (for a general discussion of asymmetrical speech, see Markova and Foppa 1991).

Men's speech—direct and indirect—is routinely reported as initiating verbal interaction. This finding with respect to sequencing is typical of reported speech in both men's and women's accounts of conflict. The least common occurrence is of a woman's direct speech at the beginning of a reported interaction. Moreover, in the accounts of *both men and women,* men control the flow of reported conversation and are more likely to engage in the first-pair parts of adjacency pairs (e.g., demands or accusations) that initiate interactions. Women provide the second-pair parts, thus responding to initial demands and accusations made by men. By assuming a reactive role, women are depicted as less able to direct interaction. In effect, men set verbal interaction into motion and control its progress. Taken overall, the speech attributed to women, through reporting by both men and women, consists of less reported verbal interaction than that attributed to men. When such interaction takes the form of compliance, it portrays a culturally meaningful image of the obedient wife who behaves appropriately, including through her speech.

Reporting Control and Compliance

Three features of reported speech are central to my analysis of who controls conversations (see Besnier 1990) and who is controlled by and through them: (1) the sequencing of speakers; (2) the patterning of adjacency pairs; and (3) variation in the form of reported speech (e.g., whether the speech produced is direct or indirect and the production of verbs of speaking). The accounts given by Rukia and Shaaban above exemplify gendered approaches. In Rukia's account, Shaaban's voice is generally more prominent than her own. The confrontation reported to have occurred around her leaving the house to go to the toilet is representative of how women respond to men's initiating utterances. Shaaban's account of the same incident also displays his control of the interaction.

In several instances in his long account presented in chapter 7, Ahmed reports speech that depicts him as initiating interactions. This pattern is evident below in an excerpt taken from his description of Amina's return from the wake (see "The Wake," appendix C):

Text 8.5

1	Ahmed:	When she came a::t *night* (1)
2		I that time I told her
3		"Now indeed you ful*fil*led that promise of yours that
4		(.) you will co::me whenever. Meaning we did not say
5		that you would go to stay at the wake. How is it that
6		you today you have- you have gone and you have *stayed*
7		(1) at the wake and you come in here in the evening,
8		it's even Monday evening and the children were here,
9		they didn't go to school since morning there weren't
10		any [school] uniforms."

Through these lines, Ahmed outlines each of his accusations about Amina's behavior, including those that he has previously made. These accusations are begun in response to her arrival rather than to any speech on her part. Reports that begin with a man's accusation of some delict are quite common even when it is claims against the man that have brought a couple to court.

Ahmed's long passage of reported accusations is extraordinarily complex in that it reports speech that is itself reported speech. Through topic naming, Ahmed reports that Amina broke a promise, then goes on to report indirectly their discussion of how long she should have stayed at the wake. He contrasts coming "whenever," presumably a quote of Amina, with their "agreement" that she would not stay long, which he reports indirectly—thereby demonstrating that Amina was able to weigh these choices. In reporting their agreement through what they *did not say,* Ahmed invests it with heavy evaluative content, both in the initial scene and in his report in Kadhi's Court. At the same time as a negative report of speech leaves vague what was actually agreed on, that agreement is also made to appear as Amina's only valid choice.

Ahmed reports no response from Amina to his accusations. Her absence as a speaker receives no comment, thus suggesting several interpretations. Perhaps she had no defense to his accusations and thus was unable to offer one. Perhaps her silence represents further disobedience in that she refuses to address her husband's concerns. By effacing Amina as a speaker in this scene, Ahmed positions his own words as those that are most important, an authoritative perspective. Throughout his long account, Ahmed initiates every reported conversation with Amina, either making requests of her or accusations (see Text 7.1, lines 10, 35, 48). Although Amina's report of the same confrontation begins similarly to Ahmed's, she includes her own self-reported speech:

Text 8.6

1	Amina:	Then I entered inside
2		I entered inside
3		I sat down.
4		He asked me
5		"How come since day before yesterday you haven't come?"
6		I started to explain to him
7		"That money that I went with had finished. Now to go
8		from there by foot to here I can't by
9		myself. The road is scary. On Sunday the wake it really

10	was finished. It was finished late afternoon I thought
11	it would be better that I sleep there. Then in the
12	morning I will get the friends who I had come with
13	there to the burial to the wake. We'll come together.
14	We'll go with each other all together those friends up
15	to Ganda where we left each other. I went to my place
16	at my father's."
17	"Now you have been brought by whom?"
18	I told him
19	"I came with dad."
20	"That's a lie you since the day before yesterday, even
21	you, there at the wake, you weren't there. You were
22	here, right here in Malindi. There at your place you
23	aren't there, and there [at the wake] you aren't there.
24	(1.2) You were right here in Malindi."
25	Here in Malindi *what* house? (2.5)

Amina's extensive report of her response to Ahmed's initiating accusations contrasts with Ahmed's intimation that she kept silent. In her own report, she repeats justifications for staying at the wake. Documenting the complex reasoning process that led her to stay longer, she displays a rationality that contrasts with Ahmed's subsequent unfounded accusations. Given the constructed nature of reported speech, it is not uncommon that two reports differ so substantially in the speech that they allege occurred. One similarity, however, is that Ahmed is depicted as initiating and controlling the interaction in both renditions.

Another similarity in the accounts is that Ahmed's initial speech is introduced with a framing device that includes a verb of speaking. He self-reports a statement; she reports a question. In this and other instances of initiating accusations or questions, framing verbs are a means whereby a speaker assumes and holds the conversational floor, thus controlling the conversation. In the latter part of the excerpt above, Amina continues to frame her speech using verbs of speaking; however, as the action advances, Ahmed's speech is quoted without framing. His utterances are also marked by a change in prosody, produced more rapidly and aggressively than Amina's self-reported speech. Moreover, Ahmed's utterances follow hers closely, almost interrupting. Here, the unframed questions are threatening and aggressive, exerting a more severe form of control over the interaction. This example suggests that, in reported speech, framing devices contribute in several ways to the establishment of conversational control. Bau-

man's description of the narrative performance of skilled Texan storytellers who get to a point in a story when the "framing devices fall away
and the quoted speech is left to stand on its own" (1986:64) is also applicable to lively Swahili narration. Yet, in instances of reporting conflict,
the falling away of framing devices can indicate more than a critical event
or an excited, engaged narrator. Rather, the absence of framings can
also indicate increased aggression and attempts to control interaction
even more firmly, as is the case in the reports by Ahmed and Amina.
Narrators face a paradox when they reach this point of the story. They
need to separate the height of escalating passion—indicated through
critical words—from signaling that a speaker was aggressively controlling interaction or speaking without thinking. Thus, depictions by
women of men controlling conversation might make use of framing devices early in an interaction and then drop them to indicate control that
has become unthinking or has transmuted into aggression.

Judging from the presentation of dialogue in court accounts,
women, for the most part, are more likely to follow men's lead by
responding to requests rather than initiating interaction. Even when
women's uncharacteristically aggressive speech is reported, it rarely
deviates from the pattern of gendered conversation. That is, when men
are trying to show that women have been verbally aggressive, they
continue to control reported conversations. The way in which an argument positions the man and woman involved as blameworthy or
abused is only one aspect of what is communicated by reported speech.
Concerns specific to legalistic fault finding are generally cross-cut by
the tendency—of both men and women—to depict the former as
someone who controls and directs and the latter as someone who com-
plies and responds.

Reported speech displays a narrator's perspective on the kinds of
speech appropriate in confrontations. This is especially the case when
the speech is framed as hypothetical or imaginary and thereby reports
conversations that a narrator wishes had occurred or plans to participate
in. Such an utterance opens a mediation involving Aisha and her husband
Omar (see "Tears," appendix C). They have been to Kadhi's Court several times previously. On this occasion, they have come at Aisha's request
after she alleges that Omar hit her. The kadhi prompts her:

Text 8.7
1   Kadhi: Now, for example, you say that he hit you yesterday for
2   what reason?

```
 3   Aisha:    Isn't it the reason,
 4             the thing about taking money (.) from [my] hands,
 5             to take from me by force,
 6             like if he would have told me gently
 7             "You now this [money] don't do anything [with it]. I
 8             will do something with' it to- I have need of that
 9             therefore don't you go anywhere with it. I will do
10             |something else."
11   Kadhi:    |Why, did he tell you [that]?
12   Aisha:    He didn't tell me.
13             He told me
14             "Give me myself my money."
15             Now what am I supposed to think?
16             Even if he tells me
17             "Another time I'll give you other [money]."
18             Lie!
19             That very time he took it in anger (    )
20             |I can't handle this anymore.
21   Kadhi:    |(    ) say matters like this
22   Aisha:    Hm.
23   Kadhi:    if they are true (      ) why, the way it's done
```

Aisha quotes an "idealized encounter" (Goodwin 1982:809)[8] that includes utterances she would have liked Omar to produce. (The kadhi
apparently mistakes her reported speech [lines 7–10] for what actually
occurred, as evidenced by his question [line 11]). This speech, though
it involves a request that any man might make, differs markedly from
the reports of men's requests by either men or women in Kadhi's
Court. The central difference is that it contains more explanation for
the request than is generally the case for men's reported speech. In
short, men need not justify their demands. When Aisha finally reports
what is allegedly Omar's quoted speech (line 14), she includes a rhetorical question to indicate her displeasure at the implications of the request. What she sought in their interaction was an explanation, a form
rarely included in men's reported speech.

Omar's account of the same incident offers an interesting departure in that Aisha is depicted as behaving with more agency than most
wives. However, Omar still retains control over the interaction, in part
through the sequencing of reported speech. This excerpt follows the
interaction above:

Text 8.8

1	Omar:	If I |( ) would have told her in in an |ger
2	Aisha:	|It's so |Huh
3	Omar:	Meaning
4		There at the house
5		there are people.
6		There's a boarder.
7		The first time I called her
8		"(Aisha), come here, where are you going?"
9		She told me
10		"I'm going (1.5) to spend that' (1) money."
11		I told her
12		"I, didn't I tell you? That [money] you should put that
13		aside, you should not use that? I told you that."
14		I told her
15		"Okay give [me]."
16		Then she (.) went out
17		you understand.
18		It shows that she doesn't like what I told her,
19		you see.
20		I told her more than six times
21		until that boarder told her
22		"You, if you don't give him that money, you'll see, if
23		he hits you, then what'll it be?"
24		Him, it's so.

Omar retains control in the interaction, which consists primarily of requests he makes of Aisha. Each of his self-reports is introduced with a framing device, and together they make his requests appear reasonable. Moreover, the number of requests and the warnings about the requests display his thoroughness, another aspect of control. His report of her speech includes a device that holds the audience in suspense, which might be attributed to her original utterance or to his report. Regardless, it suggests the unusual nature of what she had to say—that she was planning to spend the money he had told her to put aside. In addition to using reported speech quite skillfully to demonstrate Aisha's culpability, Omar underlines this conclusion through his assessments of her.

Omar's display of the participation structure of the reported interaction identifies witnesses to the conflict. Reporting the speech of one witness, the boarder, establishes him as present at the incident. More-

over, in Omar's report, the boarder predicts the beating and suggests
that Aisha should expect it. Omar thus demonstrates that Aisha had
knowledge of the consequences of her action yet invited a beating.
More importantly, perhaps, it demonstrates that his own actions appeared reasonable to at least one other individual, thereby reducing
his own culpability. Parmentier (1992) has argued that, by reporting
the speech of others, narrators reduce their own responsibility (see also
Hill and Irvine 1992; Hill and Zepeda 1992; Irvine 1992). In effect,
they allow others to say things that they themselves are reluctant to
say (see also Conley and O'Barr 1990; Philips 1986). Framing an accusation in reported speech allows the narrator to tell the story "without
assuming full responsibility for it" (Duranti 1994:137). Although an
option in Kadhi's Court, very seldom do Swahili men include third
parties in their accounts, even to deflect blame.

Similar to accounts from other men accused of violence, Omar's
story becomes vague when he describes the incident for which he is
most culpable:

Text 8.9

1	Omar:	Even if she's hit,
2		she doesn't want to give those [the money] up.
3		It's necessary, she wants to go out.
4		(Now and I) told her
5		"You give me that money"
6		if it doesn't and
7		in taking it [the money]
8		now, she, indeed (that) she's really pinching me,
9		she's really biting me.
10		|You understand?
11	Aisha:	|Even I didn't bite him at all it's not like that at
12		all.
13	Omar:	|Now it's necessary ( )
14	Aisha:	|Now after taking *his* money
15		I took the kid
16		he's cry:ing.
17		I'm nursing him.
18		After nursing him now
19		he starts to play with him.
20		I told him
21		"Now you've come to do what here?"
22		I pushed him like this.

23		"You, doesn't my kid (.) have need [of me]? Why:: don't
24		I play with him? And, me, too, it's my kid, it's not
25		your kid alone."
26		I told him
27		"No way. I'll go out with the kid."
28		I told him
29		"I'm going okay to my mother's, that my mother ( )?"
30		Okay now I (couldn't decide) that to-
31		Where I will go
32		like, like I will come here
33		like to go to the house or something.
34		(leave) the kid if I go with him
35		or I will go out with him.
36		Okay then he started to raise a fuss.
37		"I will beat you. You can't overcome me. I, if I beat
38		you, you don't know. I didn't- you can't overcome me."
39		Now indeed he started a war that time.
40		( ) beat.
41	Kadhi:	Indeed it's like that but fighting ( )|has no
42		meaning . . .
43	Aisha:	|and
44		every day Mama is forbidden from the house.
45	Omar:	-Every day I tell her-
46	Kadhi:	Meaning, if you bring a war, it will be you
47	Aisha:	First off, it's shameful.

Omar indicates that his request for Aisha to return the money occasions a violent response. Thus, he blames her for starting the violence. Aisha wins the struggle for the conversational floor and tells a version of the incident that minimizes her contribution to the violence; she depicts the beating as Omar's response to her reasonable attempt to leave. In reporting her own speech, she produces framing devices and offers her perspective at the time. She reports his speech with no framing, insinuating aggression on his part.

Through the speech produced in both her own and her opponent's accounts, Aisha is presented as a woman with agency. In Omar's account her actions, albeit carried out in silence, are forms of agency that both react to his requests and further escalate the conflict. Aisha's self-reported speech is more agentive than is typical for Swahili women. She depicts herself as initiating interaction, though Omar retains control even as he encourages her to take an active role in their marriage. After having reported that Aisha bit him for no reason, Omar says the following:

Text 8.10

1	Omar:	Yes, people definitely they will say, this way,
2		and there many people will say there,
3		that I hit her.
4		I told her words
5		"You bite me, if I feel pain, necessarily I defend
6		myself."
7		You understand?
8		It's not like it's the first time.
9		You see this.
10		There are scars from before.
11		I didn't hit her until she
12	Aisha:	You have slapped |me when I hit you.
13	Omar:	|And another scar is this one.
14		You hurt me for something that hasn't any meaning.
15		|It's so-
16	Kadhi:	|Okay okay-
17	Omar:	-By God again.
18		Every day I tell her, me,
19		I tell her
20		"You were married the first time, it's you who should
21		teach me, people do like this and like that. It's not
22		everyday to fight with each other and the like and
23		yelling and screaming."

Behind Omar's warning that he will defend himself if hit lies the assumption that violence is the proper response to violence. In self-reporting the warning, Omar mitigates his blameworthiness: Aisha was warned and could have avoided being hit by not biting him. The aside, reinforced by tag questions, further displays Aisha's culpability.

Finally, Omar contends that Aisha should take more authority in their marriage, given that she was married previously. This signals a move from the disruptive fighting he has described to what Briggs (1988b:481) calls "counseling speech" in his analysis of Warao dispute mediations. Omar demonstrates that he is capable of substituting exhortative counseling for fighting words, thereby signaling that he has already tried the very shift that the kadhi is attempting. His manner of suggesting an expanded role for Aisha in fact reveals his own control in their relationship. The initial "I tell her" suggests that he directs

their interaction even as he grants her authority. By reporting his offer
that she guide their marriage, Omar makes the subtle critique that she
fails to assume agency. Aisha herself is caught in this paradox. To assume authority in their marriage goes against norms of gendered interaction; to abdicate this responsibility defies her husband.

Women are also invested in maintaining the image of their compliance, and they sometimes describe that compliance in relation to third
parties. Women report the speech of third parties more often than do
men and in much the same way that they report dialogue with their
spouses. That is, they report the requests of the third party and their
own responses to and compliance with them. They advance the excuse
that they behaved in a manner—now seen as blameworthy—because
they were told to. In general, however, they demonstrate more indirectly, through the replay of conversations, that they are the type of
person (e.g., proper woman) who takes direction from authorities. For
Swahili women, compliance is an admirable quality to demonstrate to
the kadhi and sometimes an issue in the dispute. They show compliance by reporting conversations in which they respond to the requests
of authority figures. Compliance can be manifest in the sequencing as
well as the substance of such reported conversations. As the epigraph
to this chapter indicates, Nasira produces a considerable amount of
reported speech in her account of a dispute with her husband, Juma,
over neighborhood gossip that leads him to insist that she leave their
house (see "The TV," appendix C). After telling how she left, she reports what her parents told her to do. This report not only justifies
her subsequent actions but also demonstrates that she readily takes
direction from those in authority:

Text 8.11

1	Nasira:	He went to his place.
2		I took my things, since he told me to leave,
3		meaning
4		I had one kid by him.
5		The others are grandchildren of mine.
6		I took my things,
7		I took my clothes,
8		"Let's go to our place, our house" (1.5)
9		When I arrived at the house
10		I went
11		I explained what had happened.
12		They told me

13		"If he has *thrown* you out, he has told you to get out,
14		he wants his house keys, if it's that he is *angry,* he
15		will come here to the house meaning, his, our place, he
16		knows [it]. But if he has be*liev*ed this thing is true,
17		he will not come. So you return, take everything that
18		you know is yours, you clear out, give him his keys.
19		Ask permission at work [for] like two weeks you come to
20		the house. Wait at our place. He knows where it is. If
21		he needs *you* 'one week' will be enough for him, he will
22		come. If he has no need of you, one week finishes, you
23		will return to work. You will seek out any place at all
24		to wait and see what to do."
25		Okay I came to work.
26		I asked permission,
27		it was 'four days.'
28		That day of Tuesday they didn't count at work because
29		it was a 'Public Holiday.'
30	Kadhi:	Hmm.
31	Nasira:	They gave me four days.
32		I returned.
33		I went to my place to the house.
34		I took my thi:ngs,
35		those things which I know are mine.
36		Those which he bought [for] himself
37		even if I wanted them
38		I left for him every thing of his.

Nasira's discussion of returning to her family for advice demonstrates how women rely on authoritative third parties to justify behavior. In announcing her decision to go home, she emphasizes "home" by repeating the reference to "our place" with an almost poetic quality (line 15). She does not quote her explanation of the conflict; however, she reports in detail her family's advice and her compliance with their wishes. Through their authority, she behaves in ways that are later questioned and criticized by Juma. Her obedience to the reported requests of every authority figure emphasizes her good character as a woman.

In Kadhi's Court, Swahili men and women are invested in depicting themselves and those around them as properly gendered speakers. Yet men and women produce reported speech in ways that catch them in paradoxes. Those women who have come to court to make accusations against men are essentially initiating a discussion, one that is public and controversial. As initiators, they risk behaving in ways that are denigrated through cultural ideologies of how women should speak. Perhaps they seek to cover this very contradiction through representing themselves as verbally compliant in their self-reports of speech in testimony. Yet, by minimizing their agency, women cast doubt on their ability to be considered agentive speakers in the courtroom. For their part, men hold back from depicting wives with whom they have fought as completely disobedient, even with respect to speech, as they need to retain control over their own impression as a man who can manage a household. Even as they report delicts such as violence on the part of a spouse, they emphasize the image of themselves as wielding authority through the gendered control of conversations.

Reports of Abusive Speech

Reports of some kinds of speech are not considered appropriate in court, even if the speech constitutes critical evidence in a claim. Abusive language includes name-calling, criticizing an addressee's family members, and uttering profanity or other conventionally recognized abusive terms. Offensive utterances are identified by the Kiswahili verbs "to abuse" *(ku-tukana, ku-shutumu)* and the noun phrases "bad words" *(maneno mabaya)*, "dirty words" *(maneno machafu)*, and "abusive words" *(matukano, matusi)*. To utter a curse *(laana)* is a related, though more circumscribed, speech act in that it often includes a specific condemnation produced in a formulaic way. Abuses and curses both have illocutionary force—their utterance performs an act. Abusive language occupies the curious position of being thought of as both useless and powerful in that it injures the recipient through insult and also anyone co-present through making them witnesses to inappropriate speech. Because linguistic ideology characterizes abusive language as threatening the *heshima* of its producers, its addressees, and anyone who hears it, such language is rare in conversations involving Swahili people. The few times I witnessed abusive speech produced in arguments outside court, I noticed that those present turned away in shame or reacted with sounds of disapproval. Children are severely admonished for using "bad words." Anyone who uses such words is said to have "no manners" and to create problems.

In severely troubled relationships, incidents of conflict that include abusive speech are not uncommon. Only persons who are very angry at one another or emotionally estranged as a couple or unstable as individuals are believed to produce such language. Abusive language, as a symptom of underlying problems, indexes extremely bad relations between spouses. Such language is considered inappropriate and provocative in a marital dispute, regardless of the context. However, uttering abusive words is not an offense that is actionable in Kadhi's Court (cf. Murphy 1990; Philips 1994a, 1995). Rather, disapproval of abusive language is framed through metalinguistic statements that, in counseling mild speech among family members, draw on Swahili ethics.

Most Swahili people want to avoid being accused of producing abusive speech. It is a direct reflection of character as much as of the state of relations between the two parties. Gender and class are critical factors that determine who might produce abusive speech. Those of the elite classes are thought to avoid it. Those of the lower classes, who are routinely depicted as diminished in *heshima*, might be more likely to produce such speech. Men produce a wider range of forms of speech and are thus more familiar with abusive language. Men who produce abusive speech are assumed to have a temper *(mkali)* that leads them to fly off the handle. Women, who are generally less likely to encounter such terms, are also less likely to produce them. A wife accused of using abusive language risks being thought of as both disobedient and having no *heshima*.

Disputants in Kadhi's Court are caught in a difficult position with respect to abusive speech. In some instances, abusive speech is central to the conflict that has brought them to court. An incident when such speech was uttered might explain the escalation of violence from words to physical action. And yet, in reporting abusive language as evidence, disputants reveal themselves to have participated in extremely noxious situations, even if they did not utter the words. Accordingly, most reports of abusive speech in Kadhi's Court accounts are made through topic naming with little elaboration of the specific words. "S/He abused me" (*Alinitukana*) is the most common phrasing for such accusations.

The few attempts to report such speech in court, and the reactions such attempts engender, portray some of the most dramatic incidents of domestic conflict. At the same time, they also reveal the cultural and legal barriers to the production of certain kinds of speech in court (see Philips 1994a, 1995). These attempts demonstrate important connections between the story world of narrated action and the event world of Kadhi's Court. In court, condemnations of abusive speech and reports of such speech are the most specific prohibitions on language. Speakers narrating reports of abusive speech are interrupted, told to stop speaking, or warned that they are speaking in disruptive ways. This suggests that responsibility for damaging speech can "leak" from the person who uttered it in the story to the narrator who reports it (see, e.g., Hill and Zepeda 1992). The metalinguistic prohibition of such speech sets the terms for how speakers can transform social relations in the event world.

The example of Atwas and Munira displays the sometimes critical role that abusive speech plays in escalations of violence (see also Philips 1995). Atwas justifies his blameworthy act of hitting Munira by describing her verbal abuse of his mother:

Text 8.12

1	Atwas:	"Munira?" "Eh." "Do you remember that I've not yet
2		divorced you?" "Ah I don't want your (stupid, stupid)
3		words stuff like dogs." "Ah I'm a dog? I ask you, good
4		word, with patience, by a careful road." She abused me.
5		You told me I am a dog, it's nothing. Tell me anything
6		but when she began to (leaving) from my room. "Me I
7		didn't call you into my room get out get out, until
8		your end." When she started to abuse my mother "your
9		mother's cunt"
10	Munira:	Don't you tell a lie.
11	Atwas:	Be quiet. I am not speaking to you I am speaking to the
12		Kadhi.
13	Munira:	I will take an oath that I didn't abuse your mother.
14		Okay why is he quiet?
15	Kadhi:	Leave it, leave it.
16	Atwas:	Don't you speak to me. Have you heard, bwana? When
17		she dared to abuse my mother "your mother's cunt" that
18		moment right then a slap came from me this moment I
19		slapped her one time.

Munira becomes agitated as Atwas indirectly accuses her of having a lover and describes a series of bad names that she called him. But she is moved to contest his account only when he reports her utterance of a severe form of abusive speech. In addition to wanting to deny the charge, there are several possible motivations for Munira's interruption. First, whether true or not, no one wants it repeated that they uttered such widely disapproved speech. Second, had Munira uttered these terms, it would have suggested that the marriage was terribly damaged.

As the example suggests, abusive words are often uttered at the very height of reporting an incident of conflict, at the moment when the narrator is most deeply engaged in performance. Pronounced with raised volume and pitch, the words convey the vehemence with which they were presumably said. An interruption pulls the narrator back into the event world where interlocutors insist that such speech should not be uttered. Indeed, Munira offers to use another speech act, an oath, to erase the assumption left by Atwas that she uttered the abusive words.[9] Atwas appeals to the kadhi in order to preserve his position on the conversational floor and also to erase Munira's interruption.

In many instances, it is the kadhi rather than a disputant who protests reports of verbal abuse. The following excerpt depicts Zulecha and Saidi, who have come to Kadhi's Court for the second time in a month for mediation of their numerous problems (see "Words," appendix C). In describing an unsatisfactory home life, Zulecha accuses Saidi of visiting another woman at night, and Saidi accuses Zulecha of listening to the gossip of others, which is full of lies about him. In the following excerpt, which comes after a long account given by Saidi, Zulecha alleges that she has been mistreated, and she is concerned to recount the resulting strained relations in her natal family:

Text 8.13

1	Zulecha:	And I have persevered a lot a lo:t with him a *who:*le lot
2		ma:ny days
3	Kadhi:	Why up to now don't you persevere?
4	Zulecha:	until it's got to thi:s. Me, it's not the first time to
5		forbid me

This example begins with a reference to Zulecha's perseverance in the face of serious marital conflict. She then describes several incidents in which Saidi behaved badly to her relatives, who are also related to him. She insists that they are fed up with his attempts to turn them against her. Through topic naming, she accuses him of having committed blameworthy acts, such as making suicide threats to her family and refusing to deliver their messages.

Text 8.14

1	Kadhi:	Yes
2	Zulecha:	"My father" he tells me. | Okay "me too it's my father
3		but ( )"
4	Kadhi:	| Yes indeed what will you do
5	Zulecha:	"And my wife ( )" teasing ( ) "Go."
6		"I will go." "Go you devil your mother's cunt
7		devil."

8	Kadhi:	Okay listen
9	Saidi:	Kadhi bwana you know this one, my wife, I am not able
10		to 'support' I tell you because many times she says her
11		things meaning she believes lies she holds by them.
12		|Until ( ) it's her thing, I
13	Zulecha:	| "your mother's cunt"
14	Saidi:	Every day I will go me
15	Kadhi:	For example like that

Just at the moment that Zulecha begins a direct report of Saidi's verbal abuse of her father, the kadhi interrupts to deflect the conversation and to suggest a resolution other than telling the full story.

Kadhis routinely interrupt and curtail abusive speech, dismissing it as "silliness" *(upuzi)* and otherwise indicating its inappropriateness. Their refusal to listen to reports of verbal abuse has little legal justification (particularly during mediations); rather, they turn to the cultural belief that such speech should never be uttered, even as evidence. They push narrators toward speech that begins to resolve the problem. Thus, from the intensity of storytelling narration, speakers are catapulted into the event world, where their participation in speech toward resolution is required. This abrupt shift indicates the proper method of handling arguments: conflict does not require full-blown descriptions of delicts but rather should move swiftly to resolution, hiding some matters. In contrast to ideological support for "disentangling" in other contexts, some words are much better left unsaid in the Swahili context (see Watson-Gegeo and White 1990; cf. Besnier 1990).

When interruptions abruptly halt narrated reports of abusive speech, getting at the truth becomes less important than protecting those present from hearing reports of such speech. The narrative event becomes the central focus of the interaction, and rules for appropriate speech assume prominence as the topical focus. The point is made both explicitly and implicitly that full narration of "what happened" stands in the way of resolution. Such examples demonstrate that the metapragmatic arrangement that holds in court can be averted at any time, including through telling the wrong kind of story.

Conclusion

Swahili couples rarely engage in screaming the worst insults at one another—either at home or through reported speech produced in court. Thus, my inclusion of the above examples requires the additional statement that these outbursts are generally reserved for profoundly debilitated relationships. They are sometimes artifice and often desperation. Cognizant that reports of abusive speech occasion reprimands and silencing from kadhis, I considered eliminating the examples or presenting them with particularly offensive terms deleted. My concern, of course, was to "hide matters" that most Swahili people would not want revealed in order to protect their *heshima*. I justify including them because presenting the words in the context of their utterance in court also demonstrates the denunciation of such speech by Swahili speakers themselves. On the one hand, it shows that Swahili people reject abusive speech and thus value other kinds of language. On the other hand, however, my inclusion of such speech and its silencing, and my own thoughts of censorship, reveals the overarching and ever-present attempt to control what is revealed about problems in Swahili homes. The hegemonic insistence on hiding abusive language has the effect of curtailing stories of conflict that men and women might tell about their lives. This prohibition falls most squarely on women, for whom the narration of conflict, which might include unpleasant incidents and words, is critical to challenging and transforming domestic relations.

Swahili women who complain in court embody a contradiction. Through their participation in cases and mediations, they generally stand in gross violation of appropriate speech, and yet, in so many dialogues, they are also routinely depicted as compliant wives. They respond, verbally and otherwise, rather than initiate. With respect to women, a multifaceted and contradictory gendered speaker is produced through different aspects of linguistic usage. For men, the image of the pronouncing husband is retained more solidly at a range of levels. This cuts two ways. On the one hand, men benefit from looking like authorities in court (unless they abuse this power and end up in confrontation with the kadhi or clerk). On the other hand, they must shoulder much of the responsibility for interaction in and out of court, including in their marriage. Gendered images that both reflect and contest the persevering wife and the pronouncing husband are revealed by examining the participant roles in court, including the roles presented in depictions of reported conversations. These multiple gendered images are motivated by ideological notions of what kinds of speech are appropriate for Swahili men and women. At the same time, through use in court, they offer metalinguistic and metapragmatic contributions to the construction not only of gender relations but also of linguistic ideology as it concerns gender and speech.

CLERK: How come you didn't say this at first, (you were just quiet)? If
          you want this man, and you don't want this man, you too say
          "I don't want him." Here is the place to- to- to want and to
          refuse, you see? There are two books here. For marrying and for
          divorcing. It's right here, the place to do both of these.

RUKIA: (We'll say, then we'll go, and he'll say something else.)

CLERK: And I have forbidden that. If he doesn't want you he says here.
          If a person doesn't want his partner, they should say right here.
          There's nothing like going and saying over there. Here indeed is
          the correct place for saying, it's not there. Here indeed is the
          place.

SHAABAN: And a person, your complaints all those there say them here

CLERK: We should finish right here.

SHAABAN: Right

CLERK: If you have- Finally, your complaints, I don't want a lot of
          words. We, if you- if you don't want your partner, you should
          say here if you want him/her.

(FROM A MEDIATION IN KADHI'S COURT)

Pronouncing and Persevering:
Ideology and Metalinguistics in Disputes

In the epigraph, each speaker makes explicit metalinguistic statements that reflect cultural and legal ideas about how language should be produced. For example, by insisting that requests for divorce are appropriately made in court (rather than at home after the mediation), the clerk defines the court as a linguistic context appropriate for Rukia's claims and thus questions why Rukia had previously remained silent when asked if she wanted to end the contentious marriage. The use of language to talk about what language does is common in Kadhi's Court and can enable speakers to articulate their claims more effectively. Not surprisingly, explicit talk about talk can also produce precisely the opposite effect by silencing some speech.

This chapter focuses on how Swahili people produce metalinguistic utterances—that is, commentary on talk—in Kadhi's Court disputes. Scholarship on metalinguistics demonstrates that ideas about language, which can be expressed implicitly or explicitly, are part of every interactional context (see, e.g., Philips 1992, 1994a; Silverstein 1976, 1979; Woolard 1992).[1] In disputes, explicit metalinguistic statements routinely articulate ideas about how disputing should occur at the same time as their deployment shapes interaction.[2] By identifying what kinds of speech are appropriate for conflict resolution, explicit metalanguage, which is ideologically saturated, not only shapes interaction but also influences the interpretation of instances of interaction at issue in disputes (e.g., reported arguments). Moreover, metalinguistic utterances can generate further conflict, which attests to their role in social transformation (Matoesian 1993; Shuman 1986). Linguistically creative social effects are possible when implicit and explicit utterances about language are juxtaposed in a context where talk is the primary activity.

Although this chapter focuses directly on metalinguistics, previous chapters have drawn attention to other aspects of linguistic ideology in the processes whereby gender is performed through speech. For example, chapters 6 and 7 interpreted the gender-patterned production of accounts of conflict in relation to ideologies that link women to storytelling and men to authoritative speech. Through producing accounts, speakers index gender, a process that relies on an idea of the relation between genres and the gendered stances they accomplish. Though culturally salient, these cultural ideas need not be expressed overtly in court in order to shape the production and interpretation of speech that indexes gender. In chapter 8, I concluded that the images of gendered interaction presented through reported speech contrast with the participant roles of the disputants producing them. The obedient wife of reported conversations presents an image quite divergent from that of the woman who exposes family conflict by telling stories in court.

Reported speech is an important form of implicit metapragmatics in that it comments indirectly on the relation between language and context. Because people are relatively unaware of the metalinguistic level of speech—especially the metapragmatic level—the explicit, articulated "theory" and the implicit "practice" can contradict one another in a given conversation. Such disjunctures offer possibilities for creative reformulation (Silverstein 1979). My focus on the contradictions among these features demonstrates my point that gendered subjects are constituted through speech that operates within and against cultural ideas about speech and speakers. Those ideas, which sometimes display contradictory images of gender, in turn set limits on how individuals engage, reproduce, and transform their gendered positions.

After a brief discussion of how metalinguistic statements operate in court to direct interaction, index gender, and contribute to the construction of gendered subjects, I analyze three cultural ideas about speech, which, when produced in Kadhi's Court cases and mediations, express the ideological devaluation of telling stories. Although this chapter examines specific instances of the production of linguistic items, drawing on cases and mediations in much the same way as previous chapters, it also summarizes the multilayered analysis of the construction of gender that I have been developing. By showing how these ideologically saturated statements devalue stories and, more importantly, storytellers, I offer the final point in my argument about how gender is constituted in multiple and contradictory ways. The argument turns on the connection between telling a story of conflict and complaining, an act that exposes or harms others. The entextualized stories of conflict that women tell in making claims are metalinguistically vulnerable to being devalued as complaints.

Ideology and Metalinguistics in Disputes

In Kadhi's Court, authoritative statements about language are enshrined in procedural and evidentiary rules, which, despite their formal
status, are only loosely applied, even in cases (see chapter 5). When
speakers produce explicit metalinguistic observations in Kadhi's
Court, they tend to draw on ones that reflect cultural, rather than institutional, conventions. The ideology of not exposing the problems of
one's family shapes how and whether disputes enter the legal arena
and, once there, how they are presented. In the course of interaction
in court, speakers express aspects of this and other ideologies about
language. This is especially the case in mediations, where the rules for
speech are open to contestation that routinely involves claims about
the forms of speech appropriate for conflict resolution.

The attention to implicit and explicit metapragmatics in Charles
Briggs's analysis of a Warao mediation provides a useful model for
my approach, particularly because Briggs (1988b) links the social creativity of language to language ideology. In a dispute described by
Briggs, a Warao man, through narrating the inappropriate behavior
of his wife, depicts his own reported speech as conforming to genres
useful in conflict resolution—that is, counseling speech and exhortative speech, rather than accusations and "bad words." Briggs makes
the point that the man's depiction of himself as counseling and ex-
horting indexes his appropriate behavior in the moment of conflict.[3]
This point is similar to the demonstration in chapter 8 of how Swahili
disputants depict themselves speaking as appropriately gendered subjects in asymmetrical reported conversations. Briggs goes further to
show that "this implicit framework is complemented by a running explicit metapragmatic commentary on particular actions and on appropriate modes of talking and acting" (1988b:461). Thus, the Warao
man presents himself as capable of operating in the appropriate metapragmatic frame for conflict resolution, and, if anyone doubts the nature of that frame, he reminds them explicitly (cf. Haviland 1988).

In Kadhi's Court, the production of explicit statements about language has directive force in shaping interaction. For example, statements that value counseling or exhortative speech over reports of gossip establish the importance of moving to the former in order to resolve
conflict. They provide a charter for appropriate speech and build a
case for the good character of whoever adopts it. As argued in previous
chapters, the shift from narration to speech forms that are directed
more pointedly at conflict resolution also typifies disputing in Kadhi's

Court. Such shifts are effected in large part by third-party mediators or adjudicators who explicitly urge disputants to forsake stories of conflict *(maneno)* and engage in other kinds of speech, such as conversation *(mazungumzo)* or counseling *(shauri)*, that might lead to an agreement. Or, in legal cases, disputants are encouraged to articulate clearly claims that address legal tasks (e.g., blaming). They are counseled to focus on speech that works toward agreement *(masikizano)*. Sometimes they are encouraged to pray rather than recapitulate scenes of conflict.

Although kadhis and clerks possess the unquestioned authority to shift the metapragmatic frame of interaction in court, litigants themselves produce speech that also encourages and effects shifts. Briggs lys out the consequences of moving from one metapragmatic frame to another: "successful mediation thus requires the transformation of 'bad words'—conflictual discourse—into counseling speech. I have argued that this process transforms the formal features of the discourse, moves the discourse from narration to exhortation, and effects a shift from token-based to type-based metapragmatic elements" (1988b: 481). Briggs notes the distinction between token-based elements, which are productions of kinds of speech, and those that are type-based, which are characterizations of kinds of speech. The movement from tokens to types typifies the route to successful dispute resolution and at the same time is fundamental to how social relations are restructured. This pattern is also common in Kadhi's Court.

Almost as an aside, Briggs notes that, in Warao disputes, only men produce tokens of appropriate disputing language (e.g., exhortative speech) or the metapragmatic devices that define and call for appropriate speech. Although male disputants as well as mediating third parties produce such speech, Briggs does not consider what this asymmetry means for the negotiation of gender in disputing. A similar dynamic of moving from narrating the events of conflict to counseling (or calls for counseling) operates in Kadhi's Court mediations and cases in gender-patterned ways. Swahili women resist the move toward speech that ignores or minimizes their narratives, such as legal pronouncements, counseling, or prayer. As Briggs would predict, Swahili women produce token-based examples of speech, especially narrative, rather than type-based observations as to what might be more appropriate speech. These productions make women vulnerable to the targeted deployment of explicit metalinguistic calls for genres to which they have limited access. At the same time, men's facility with explicit metalinguistics and with the various type-based forms of mediating discourse indexes and extends their authority.

In Kadhi's Court, men comment on the conflict and the disputing context, while women are occupied with telling stories of conflict. Accordingly, men are more likely to produce metalanguage.[4] Women, through particular forms of token-based speech, index themselves as narrators and, by extension, as narrators who risk exposing household problems through their stories. By narrating in the face of metalinguistic calls for speech *other* than stories of conflict, Swahili women risk not only defying their interlocutors (some of whom hold considerable authority over them) but also being viewed and labeled as dangerous complainers and exposers.

To be targeted metalinguistically as someone who produces inappropriate speech can be a serious accusation. Yet Greg Matoesian (1993) makes the important point that "complaints about complaining" are a fundamental feature of disputing discourse, a conversational resource that commonly occurs as a response to an initial statement of complaint. The speaker who responds produces a complaint about the initial complaining statement in order to deflect attention. According to Matoesian (1993:44), the second utterance "represents an elegantly designed and multiplex conversational strategy in which the impact of a prior complaint is mollified and its texture of relevance altered by topical and interactional transformations performed on it."[5] The entire sequence is a "topic slift" that "lifts the relevance of a reply to topic and slips in a response to flaws concerning the actions, motives, or character of the complainant." The shift from conflict stories told to accuse or complain to "complaints about complaining" is a "transituational" possibility in conversation, especially disputes (45).

I draw on Matoesian's example to suggest that the routine conversational gambit of complaints about complaining can operate in tandem with the multiple strategies for shifting metapragmatic frames identified by Briggs. Complaints about complaining may be among a range of ways that accomplish the shift away from conflict stories. I am suggesting that complaints about complaining operate not only as conversational gambits but also at a broader discursive level in mediations and cases to afford those who are the object of complaint the possibility of shifting the topic to the blameworthy actions or character of their accuser. At the discourse level, these complaints gain their force from cultural understandings about complaining and its appropriateness in a given interactional and cultural context (cf. Matoesian

1993). In Swahili disputing, for example, shifts from stories to metalinguistic talk—especially the shifts that rely on complaints about complaining—gain their force from the strong ideology of complaining as inappropriate, particularly when it exposes problems in the household. Moreover, as shown in the examples below, only some speakers are positioned to effect these shifts, and their deployment is subject to cultural understandings about complaints and conflict talk and who is entitled or expected to produce them.

Explicit Metalanguage in Kadhi's Court Disputes

Much of the metalanguage produced in court explicitly and implicitly calls into question the validity of telling stories of conflict as a means of making claims toward resolving the problem. The descriptions of Swahili cultural beliefs about speech in earlier chapters directed attention to the problems attributed to speech about conflict. They suggested that speech about conflict should be limited, especially when produced by women, as they are most suspect with respect to revealing the secrets in Swahili houses. I discuss three of these beliefs—words have no end, words expose, and words harm—which are produced to justify approaches to conflict resolution and which reflect Swahili cultural understandings that prefer hiding matters of conflict. All three also draw on the concept of *maneno*, which translates most literally as "words" but can also refer to gossip, complaints, accusations, and useless talk (see chapter 3). When produced in disputes, these ideas blur the differences among the generic forms referred to by *maneno* and thereby devalue narrative generally. These deployments implicate storytellers as causing problems. Moreover, because women's stories focus on entextualizing tales of conflict that index the link between narration and the gendered exposure of household problems, these metalinguistic deployments, which reflect underlying ideology, facilitate devaluing women as complainers.

By preferring discussions that move toward resolution and thereby avoid additional descriptions of conflict, the kadhi's agenda relies on the type of discourse engaged in by men. Such agendas authorize metalinguistic discussion in the post-account phase of dispute resolution as the appropriate form of speech. Even though many issues put forward by both men and women are ignored, women's stories and women's voices, which are focused on the narrated story, are positioned precariously. Men, like the kadhi, use metalinguistic remarks to gain control over the discussion of conflict and supervise resolution, thereby in-

dexing their authority in court. In bypassing the story and thus subordinating the way in which women discuss conflict, the kadhi privileges
the discourse of men. Although the kadhi occupies a participant role
vested with significant influence, male and female disputants also contribute to the move past conflict talk.

Words Never End

The first of the three Swahili beliefs about language mentioned above
is the notion that words, or talk, necessarily lead to further talk. A
story of an incident can always be followed by another, perhaps contradictory, story or even by the history behind the story. Because they
involve people and social life, stories also have various trajectories of
analysis, any of which might be pursued in the conversation following
an initial telling. The idea of words having no end comes into play in
dispute resolution, where the stakes of getting across certain versions
of a story are high and managing how stories are told or interpreted
offers a critical means of intervention. This idea can be the justification
for some participants to deploy metalinguistic statements to curtail discussion that—because no end is possible—would impede resolution.

Even when disputants present diametrically opposed versions of
an incident, kadhis try to move past words that have no end, particularly narrated stories, and toward speech that will resolve the problem.
In a mediation heard by the kadhi, Juma and Nasira present accounts
of their conflict, which has led Nasira, the wife, to stay with her parents (see "The TV," appendix C). In her account, Nasira claims that
Juma's daughter has abused her verbally. She says that misunderstandings escalated the conflict when she appealed to Juma to resolve
the matter, and, ultimately, he threw her out of their house. Juma
counters that, when he tried to verify the accusations against his
daughter, Nasira began hurling abuses. Yet he insists that he did not
throw her out. In the following excerpt, the kadhi attempts to make
sense of the long narratives in which they made these claims:

Text 9.1
1	Kadhi:	Now. Those are two different words.
2	Juma:	Eh [affirmative]
3	Kadhi:	She said she was thrown out by you because of words/
4		gossip.
5	Nasira:	Eh. [affirmative]
6	Kadhi:	And he says he didn't throw you out. Words/advice he
7		told you truly.

8   Juma: | Yes.
9   Nasira: | He threw me out.
10 Juma: I didn't throw her out.

Nasira offers more information about her departure from the house, which the kadhi interrupts. His lack of interest in pursuing the truth of either account reveals his preference for a reconciliation that would eliminate any further consideration of words about the incidents. Nasira's insistent return to the issues prompts the kadhi's turn to metalinguistics:

Text 9.2

1   Nasira: And those [abusive] words began long ago, like we
2   Kadhi: Yes, now, those words, if you search after words,
3   meaning, words, every day, they don't end.
4   Juma: 'Yeah.'
5   Kadhi: And people are able to waste their time, or waste their
6   lives, because of words. Meaning, words aren't a thing for
7   a person to cling to nor to depend on. A person should
8   hold on to your own ways. You, like a wife, to look after
9   your husband, "How's it going?"
10   Leave words aside.

By insisting that words are undependable and unending, the kadhi justifies his agenda, articulated soon after the passage above, that the couple should put aside the bad things that transpired between them and agree to reconcile. This approach, regularly pursued in Kadhi's Court cases and mediations, ignores disputants' claims—even directly contradictory ones—in setting the agenda for more appropriate conflict resolution.

Although in expressing skepticism about words the kadhi refers specifically to the gossip alleged to have started the problem, he effectively disparages speech about talk more generally. His remarks extend to Nasira's own words of accusation—in court—about the events of the conflict. The connection between the argumentative words produced in disputing, including disputes heard in Kadhi's Court, and the words of the original gossip leaves a problematic image of narrations of conflict. When, as in this example, the kadhi expresses disapproval of gossip, he devalues the gossip, subsequent reports of that gossip, and also, by extension, the act of relating *maneno* about events of conflict. I emphasize this point to direct attention to the fine line between the stories of disputing presented in court and the stories of gossip that sometimes occasion conflict.

A second example draws out different uses of the cultural belief that words have no end. Prior to the excerpt presented in the epigraph, Rukia has been sitting in silence, refusing the clerk's attempts to solicit her agreement to a divorce. When she finally responds, she is chastised for not speaking openly.[6] Rukia's observation that conversation about the conflict will continue beyond the courtroom corresponds to the notion that words have no end. The clerk attempts to avert the possibility that Shaaban will raise the same issues outside court by making clear that their speech in mediation should settle the matter. Shaaban agrees and then extends the idea that the court is the appropriate place for speech about conflict by insisting that all complaints should be stated in court, presumably also in order to "finish" the matter once and for all. The notion that words have no end includes the belief that, left to their own devices, people have a difficult time bringing words to an end. Yet the clerk and Shaaban do not entirely agree on the kind of speaking context the court should provide. Shaaban insists that everything be said in court, so that no other talk can start outside court. The clerk tries to circumvent a situation in which he will have to hear every complaint. Characterizing court as a place to speak openly about conflict, the clerk suggests that making demands rather than telling tales is appropriate.

Clerks and kadhis express their intolerance of excessive speech by interrupting disputants with statements like "We don't like long matters here, we like short matters" and "There are not a lot of words here. I want to finish and everyone go to his/her place."[7] In some instances, kadhis cut off disputants when they want most desperately to articulate their story. The preference for brevity and the active limitation on speech disadvantages women, who use long narratives to convey the experience of repetitive oppression. In one sense, the tactic helps women by relieving them of the burden of exposing themselves and their households. But in the end, the story of what happened is their real source of power, all they have that no one else knows.

Words Expose

The Swahili notion of "hiding matters" includes the idea that exposing household problems is damaging to family members and should only be risked with good reason. Narrating sensitive information exposes everyone, including the speaker, and people express their recognition of the shame through body language (e.g., veiling the face) or dismissive sounds (e.g., sucking teeth). This idea is a central force behind complaints about disputing in public, including in courts, where male disputants are the most likely to raise it.

Men make the point that words expose in several ways, including through reference to prior incidents of inappropriate discussions of conflict in which troubled domestic lives were exposed. In the following excerpt, Omar is angry at Aisha, his wife, because she complained to a relative about financial problems in the household (see "Tears," appendix C). His fury at being exposed through her stories leads him to a metalinguistic articulation of his preference for silence about controversial domestic matters.

Text 9.3

1	Omar:	It's shameful like that. People stay, they- they
2		conceal together about
3		anything they have, they don't have.
4		Indeed, this is how people get along.

Omar indicates his belief that it is shameful for people to fight regularly (line 1). Moreover, his view of how people should treat one another includes the idea that they should conceal their home lives. Not only does Omar take the opportunity to suggest that couples should suffer together in silence, but also he presents it as a general statement, which can be extended well beyond the incident to which he objects to disapprove of any act that fails to conceal domestic problems. The act in which Aisha is currently engaged—seeking assistance in court—is a primary instance of that delict.

The example below illustrates the use of a narrative to accomplish a complaint about complaining. The excerpt is taken from the mediation between Ahmed and Amina profiled in chapter 7 (see "The Wake," appendix C) and comes late in the mediation, after many issues have been raised and resolved. Ahmed, in a gambit to make Amina look bad, relates the following:

Text 9.4

1	Ahmed:	And also I have one thing like an accusation
2		that's still here, Kadhi.
3		You know, this woman
4		it's- she has spoken about clothes.
5		It's those clothes to say those very clothes
6		but there, she is *wearing* clothes.
7		And that's not all.
8		She took the opportunity to- to bring my brother-in-law
9		to the house and to mention these matters.

10	Even saying, I haven't bought, I don't know, even her
11	*underclothes.* Also I didn't buy.
12	When that brother-in-law, I had words about him,
13	I don't want her speaking to him about anything
14	at all.

Ahmed expresses his anger that Amina spoke to the brother-in-law about their domestic problems. It is not clear if Ahmed objects because she spoke to a man with whom she might be illicitly involved or because it is shameful no matter whom she told about a problem like his inability to provide his wife with underclothing. Hesitancies in his speech suggest that he feels the shame even in repeating the claims. His example, a discourse-level complaint about complaining, suggests that complaining can be an inappropriate act, thereby casting suspicion on Amina's complaints.

In their speech, women reflect a concern to limit exposure of domestic conflict, and they generally refrain from making overt statements about the problem or complaints about complaining. The organization of women's accounts of conflict, particularly the tendency to hold back controversial information until very late in their accounts, suggests that limiting exposure is important to them, too (see chapter 5). This is very difficult to establish, but I would argue that they are struggling with the intention to tell in order to get relief and yet, at the same time, the desire to hold back from exposing family matters so shameful that they will tarnish their own reputations through the very utterances. Depending on their own predilections, kadhis refuse to hear some matters (e.g., accusations of adultery) unless there is eyewitness evidence.

Though kadhis routinely try to move beyond reports of conflict, they express ambivalence with respect to the value of exposing conflict. Their primary task in court is to resolve conflict that has been exposed, and this means that they must obtain information by encouraging exposure. Yet they do not advocate unlimited revelation. Below, the kadhi exhibits this ambivalence as he gives advice to Saidi, whose wife, Zulecha, expresses jealousy. The kadhi prods the man by offering a hypothetical involving a husband who behaves in secretive ways that evoke unspoken bad feelings:

Text 9.5

1	Kadhi:	And you, I want you to see (it's a good thing) that [a wife
2		be exposed to a husband's affair]? Is there a person who
3		doesn't feel pain? Meaning, there isn't. A person is able to

4   hide, mashallah[8] a wife asks him nothing at all. Now that's
5   what kind of achievement? Meaning, she isn't happy, nor
6   are you. She doesn't have love for you.

The kadhi urges the man to recognize that, if his wife suffers in silence
by asking him "nothing at all," they may have more serious problems
than if she voices her dissatisfaction with him. Thus, the kadhi affirms
that some problems are necessarily spoken about, at least outside
court, in order to work toward resolution or to live peacefully.

The kadhi engages directly the belief on the part of many male
disputants that the complaints of women are the "cause" of marital
problems. This accusation, typically made in court and out, is a complaint about complaining that links women's speech about problems
and inappropriate language. This is precisely the point that undercuts
women's claims in court.

Words Harm

A third metalinguistic comment used when kadhis curtail speech about
conflict asserts that such speech, particularly graphic reports or abusive words, is harmful to those who produce and hear it. Related to
a broad ideology that speech about unpleasant matters creates an atmosphere of vulnerability to evil, the view that "words harm" entails
the notion that some speech "invites devils"—in effect, encourages evil
spirits who might cause more trouble. Thus, speech about bad acts
literally creates a bad or destabilized atmosphere in which further
problems might occur. In some instances, kadhis treat the recounting
of conflict—in the form of reported abusive speech or descriptions of
scenes of conflict, or even accusations of wrongdoing—as contrary to
the goal of ridding a couple of their problems and liable to create or
increase vulnerability to new trouble.

The belief that bad words "cause" bad events is widespread in
Swahili culture. In court, comments to that effect are produced primarily by kadhis, particularly in those instances when they want to persuade disputants to refrain from retelling stories of conflict. In the following example, however, a male disputant, Juma, refers to this view
when he reports his comments after a fight with his wife:

Text 9.6

1   Juma: I said
2   "I am going out and I will return with those children."
3   I (   ) I went out to avoid this evil.
4   I went on my way.

Juma's concern to leave the house in the midst of an argument is a recognition that he is vulnerable to evil or devils at the moment of fighting. This means more than just the obvious—that he can be accused and perhaps injured verbally or physically, or at the very least exposed as culpable in front of others. It means also that, in a fundamental way, he would be compromised by the utterance of evil words—that is, words of conflict—no matter who spoke them.

Kadhis use the specter of devils and evil spirits to warn about the potential harm of words of conflict. In the following example, the kadhi has heard Aisha's account of being beaten by Omar and also his defense. They discuss the claims, and the kadhi convinces them to reconcile and provides advice:

Text 9.7

1	Kadhi:	But don't- don't you, don't you, be ready all the time to
2		(cause) [trouble], meaning, it's bad to argue. This isn't
3		good. A person goes by any means possible, a person
4		follows. If a person gives you an opportunity, necessarily
5		you must take it, indeed. This one, indeed, I am begging
6		you. That one, it has passed. Go away devils, you
7		understand? It's indeed this way that we pray ( ) at the
8		house, but search after lots of things that don't have any
9		meaning. Those that passed she (had) pain, she was hurt.
10		And you the same, that pain, you were hurt. Now forgive
11		each other. Meaning, you, you weren't yourself, and she
12		wasn't herself. But now another day you will understand
13		each other. Each one will see that all this makes no sense.

The kadhi tells Aisha and Omar that they should avoid speech about conflict and thereby protect themselves. For him, words themselves are problematic and potentially cause conflict. Moreover, he counsels them to chase away evil spirits. Soon after this passage, he leads them in prayer.

By ending their mediation with a prayer—as is often done—the kadhi produces religious discourse that is culturally recognized as cleansing, as an antidote to the bad words that encourage evil spirits.[9] The recitation of a prayer creates an atmosphere of peace as well as an end to the discussion of conflict. People who are vulnerable to evil spirits are counseled to wash as if for prayer, and pray after that. The efficacy of washing for prayer comes from the belief that, as one Swahili practitioner said, "The medicine for fire is water."[10] The devils cause heat or fire, which is easily extinguished by water. Bad (or hot) words are similarly extinguished by the cooling effect of prayer. Inter-actionally in court, the prayer silences discussion or protest, as every-one participates in praying, even if they keep silent. Thus, they also participate in the decision that its production seals. Prayer, the ulti-mate good words, ends talk about conflict, which, with the exception of curses, constitutes the ultimate bad words.

The metalinguistic observation that words can harm is particularly relevant to words of abuse or insults, which are believed to harm in their original utterance and also in their repetition. This is why kadhis so often bar the repetition of such words in court (see chapter 8). Ex-pressing the point that everyone is made vulnerable when they hear bad words is a powerful metalinguistic means of limiting speech. Typi-cally, kadhis interrupt a narrated story at the very point when the wife quotes her husband's abusive speech, with statements like "Leave aside these careless words" and "Don't say those things here." [11] In prohib-iting reports of abusive speech, kadhis may be guarding against the trouble brought by the original utterance with the belief that repeating the words will "bring trouble" *(tia dhiki)*.

Linguistic Ideology and Courtroom Interaction

A central point of this book is that the ideological level of language plays a significant, though largely underrecognized, role in the con-struction and transformation of gender and that this interactive pro-cess is especially critical in disputing contexts. In court, the production of the three ideologies described above has directive force in shaping interaction, particularly in limiting stories of conflict. The force comes in part because the ideologies operate not only through explicit state-ments that propose moving the metapragmatic frame away from sto-ries but also in more implicit ways that are displayed through the struc-ture of stories and reported conversations. Through these several tactics, metalinguistic statements make the preferred metapragmatic frame explicit; most importantly, they facilitate and rationalize the shift to frames other than "performing the story," an effective limit on narration and the attention afforded stories of conflict. In the Swahili context, the deployment of these ideologies suggests that moving past the story is the central outcome and ideal.

Even though speech that directs interaction is associated with the court's authority and with its mission of organizing the presentation of claims and of resolving rather than just airing them, I am not arguing that the deployment of these ideologies primarily reflects prerogatives of the court or legal discourse (Islamic or state). Rather, I propose that the use of these three statements to limit utterances in court emerges as much from broader cultural ideas as it does from the discursive trappings of official court speech. Even though, for example, the idea that "words never end" plays out the court's endeavor not to dwell on any one conflict—a bureaucratic problem in any crowded court calendar—the role culture plays in motivating its production cannot be discounted. Historical and cultural factors particular to the Swahili coast not only shape the claims addressed in Kadhi's Courts but also motivate how claims are presented and resolved.

Even as I direct the attention of scholars of language and law to the critical role of cultural ideas about language in shaping interaction, I am aware that the move from token-based speech, especially narrative, to type-based speech, especially the mention of other forms of resolution, is common in mediations across a wide range of cultural contexts. That is, the desire to restore "order" to a dispute means that there is a routine and patterned move from stories of conflict to explicit metapragmatics and to speech that orders interaction and social relations. Even though this shift is a widespread phenomenon—perhaps a basic discursive pattern in dispute resolution—accomplishing it poses a difficult task, particularly in mediations (as opposed to cases), where the lack of institutionalized rules of interaction makes contestations over language (and attempts to control it explicitly) even more likely.

Despite the potential universality of this pattern, I want to reiterate the claim that the configuration of discourse in Swahili society enacts this process in a way that calls into question a transituational organization of interaction in disputes. The move to forms of speech that bring order to stories is also accomplished in relation to ideas about language that are particular to a cultural context, and understanding the particularities requires taking into account many forms of speech. In Swahili society, the central role of stories as a means of articulating claims establishes a metapragmatic frame that subsequent utterances operate to dismantle. Moreover, the metalinguistic comment that decries exposing household conflict in Swahili culture perhaps means that stories are curtailed more swiftly than in other places where, for example, ideologies of "disentangling" or of speech as therapeutic might be common in conflict resolution. Although comparative projects would usefully explore some of the similarities in how disputes provide order, subtle differences can only be seen by careful ethnographic and linguistic analysis of speech about conflict, and ideologies about that speech, in court and out.

Courtroom Discourse and Constituting Subjects

In chapter 1, I reviewed recent literature from pragmatics that explores how linguistic ideology is central to social creativity through speech. My main concern was to develop an approach that examines such creativity with respect to gender and that can be applied to legal contexts. In applying my approach to Swahili disputes, I came to focus on narrative as a critical linguistic genre through which gender is indexed and enacted in disputes, allowing for the possibility of social creativity in its production. The several preceding chapters, which focused on analyzing speech in disputes, demonstrated that the speech of men and women in court indexes gender primarily through the gender-patterned production of narrative. By entextualizing stories of domestic trouble, women point to the cultural ideas that characterize them as telling stories. However, indexing gender through narrative also entails the Swahili idea that those who narrate might do so inappropriately, in ways that expose family problems.

The close link between women and narratives on the one hand and between men and other forms of language and metalanguage on the other hand means that the shifts in metapragmatic frames in Kadhi's Court disputes highlight men's authority as speakers and legal actors. Men's metalinguistic utterances operate in several ways to identify women as narrators, and, as this chapter demonstrates, their production of metalinguistic commentary during disputes emphasizes a negative image of women and women's speech. This image plays on the suspicion that women might narrate family problems in ways that violate *heshima*. Less a problem for individual women narrators, who usually win their claims, the depiction of women's speech as negative perpetuates and deepens a problematic cultural idea about gender and speech. Thus, narratives of conflict produced by women in court contradict the expectation that women will hide matters in order to protect *heshima*. This contradiction is built into the court process in that Kadhi's Courts primarily offer women contexts to voice claims against men. What is most interesting in the postcolonial period is that this does not appear to *prevent* women from narrating; rather, they narrate and in the process transform their relation to the image of the persevering wife.

It should be no surprise that, as Swahili women call into question the terms of gender relations through winning their claims in court, their efforts are denounced and their character questioned. This kind of "backlash," one way of characterizing the effects of a "complaint about complaining," generally follows when those who confront powerful adversaries achieve some relief or advantage. My analysis of the denunciation of women's narratives in court directs attention to the role language plays in providing not only the vehicle for women's successes in confronting domestic relations but also the specific target for the backlash that condemns them as women who speak inappropriately. More generally, language is always available as a target on which to focus in condemning the actions of the least powerful populations or those who try to effect change. They can be denounced through their use of language, which is a routine and powerful strategy for negating their words or silencing them. This possibility makes it all the more important that scholarly and political attempts to understand how hierarchies (e.g., gender) are perpetuated continue to examine the role of discourse and, perhaps more importantly, ideas about language in struggles to transform social life.

The cultural ideals of the pronouncing husband and the persevering wife give little indication of the tremendous struggle over gender relations waged through discourse and ideas about its preferred production in Swahili society. My argument has depended on the notion that these subject positions symbolically embody important cultural beliefs that guide the production (or lack thereof) of speech about conflict and the interpretation of that speech.

The persevering wife is a challenging ideal for Swahili women to sustain in the strained economy since the early 1980s. When she speaks, the persevering woman produces the voice that she knows; she narrates. By telling stories of conflict, however, she transmutes into her evil twin—the woman who exposes the underside of life in the family home. Such a woman, also a salient image in Swahili society, is derided for her lack of *heshima* and lack of commitment to hiding family secrets. She is the consummate complainer, subject to metapragmatic reminders that complaining reflects her deficient character. Her case is made only if she has shown that she was previously a persevering wife, and explicit ideological comments push some women back toward perseverance by making clear that their complaints are not desired, at least not in public contexts. Thus, the image of the persevering wife implies an ability to speak, which must be contained. Both of these relations to language are central to the construction of gender in Swahili society. The struggle a woman faces in attempting to live up to the ideal is reminiscent of the difficulty all Swahili women face in attempting to maintain *heshima*.

For their part, men also speak within and against a gendered image—the pronouncing husband. In comparison to women, however, they are less likely to shift so abruptly between opposed images. Through multiple forms of linguistic usage, including the production of narrative, men index their authority, which links them to the kadhis and to Islamic law. By and large, their speech in court reaffirms their roles as men with the authority of legal pronouncement; however, their lack of success with respect to case decisions means that they lose the struggle over authority to the kadhis who intervene to refigure their domestic lives. Nonetheless, in losing cases and mediations, men are not silenced. Rather, overt struggle with an authority figure tends to strengthen their authoritative position. The image of an abusive man, one who uses speech to harm his wife, is often invoked in women's narratives of conflict, but this image disappears as the story is effaced through metalanguage. Recounting abusive speech is inappropriate in court, even if it ultimately leads to legal decisions against men.

My attention to the figures of the persevering wife and the pronouncing husband is motivated by their prominence in Swahili cultural understandings and, as well, by their resemblance to stereotypes of Islamic gender relations that circulate globally. Returning to these images throughout has allowed me to make the point that Swahili people who speak in court are gendered, legal, and linguistic subjects all at once and that the performance of gender is refracted through and in relation to these subject positions. Dismissing the notion that the images reflect a singular reality of gendered behavior for Muslim men and women, I contend that they are guides for the performance of gender and sites of transformation. As cultural creations, these images do not describe real subjects but rather identify commonly recognized subject positions. Accordingly, Swahili people perform gender *in relation to* these images and to others situated in opposition to them. The ideals of gender, discourse, and conflict configured together in the images of the persevering wife and the pronouncing husband provide a symbolic background against which the speech of Swahili people is produced and interpreted. In this dynamic process, multiple factors relevant to the performance of gender merge, sometimes uneasily, in the speech of gendered subjects.

Gender is always configured in part through cultural understandings about how gendered subjects stand in relation to language and its availability to them. The treatment of the images in speech thus indicates how language and gender connect, and who people are as gendered beings also includes how and whether they should use language and for what purposes. In order to understand the interactive constitution of gender in real contexts, feminist scholars should examine how speech operates against certain ingrained ideas about language and against specific images of subjects. In the face of gender hierarchy, mapping the dynamic struggle of performing gender through speech is critical to developing a politics of social transformation that takes discourse seriously.

Conclusion

Outside court, many Muslim men complain bitterly about cases or mediations that did not go their way and about the kadhis' alleged tendency to favor women. The Kadhi's Courts have lost legitimacy in the postcolonial period, and kadhis are routinely criticized for their connection to the state as well as their partiality. Men's inability to retain control and authority in Kadhi's Court is often attributed to the illegitimate intervention of the secular state, thus suggesting that, if the courts were really Muslim, men would have even more power over their wives. In 1992, a man disgruntled by a kadhi's decision to grant his wife a divorce accosted him on a Mombasa street and stabbed him several times. The kadhi, who returned to court once his wounds had healed and his nerves toughened, admitted that many men are unhappy about what happens to them in court, but he resolved to continue doing justice for women, in the name of Islam. In Kenya, and many other nations, the postcolonial courts offer sites for the complex reworking of gender relations. This happens in part because these courts stand at the intersection of multiple discourses that configure conflict and the subjects who engage in it in quite divergent ways. The gaps opened through unresolved tensions and contradictions in the meeting of these discourses create possibilities for significant changes in social relations. Swahili women turn to the Kadhi's Courts in part because the institution destabilizes male authority in the community. Women are thus provided the space to rework gender relations, and the results, which often change their lives, are mixed.

Heshima kwa wanawake.
Respect for women.

Conclusion

I was in Mombasa in December of 1992 during the first multiparty presidential and parliamentary elections in Kenya since the early 1960s. The nation was emerging from a decade of repressive one-party rule, and the mood was one of openness and yet foreboding. In coastal towns, tension was heightened by a struggle pitting Muslims against the government, which had refused to recognize the newly formed Islamic Party of Kenya (IPK)—an amalgam of Muslims from a range of ethnicities, including many young Swahili men. For a Muslim minority community that has steadily lost power since the nineteenth century and has tended to avoid dealings with the secular state, forming such a party was a significant political undertaking. The secular government's denial of party registration infuriated some Swahili Muslims, radicalized others, and revealed divisions of ethnicity, color, class, politics, and religious sect. Several weeks after the election, I walked through an IPK stronghold area in Mombasa. Every house was painted with IPK slogans. Support for the party had only grown in the wake of the election, which was thought by most Kenyans (and international observers) to have been rigged to reelect ruling-party candidates. One small sign hanging high on an electrical wire caught my eye: "Heshima kwa wanawake" (Respect for women). My mind started racing—was this an indication of a link between politicized Islam (perhaps fundamentalist) and a new, restrictive politics of gender? When I pointed to the sign and inquired whether the IPK had made statements about women's social position, my Swahili friends laughed at me: "Of course you would notice that, you're always interested in women." They admitted that IPK leaders did, at times, discuss the appropriate forms of behavior for pious women and men, but they also reminded me that coastal Muslims have always told each other to have respect for women as a basic tenet of the system that maintains family status and honor.

Later, I remembered another place I had encountered the "Heshima kwa wanawake" slogan. It was prominently featured on the cloth *(leso)* produced in honor of the 1985 United Nations Decade for Women Conference in Nairobi, and I had purchased one during my first week in Kenya when I began this research project. The commemorative cloth, bought by many conference attendees, is one of the few examples of global feminist material culture. Many women's centers in North America prominently display one of these brightly colored cloths with the UN peace symbol. Reassured by this avowedly pro-feminist and pro-woman use of the slogan, I questioned my initial panic over potential fundamentalist oppression of coastal Kenyan Muslim women. My friends were right; "respect for women" is an enduring ideal for Swahili Muslims as well as for many other people, invoked in situations involving widely divergent configurations of gender. I needed to remember the multiple meanings of such expressions. To have respect for Swahili women can mean to protect them from strangers, to buy them fancy clothes, to contribute to their bridewealth so that they might support themselves upon divorce, to refrain from beating them, or to provide them with education.

In a critique of representations of pro-democracy rallies and state violence in Tienanmen Square, Rey Chow (1991:82) allows that in moments of political crisis, "academics cannot see the world as scholars, but rather become journalists." Unaccustomed to this role, we make just the sort of interpretive misjudgment that I did in seeing the IPK sign, lapsing into "repetitive narratives" that often have limited relevance to issues underlying the crisis. Yet the crisis and the experience of misjudgment can make us "suddenly aware of the precarious, provisional nature of our discourse" (ibid.). The repetitive narrative that I readily embraced is all too familiar in the long wake of the Iranian revolution, during which the call for a politics based on Islam is routinely and often wrongly interpreted as being motivated by fundamentalism and committed to women's legal subordination. While this narrative has been a quite accurate description in some contexts, this book offers an example that is intended to disrupt stereotyped assumptions and repetitive narratives of how Islamic law configures Muslim women's lives. I am not denying that many women across the globe have been oppressed in the name of Islam (and other religions); rather, I direct attention to the particular struggles of gender and law taking place in postcolonial Kenya to illuminate the culturally specific processes through which gender can be reinforced or transformed in the name of Islam. Such an example is intended to demonstrate the varieties of Islamic experience.

The Kenyan Kadhi's Courts provide a context for the performance of gender that, prior to the past two decades, Swahili women rarely used on their own initiative. Thus, innovative performances of gender have emerged in the postcolonial era. The increased use of the courts by women means, among other things, that important struggles about gender are carried out in a public context in which the state enters into the relations between Swahili people. This exhibition before the state solidifies gender differences and gender antagonisms more firmly. The publicly performed negotiation of gender relations in court has meant that the image of the Swahili woman narrator as a dangerous complainer who exposes family problems enters a discursive realm in which it operates according to new rules and is publicized more widely than in the past. Moreover, the negative connotation is greater given that women who complain bring their families not only into a public arena but also closer to the distrusted secular state. By suggesting that women further establish a negative image through speaking in the courts, I do not mean to diminish their considerable success with respect to altering individual circumstances and paving the way for other women to confront problems at home. Most Swahili women will never make a claim in Kadhi's Court, yet gender relations are being influenced and transformed by decisions in cases and mediations. Word of women's successes in court trickles out, even though concerns about *heshima* make most people unwilling to speak openly about their day in court. As women use language in courts and other contexts connected with the state (e.g., schools and offices) in increasing numbers, their voices may begin to sound less out-of-place or threatening.

Several factors account for the complex process taking place in Kadhi's Courts. First, none of the four discourses used to frame the domestic problems of Swahili people is hegemonic in shaping approaches to gender and law. Thus, claimants and third parties struggle and strategize among different normative orders and diverse disputing practices; the mixture of discourses opens possibilities. At the same time, these discourses reflect relations of power that set the possibilities and limitations for what parties to a dispute can achieve—that is, for how they can remake their subject positions. Second, kadhis and clerks, often at odds with local, more conservative male elders, listen with sympathy to women's claims of perseverance and defend their own authority when challenged by men. Moreover, these third parties are as likely to apply ethical principles associated with coastal practice as they are strict Islamic or secular legal rules. Their flexible use of the discourses, including the application of ethical discourse, tends to recognize and provide relief for the kinds of claims brought by women, particularly concerning emotional abuse. The concept of *heshima,* in the sense of displaying respect for others, underpins the ethical discourse that is invoked in court.

Although I emphasize the particularity of Swahili culture and the Kenyan context in shaping disputes in Kadhi's Court and their consequences for gender, the example is useful for broader intellectual and political projects. For instance, my depiction of the Kadhi's Courts destabilizes stereotypes of Islamic law in relation to gender. In addition to challenging the image of Muslim women as persevering in silence, I go beyond studies that have located their agency primarily in behind-the-scenes manipulation. I hope to have demonstrated that Muslim women are capable of altering their lives by turning to authorities, both national and religious. I hope as well that this example will be useful to the set of scholars, generally feminist Muslims, who are re-fashioning Islamic law by emphasizing ethical principles overlooked in the exegesis of Muslim legal scholars (see, e.g., Ahmed 1992; Mernissi 1991). Although these admirable projects focus primarily on developing legal doctrine that treats women equitably and yet in accordance with Islam, they might find this example useful in illuminating the results of the mixture of discourses in situations of legal pluralism. Rethinking how law, including Islamic law, operates in action is an inseparable counterpart to doctrinal analysis and statutory reform. As a non-Muslim, I must remain a bystander on the sidelines of the developing politics around Islamic law and gender relations, which promises to extend the potential for transforming the lives of women and men living under Muslim law.

Similarly, I am under no illusions that this volume addresses the conscious political goals of Swahili people, men or women. Many expressed to me their interest in my production of an account that would educate non-Muslims about coastal Kenyan Islam, and I believe I have provided that; but some are certainly unsettled at the extent to which this project exposes the difficulties of life in Swahili households, which should, of course, be concealed. As I suggested earlier, scholarship focusing on gender, which must confront directly the tensions of unequal relations, has tended to produce narratives that expose those aspects of Swahili social life that some Swahili people and most scholars endeavor to keep hidden. Partial exposures always involve risk, but, as the Kadhi's Court example suggests, their consequences can include transformative visions, as well as backlash.

Judging from the spirited conversations I had about married life with Swahili people, many share my interest in understanding and resolving the problems of living in intimate relationships. This point leads me to the final aspect of the intellectual and political agenda that I have pursued in this volume—that is, to analyze in detail and develop theory about what happens when ordinary, often subordinate people appeal to the state, specifically the legal system, to help them repair or reconfigure their relationships with others. The serious risks of turning to the state are balanced against the enormous possibilities, particularly for those seeking relief from lives of abuse. Following other scholars, I have found that many of the difficulties people face in court emerge through their unfamiliarity with the discourses of law and legal processes. Problems lurk in the "word vaults" (Williams 1991) that obfuscate important concepts and in the "unnatural" rules of interaction that face those presenting claims. These observations, which have tended to illuminate how legal discourse poses problems for people in court, need to be complemented by considerations of the local character of disputing and the contribution of cultural factors to the procedural (and substantive) injustices that reinforce unequal relations in legal contexts. Moreover, the closer we listen to the language of disputants across a range of contexts, the more likely we are to hear and identify problems in new realms of language, such as the ideas about language through which interaction is characterized and controlled. Further study of metalinguistic elements will allow us to engage more directly questions of the consequences of disputing and the development (and content) of legal consciousness.

This example from a vibrant postcolonial Islamic society demonstrates that the participation of Swahili Muslim men and women in legal processes alters their domestic positions as individuals and perhaps, as the decisions favoring women accumulate, transforms gender relations more generally. Yet, by acknowledging that such transformations are effected against idealized versions of Islamic law and its expressly patriarchal forms in some cultural contexts, I demonstrate that domination through institutional definitions of subjects is never complete, perhaps especially when multiple legal systems intersect (see also

Hirsch and Lazarus-Black 1994). There are always gaps to be exploited by those who seek a hearing for their experiences. Some voices do break through and succeed in remaking categories of personhood and recreating conditions of possibility. This volume tells a story about some Muslim women whose voices are heard, silenced, and transformed ideologically in disputes, in part to confirm oppression, but in part to deny subservience, to assert creativity, and to inspire hope.

Appendix A: Glossary

The following is a list of Kiswahili terms used frequently in the text. The glosses are taken in part from *A Standard Swahili-English Dictionary* (Johnson and Madan 1939) and *Kamusi ya Kiswahili Sanifu* (Department of Kiswahili Studies, University of Dar es Salaam, 1981).

bidhaa: innovative practices (i.e., those not done during the life of the Prophet Mohammed)
buibui: black cloak and veil worn by women outside the home
bwana: term of reference or address for a man, e.g., guy, man, sir
dawa: medicine, including Swahili and/or Islamic traditional medicine
edda: period of seclusion for widows (for four months, ten days after the husband's death) and divorced women (for three months after the divorce)
fiqh: Islamic law
haki: right, justice, privilege
harusi: wedding
heshima: respect, honor, modesty
Idd: Islamic holiday
jini (pl. *majini*): spirit
kadhi (pl. *makadhi* or *kadhi*s): Islamic judge
Kiswahili: the Swahili language, spoken widely through East and Central Africa and the first language of coastal Waswahili people
lian (Ar.; also *laana*): oath
liwali (pl. *maliwali*): leader, governor
mahari: bridewealth payment, agreed on at the time of marriage; to be paid by a Swahili man to his prospective wife
maneno (s. *neno*): words, gossip, expression, message
mapenzi: love

Mswahili (pl. *Waswahili*): a Swahili person, a coastal person of
  Afro-Arab origin
mwalimu (pl. *walimu*): teacher, learned person
mzee (pl. *wazee*): elder
ndoa: marriage
-oa/-olewa/-oana: marry (for a man)/be married by (for a woman)/
  marry with each other
sharifu (pl. *masharifu*): descendant of the Prophet Mohammed
sheikh (pl. *masheikh;* also *shayikh/mashayikh*): learned person,
  elder
sheria: law, a law
shetwani (also *shetani*): evil spirit, devil, being with supernatural
  power
somo (pl. *masomo;* also *kungwi*): advisor at the time of puberty
-stahimili: persevere, have patience
tabia: nature, condition, character
tafsir: Koranic exegesis
talaka: divorce
-tamka: pronounce
-tukana: abuse verbally, curse, insult
ulama (Ar.): scholar class
wakili: representative, proxy, attorney
wivu: jealousy, envy

Appendix B: Features of Transcription

The transcription features I have used reflect the conventions developed by several scholars (Goodwin 1990; Jefferson 1978; Moerman 1988).

(2.5)	pause of 2.5 seconds
(.)	very short pause
word	emphasis or stress
( )	inaudible on tape
(word)	tentative guess at word
word = word	"latched" words with no time gap between them
WORD	increased volume
word::	lengthened syllable
word'	rising intonation characteristic of Swahili speech
word | word | word	simultaneous speech from two speakers, sometimes interruptive
[word]	word not in original but included to facilitate understanding
"word"	reported or quoted speech
'word'	foreign word, generally English
word-	word cut short by speaker

Appendix C: Case Summaries

Abandoned

Both parties agree that Ali divorced Mariamu by letter. Several weeks after the divorce, Mariamu asks the assistant registrar for assistance in compelling Ali to provide her with a certificate of divorce and *edda* maintenance. She is especially concerned to arrange for support given that she is pregnant at the time of the divorce and expects to receive child-support payments. The assistant registrar counsels Mariamu to wait until the end of the *edda* period (the time of the birth of the child). After that time, on the advice of the assistant registrar, she travels frequently to Mombasa in order to contact Ali and demand child support. She becomes frustrated after numerous trips fail to result in a meeting with Ali. She comes to Kadhi's Court to discuss the matter with the kadhi. The kadhi instructs her to file a case requesting a divorce certificate. About one week later, she and Ali appear before the kadhi. Mariamu makes claims for a divorce certificate, *edda* maintenance, and child support. At first, Ali is reluctant to agree that he has any obligations at all. At the kadhi's urging, he agrees to sign a divorce certificate and to pay *edda* maintenance, but he refuses to support the child, who he claims is not his. The kadhi supervises preparation of the divorce certificate and advises Mariamu to file a separate case to demand child support. Three months later, Mariamu had not yet filed a case for child support.

The Wake

Ahmed, a man in his forties, comes to Kadhi's Court alleging that Amina, his wife, has disobeyed him several times and, after a confrontation between them, has left the matrimonial home. He asks the clerk to summon her to court. The clerk counsels him to wait several days

250

in case she returns on her own. Ahmed leaves court and prepares an official-looking letter summoning Amina to appear before the kadhi. Amina comes to Kadhi's Court on the day indicated in the letter, and Ahmed appears with her before the kadhi. Ahmed alleges that Amina stayed for several days at a wake when they had agreed that she should return sooner. When she returns home, they have confrontations. Amina defends her actions by saying that they did not agree that she should return early and that Ahmed did not give her enough money to return by herself at the earlier time. They both report that after one of their arguments, Amina left the house. Amina alleges that Ahmed has been abusive to her for a very long time and that he has not maintained her with clothes. She also accuses him of seeing other women. In court, Amina's father reiterates her claims and expresses his desire that the two be divorced. The kadhi conducts mediation in which he focuses on the need for them to reconcile for the sake of their children. He blames many of their problems on evil spirits. They agree to reconcile after an hour of mediation.

The Beating

Atwas and Munira have been married for one year, although they had three children together when unmarried. Munira comes to court alleging that Atwas owes her maintenance and *mahari*. She also says that he is abusive to her. Her claim is granted in a formal case heard *ex parte*, even though the kadhi concedes that she produced little evidence. After several months, Munira files a notice to show cause alleging that Atwas has suspended payments. They come to court. Atwas claims that he began payments after the court case but discontinued them when Munira moved from his house. Munira counters that she left home because a former girlfriend of Atwas habitually came to see him at their home. Atwas agrees to pay, but Munira refuses to return to his home. About a month later, they return to court. Munira is still living with a relative, and Atwas wants her to return home. She informally appeals the kadhi's decision that she return home by going to the Chief Kadhi. He consults with the original kadhi and accepts his assessment that there was a chance that Munira still wanted to be with Atwas. One month after that, Munira comes to court alleging that Atwas beat her. She claims that, in front of witnesses, Atwas said that he would divorce her if she gave him custody of their children. She brings her children to court and has left word with him that they are there. Atwas does not come to court. Munira asks for the dissolution of their marriage and the money owed to her. On the advice of the kadhi, she also files a complaint of assault with the police. Atwas comes to court the following day. He explains having beaten Munira by claiming that she insulted him and his mother. Also, he claims that she has not been accepting money from him for maintenance. The kadhi attempts to bring them to an understanding that they should divorce. Atwas refuses at first and then agrees to divorce her, admitting that they cannot live together peacefully. They divorce. Munira continues the assault claim.

Certificate

Malik, a man in his mid-thirties, and Halima, a woman in her twenties, have been married for several years. Halima comes to court alleging that Malik does not maintain her and treats her poorly. She says that she was ill in the hospital, and he failed to visit her. When she returned home after her illness, he divorced her. She claims for maintenance and the divorce certificate. Malik admits to bad behavior, and the kadhi convinces them to reconcile. The next day, Halima returns to court with her brother, who accuses the kadhi of not being harsh enough with Malik. He claims that Malik has had a history of treating Halima poorly. The kadhi stands by his decision. One week later, Malik comes to court to obtain the divorce certificate. The kadhi refuses to allow him to take the certificate without Halima's signature. Malik and Halima come to court. Malik alleges that Halima came to see him after their mediation, reconciled with him, then left and has not returned since. Halima says it was her understanding that Malik would come to see her at her home, and she has not heard from him. Malik insists that he can bring witnesses to say that Halima came to see him. They return that afternoon with witnesses. Halima repeats her claim that she did not visit Malik at their house. Malik's witness says that he saw her there. Halima says that the witness cannot be believed because he "eats from the same plate" as Malik and thus would protect him. Halima's witness says that she did not go to see Malik. The kadhi becomes very angry that someone is lying over such a small matter. Halima becomes very upset and pleads with the kadhi to dissolve the marriage. The kadhi convinces them to think it over for another night and return the next day. They return and discuss the conflict but reach no resolution. One week later, they come in to divorce and prepare the divorce certificate. Out of court, Malik claims that Halima's parents wanted the divorce.

The Knife

The young couple, Shaaban (the husband) and Rukia (the wife) have gone before elders and the subchief many times for reconciliation. They come to speak to the Kadhi's Court clerk about their latest conflict. Shaaban reports that they had been living apart because of their employment in different towns. Shaaban returned home when he heard that Rukia was seeing another man. He found some of her activities, like going out to the toilet late at night, very suspicious. They had several confrontations. Her father intervened in one and beat Rukia as punishment for disobeying her husband. Shaaban claims that Rukia does not behave like a wife (i.e., she does not cook and clean for him) and that she goes out late at night. Rukia insists that she goes out to the toilet some distance from their house because they do not have the proper accommodations any closer. She says that Shaaban insults and beats her and once threatened her with a knife. Shaaban vehemently denies that he threatened her with a knife and alleges that she is meeting with other men. He is frustrated because she refuses to go to the elders to reconcile. She insisted that they come to Kadhi's Court. The clerk mediates by telling them that they have both behaved badly and that jealousy is at the root of their difficulties. Rukia insists that they appear before the kadhi and refuses to respond to the clerk's question of whether she wants her husband or not. Later that day they appear before the kadhi. They tell essentially the same stories. After about forty-five minutes of mediation before the kadhi, they reconcile and leave together.

The Letter

Moussa and Leila, a couple in their forties, marry and go to Mombasa to live. They have been married only briefly when Moussa gives Leila a letter of divorce. Leila's mother helps them to reconcile. After their reconciliation, Moussa leaves to spend the month of Ramadhan with his other wife. On his return, he insists that the letter of divorce is in effect again. Leila waits to receive her bridewealth payment and divorce certificate. She enlists the assistance of the local chief and her brother to obtain them. They suggest that she go to the kadhi. When

Leila asks Moussa to get the certificate from the kadhi, he tells her that the kadhi is away. In the meantime, Moussa comes to the court and attempts to get a divorce certificate. The kadhi refuses to sign the certificate as Moussa indicates that he owes no bridewealth. The kadhi insists that when a claim of no bridewealth is made, it is necessary to have the woman come to court to verify that she is owed nothing. Leila appears in court without being summoned and without knowing that Moussa has tried to obtain a certificate that fails to indicate his debt to her. The kadhi assists her in listing Moussa's debts and in agreeing to finalize the divorce. She obtains a divorce certificate and files a claim for the money owed her.

Soap

Najima, a woman in her twenties, comes to Kadhi's Court to report that her husband has not been maintaining her for over a month. She claims also that he has not responded to her protests against sharing a house with his other wife. She reports that when she complained to him and asked him for separate accommodations, he told her to leave if she wanted to or to stay under the circumstances. He also said that, if she wanted a house, she could build it herself. Najima then went to her parents' home, taking their children. Her father and brother entered into the dispute, but her husband refused to listen to any of them so long as Najima remained away from his home. She complains of having to borrow money from her brother for basic necessities, including soap. The kadhi counsels her to file a case for maintenance. She files the case.

Tears

Aisha comes to see the kadhi to report that Omar, her husband, beat her earlier that day. She explains that he had asked her to return some money that he had given her. She did not produce the money when he requested it, and he beat her severely. The kadhi, outraged, summons Omar to court. Omar and Aisha appear before him the next day. Omar agrees with Aisha's claims that he was angry when the money was not returned; however, he insists that she hit him first and thus began the fight that led to his beating her. Aisha asks to be divorced. Omar claims that he wants to stay with her and is ashamed of their fighting in this incident and others. The kadhi attempts to reconcile them. Aisha makes an additional claim that Omar never allows her mother to visit at their home. The kadhi secures Omar's promise that he will reform his behavior. They agree to reconcile, and the kadhi offers a prayer before they leave.

Thrown Out

Aziz, the husband, and Hawa, the wife, have a long history of conflict and resolution through Kadhi's Court. They have come four or five times for mediation. This is a second marriage for both of them. Aziz tells the clerk that Hawa has thrown him out of the house that they were living in, her brother's house. The clerk summons Hawa by letter. They appear before the clerk the next day. Aziz repeats his claim that he has been thrown out of the house. Hawa alleges that Aziz visits his ex-wife. She wants to be divorced. Aziz swears that he does not visit his ex-wife and offers to take a formal oath on the Koran. The clerk mediates the discussion for over an hour. Hawa refuses to agree to his return. The clerk convinces them to return the next day after thinking about their options. He is not convinced that Hawa wants a divorce, and he suspects that someone in her family is compelling her to pursue it. They return the next day. Hawa refuses to reconcile. Finally, Aziz agrees to divorce her. As they prepare a divorce certificate, several observers in the office counsel them against divorcing, especially during Ramadhan, the holy month.

The TV

Nasira and Juma were married in 1981. At that time, Nasira converted from Christianity to Islam. She was then in her early thirties, and Juma, well known for his skills in Swahili medicine and magic, was considerably older than she. The couple come to Kadhi's Court alleging problems that resulted in Nasira's leaving the matrimonial home. In court, they offer very different stories about the conflict. Nasira alleges that Juma's grown daughter (from a previous marriage) gossips about her to people in the neighborhood. When she convinced Juma to investigate the problem, it resulted in a fight. During the fight, Juma told Nasira to leave the house and not to use the TV. Nasira claims that Juma's children came for his belongings. She gathered her own things and left with her children. Juma says that he knows nothing about the gossip that supposedly started the problem. He says that he did not order Nasira out of the house, but rather they fought and she left. During mediation, Juma says that he is no longer interested in Nasira. She is not interested in divorcing; however, she admits being reticent to return to Juma given their conflict and his magical powers. The discussion continues until Juma decides to divorce Nasira. At first, he refuses *edda* maintenance, citing her contribution to their divorce; at the kadhi's insistence, however, he agrees.

Words

Saidi, the husband, and Zulecha, the wife, come to Kadhi's Court with allegations of general problems at home. Zulecha thinks that Saidi has brought her to court to divorce her, but he intends that they be reconciled. Zulecha says that Saidi visits a woman by pretending to go to see the woman's husband, his friend. Saidi says that he goes to that neighborhood because his mosque is there and also to see his friend, the husband of the woman. He claims that he is not interested in the woman. At the kadhi's urging, Saidi agrees to switch mosques and says that if Zulecha finds him at the house of the woman, he will divorce her immediately. About one month later, they return to court after a confrontation at home. Zulecha insists that Saidi has gone to see the woman. She claims that she followed him there and, though she did not see him in the house, she heard him laughing. She also accuses him of abusing her father and generally treating her poorly. Saidi says that he did not go to the house and that Zulecha listens to the gossip of other people. The kadhi counsels Zulecha not to listen to gossip, and they reconcile.

Appendix D: Kiswahili Texts

Text 6.1

1	Mariamu:	Shida yangu vile:: aniacha na mimba. Nikaenda
2		kwetu. Nikalea mimba yangu mpaka
3		nikazaa. Kabla sijazaa nikapata barua ya- kwake
4		kuwa aniata. Nikakaa::: mpaka nilipomaliza
5		nikaenda kwa Shariff Abdallah. Kaenda. Kamweleza
6		kamwambia maadamu ameniata na sasa nina- mimi
7		"mpaka uzae ndiye utamaliza edda kuachwa.
8		Utakaa. Ulipomaliza edda ulipozaa."
9		Kisha edda yangu. Nikienda. Nikamweleza
10		(.) habari ya: cheti. Akaniambia "bas nitamwandikia
11		barua." Akamwandikia barua mbili Sha faa Shariff
12		Abdallah. "Nishaandika barua yake
13		amenijibu yuwaje." Kake:::ti. Mwisho
14		akaniambia afadhali niende kwa Mombasa.
15		Maana yake yuko Mombasa na mimi na mtoto mchanga
16		na kila siku panda magari nikishuka. Kienda zangu
17		mpaka kule. Niki- nikienda zangu nikamwandikia
18		barua. Nikimwita haji. Siku ya ile afike kule
19		Jumanne. Jumanne mimi nikakaa.
20		Nikamsubiri. Hakuja. Nikamwambia "bas we nenda
21		siku nyingine ufike kila baada ya wiki uje umjulie."
22		Sasa ikawa mimi kibarua changu kila siku kwenda
23		kwa kumjulie. ( ) Hayuko. Nikaenda mara ya
24		mwisho. Nakamwambia "basi afadhali niende
25		Malindi." Ndiyo nikaja.

Text 6.2

1	Mariamu:	Niki- nikienda zangu
2		nikamwandikia barua.

3   Nikimwita
4   haji.
5   Siku ya ile afika kule Jumanne.
6   Jumanne, mimi nikakaa.
7   Nikamsubiri.
8   Hakuja.
9   Nikamwambia . . .

Text 6.3
1   Mariamu: Kake:::ti. Mwisho
2   akaniambia afadhali niende kwa Mombasa.

Text 6.4
1   Zulecha: Na mimi nimestahimili sana sa:na kwake *sa*:na
2   siku *nyi*:ngi
3   Kadhi: Kwa nini mpaka sasa hustahimili?
4   Zulecha: Mpaka imefikilia ha:pa

Text 6.5
1   Munira: (3.3) Yeye alipomaliza kunipiga |nasikia (   ) moto
2   Kadhi: |lini? lini? lini?
3   Munira: ilikuwa siku ya:: Iddi nne (4.2)
4   maanake si::
5   watu walianza (   ) siku ya juma ngapi siku ya
6   Idd maanake ni siku ya Jumatano
7   nilikwenda Mombasa.
8   Kwenda Chief Kadhi.
9   Niliporudi Mombasa usiku wake
10   ndio akaja kunipiga siku ya jumatano
11   siku ya watu waanze kazi siku ya Idd.

Text 6.6
1   Shaaban: Na mimi nikaacha ile kazi
2   nikaja nyumbani.
3   Nilipokuja nyumbani
4   nikaona bibi yangu . . .

Text 6.7
1   Mariamu: Nikimwita
2   haji.

3   Siku ya ile afika kule, Jumanne.
4   Jumanne, mimi nikakaa.
5   Nikamsubiri.
6   Hakuja.

Text 6.8

1   Kadhi: Wewe, wasemaje? Eleza ile habari yako.
2   Munira: Habari yangu mimi (1.4) ni ile nilikuambia kama
3   mimi nataka kuatwa.
4   Kadhi: Uh huh (2.8) Bas. (2.5) Ndiyo habari yako lile jambo
5   huna lingine?
6   Munira: Ninayo. Sivo jeuzi alipokuja ku:nipiga hata
7   nikaenda polisi nilipawa P Three. Nikajaza
8   jana nikaregesha polisi. (1.6) Akaniumiza ni
9   (   ) mbavu na figo. (   ). Ameniumiza
10   sana.

Text 6.9

1   Kadhi: Asema huyu bibi unampiga.
2   Atwas: Ni kweli lakini kwa sababu yake. Na sikusudi yangu
3   kutaka kumpiga siku ile lakini nilipotoka kwa safari
4   nilipokuja mimi- yeye alikuwa amehama katika ile
5   nyumba ambayo yuko. Alihama. Yuko nyumba
6   nyingine hapo juu karibu na pale. Nilikuwa nikifanza
7   mimi kazi ilikuwa mimi nilihama pale nyumba ya juu.
8   Sasa baada pale nimehama ile nyumba ya juu ile
9   nyumba ya juu vile nilikuwa nikaenda vilevile. Peleka
10   senti mpelekea kule chumbani kwake. Ikawa kila saa
11   mara na anitusi matusi machafu machafu machafu
12   ikawa tumekuwa mbalimbali. Kwenda kamwita
13   nyanyake saa nyingine kumpatia senti. Mpaka
14   mwenyewe asema "haiwezikani. Haitawezekana
15   maana yake wewe hapa nyumbani ni mtu na mtoto
16   wako lazima ufike, ushasikia?" Basi ikawa mimi
17   nimeanza kwenda. Ikawa yeye maneno machafu
18   ameyaacha. Nanikaa nikamwelezea "kama umeacha
19   maneno machafu." Nikamkienda. Nikienda nikienda
20   nikienda nikienda mpaka akagura tena katika hiyo
21   nyumba alioko sasa tena. Akanirudi katika ile
22   nyumba ya kule kule mahali patupoishi vile vile. Ule

23   nyumbani kwa mamake kwa mjombake. Akaregea
24   nyumba ile tena. Sasa aliporegea pale nikawa- mimi
25   nenda pale nyumbani kama kawaida, ushasikia,
26   kupeleka senti kama kawaida.

Text 6.10

1   Atwas: Sasa siku hiyo mimi nikawa nikwenda safari nikaja
2   usiku. Kama vile wakati wa saa mbili mbili.
3   Nilipokuja kutoka safari naenda zangu. Mimi niliingia
4   sikusikii (mume) kwanza nisikia mume wa shemeji
5   yangu Mariamu. Nakakaa pale. Na shemeji yangu.
6   Nikala chakula nikamaliza. Nilipomaliza kwa muda
7   wa saa tatu u nusu nne akaja jamaa mmoja. Na
8   mimi nijua huyu jamaa ni rafiki yake. Alipobisha
9   ndani ya nyumba. Mimi sikumwitikia. Nikamwambia
10   "wewe" shemeji yangu. Nikamwambia "(   ) na
11   wewe nenda kumfungulia huyu ni nani." Ushasikia.
12   Alipokwenda yule jamaa kumfungulia ule mlango
13   shemeji yangu akamuliza "Munira yuko?" Yule
14   shemeji yangu yule shemeji yangu akamwambia
15   "bwanake yuko hapa." Atoka jamaa huyo lakini
16   ilikuwa nishajua ni hayo ushasikia. Nikamwambia
17   huyu "nishajua hayo. Mimi namjua wewe jamaa
18   kwamba ameafikana na huyu Munira" lakini (   ).
19   Nikae makini.

Text 6.11

1   Atwas: Kaondoka, nikaenda mpaka kule room yake na
2   (nilipolewa) nikaenda kwa room yake kwa nilikwenda
3   kumpa senti lakini nilipofika pale kamuuliza
4   "Munira?" "Eh." "Unakumbuka mimi, wewe
5   sijakuacha." "Ah mimi sitaki maneno yako ya
6   kishoga shoga mambo ya kimbwa mbwa." "Ah mimi
7   ni mbwa? Nakuuliza neno zuri kwa pole pole kwa
8   ndia taratibu." Ananitukana. Waniambia mimi ni
9   mbwa si neno. Nambia vyo vyote lakini alivyofikana
10   (kutoka) mimi na room yangu. "Mimi sikukuita ndani
11   ya room yangu toka toka mpaka mwisho wake."
12   Alipoanzalia kunitukania mamangu "kuma mamako."
13 Munira: Usiseme uwongo
14 Atwas: Nyamaza. Sisemi na wewe nasema na

15		kadhi.
16	Munira:	Nitakula kiapo kama mimi nimekutukana mamako.
17		Haya mbona hasemi.
18	Kadhi:	Wacha uache.
19	Atwas:	Usisemi na mimi. Ushasikia bwana? Alipodai
20		akumtukana mamangu "kuma mamako" saa hiyo
21		hiyo lilinitoka kabisa kofi saa hii nikampiga kofi
22		moja. Sikumzidisha. Nikimpiga hata.
23		Akanipiga ubao. Damu zikaanza kunitoka.
24		Mimi ningaliingiliaje kama vita sivijui.
25		Ushasikia? Hapo ndiyo mwanzo asema
26		yeye kwamba kama mimi nilimpiga. Kweli hapo
27		nilimpiga maana yake' alipotajaliwa kunitukana
28		mamangu saa hiyo hiyo kofi tayari.

Text 7.1

1	Ahmed:	Maanake:: (1.4) mambo yake ni:: kudharau. (3.0)
2		Asili ya kusema hivo ni kwamba:: (2.3)
3		ni wakati ambao si m:uda mrefu sana
4		ali:fewa na nyanyake.
5		Sasa ikawa: ataka kwenda kuzika.
6		Mimi nikampatia senti za kwenda (2.2) mazishini
7		ikawa sina senti zaidi.
8		Sasa ilikuwa: amekwenda.=
9		Kabla hajakwenda
10		mimi nikamuuliza (.) ambao
11		"utarudi lini?"
12		Amesema
13		"mimi nitarudi wakati wo wote."
14		Nikamwambia
15		"kwa vile utarudi wakati wo *wote* (.)
16		mimi sikupe."
17		(Ikiingia) kwamba: hatafanya hii.
18		Kama itakuwa wakati wo wote nini hini
19		mtu atakwenda helafu' (.)
20		mimi maoni yangu alikuwa aje siku ile ile
21		halafu karudi. (1.5)
22		Na hakufanya hivyo.=
23		Yeye a*ken*da (1.5)
24		alipokwenda kule

25		akawa ataketi
26		mpaka matanga imemaliza.
27	Kadhi:	Hmm
28	Ahmed:	Alipokuja siku hiyo
29		akaaingia usiku.
30		Na yeye anajua kwamba akaniwatia watoto wangu.
31		Watoto wataka kwenda skuli.
32		Na hakujali mambo hayo
33		alipokuja na:: usiku (1)
34		mimi wakati ule nikamwambia
35		"Sasa ndiyo umetimiza ile ahadi yako kwamba (.)
36		uta::kuja wakati wo wote. Maana yake hatuku:sema
37		kwamba wewe utakwenda keti matanga. Ni vipi wewe
38		leo ume- umekwenda na umekaa (1)
39		matangani
40		na umeingia hapa usiku ni Jumatatu
41		tena usiku na watoto walikuwako, hawaendi
42		skuli tangu asubuhi hakuna uniforms."
43		Bas
44		na mimi ni mtu ambaye siwezi (.) kuketi nao watoto
45		nikawa hifadhi kama vile ambavyo yeye.
46	Kadhi:	Hmm. (1.5)
47	Ahmed:	Bas. (1.4)
48		Yeye kitu nilichomwambia (.) wakati huo (.) wa usiku
49		nimesema "Bas tulale. Asubuhi (1.2) nita' (.)
50		nitakwenda kwa kadhi. Na kuuliza kwamba kuna
51		sheria ya mtu aweza kujitoa mwenyewe na
52		akatukua hatua yake mwenyewe bila ya-a-a mume
53		kuwa (mutaafikiana). Tutakwenda kujua."
54		Mimi nikatoka.
55		Nilipotoka wakati wa ule usiku
56		nikawa na kazi zangu saa nyingine biashara biashara
57		yangu ( ).
58		Duka (ambalo nilichukua)
59		kuna mali ambayo nitaipeleka shamba.
60		Sikumwambia (.) kwamba mimi nitakwenda.
61		Mimi niliporudi asubuhi
62		maana yake mimi nilikwenda
63		mimi' (.) nikalala.
64		Niliporudi asubuhi

65   ikawa (.) hayuko yeye
66   ameweka ufunguo na
67   ametoka
68   amekwenda (1.5) zake. (2.0)
69   Bas.
70   Nikaona sasa huyu amekwenda zake
71   salimie vipi?

Text 7.2

1 Kadhi: Mama umesikia asemavyo.
2 Amina: Nimesikia lakini
3   yote aliyosema ni uwongo.
4 Kadhi: Naam.
5 Amina: Huyu bwana jambo la kwanza (.) vita vya
6   mwanzo hataingilia mambo ya matangani.
7   Huyu bwana halipi nguo mpiya.
8   Hili jambo la pili maneno mazuri hana.
9   Jambo la tatu nyumbani ndiyo halali
10   kabisa.
11   Akitoka asubuhi saa tano
12   mpaka siku ya pili saa tano.
13   Akitoka saa mbili
14   mpaka saa mbili siku ya pili.
15   Akija mapema ni saa nane saa tisia
16   ndiyo alale.
17   Ukimuuliza
18   ni mkali.
19   Alifanya hivo mara ya kwanza
20   akafanya tena mara ya pili
21   akafanya mara ya tatu.
22   Mara ya nne akaja siku ile saa tisia.
23   Nikaja
24   nikamuuliza.
25   Akaniambia
26   "Mimi siwezi kusema na wewe (.) kuondoa.
27   Wewe kama una kwenu (   ) wewe nenda.
28   Siku zote mimi nikamfukuza 'wewe enda
29   zako kwenu' uko hapa tu."
30   Nikamwambia
31   "basi wewe ngoja" babake

32		Ananiambia
33		"hata kumwite" babake
34		"hatutafanza lo lote."
35		Yaani mimi nikayawacha.

Text 7.3

1	Amina:	Ikawa nimeletewa na habari kama jioni.
2		Huyu bibi alisema kwamba ni kweli
3		ni bibi yangu. Ni mamake mamao. (.)
4		Nikamwambia
5		"Basi yule bibi aliyekuwa mgonjwa. Amekufa."
6		"Atazikwa saa ngapi?"
7		Nikamwambia
8		"Atazikwa pengine saa nne maana yake amekufa
9		mapema." (1)
10		Tukalala.
11		Asubuhi nikaketi
12		mpaka alinipatia nauli
13		mimi nikenda.
14		Nikienda
15		nilipofika ku:le
16		tiketi alionipatia ni shilingi ishirini.
17		Nilipofika kule
18		tiketi ni shilingi tano
19		kutoka hapo mpaka huko.
20		Nilipofika huko
21		kuna tangiza.
22		Matanga ni yetu.
23		First shilingi tano kwenye ishirini ilibakia nini?
24	Kadhi:	Kumi na tano.
25	Amina:	Ibakia shilingi kumi.
26		Tiketi shilingi tano kutokea hapo mpaka huko.
27		Kufika kule kuna tangiza ni shilingi tano.
28	Kadhi:	Yes shilingi kumi.
29	Amina:	Halafu shilingi kumi.
30		Ibakia kitu.
31		Na kutoka huko na miguu na jioni
32		mimi siwezi mpaka kufika huku.
33		Nikalala.

34	Siku ya pili asubuhi nikakosa mtu akuja naye
35	na kushuka barabara peke yangu siwezi.
36	Ndia zatisha.
37	Nikalala.
38	Siku ya pili matanga yaondoka.
39	Nikaona afadhali niondoshe kabisa
40	halafu niende
41	maana yake si mara ya kwanza.
42	(Ilitukia)
43	tukafiliwa
44	na nikienda
45	na nikakaa
46	mpaka matanga yakamalizika
47	sijasikia na balaa hii.
48	Nikaja sasa.
49	Nilipokuja zangu
50	nikapisha nyumbani kwa mamangu kwa miguu
51	kutoka Kakuyuni mpaka Ganda ndiyo ni kwetu.
52	Nikapitia nyumbani kwa baba.
53	Nikaenda
54	nikamweleze:a
55	akaniambia
56	"basi sasa wewe keti kwa sababu ma*ba*si hayapiti
57	kwa *huku*. Wakati wa jioni nitakupeleka."
58	Tukaketi mpaka saa kumi na moja
59	tukafuatana na baba
60	tukaja sote mpaka kwa Bakshweni.
61	(Tukifika) kwa Bakshweni
62	ilikuwa usiku.
63	Akanambia
64	"Sasa mimi nimepata wenzangu ambao wamerudi
65	nyumbani kwa miguu. Wewe nenda."
66	Mimi nikashika njia
67	nikaenda zangu mpaka nyumbani.
68	Nilipofika nyumbani
69	huyu bwana ametia kufuli.
70	Hayuko.
71	Nikauliza wenzangu ambao tuwakaa sote
72	"Ameniwachia ufunguo?"

73	Wakaniambia
74	"huh."
75	"Ametoka saa ngapi?"
76	Huyu amesema
77	"ametoka kitambo kidogo."
78	Mimi nikakaa.
79	Nikakaa halafu
80	mimi nikatoka
81	nikaenda jiranini.
82	Nikaketi jiranini
83	hata nilipokuja' (.7)
84	na yeye yuwaingia.
85	Alipokuja
86	aka- akaambiwa
87	"Mama amekuja."
88	Basi vile akamwambiwa kama mimi nimekuja
89	aliudhika hapo hapo mlangoni
90	kabla hajaingia ndani.
91	Akaingia ndani
92	na mimi niko nyuma
93	nikaingia.
94	Vile nashika mlango
95	nataka kuingia chumbani
96	akaniambia (1)
97	"kwa nini wafunga mlango kama mtu mwizi?
98	Umeichelewesha usiku kusudi kupata
99	kupeleleza wapeleleza nini?"
100	Mimi nikakataa
101	shangaa kwanza.
102	Nasema
103	"ilianzaje?"
104	Helafu mimi nikaingia ndani
105	nikaingia ndani
106	nikakaa.
107	Akaniuliza
108	"Mbona tangu juzi hujaja?"
109	Nikaanza kamweleza
110	"zile senti zilikuwa nazo zimekwisha. Sasa kutoka
111	kule na miguu mpaka huku siwezi peke
112	yangu. Barabara zatishe. Jumapili matanga

113		ndio yaondoka. Yameondoka jioni. Nikaona
114		afadhali nilale. Helafu
115		asubuhi nitapita wenzangu ambao tutakuja pale
116		mazishini matangani. Tutakuja sote.
117		Tutafuatana sote wale wenzangu
118		mpaka Ganda tukaatana. Mimi nikaenda zangu
119		kwa baba."
120		"Sasa umeletwa na nani?"
121		Namwambia
122		"Nimekuja na baba."
123		"Uwongo wewe tangu juzi hata wewe
124		huko matangani hukuweko. Ulikuweko
125		hapa hapa Malindi. Huko kwenu
126		huko na huko
127		huko. (1.2) Uko hapa hapa Malindi."
128		Hapa Malindi nyumba *ga:ni?* (2.5)

Text 7.4

1	Kadhi:	Sikia MaAmina. Muna watoto.
2	Amina:	Tuna watoto.
3	Kadhi:	Wangapi?
4	Amina:	Watano.
5	Kadhi:	Watoto watano.
6	Amina:	Mmm. [affirmative]
7		Na si mara ya kwanza.
8		KILA ANAVYOKUWA NA MWANAMKE WA NJE
9		KAZI YAKE NI *HII HII HUU.*
10		|Si mara ya kwanza kabisa-
11	Kadhi:	|Mpaka sasa munao watoto watano
12		akili zenu namna hii?
13	Amina:	Mi sina makosa.
14		Makosa yaje na huyu
15		kwa sababu ya wanawake wa nje.
16		*Hizi* basi- balaa zake ziki- zikianza balaa
17		ni mwanamke wa nje.
18		Saa hizi anaye.
19		Mara nyumbani halali. (3.5)
20		Halali *kabisa* nyumbani.
21		Alisema maneno uwongo.

Text 7.5

1	Amina:	"Mbona tangu juzi hujaja?"
2		Nikaanza kamweleza
3		"zile senti zilikuwa nazo zimekwisha. Sasa kutoka
4		kule na miguu mpaka huku siwezi peke
5		yangu. Barabara zatishe. Jumapili matanga
6		ndio yaondoka. Yameondoka jioni. Nikaona
7		afadhali nilale. Halafu asabuhi nitapita wenzangu
8		ambao tutakuja pale mazishini matangani.
9		Tutakuja sote. Tutafuatana sote wale
10		wenzangu mpaka Ganda tukaatana.
11		Mimi nikaenda zangu kwa baba."
12		"Sasa umeletwa na nani?"
13		Namwambia
14		"Nimekuja na baba."

Text 7.6

1	Amina:	". . . tangu juzi hata wewe huko matangani
2		hukuweko.
3		Ulikuweko hapa hapa Malindi.
4		Huko kwenu huko na
5		huko huko. (1.2)
6		Uko hapa hapa Malindi."
7		Hapa Malindi nyumba *ga:ni.*

Text 7.7

1	Amina:	Huyu bwana jambo la kwanza (.) vita vya mwanzo
2		hataingilia mambo ya matangani.
3		Huyu bwana halipi nguo mpiya.
4		Hili jambo la pili maneno mazuri hana.
5		Jambo la tatu nyumbani ndiyo halali
6		kabisa.
7		Akitoka asubuhi saa tano
8		mpaka siku ya pili saa tano.
9		Akitoka saa mbili
10		mpaka saa mbili siku ya pili.
11		Akija mapema ni saa nane saa tisia
12		ndiyo alale.
13		Ukimuuliza

14	ni mkali.
15	Alifanya hivo mara ya kwanza
16	akafanya tena mara ya pili
17	akafanya mara ya tatu.
18	Mara ya nne akaja siku ile saa tisia.

Text 7.8

1	Kadhi:	Yeye akajua namna ya kufikiria. Mufanza jambo
2		kama kitoto.
3	Ahmed:	Basi ni yeye kama vile ambavyo amenieleza bwana.
4	Amina:	Kwani? Yeye ametia dhiki. Na wewe walala nje kila
5		siku.
6	Kadhi:	Sasa nyinyi mbele ya Mungu kuwa weka na watoto
7		watano. Utamjibu nini Mwenyezi Mungu? Nafikiri au
8		ile ambapo tutasikiza kwenu akija taabu hii
9		yamshukia ni nani? Si watoto?
10	Ahmed:	Ni watoto.

Text 7.9

1	Kadhi:	Mtukuliane akikukosa. Mchukulie mamake mama na
2		huyu mwenziwe akikosa mchukulie babako.
3		(Mwakinishe). Enda nje kwa kishindwe upande kadhi
4		nini. Mutengeneza nyumba yenu.
5		Muangalie watoto vizuri.
6	Amina:	Huyu hayuko kazini. Hayo maneno asemao ni
7		uwongo huyu.
8	Kadhi:	Ah ndiyo lakini sasa mimi sijasema maana yake haya
9		hatuwezi kuthibitisha ni kweli au uwongo. Lakini sasa
10		tusemaje. Akiwa yeye asema "mimi nakwenda kazini"
11		utamwambia mtu hakwenda kazini. Utasema maneno
12		namna hayo? Na hata kama namna hivo. Wewe si
13		juu yako kukaa kila mara sikizanisha namna hivo?
14		Maana yake itakuharibia.

Text 7.10

1	Kadhi:	Sasa wewe, sababu yako umetukua siku zaidi eh
2		amekaa siku zaidi lakini amekwenda filihali maskini.
3		Ni mnyonge nenda kwao na wewe mume wake.
4		Ikitaka unue uso wako.

5	Ahmed:	Maana yake amefanya kitu kiriba. Hakusema kitu
6		ameanza kusema nyumbani kwamba "mimi sijui siku
7		yote nitakaa ndiyo siku nataka kuja."
8	Kadhi:	Ndiyo hivo maana yake
9	Ahmed:	Anatimiza ule wajibu atakaa.
10	Kadhi:	Nakuambia ende ( ) ndiyo hivo na wewe hukum-
11		sharitiza kwamba "la nilikuambia urudi kesho."
12		Ulimwambia? (2). Mulikwisha hivo hivo. Bas.
13	Ahmed:	Hayo ajibu hivo ndivyo nakaona umesema kwamba
14		ni: atachukuwa ni maneno tu. Na akatimiza
15		yule bibi.
16	Kadhi:	Sasa akatimiza lakini wewe ukashamtimiza
17		kumwambia yule endao atakuja siku yo yote lakini
18		hukumwambia "urudi kesho."
19		Hukumwambia. Shafahamu? Sasa hayo.
20	Ahmed:	Ionyesha wazi kwamba hata kama ningemwambia
21		yeye hangekuja.
22	Kadhi:	Uh uh lakini at least singalikuwa na saba:bu? Ndiyo
23		kumwambia ikiwa mtu kama hivi akunimwambia
24		"mimi niende mahali. Sijui nitarudi lini." Na wewe
25		ukamkubalia. Bas. Huwashakuwa permitted? Na
26		huwezi kumtia katika makosa.

Text 7.11

1	Shaaban:	Nikarudi kwangu.
2		Niliporudi
3		mimi nikaona kwamba akakaa pale pale nyumbani.
4		Siyo maana yake ukikosana na
5		bibi yako
6		si lazima atakaa pale?
7		Mukipatana
8		mutapatana mbali?

Text 7.12

1	Shaaban:	Nikakaa tena kama siku saba hivi
2		nikasema
3		"Hapana."
4		(kaje)
5		mimi nikamwita jamaa
6		nikasema

7		"Bibi yangu haina haja tuende kwa kadhi
8		ushaona.
9		Tuende zetu
10		tuelewane tena."
11		Tukakae
12		maana yake hii itakuwa ni taabu sisi ( ) taabu
13		(kaa) mbali jamani huko.
14		Maisha kweli imeharibika
15		siyo bwana?
16	Kadhi:	Hmm
17	Shaaban:	Nikasema
18		"haina haja."

Text 8.1

1	Munira:	Sasa yeye alipo alipo alipo maliza (.) kunipiga
2		alisema
3		"Oh mimi sikuwate mpaka unipewe: mtoto wangu.
4		Si u- ukinipa watoto mimi nitakuata."
5		Saa saba juzi siku ya Jumanne
6		ndiyo ilikuwa ni::-
7		nimekuja nao hao watoto wote.
8		Nikaja.
9		Nikaketi nao
10		na yeye hakuja.

Text 8.2

1	Shaaban:	Nikamuuliza
2		"Wewe watoka wapi?"
3		Akasema
4		"Mimi natoka chooni."
5		"Wewe watoka chooni na mimi niko kwenye hoteli
6		hapa. Kwa nini hukupeleka mtoto kwenye choo? Kwa
7		nini alie? Usiingie hapa?"
8		Pale chooni waona akaanza kurudi
9		tena
10		(kamfuata).
11		Nikajaribu kumpiga makofi matatu (.)
12		ushaona bwana?
13		Nikarudi kwangu.

Text 8.3

1	Rukia:	Nikatoka
2		Nikaenda zangu choo.
3		Saa hiyo hiyo nikarudi.
4		Niliporudi
5		Yeye amekaa
6		"Watoka wapi?"
7		"Chooni."
8		"Watoka wapi?"
9		"Natoka chooni"
10		Mimi nikanyamaza.
11		Akanipiga kofi la kwanza hapa na hapa.

Text 8.4

1	Shaaban:	Niliporudi mimi
2		nikaona kwamba akakaa pale pale nyumbani.
3		Siyo maana yake
4		ukikosana na bibi yako
5		si lazima atakaa pale?
6		Mukipatana
7		mutapatana mbali?
8		Akahama huyu.
9		Asiende kule hoteli
10		ushaona.
11		Na sasa nimeshajua
12		akaa huko kwa
13		kaa hoteli
14		ushaona.
15		Mimi nikakaa siku ya kwanza siku ya pili siku ya tatu
16		nikaenda kamwita mamake bwana
17		( ) Mimi, tusikizane na bibi yangu
18		maana yake mimi sioni mbaya
19		maana yake sianze mimi bwana
20		kila mtu afanze bibi yake ( )
21		pale mimi nikamfanya bibi yangu kazi yangu.
22		Ashajua.

Text 8.5

1	Ahmed:	Alipokuja na:: us*i*ku (1)
2		mimi wakati ule nikamwambia
3		"Sasa ndiyo umet*imiz*a ile ahadi yako kwamba (.)

4		uta::kuja wakati wo wote. Maana yake hatuku:sema
5		kwamba wewe utakwenda keti matanga. Ni vipi
6		wewe leo ume- umekwenda na ume*kaa* (1)
7		matangani na umeingia hapa usiku
8		ni Jumatatu tena usiku
9		na watoto walikuwako, hawaendi skuli tangu asubuhi
10		hakuna uniforms."

Text 8.6

1	Amina:	Halafu mimi nikaingia ndani
2		nikaingia ndani
3		nikakaa.
4		Akaniuliza.
5		"Mbona tangu juzi hujaja?"
6		Nikaanza kamweleza
7		"zile senti zilikuwa nazo zimekwisha. Sasa kutoka
8		kule na miguu mpaka huku siwezi peke
9		yangu. Barabara zatishe. Jumapili matanga ndio
10		yaondoka. Yameondoka jioni. Nikaona
11		afadhali nilale. Halafu
12		asubuhi nitapita wenzangu ambao tutakuja
13		pale mazishini matangani. Tutakuja sote.
14		Tutafuatana sote wale wenzangu
15		mpaka Ganda tukaatana. Mimi nikaenda zangu
16		kwa baba."
17		"Sasa umeletwa na nani?"
18		Namwambia
19		"Nimekuja na baba."
20		"Uwongo wewe tangu juzi hata wewe huko
21		matangani hukuweko. Ulikuweko
22		hapa hapa Malindi. Huko kwenu
23		huko na huko huko.
24		(1.2) Uko hapa hapa Malindi."
25		Hapa Malindi nyumba *ga:ni?* (2.5)

Text 8.7

1	Kadhi:	Sasa kwa mfano wewe unasema amekupiga
2		jana kwa sababu gani?
3	Aisha:	Si sababu habari ya
4		tukulia pesa (.) mkononi,

5		kunipokonya kwa nguvu,
6		kama angeniambia kwa upole
7		"Wewe sasa hizi usifanye jambo fulani.
8		Nitakazifanya' ku- nina haja nazo
9		kwa hivyo usiende nazo po pote. Nitafanya
10		|jambo lingine."
11	Kadhi:	|Kwani alikuambia?
12	Aisha:	Hakuniambia.
13		Ameniambia
14		"Nipe mwenyewe pesa *za*ngu."
15		Sasa mimi nitafikiriaje?
16		Hata kama ataniambia
17		"Saa nyingine nitakupa nyingine."
18		Uwongo!
19		Saa saa ile ametukulia hasira ( )
20		|siwezi tena.
21	Kadhi:	|( ) sema mambo kama haya
22	Aisha:	Hm.
23	Kadhi:	ikiwa ni kweli. ( ) kwa nini ilivyofanza

Text 8.8

1	Omar:	Kama mimi |( ) ningemwambia kwa kwa hasi|ra
2	Aisha:	|Ni hivo |Huh
3	Omar:	Maana yake
4		Huko nyumbani
5		kuna watu.
6		Yuko mpangaji.
7		Mara ya kwanza nilimwita
8		"Fulani ndoo nenda wapi?"
9		Akaniambia
10		"Naenda (1.5) kulipa zile' (1) pesa."
11		Nikamwambia
12		"Mimi si nikuambie? Zile uziweke usizitumie?
13		Nilikuambia hivo."
14		Kamwambia
15		"Basi lete."
16		Akawa yeye (.) yuwatoka
17		ushafahamu.
18		Ikaonyesha kuwa hataki ile nilivyomwambia
19		waona.

20   Nikamwambia zaidi mara ya sita
21   mpaka yule mpangaji akamwambia
22   "Wewe sikumpe hizo pesa uangalia akikupiga hapo
23   itakuwa nini?"
24   Yeye ndiyo.

Text 8.9

1   Omar: Atakapokupiga
2   hataki kuzitoa hizo.
3   Ni lazima ataka kutoka.
4   (Sasa na mimi) nikamwambia
5   "Wewe nipe hizo pesa"
6   isipokuwa na
7   katika kuzitukuwa
8   sasa yeye ndiyo (kwamba) mbali yuanifinya
9   mbali yuaniuma.
10 |Ushafahamu?
11 Aisha: |Hata mimi sikumwuma hata si hivyo
12   kabisa
13 Omar: |Sasa ni lazima (   )
14 Aisha: |Sasa baada ya kuchukua pesa *za*ke
15   nilimchukua mtoto
16   yuwali:a.
17   Namnyonyeshe.
18   Baada ya kumnyonyesha sasa
19   akaanza kuteza naye.
20   Nikamwambia
21   "Sasa umekuja fanya nini hapa?"
22   Nikamsukuma hivi.
23   "Wewe kwani mtoto wangu (.) haina haja? Kwani::
24   mimi nateza naye. Na mimi pia ni mtoto wangu si
25   mtoto wako peke yako."
26   Niambie
27   "Hapana. Mimi nitatoka naye mtoto."
28   Nilimwambia
29   "Naenda haya kwa mamangu kuwa mamangu ni
30   (hayo)?" Basi sasa sikuniacha kama ku-
31   mimi nitakwenda wapi
32   kama kama nitakuja huu
33   kama kwenda nyumbani na nini.

34		(acha) mtoto nikienda naye
35		au nitatoka naye.
36		Basi haya akaanza kuleta vita.
37		"Mimi nitakupiga. Huniwezi. Mimi nikikupiga hujui.
38		Siku- wewe huniwezi."
39		Sasa ndiyo akaanza vita hapo
40		( ) piga.
41	Kadhi:	Ndivyo hivyo lakini vita ( ) |havina
42		maana . . .
43	Aisha:	|Na kila siku mama
44		akatazwa nyumbani.
45	Omar:	-siku zote mimi nimwambia-
46	Kadhi:	Maana yake ukileta vita itakuwa wewe
47	Aisha:	Kwanza ni aibu.

Text 8.10

1	Omar:	Ndiyo watu lazima watasema hivyo
2		na huko watu wengi watasema huko
3		mimi nampige.
4		Mimi namwambia maneno
5		"Wewe waniuma mimi nasikie utungu lazima mimi
6		nijitetea."
7		Ushafahamu?
8		Siyo kwamba ni mara ya kwanza.
9		Unaona hii.
10		Kuna alama za kitambo.
11		Mimi sikumpiga mpaka yeye
12	Aisha:	Umenipiga |makofi ndipo mimi nikakuuma.
13	Omar:	|Na alama nyingine ni hini.
14		Ukaniuma kwa jambo ambalo halina maana.
15		|Ndiyo-
16	Kadhi:	|Bas bas-
17	Omar:	-Wallahi tena.
18		Kila siku namwambia mimi
19		namwambia
20		"Wewe umeolewa cheo cha kwanza ni wewe
21		unifundishe mimi watu waenda hivi waenda
22		hivi. Sio kila siku kupigizana na nini na
23		mayowe na makilele."

Text 8.11

1	Nasira:	Akenda zake.
2		Mimi nikachukua vyangu vile alivyoniambia nitoke
3		maana yake
4		nazaa naye mtoto mmoja
5		wengine (ni) jukuu wanangu.
6		Nikachukua vyangu
7		nikachukua nguo zangu
8		"Twende zetu nyumbani kwetu." (1.5)
9		Nilipofika nyumbani
10		nakenda
11		nakaelezea vile ilivyotokea.
12		Wakaniambia
13		"Ikiwa amekufu*kuza* amekuambia utoke ataka
14		ufunguo zake za nyumba ikiwa kuwa ana ha*sira*
15		atakuja hapa nyumbani maana yake kwenu
16		yuwakujua. Lakini ikiwa ame*amini* hicho kitu ni
17		kweli hatakuja. Kwa hivyo wewe urudi ukachukua
18		kila ambacho ujue ni chako uondoe mpe ufunguo
19		zake. Uombe ruhusa kazini kama wiki mbili uje
20		nyumbani ukae. Yeye kwenu yuwakujua ni wapi.
21		Ikiwa ana haja na *wewe* one week yamtosha atakuja.
22		Ikiwa hana haja na wewe wiki moja ikisha utarudi
23		kazini. Utafuta mahali popote ukae utafuta jambo la
24		kufanya."
25		Basi mimi nikaja kazini
26		Nikaomba ruhusa
27		ikakuwa four days.
28		Ile siku ya Jumanne hawakuhesabu kazini
29		kwa vile ilikuwa ni Public Holiday.
30	Kadhi:	Hmm.
31	Nasira:	Wakanipa siku nne.
32		Mimi nikarudi.
33		Nikaenda zangu nyumbani.
34		Nikachukua vitu vya:ngu
35		vile ambavyo najua ni vyangu.
36		Vile ambavyo alivinunua yeye mwenyewe
37		kama nikazitaka
38		nikamwachia kile kitu chake.

Text 8.12

1	Atwas:	"Munira?" "Eh." "Unakumbuka mimi, wewe
2		sijakuacha?" "Ah mimi sitaki maneno yako ya
3		kishoga shoga mambo ya kimbwa mbwa." "Ah mimi
4		ni mbwa? Nakuuliza, neno zuri, kwa pole pole kwa
5		ndia taratibu." Alinitukana. Waniambia mimi ni
6		mbwa si neno. Nambia vyo vyote lakini alivyofikana
7		(kutoka) mimi na room yangu. "Mimi sikukuita ndani
8		ya room yangu toka toka mpaka mwisho wako."
9		Alipoanzalia kunitukania mamangu "kuma mamako."
10	Munira:	Usiseme uwongo
11	Atwas:	Nyamaza. Sisemi na wewe na sema
12		na kadhi.
13	Munira:	Nitakula kiapo kama mimi nimekutukania mamako.
14		Haya mbona hasemi.
15	Kadhi:	Wacha uache.
16	Atwas:	Usisemi na mimi. Ushasikia bwana? Alipodai
17		akumtukana mamangu "kuma mamako"
18		saa hiyo hiyo lilinitoka kabisa kofi
19		saa hii nikampiga kofi moja.

Text 8.13

1	Zulecha:	Na mimi nimestahimili sana sa:na kwake *sa*:na siku
2		*nyi*:ngi
3	Kadhi:	Kwa nini mpaka sasa hustahimili?
4	Zulecha:	Mpaka imefikilia ha:pa. Hao mimi si mara ya kwanza
5		kunikatazana

Text 8.14

1	Kadhi:	Naam
2	Zulecha:	"Babangu" aniambie mimi.|Haya "mimi pia ni
3		babangu lakini ( )"
4	Kadhi:	|Hii ndiyo utafanzaje
5	Zulecha:	"Na mke wangu ( )" bembeleza ( ) "Kwenda."
6		"Nitakwenda." "Kwenda shenzi kuma mamako
7		mshenzi."
8	Kadhi:	Haya sikia.
9	Saidi:	Kadhi bwana wajua huyu, bibi yangu, mimi siwezi
10		kumsupport nakuambia kwa sababu mara nyingi
11		asema maneno yake yaani achukua uwongo

12   ashakasirika. |Mpaka (   ) kazi yake mimi
13 Zulecha: |"Kuma mamangu"
14 Saidi: Kila siku nitakwenda mimi
15 Kadhi: Kwa mfano kama hayo

Text 9.1

1 Kadhi: Sasa. Hio maneno mawili mbalimbali.
2 Juma: Eh.
3 Kadhi: Yeye amesema amekufukuzwa kwa sababu ya
4   maneno.
5 Nasira: Eh.
6 Kadhi: Na yeye asema hakufukuza. Maneno amekuambia
7   kweli.
8 Juma: |Naam
9 Nasira: |Alinifukuza.
10 Juma: Sikumfukuza.

Text 9.2

1 Nasira: Na hayo maneno yalianza muda mrefu kama sisi
2 Kadhi: Ndiyo sasa hayo maneno ukiyatafuta maneno
3   maana yake maneno siku zote hayana mwisho.
4 Juma: Yeah.
5 Kadhi: Na watu waweza kupoteza wakati wao au kupoteza
6   maisha yao kwa sababu ya maneno. Maana yake
7   maneno si kitu cha mtu kushiriki wala kutegemea.
8   Mtu kushiriki mwendo wako. Wewe kama mke
9   kumtazama mume wako, "Endelea vipi?"
10   Maneno wacha kando.

Text 9.3

1 Omar: Ni aibu namna hiyo. Watu waketi wa-
2   wakasitiriana kwa chochote
3   wanacho hawana.
4   Ndivyo watu wanavoenda.

Text 9.4

1 Ahmed: Na pia nina kitu kimoja methali ya maneno bado
2   yuko hapa Kadhi.
3   Wajua huyu bibi
4   ni- ametaja habari ya nguo.

5	Ni hizo nguo kusema nguo vile pale
6	alipo yeye ame*vaa* nguo.
7	Na si tu.
8	Aliwahi kum- kumleta shemeji yangu
9	nyumbani na kamtajia maneno haya.
10	Mpaka asema mimi sijanunua sijui mpaka
11	nguo yake *ndani*. Pia sikununua.
12	Ambapo yule shemeji mimi nishafanyia maneno
13	kuhusu yeye sitaki awa na waliozungumza kitu
14	chochote.

Text 9.5

1	Kadhi:	Na wewe nataka uone (kwa ni fakhari hivo)?
2		Kuna mtu ambaye haoni utungu?
3		Maana yake hakuna. Mtu anaweza
4		kujificha mashallah mke hamuulize lo lote.
5		Sasa ni sifa gani? Maana yake hana raha wala wewe.
6		Hana mapenzi na wewe.

Text 9.6

1	Juma:	Nikasema
2		"Mimi natoka na nitarudi na wale watoto." Mimi
3		( ) mimi nikatoka kwa kuepusha huyu
4		shetwani. Nenda zangu.

Text 9.7

1	Kadhi:	Lakini usi- usiwe usiwe tayari sana
2		kujifanza maana yake ubaya kuteta. Hii
3		si nzuri. Mtu apendalee kwa ndia yo yote
4		itapita. Mtu kitu akikupa lazima ukitukua
5		hayo ndiyo. Hili ndilo naloomba. Hayo yalipita.
6		Nendani shetwani unafahamu? Ni hivo ndivo
7		tunavyoomba ( ) nyumbani lakini usitafute mengi
8		yasikuwa na maana. Haya yalopita yeye
9		(anakuwa na) utungu ameumia. Na wewe ulionana
10		utungu hapo umeumia. Sasa musameheana. Maana
11		yake wewe akili si zako na yeye akili si zake. Lakini
12		sasa siku nyingine mushasikizana. Kila moja
13		ashaone kile kitendo hakina maana.

Notes

Chapter One

1. My translation of the saying in the epigraph reflects the two meanings of "goodness" in the definition offered by Johnson and Madan (1939: 547) under *uzuri*: "beauty—mainly external, and appealing to the senses, and so often of things concrete, an ornament, decorative work, a work of art, a perfume, a cosmetic, &c. But also of 'excellence', and even 'moral goodness', considered rather as good taste than good principle *(wema)*."

2. Many feminist scholars have contributed to this debate (see, e.g., Alcoff 1988; Barrett 1992; de Lauretis 1990; Ferguson 1993; Fisher and Davis 1993; Mahoney and Yngvesson 1992; H. Moore 1994). They proffer a variety of approaches to the problem of the gendered subject, such as positionality and strategic location. As Ferguson (1993:163) has argued, it cannot be assumed that gendered subjectivity is unproblematic either in theory or in its lived enactment: "Even the hegemonic insistances that we *be* a certain way must be negotiated, not simply absorbed and regurgitated."

3. By depicting gender as a "performance," Butler (1993) faces the problem of discourse and agency head on, treating the discursive construction of gendered subjectivity as a dynamic process. Moreover, Butler theorizes the gendered subject as prior to the human subject, arguing that materiality is itself part of discursive practice. Recent responses to the debates over gendered subjectivity turn to culturally specific and locally constituted examinations of lives in order to display both how subjects are constituted prior to interaction and how they are transformed through their actions (see di Leonardo 1991; H. Moore 1994).

4. This broader sense of discourse follows Foucault's notions of discourses as ways of speaking and "knowing" that are linked to specific forms of knowledge production (1980, 1983). Foucault's approach identifies the connections among discourse, knowledge, and power. The vocabularies, interactional routines, and epistemological assumptions associated with discourses have historical specificity. Although discourses develop in relation to the institutions of modern society (e.g., the law), the operation of any discourse extends institutional and disciplinary reach. Discourse in the Foucauldian sense is distinct from interactional speech, yet the two forms are

inextricably related (see Ferguson 1984; Merry 1990; Mertz 1992a; Wagner-Pacifici 1994).

5. Gal (1991:189) draws on Bourdieu to make a similar point: "Forms that diverge are devalued by the dominant ideologies. . . . Despite the resistance demonstrated in women's linguistic practices, Bourdieu's (1977b) remark about the effects of this kind of linguistic domination applies: by authorizing some linguistic practices and not others, the institution appears to demonstrate the inferiority of those who use unauthorized forms and often inculcates in them feelings of worthlessness."

6. Brenneis and Myers (1984:19) make the important theoretical move of separating the intentional exercise of power from the reproduction of relations of domination: "We are not saying that actors are trying to reproduce the relations of domination but that, in the act of accomplishing something they do intend, such as resolving a dispute or winning a debate, the meaning of their acts and utterances may come to be more, or other than, what was the simple intent." For Brenneis and Myers, the intentional exercise of power is not correlated absolutely with reproducing domination. Their approach to agency considers the political contribution of speakers who are not consciously aware of their acts.

7. Reviews of the legal anthropology literature note that interest in the study of disputes as a means of understanding law's role in society reoriented the subdiscipline away from treating law as a system of static rules embedded within an equally static social order (Comaroff and Roberts 1981; Conley and O'Barr 1990; Hirsch and Lazarus-Black 1994; Just 1992; Moore 1986; Nader 1969, 1990; Roberts 1979; Starr and Collier 1989; Vincent 1990). When they took up the analysis of small-scale hearings, Gluckman, Bohannan, and Pospisil focused on "the customary content of the disputes themselves and the rules and concepts employed" (Moore 1986:9). Their studies depicted disputes as normative displays of intricate legal logics distinct from, yet as elaborate as, Western legal traditions and processes. This "stream of analysis" shifted as other anthropologists began to focus on disputes as arenas of strategic and political action undertaken by individuals pursuing particular interests (ibid.). Motivated from a distance by Malinowski's pioneering work on crime, these scholars addressed, albeit in different ways, the issues of strategy, individual choice, and case outcome and moved studies of disputing well beyond earlier concerns with rules, customs, and systems. It was through these processually oriented approaches that "the unfolding of a case over time entered the models of disputing" (ibid.:10). Moore (1986) notes that attention to disputing paralleled the trend toward studying process in anthropology and social theory more generally.

8. Studies of comparative dispute processes and dispute transformation have demonstrated that, as people with grievances engage in the processes of "naming, blaming, and claiming" associated with the development of disputes, they move from one disputing context to another and from one way of articulating a problem to another (see, e.g., Felstiner, Abel, and Sarat

1980; Mather and Yngvesson 1980). The focus on "styles" of disputing analyzed how dispute processes are conditioned by cultural and social forces and, as well, how they reflect individual interests (see, e.g., Nader 1969, 1990; Nader and Todd 1978). For example, a disputant's choice to take a conflict to a particular disputing forum or to avoid conflict by "lumping it" can be understood, at least in part, as evidence of conformity to a cultural style of handling conflict and thereby ordering society. In some contexts, cultural notions such as "harmony ideology" shape disputants' strategies, and, as Nader has argued, these ideologies emerge over time as cultural responses—sometimes counterhegemonic—to broad historical shifts of power (Nader 1990; see also Chanock 1985; Moore 1986). Other cultural understandings or ideologies, such as "praying for justice" (Greenhouse 1986), "disentangling" (Watson-Gegeo and White 1990), or "bargaining for reality" (Rosen 1984), have been identified by ethnographers of law who, though influenced by the disputing paradigm, take a range of approaches to culture's role in legal processes (see also Geertz 1983).

9. Moore (1986:10) identifies several tendencies in the study of disputing. These include the focus on particular cases and disputing; plural legal systems in postcolonial societies; the evolution of law and legal processes; cultural assumptions embedded in legal systems; and law's role in history and change. Just (1992) describes two key approaches in legal anthropology that lead scholars to focus on law and cultural practices or, alternatively, law and its relation to history and social change. His review of the legal anthropology literature indicates as well that disputing has remained significant to both groups of scholars (see also Vincent 1990).

10. At the conclusion of their analysis, critique, and ultimate disavowal of legal anthropology, Comaroff and Roberts (1981:248–49) portray the paradox in theory and method of their own approach to disputing: "On the one hand, the logic of dispute is ultimately situated in the encompassing system and can be comprehended only as such. But, on the other, it is in the context of confrontation—when persons negotiate their social universe and enter discourse about it—that the character of that system is revealed."

11. Over the past several decades, there have been numerous studies of the discourses of disputing and law. Many have considered the relation between the forms of courtroom speech and the social characteristics of the speakers who produce them. A central finding of this research is that certain genres of speech (characterized by lexical items and patterns of interaction) are routinely produced by legal professionals. Moreover, some studies explore the rules for interaction in legal contexts to which all participants are compelled to conform. Conversation analysts have been particularly interested in the ways that rules of evidence and procedure violate the commonsense understandings about language with which speakers generally operate. A number of empirical studies describe how the language of legal institutions, particularly the structure of interaction, constrains speakers. Atkinson

and Drew (1979) present an extensive description of the differences between ordinary conversation and the language of legal cases (see also Goldman 1983; Moerman 1988; O'Barr 1982). By delineating particularities of the organization of courtroom conversation (such as question-and-answer sequencing), they show how some very fundamental tasks (such as blaming) occur differently under the rules (formal and informal) that guide interaction. Some studies claim that, out of their unfamiliarity with conventions of speech in court, some disputants are linguistically disadvantaged (see, e.g., O'Barr 1982). Experts and, ironically, some repeat players have great facility with courtroom language. Those most socially marginal in court (i.e., women, individuals with low social status or limited education) face the greatest difficulties in producing effective court speech (O'Barr 1982; O'Barr and Atkins 1980). Several studies investigate differences among disputants in the specific features of speech produced in court. These include syntactic or lexical differences (see, e.g., O'Barr 1982 on powerful and powerless speech; see also Danet 1980; Philips 1987) and discourse-level differences (see Conley and O'Barr 1990 on rule-oriented and relational speech). Adelsward, Aronsson, and Linell (1988) claim that the organization of blaming and justification in criminal cases depends in part on the severity of the crime. Thus, a range of factors contribute to differences in the speech produced by disputants and other participants in a legal proceeding. Whether, as Brenneis (1988) suggests, these studies assume that disputants create social relations through interaction (the conversation-analysis tradition) or that they speak from preexisting social roles or relations (the ethnography-of-speaking tradition), there is the corollary assumption—largely implicit in most studies—that speakers rework the conditions under which present and future speech occurs.

    12. Several cross-cultural studies explore gender differences in the speech genres produced by men and women engaged in conflict resolution (see, e.g., Brown 1993; Gal 1991; Keenan 1974). Based on ethnographic and linguistic research in Madagascar, Elinor Keenan's influential article "Norm Makers and Norm Breakers: Uses of Speech by Men and Women in a Malagasy Community" describes how Malagasy men and women produced gender-patterned linguistic responses to conflict (Keenan 1974). Men upheld cultural norms by speaking indirectly and formally, even when faced with disturbing incidents (e.g., thefts). On the rare occasions when they voiced accusations against others, they did so through veiled claims. By contrast, women were said to have "long tongues" with which they spoke boldly and directly. They made public accusations and engaged openly in disputes. Both men and women believed women's direct speech to violate socially recognized norms that entailed avoiding conflict and offensive speech. Although both genders valued these ideals, women explicitly violated them and, consequently, suffered social disapproval. For their part, men recognized implicitly the value of direct confrontation, as they routinely compelled women under their control to make accusations that they themselves refrained from

voicing. An early contribution to feminist anthropology, Keenan's article makes the important point that, although men and women produce contrasting speech genres, this difference can only be understood in relation to cultural beliefs about the value of each genre. But neither speech differences nor the cultural devaluation of those differences are evidence of lack of social power. Rather, Keenan's assertion that "women use one kind of power and men another" (139) implies that women are capable of playing important roles in social life, even though they rely on different linguistic means.

13. If there is a canonical work in language and gender, it is Robin Lakoff's *Language and Woman's Place* (1975). It has attracted considerable attention (much of it critical) from a popular as well as scholarly audience, and it continues to serve as a starting point for reviews of language and gender scholarship. Lakoff describes women's language as less influential in comparison to men's by virtue of the speech features produced by women speakers. Based on her observations of speech in the United States and examples drawn from native-speaker intuition, Lakoff furthers the notion that ways of speaking are gendered, and she calls attention to the corresponding disadvantage to women in most circumstances. Lakoff was among the first scholars to examine women's roles in "ordinary" conversation. There have been numerous critiques of Lakoff's model of women's speech, particularly of the lax methods used to select and interpret the features that characterize women's language. Her approach was narrow in at least two ways. Her focus on gender meant that she failed to consider the roles of class, race, and education in the speech of her subjects, who were generally white middle- or upper-middle-class women. Also, her theory of the relation between speech forms and power was inadequate, leaving readers to assume that language merely reflects immutable social hierarchies. This aspect of Lakoff's work is curious given that, at the same time, activists were advocating changes in language in order to alter women's position. Lakoff's study sparked a virtual flood of language and gender research. The empirical testing of her claims, undertaken by other scholars who manipulated variables of the speech event, falsified and questioned her findings and contributed to the growing field of sociolinguistics.

14. The features that they examined were hedges, polite forms, tag questions, speaking in italics, empty adjectives, hypercorrect grammar and pronunciation, lack of a sense of humor, direct quotations, special lexicon, and question intonation in declarative sentences.

15. In an experimental phase of the research, mock jurors reported that speakers who exhibited the features of powerless speech were less reliable, less convincing, less truthful, and less intelligent than those who spoke powerfully.

16. In "On Being the Object of Property," Williams (1991:225–26) explores how the language of contract enslaved her great-great-grandmother, offering the young woman no recourse when she was raped and impregnated by the white lawyer who had purchased her. Williams makes a deft compari-

son between her ancestor's plight and that of women engaged in more recent
battles over contract, parentage, and bodily integrity:

> the rhetorical tricks by which Sara Whitehead became Melissa Stern seem
> very like the heavy-worded legalities by which my great-great-grandmother
> was pacified and parted from her child. In both situations, the real mother
> had no say; her powerlessness was imposed by state law that made her and
> her child helpless in relation to the father. My great-great-grandmother's
> powerlessness came about as the result of a contract to which she was not
> a party; Mary Beth Whitehead's powerlessness came about as a result of
> a contract she signed at a discrete point in time—yet which, over time,
> enslaved her. The contract-reality in both instances was no less than magic:
> it was illusion transformed into not-illusion. Furthermore, it masterfully
> disguised the brutality of enforced arrangements in which these women's
> autonomy, their flesh and their blood, was locked away in word vaults,
> without room to reconsider—ever.

By directing attention to the "word vaults" that perform and conceal
the magic of legal contract, Williams emphasizes the power of legal discourse
to constitute identities and to effect painfully unequal relationships. From
this perspective, law is a crucial factor in inhibiting narrations that describe
the complex and debilitating positionings of some persons.

17. Some sociolinguists would posit that forms of speech reflect commonly accepted categories of social relations that operate almost at the level
of the Durkheimian social fact. By contrast, ethnomethodologists view
speech as the vehicle through which social relations and social life are created
anew in every interaction. They resist treating speakers as members of social
categories who routinely produce particular kinds of speech. Though these
are radically different approaches, they share similar limitations. First, neither approach attends to the range of phenomena associated with language
use. That is, they focus on only a few linguistic forms and conceptualize
linguistic meaning narrowly. Second, neither approach fully appreciates language as produced in particular historical, political, and cultural contexts.
The brief caricature offered here is not intended as a full analysis of the
epistemological positions in sociolinguistics, a task that is beyond the scope
of this volume (for such an analysis, see, e.g., Levinson 1983; Schiffrin 1994).

18. Cameron also uses the term *folklinguistics* to refer to linguistic ideology. She defines folklinguistics as "that collection of beliefs about language
which are accepted as common sense within a society. These beliefs serve
both to regulate linguistic behavior, and to explain it to the ordinary language user; some of them are fairly accurate, some quite false" (1985:31).

19. Although pragmatics has several distinct intellectual trajectories
(e.g., speech-act theory, semiotics, conversation analysis), those who study
pragmatics from the perspective with which I am concerned share a commitment to examining the relation between language and its use in context. A
number of scholars in this area focus on the performative force of language.
Speech-act theory focuses most narrowly on the functions of certain linguis-

tic forms (such as promises). In response to critiques of speech-act theory, scholars have looked more broadly at how a wide range of linguistic forms and usages "do things" in social life (Mertz 1985; Mertz and Parmentier 1985; Silverstein 1976). The distinct approach developed by Silverstein following the work of Bakhtin and Jakobsen has been very influential (see, e.g., Lucy 1992; Mertz and Parmentier 1985; Silverstein 1976, 1985). Silverstein (1985:222) defines pragmatics as the study of "usage as discourse in actual situations of communication, looking for regularities of how 'appropriate' linguistic forms occur as indexes of (pointers to) the particularities of an intersubjective communicative context and how 'effective' linguistic forms occur as indexes of (pointers to) intersubjective consequences of communication." Levinson's chapter-long definition of pragmatics (1983) sticks close to the particular American school that follows from Morris. By contrast, Mey (1993) emphasizes Continental approaches.

20. Mertz (1994:439) outlines the three structuring principles of language that allow for its socially creative capacity: "First, language operates against a backdrop of presupposed social knowledge that is variously encoded and enacted in indexical usage. Second, language use is continuously socially creative in its ongoing operation against that backdrop—deploying and rupturing expectations, playing with categories and generating ambiguities, expressing and forming the fluid polyphony of social interaction. Finally, another key aspect of language is its ability to represent and refer to itself—its meta-level capacity."

21. My brief discussion of this important article neither does justice to Silverstein's complex and subtle theoretical point that people construct ideologies of linguistic structure in "predictable" ways nor does it take him to task for his limited discussion of the struggles over linguistic ideology and political strategy among feminists, including feminist linguists. Rather, I am concerned to highlight Silverstein's demonstration that some usages of speech index ideologies that are pivotal to the negotiation of gender relations (see also Kulick 1992; Ochs 1992).

22. In an excellent review of scholarship on language ideologies, Woolard and Schieffelin (1994:57) point out that a critical division among scholars of ideology, including language ideology, is whether they treat ideology as "neutral" (i.e., a way of characterizing all systems of representation) or as holding "critical" value directly connected to politics and power relations. In this work, I take a broad view of ideology; yet, because my area of concern is specifically around gender, the connection to politics and power relations is inherent.

23. The following quote from Silverstein (1992b:320) delineates his approach to this form of linguistic ideology:

> Such a metadiscourse is semiotically situated to advantage in being a mode of rationalizing explanation, representing de-contextualizable characteristics as the basis of how indexical signs instance *types* of meaningfulness. Thus, any accounts of how characteristics of individuals recruited to the

roles in semiotic events are indexed by certain linguistic forms, have this
characteristic: women vs. men engage in, or are skilled at, distinct genres
of discourse—extensional observation—because, women are such-and-
such and men are so-and-so—intensionalization in another etiological
schema giving the 'essence' of the social category; these are the valued vs.
devalued forms of language because they are in keeping with tradition or
the way of the ancestors or not.

Silverstein goes on to argue that "elaborate metalinguistic ideologies" are
"one place for the social scientist to start in figuring out the nature of the
indexical dialectic that is the sociocultural object of investigation" (320).

24. Ochs makes the point that Silverstein succeeded in directing attention to the ways in which social context is indexed nonreferentially. Drawing
on Silverstein, she argues that there are fewer referential indexes of gender
than nonreferential (1992:339).

25. Ochs (1992) refers to three aspects of the relation of language to
gender to establish her contention that gender indexing is not direct: the
relation is nonexclusive, constitutive, and temporally transcendant.

26. Ochs (1992:343) makes the point that

One of the major advances in language and gender research has been a
move away from relating isolated linguistic forms to gender differences and
toward specifying clusters of linguistic features that distinguish men's and
women's speech in society. This shift represents a move toward defining
men's and women's communicative styles, their access to different conversational acts, activities, and genres, and their strategies for performing similar acts, activities, and genres.

27. In an analysis of language, gender, and emotions in Gapun, Papua
New Guinea, Kulick (1992:295) insists on recognizing the complexity of
linguistic ideologies: "Language ideologies seem never to be solely about
language—they are always about entangled clusters of phenomena, and they
encompass and comment on aspects of culture like gender and expression
and being civilised. Furthermore, this inherently snarled and delicately-
layered nature of language ideology can in effect provide a point of entry
for colonial discourses of Christianity and modernity to penetrate and . . .
enmesh themselves with linguistic practice and with local ideas about gender,
affect and language."

28. Briggs 1992a, Kulick 1992, and Philips 1992 also distinguish between implicit and explicit ideologies in their work, as I have been doing in
this section.

29. In English usage, the term *story* denotes a broad category of forms
of speech that includes narratives, observations, fictional tales, justifications,
explanations, and accounts. Several of these terms refer to forms commonly
produced in disputing contexts.

30. Briggs (1988b:272–73) identifies two shifts in the study of narrative. The first was the shift to studying genres other than myths and folktales.
The second was the shift away from content analysis. Both of these have

been enhanced by attention to narrations of conflict (see also Mertz 1994: 443).

31. The connection between these worlds has been of interest to several linguists studying narrative (see, e.g., Bauman 1986; Hymes 1981). Those scholars whose central concern is pragmatics have offered important contributions to this literature. Shuman's study of fights in schools provides an excellent example of the direct connection between the narrated world and the event world, as telling a story about a fight is an act produced in the event world that connects to and extends the conflict begun in the story world (Shuman 1986; see also Goodwin 1984).

32. A wide variety of scholarship indicates the centrality of narration to legal processes (Abrams 1994; Briggs 1988a; Conley and O'Barr 1990; Ewick and Silbey 1995; Mertz 1994:443; Minow, Ryan, and Sarat 1992). Several studies focus on the technical linguistic production of narrative (Berk-Seligson 1990; Goodwin 1990; O'Barr 1982). Others are more concerned with narration as a problem of telling one's story in court (see, e.g., Bumiller 1991). Still others have treated narrative as more implicitly embedded in legal processes, underlying presentations of information that might take a variety of forms (Bennett and Feldman 1981; Cobb 1994; Sarat 1993).

33. Bauman and Briggs introduce these concepts to replace the limited and static notions of "text" and "context" in performance studies.

34. Studies of reported speech in narratives and interactive talk document its several forms (e.g., direct, indirect, indirect libre) and multiple functions (Coulmas 1986; Lucy 1992; Philips 1986). Because reported speech consists of language that comments on a prior use of language, it constitutes a reflexive linguistic act, one that assesses the communicative process. Several scholars have studied reported speech to understand linguistic metapragmatics, and I draw on their work (Lucy 1992; Silverstein 1992a).

35. Coulmas (1986:56) points out that

> The reported speech in indirect discourse is processed by the reporter. It presupposes his [sic] analysis. "Analysis," says Voloshinov (1973:129), "is the heart and soul of indirect discourse." The reporter's analysis consists in distinguishing illocutionary function and propositional content of the reported utterance, and it may include an interpretation of the reported utterance as it is to be understood in the light of the reporter's knowledge of the world.

The reporter's analysis embedded in the report of speech can convey character information about several participants in the original speech act and the speech act of the report.

36. Studies of the construction of "battered woman" as a category that has gained legal salience demonstrated that feminist efforts to redefine gendered subjectivity in legal contexts could succeed in refiguring relations of power. However, the perversion of the category through continued use in legal processes stands as evidence as well of the limits of legal discourse as a vehicle for feminist projects (see Fineman and Mykitiuk 1994). It is precisely

around the use of language that the category "battered woman" becomes problematic. The designation itself often implies that the victim has been silenced over an extended period of time. This serves to explain why she failed to speak to authorities or, more generally, why she did not leave a relationship that exposed her to violence. Yet these assumptions conflict with the expectations placed on her in the context of the courtroom, where she is supposed to not only tell her story publicly but also speak authoritatively. This example alone shows that only a theory of discourse that understands subjectivity as encompassing the notion of subjects as speakers will begin to illuminate how gender is constructed in legal processes.

37. Steedly's analysis is mindful of the power relations that structure narration: "The politics of narrative experience defines not only the expressive resources for subject-production and the relative access of various persons to those resources, but also the public (and private) recognition or nonrecognition accorded to their varied efforts" (1993:28).

Chapter Two

1. The "old court" in Mombasa is located near Fort Jesus, not far from the new Mombasa Law Courts building. Most cases, including Kadhi's Court cases, are heard in the new complex, although the Court of Appeal still meets in the old building. The law library and some offices are also maintained in the old building, which has been made into a historical monument and is scheduled for renovation and expansion.

2. I was the first of many researchers to live for an extended period (two months) with this family, which was already well acquainted with groups of foreign students studying Kiswahili at the coast.

3. Both Swartz (1991:xi) and Fuglesang (1994:84) mention the Swahili concept of "hiding matters."

4. Steedly (1993:135) uses a concept similar to partial exposure to describe the stories of subordinate Karo people, particularly those stories told to counter official discourses or versions of events:

> These stories are always—and in both senses of the word—partial. That is, they are on one hand explicitly *partisan,* interested accounts, and, on the other, they are *incomplete,* fragmentary. . . . This narrative uncertainty is more than some epiphenomenal residue of official processes of exclusion or incorporation. Rather, it seems to me that this interpretive indeterminacy is the defining feature of an unofficial vision, and that this more than anything else, is what makes it both subversive and open to official subversion.

Considering ethnography as partial exposure raises the interesting problem of what constitutes official discourse.

5. The history of the presence of Swahili people as an ethnic group in the small towns along the coast of Kenya has been well documented (see, e.g., Allen 1973, 1993; Horton 1987; Kirkman 1964; Nurse and Spear 1985; Pouwels 1987; Stigand 1913; and bibliographies and bibliographic essays

in Bakari 1981; Strobel 1979). Cooper (1977) contrasts two types of coastal slavery (plantation and household) and describes the involvement of coastal people in the slave trade. He charts the transition from a slave economy to wage labor through the colonial and postcolonial periods (1980, 1987; see also Glassman 1991). Histories of individual towns on the coast suggest variations in their political and economic development (for Mombasa, see Berg 1968, Strobel 1979, and Willis 1993; for Malindi, see Martin 1973, 1975). Salim (1973) describes coastal political history, including the Mwambao secession movement in the early post-Independence period (for earlier political history, see Nicholls 1971). Pouwels (1979, 1987) offers a comprehensive historical study of Islam on the coast, and other discussions of coastal Islam are most valuable (El-Zein 1974; Lienhardt 1959; Martin 1971; Nimtz 1980). Strobel (1979) provides the first consideration of the history of women in Swahili society (see also Mirza and Strobel 1989).

    6. Prins's volume on the "Arab, Shirazi, and Swahili" of the East African coast in the *Ethnographic Survey of Africa* series identifies basic Swahili traits "thought to pervade large sectors of the life and literature and account for the distinctive style or pattern of Swahili culture . . .: pragmatism, inquisitiveness, looseness of structure, adaptability, absence of norms, ambivalence, inclination towards risk, competitiveness" (1961:x). El-Zein (1974) and Caplan (1975) offer general ethnographic descriptions in the context of community studies on Lamu and Mafia Islands respectively (see also Mbaabu 1985; Russell 1981). Several early indigenous ethnographies provide extensive information about Swahili life (e.g., rituals of birth, death, and marriage; laws; kinship) but are shrouded in controversy as to who authored them and whether some authors presented politically motivated views (Bakari 1981; Ruete 1886; Werner 1934). Swahili literature offers ethnographic and historical information about Swahili society (see, e.g., the poem *Al- Inkishafi* in Nasir 1972; Knappert 1967), and several scholars advise readers on how to evaluate Swahili literature given its tendency to romanticize, idealize, and generally wax poetic (so to speak) about Swahili culture (Abdulaziz 1979; Knappert 1979; Mazrui and Shariff 1994; Strobel 1979).

    7. Middleton asserts the importance of the distinction between stone towns and country towns. The former are those port towns populated in previous times by patrician families where fishing and trade were the central economic activities. Country towns are generally smaller in size and population; farming and fishing, rather than trade, have been their primary activities (see Middleton 1992:23).

    8. Middleton argues that "the Swahili are often accused of being culturally nostalgic, bewailing the vanishing of past glories; this condescending view bears little relationship to the actuality of ongoing Swahili society. Pride in the past is used as a source of ambition and as a weapon of protest, and does not imply lack of concern or excitement for the present and future" (1992:ix).

    9. Mazrui and Shariff (1994:19) make the point that "the Swahili today

are a living expression of an African-Arab process of intermarriage which may have started even prior to the Christian era." By contrast, Allen (1993) claims that people may not always have been so willing to offer up their daughters for marriage, particularly to foreign traders.

10. Mazrui and Shariff's history quite consciously locates Swahili people as an indigenous East African population which, having undergone many transformations by virtue of geographical position, is well described as an "Arab creole community of African origin" that has continued to evolve as a "multidimensional ethno-cultural continuum" (1994:52).

11. For discussions of the Mijikenda peoples who have interacted with Swahili societies, see, e.g., Bergman 1996; Parkin 1972, 1989; Spear 1978; and Willis 1993.

12. Pouwels (1979:72) argues that the definition of *uungwana* has shifted over time. In the mid-nineteenth century, the term was used to compare "African" to "civilization." Later, it came to mean "Arab culture."

13. *Tribe* in this context does not reflect the standard, though quite problematic, usage developed by colonizers and ethnographers. Here it refers to subgroups of the Swahili population and is based primarily on genealogical connection to ancestors from a particular area of the coast. Mombasa is characterized by the Three Tribe and Nine Tribe groups. The three tribes are Wakilindi, Wachangamwe, and Watangana. The nine tribes are Wamvita, Wajomvu, Wakilifi, Wamtwapa, Washaka, Wafaza, Wagunya, Wapate, and Wakatwa. Sk. Ahmed Nabahani divides the groups somewhat differently. He argues that there are others not mentioned by most scholars: Waamu, Wapate, Wasiu, Watikuu/Wagunya/Wabajuni, Wamalindi, Wakilifi, Wamutafi, Wamvita, Watangana, Wachangamwe, Wajomvu/junda, and Wakilindini (personal communication).

14. Mazrui and Shariff (1994) show the impact of colonial laws based on racist notions of identity as "exclusive" rather than "incorporative," which assigned non-native status to "Arabs" and "native" status to Swahili people. Depending on the consequences of identification (e.g., taxation), Swahili people sometimes switched affiliation. These laws had devastating effects on relations among Swahili people, dividing them along lines of ethnicity, color, and birth.

15. There are few studies of the economy of the coastal region (see, e.g., Constantin 1989; Cooper 1987; Kitching 1980; Le Cour Grandmaison 1989).

16. In the 1980s, tourism expanded throughout Kenya, in part because of the government's interest in obtaining foreign exchange. Although the coastal beaches are prime tourist sites, the impact of tourism on the lives of coastal Swahili is not positive, as they receive limited economic benefits from its expansion and are generally appalled by the dress (or lack thereof) and comportment of tourists (Migot-Adholla, Mkangi, and Mbindayo 1982; Peake 1989).

17. In the 1980s, the few Swahili politicians were regarded as serving

the state's or their own needs rather than those of Swahili or Kenyan Muslims of other ethnicities. In a hotly contested election in 1988, several Swahili candidates regained seats in Mombasa and Malindi from non-Muslims who had held them for years. This was talked of as a revitalization of the community as a political force. The political scene changed even more dramatically with the move to multiparty "democracy" in the early 1990s. Elections held in 1992 fueled coastal interest in politics. The Islamic Party of Kenya emerged, though it was denied party registration by the Kenyan Board of Elections (Hirsch 1993; Mazrui and Shariff 1994; see also Constantin 1993).

18. I follow Mazrui and Shariff (1994) in using the term *Swahili nationalists* to refer to a diverse group of people who most likely would not label themselves as such. The term can include people who seek coastal political autonomy or recognition for coastal society in other ways, such as adoption for educational purposes of a version of Kiswahili that resembles coastal usage (see Khalid 1977). The projects of Swahili nationalism vary: some promote Arab elements, while some recapture the distinctly Swahili customs that tend to reflect African origins. Young people, such as those active in the Islamic Party of Kenya or in religious groups, adhere to quite different nationalist ideologies, some supported by international discourses and organizations. These are known as reformist movements (see Fuglesang 1994).

19. Scholars generally agree that the coastal population has included Arabs (from Oman and the Hadramaut), Shirazi (possibly Persians, more likely Somalis who migrated south [Nurse and Spear 1985]), and Africans from inland areas as well as the coast. Whether people from any of these groups contributed to or were incorporated into a uniquely "Swahili" culture is much debated (see, e.g., Arens 1975; Eastman 1971). Summaries of the debates over who is an Mswahili—that is, a Swahili person—and how the term *Waswahili* (Swahili people) should be applied are offered in many texts (see, e.g., Allen 1993; Bakari 1981; Constantin 1987; Mazrui and Shariff 1994; Russell 1981; Salim 1985). Discussions of how colonial favoritism toward Arabs caused coastal people to drop the appellation "Swahili" in favor of "Arab," only to readopt it after Independence as a mark of African nationalism, make the Swahili situation a prototype for analyses of ethnic boundaries and the shifting meaning of ethnic-group terms.

Scholars disagree on the utility of "Swahili" as an ethnic category: Spear (as cited in Eastman 1988:7) counsels that Waswahili are an amalgam of groups, while Swartz (1979) insists that they have a distinct culture. Several authors refuse to refer to "Waswahili" or "the Swahili," preferring "Swahili" as an adjective (Russell 1981). I use "Swahili people" or "Waswahili" to refer to those coastal Muslims of African, Arab, Asian, or mixed ancestry who would agree that "Mswahili" is one term that *could* be used to identify them in at least *some* contexts (cf. Russell [1981:26], who prefers "Afro-Arab" to "Swahili"). In summarizing and criticizing the many approaches to Swahili ethnicity, Salim (1985:216) concludes: "I would say a 'Swahili person is one who has inherited or adopted Swahili culture, etc.' i.e. putting inheritance first to reflect the existence of the original, core Swahilis to whom, over generations, and through the process of Swahilization, others who have come and adopted Swahili culture were added: many Arabs and some Indians, Pakistanis and Iranians from overseas, many Africans from surrounding areas as well as from more distant places."

Mazrui and Shariff (1994) make the point that the quest to determine the criteria and boundaries of Swahili culture has frequently reflected racist, empiricist, or paternalist ideologies of identity, which have led to the conclusion that Swahili people are perplexed about who they are culturally. Mazrui and Shariff reject the idea that Swahili people are confused, arguing that they "recognize a geographical contiguity, a quasigenetic historicity and a cultural commonality that, in their consciousness, easily define their collective identity" (1994:8). Shariff (1973) suggests that European scholars, overly concerned with Swahili identity, have distorted the importance of the ethnicity question.

20. The principles of coastal Islam are outlined in pamphlets distributed locally (see, e.g., Bakari and Yahya 1995; Farsy 1965; Shee 1984). Nonindigenous scholarship on Islam includes Anderson 1955; Caplan 1975; Lewis 1966; Martin 1971; Strobel 1979; Trimingham 1964; and, for Tanzania, Nimtz 1980.

21. Ninety-five percent of Kenyan Muslims are Sunnis. The others are Shia from South Asia. In the Swahili community, there are also some who follow Saudi Arabian Wahaabi Islam.

22. Parkin makes the important point that "the Swahili see themselves as facing the problem of how to combat the forces of African animism which threaten their religious hierarchy of morality. This is a problem for the Swahili because, whether or not they are always willing openly to admit it, their culture operates at two levels: the Islamic and the animistic." He goes on to explain this dualism in concrete terms:

> On the one hand, Swahili wish to be as devout Muslims as possible, and to demonstrate to each other their piety, increasing as far as possible their religious status and even, through the marriages of daughters to high-born Swahili or Arabs, improving the religious pedigree of their grandchildren. On the other hand, they see animism as providing immediately understandable and seemingly effective explanations and cures of misfortune as well as the predictions and good luck needed for future events (1985:234).

23. Prins (1961:xi) notes the early abundance of language studies on Kiswahili and includes a number of references. The extent of more recent research on Swahili language, linguistics, and literature makes a comprehensive set of citations beyond the scope of this volume. Kiswahili has received considerable attention for several reasons, including its status as an East and Central African lingua franca, its literature and historical documents, and the interest of African American nationalists in Kiswahili terms and concepts.

24. It may be somewhat romantic or paternalistic to claim, as does Allen (1973:309), that Swahili people exhibit an "extraordinarily high level of articulacy." But, similarly, Russell (1981) makes the appreciative point that Waswahili take great pride in their language because of its rich literary tradition and the skill of its speakers in storytelling and word play.

25. Several scholars draw a parallel between hierarchical gender relations and the dichotomized relations of power pervading Swahili social life that firmly links women with devalued aspects of Swahili society (e.g., slavery, Africanness, and orality). Eastman (1984a) argues that this parallel has resulted in women's expressive culture being largely ignored as representative of Swahili society, while male high culture has been acclaimed by Swahili people and scholars (see also Swartz 1991). By contrast, Middleton (1992) argues that the connection between women and slavery has been overemphasized and that Swahili people themselves do not recognize it. Resolving this controversy would require data that I do not possess; however, it is the case that men's contributions to Swahili society are more highly valued than women's and less likely to be characterized, by Swahili people, as having slave origins.

26. For example, elements within Swahili society are currently struggling over the status of new forms of Kiswahili prose and verse, especially free verse, which challenge those who would continue their tight control over the definition of Swahili expressive culture (see Mazrui and Shariff 1994:130).

27. According to Strobel (1979:21), "Swahili society's genius for absorbing and Swahilizing people has not brought equality and homogeneity. Social hierarchy remains, even while status differences between people of slave and free ancestry diminish. But the evidence from wedding celebrations indicates that the stigma of slavery is waning as people from all classes absorb the cultural heritage of slaves. It further suggests that women, because of their position in Mombasa society, have been agents in the integration of different elements into Swahili culture."

28. Bakari's manuscript offered detailed descriptions of Swahili practices, such as the life-cycle rituals of birth, initiation, marriage, and death; cultural conventions, such as manners, greetings, and attire; the events of daily existence; and the rules of law. Velten published minimally edited Swahili and German versions in 1903 at Göttingen. In the preface to the 1981 English translation of Desturi, the editor praises Velten's final product: "Far more than being a mere listing and description of the customs and picturesque gyrations of a far-off people, the outcome of [the collaborator's] efforts is a piece of writing couched in Swahili of such excellence that it has become the model for the best in Swahili prose" (King 1981:xi).

29. Noel Q. King, who wrote the preface to the English translation of Desturi after the death of the editor, J. W. T. Allen, anticipates that Western women will be disappointed because Bakari provides little information on

Swahili women. He excuses the inattention to women as reflecting the approach of men of Bakari's time: "If we judge [Bakari] by the standards of modern-day California, we can only say his writings in a number of places show a certain asymmetry in dealing with the sexes. One has to add it is unscientific to fiddle with chron(e)ology and standards" (King 1981:xiii–xiv). I have no desire to judge Bakari by the standards of any American state in terms of equal treatment, but the meta-ethnographic apologia warrants comment. By assuming that conflict along gender lines began in the 1960s, the editor misses the opportunity to consider how an emerging struggle between men and women in late-nineteenth-century Swahili society, a struggle connected to colonization, might have influenced the content of *Desturi* (see Strobel 1979).

30. Swahili women have worn long black cloaks since the nineteenth century. Women from the most prestigious Lamu families walked inside a *shiraa,* a tentlike enclosure carried by servants, until this practice was outlawed by the British (Middleton 1992:215 n. 39).

31. *Mwana Kupona,* the widely recited Kiswahili poem advising young women about proper behavior, was published as the work of a nineteenth-century Siu woman (Werner 1934); however, it has recently been suggested that her husband, interested in preserving patriarchal relations, was the more likely author (Eastman 1984b).

32. Middleton (1992:192) makes the point that for Swahili people, purity contrasts with pollution in virtually the same ways as it does in many other societies. However, Swahili people understand *heshima* as represented by an individual's charity, good descent, propriety in behavior, and cleanliness. In contrast to Middleton, who links *heshima* with men and *usafi* with women, I would argue that *heshima* has become the primary means of talking about the moral character of women, perhaps to direct attention away from virginity. My impression is that the ideal of *usafi* in the sense of sexual purity is less influential than it was previously, and the term is used less frequently.

33. "Jambo kubwa Sheria ya Islamu inalotaka kwa Mwanamke ni hishima na adabu ya Kiislamu wakati anapo kuwa nyumbani na nje ya nyumbani." Unless otherwise noted, all translations are my own.

34. Middleton (1992:194) offers a good description of how *heshima* operates within a Swahili honor complex: "By behaving with courtesy, sensitivity, and goodness toward someone else, a person both acquires *heshima* himself and bestows it on the person addressed, who, by responding seemingly and graciously, in turn affirms his own *heshima* and emphasizes its possession by the original giver."

35. Swahili women address their moral ambiguity through a variety of means. Some try to live outside of the hegemony of the *heshima* complex by becoming involved in secular employment pursuits, although this is an extreme approach. Others turn to religious education. Participation in spirit-possession cults allows women to display the terms of their ambiguous posi-

tion. Giles (1987) and Middleton (1992) make the important point that these cults should not be understood as peripheral to Swahili Islam but rather as the expression of the diversity and ambiguity at its core.

36. Fuglesang (1994:90) delineates the disjuncture between ideal and actual roles: "Women in the upper strata have been more constrained by sexual segregation and seclusion. Their access to forms of education, occupation, individual wealth and formal power has been curtailed. Lower-strata women on the other hand, have been constrained by economic poverty, although they have always taken a more active role in providing for the family." Although my observations suggest that this is, for the most part, an accurate description, it is also the case that upper-status women were among the first to have access to education. Moreover, claims to status sometimes involve masking or denying one's practices. Claims to status enacted through religious piety can be undertaken at any class level and often involve women's seclusion.

37. Although the wives of the Prophet were encouraged to wear modest clothing, veiling was not inscribed in the Koran as an imperative for all Muslim women.

38. In a sensitive discussion of the meaning of veils for Egyptian Bedouin women, Abu-Lughod (1986) identifies a salient function of the veil as concealing women's sexual shame. The sexual shame arises from the particularities of the affinal relation whereby daughters-in-law, as women from other clans and villages, are married into strong patrilineal family units. The sexuality of these female strangers is marked as potentially shameful. Abu-Lughod asserts a connection between the destabilizing sexuality attributed to the daughters-in-law and the potential disruption they can cause to the relations among brothers and other male relatives by making inappropriate demands on their husbands. The Swahili concept of *heshima* includes the notion of covering sexual shame, particularly the shame accompanying inappropriate sexual behavior, although the difference between marital patterns in Swahili society and for the Bedouins makes veiling somewhat different in the two contexts.

39. Although the *kanzu* remains the primary mode of dress for a few older men, others wear it only to pray at the mosque and for religious occasions such as holidays and weddings. Wearing a *kofia* is more common and marks not only a man's belief in Islam but also his identification with Swahili culture via its tradition of fine needlework.

40. These women (called *wanawali*) are assumed to be virgins. Because marriages tend to take place later than in the colonial period, women are often in their later teens or their twenties. As an unmarried woman ages, she may stop attending weddings with these groups and will certainly desist from rambunctious behavior. An older never-married woman is out of place at a wedding. At the marriage of a young woman from a prominent Malindi family, guests quietly expressed great sympathy for a woman in her forties who, because she had never married, was unable to attend the wedding of

a beloved niece. Clad in cloths called *leso*s draped around her waist and head, she watched the guests dance from about twenty yards away, peering over the heads of the large crowd of unmarried women in *buibui*s. The scene was poignant in that family members convinced me, an unmarried woman, to participate in the dance, my status as foreign clearly overriding my status as never married.

41. Fuglesang (1994) reports that these young women call themselves "ninjas" to reflect both their dress and their aggressive behavior. (The term *ninja* is also used to refer to small masks tied around the eyes, nose, and mouth, which are worn as a veil by a very small number of women.) The young women at an overcrowded wedding I attended in Malindi were not admitted to the Cleopatra Theater, a large movie hall in which one of the celebrations was being held. Having been told that there was no room, even to stand in the back, they pushed against the doors, shattering them. On leaving the event, I was pinched, quite hard, by someone in the crowd. To my surprise, a young, very shy woman admitted several days later that she had done the deed. Because of the damage to property, this incident led many people to argue that young women should not be allowed to attend weddings.

42. Porter (1992b) explores another aspect of the public/private dynamic when she argues that women have routinely "privatized" public areas, making them spaces for women to engage in activities without the fear of "breaking *heshima*." For example, families put up barriers in order to seclude wedding guests from the gazes of those in the street. She makes the further point that it is the gender of the participants, rather than the actual space, that makes an area private or public. Indeed, one's home can become public when a number of men enter.

43. Within Swahili houses, the most private areas are designated as inside *(ndani)*, generally the bedrooms entered only by family.

44. Because of the rise in the crime rate in Mombasa, women sometimes send their gold jewelry by car rather than wear it as they walk in the street (Mary Porter, personal communication).

45. Both the jasmine and incense used to perfume clothing offer olfactory evidence that a woman has the wealth and status to attend a wedding resplendent in finery.

46. Men also dress specially for a wedding. Depending on the event, they might don a *kanzu* or a fancy, brightly colored polyester shirt and spray on perfume. Some prepare for the subsequent sexual encounter by chewing a popular stimulant called *miraa*.

47. Women who work outside the home remove the black outergarment when they reach work, where they wear a long robe and trousers or a dress, with or without the scarf, depending on the work context or the demands of authorities (e.g., husbands or bosses). Another example of women's agency with respect to veiling is Porter's description of how young Muslim women in coastal secondary schools performed a song to mark the adop-

tion of long dresses, trousers, and headscarves as their school uniform (1992a).

48. Macleod's use of the terms *resistance, accommodation,* and *protest* to analyze the new veiling in Cairo perhaps overstates the political agency behind Cairean women's choices of dress. Further discussion of the politics of Islam and of feminism within Egypt might have bolstered her claims that these terms should be applied (Macleod 1991).

49. The verb "to marry" *(kuoa)* is used differently depending on the gender of the subject of the sentence. A man "marries" (active form), while a woman "is married" (passive form). It is possible as well to say that the two "marry each other." I reflect these usages throughout the text.

50. When married by her father's brother's son, a woman becomes the instrument for retaining familial wealth, including heritable moveable and immovable property. Postnuptial residence with the bride's family, also rare, means that women literally stay inside their houses (Middleton 1992).

51. Several scholars have written of the importance of matrilineal ties in Swahili kinship, although it is generally acknowledged to be patrilineal (Caplan 1975, 1976; Middleton 1992; Porter 1992b). Prins (1961:80) writes of the issue of kinship, "The whole subject is somewhat intricate and confused." In part, this is because of the extensive terminology used in various ways. Caplan (1975) describes cognatic descent and inheritance for the Waswahili of Mafia Island. Swartz (1983) claims that, for the most part, residence is in nuclear families and that the nuclear family is the primary reference group for most individuals.

52. Marriages between the children of sisters do, however, occur. A woman from a high-status family in Malindi explained to me that she had been criticized widely for arranging the marriage of her son to her sister's daughter. Not only was she uniting these maternal parallel cousins, but she had been the foster mother of her sister's daughter, raising her in her own home alongside her son. She explained to me that her son was older than the girl and that they behaved as brother and sister together as they were growing up. The son left quite young to work in another country. When he decided to marry, he asked his mother to choose a Swahili woman as his bride. She suggested the cousin with whom he had been raised, and he immediately agreed. They believed that, since the two had not seen each other for many years, the match would avert charges of incest, but this was not the case.

53. A small percentage of marriages are contracted between a coastal resident and a spouse from a foreign country. The historically common pattern of marriage between Swahili women and husbands from the Middle East continues as men from Saudi Arabia and Oman seek Kenyan brides rather than women from their own communities. Marriage to a Middle Eastern Muslim woman requires higher marriage payments than for a Kenyan woman. Swahili people recognize that many foreign grooms marry for the convenience of having a wife while in Kenya and often abandon these

women when they return home. Even though women face potential abandonment, this type of marital alliance is attractive, as it holds the possibility of status and wealth for a woman's family.

54. Hypergamy—marriage involving a woman of lower status than the man—is more common than its opposite, hypogamy, although the latter is not unknown (see Porter 1992b:58).

55. A customary amount for bridewealth is 212 Kenyan shillings (KS). Middleton (1992) writes that this is paid from one lineage to another, but it is supposed to go only to the bride, in order to protect her. Kadhis insist that all marriage payments belong to the bride, and she is given the promised money if it is still unpaid at the time of divorce. In practice, some families take the marriage payments.

56. The amount of the larger payment, which varies from 100 KS or less to over 30,000 KS ($1,875), is agreed on at the time of contracting the marriage. Porter (1992a) offers similar figures for *mahari* in Mombasa. Fuglesang (1994:267) summarizes the literature on bridewealth amounts, charting a rise from several thousand shillings in the 1960s to 30,000 in the 1980s. In Malindi in the mid-1980s, 20,000 was considered obligatory for a good marriage, although families aspired to 50,000. The highest *mahari* amounts in Malindi are slightly lower than those in Mombasa.

In a Mombasa Kadhi's Court case, a man had agreed to *mahari* of 55,000 KS. His family and the family of the bride began preparations for the wedding, and he paid 35,000 KS up front. Shortly before the wedding, he announced that he did not want to marry the woman. He wrote a note to the bride's father indicating that they could keep the initial *mahari* payment. The father was so angry that his daughter had been rejected publicly that he went to the kadhi to demand his rights. The kadhi appreciated the amount of fuss that the father and the rest of the family had been through, and he ordered the young man to pay compensation for the cost of the wedding preparations.

57. At one elaborate Malindi wedding held at a large cinema, entertainment was provided by Bhalo, a Mombasan musician and singer whose poignant love songs are legendary on the coast. Several women, overcome in the excitement of the celebration, joined him on stage, performing *chakacha*, which resembles bellydancing. A lecture delivered the next week at the local mosque denounced their behavior, particularly the fact that they danced in front of men—Bhalo and the men in his band as well as men from the community who were hiding upstairs in the projection booth. According to Fuglesang (1994:238), women dance "out" the anxiety of events that emphasize sexuality and thus accentuate their ambivalent status.

58. Same-sex sexual activity is illegal under Kenyan law and remains quite hidden. Homosexual men face the greatest disapproval from non-Swahili people, who link homosexuality with Islam and coastal culture. Media stereotypes emphasize the role of young Swahili men as sexual partners of foreign tourists, as well as of other Swahili men (see Porter 1995). Middle-

ton (1992) counters this stereotype by arguing that most of the "beachboys" who make their living by escorting tourists are not Swahili, although my own observations suggest that Swahili beachboys are quite prevalent (see also Peake 1989).

59. The few men who change wives frequently are thought of as little better than the "playboys" known to seek sex with prostitutes or foreign tourists. If a woman has been married numerous times, she acquires a reputation for being difficult to live with.

60. For discussions of the "postmodern turn" in feminist anthropology, see, e.g., di Leonardo 1991; Mirza and Strobel 1989; Personal Narratives Group 1989; Quinn 1996; Strathern 1987; Wolf 1992.

Chapter Three

1. Attitudes about language expressed by indigenous scholars are an especially rich source of prescriptive data, although they are sometimes presented as descriptions of reality (see, e.g., Bakari 1981; Werner 1934).

2. In making this point, Russell does not explain that women often repeat lectures for the benefit of women who were not present to hear them. Some women do not attend mosque because of restrictions on their movement outside the house; others miss lectures when they have their menstrual periods. Swahili Muslim women do not pray, enter mosques, or touch the Koran when they are menstruating.

3. According to Makhlouf, speech about "trivialities" at afternoon visits *(tafrita)* among Yemeni Muslim women empowers them amidst severe gender hierarchy. Makhlouf (1979:27) writes:

> In the traditional *tafrita,* when they are not making jokes, telling stories or dancing, women are engaged in conversation about children, husbands, close and distant relatives, recent marriages, births or divorces, which are topics of common interest and tend to reinforce female identity and community. But conversation is not only verbal exchange; it also has a silent language. Equally important is the implicit part of the conversation, the fact that it takes for granted, or perhaps pretends, that participants belong to the same social world. Thus, it may provide a means of expressing, without verbalising, potential unity, and may reaffirm the reality of the culture.

Her further interpretation that men are more excluded from women's culture than the other way around fails to recognize that men define the meaning of who is excluded and set the terms for how interaction occurs.

4. A pamphlet on Muslim women's roles counsels women to avoid "pretending to be busy or wasting time by going to the cinema and to weddings and to funerals where there is gossip and mutual backbiting through speech, things that are forbidden by Sheria [Islamic law]" (Shee 1984:37).

5. Mtoro bin Mwinyi Bakari, the late-nineteenth-century indigenous Swahili ethnographer, offers a portrait of a Swahili woman whose speech exacerbates the troubles in a marriage: "[a] young woman does not under-

stand such things [her husband's lack of interest in her]; but she has a confidant [*sic*] who tells her about going astray. She says 'One man cannot fill a basket,' or 'If you till a field, you must have your own allotment.' So she opened the woman's ears" (1981:131). The friend's words cause the woman to lapse in her behavior as a dutiful wife, and eventually she and her husband divorce. Although Bakari wrote about a community far removed from present-day Swahili society, informants routinely echo his claim linking women's words to domestic conflict.

6. Other terms for a person who gossips include *mdakizi* and *msengenyi* (backbiter). Terms for gossip include *maneno* (literally, "words"), *maneno maneno* ("words words"), and *mazungumzo* ("conversation").

7. For Briggs (1992b), this approach helps scholars to avoid "naturalizing" their own interpretive authority by virtue of having grasped the dominant ideologies. Making the point that "linguistic ideologies do not simply constitute underlying frameworks that implicitly shape the discourse of particular individuals or social groups," Briggs argues further that "linguistic ideologies are crucial resources for according social power to strategies for the production and reception of discourse" (399).

8. For example, I raised no protest at a story about a funeral for a relative of my host family in which I was depicted as having engaged in ritual crying, which had not been the case. This story was told to relatives not present at the funeral in order to demonstrate my position in the family.

9. Goldman's vivid criticism of legal anthropologists' tendency to present only summaries of the cases they have researched is worth quoting in detail:

> Disregarding the possibilities offered by providing even *one* complete dispute transcript, researchers have created a veritable cemetery of skeletal cases. These are rarely exhumed for the purposes of pathological examination, precisely because their corporeal form cannot serve to answer the questions engendered by detailed post-mortem inquiries. Such descriptive reports are specifically designed in accordance with the prior interests of the ethnographer, and his or her evaluations of what is important about any stream of events. Whilst cross-disciplinary interests are frequently thwarted by the format of data presentation, each new study generates further dead matter (1983:2).

10. The announcement is also called an abstract (Labov) or a preface (Goodwin 1984). For further discussion, see Linde 1993:69.

11. Linde (1993) makes the important point that studies of narrative increasingly combine structural and functional considerations, as does her own work. Using the example of the Goodwins' focus on conversation analysis, she asserts that even their attention to how linguistic structure emerges through conversational interaction relies on some assumptions about the presence of specific features. She argues that the Goodwins "make use of such subunits of narrative structure as preface, background, climax, and parenthesis sections as part of the task of the participants, who must exhibit

different types of reactions in different sections." She goes on to make a further point: "These studies show that a purely structural approach to discourse is possible but barren, while a purely functional approach is not possible at all, since some form of internal linguistic structure must be posited (if only covertly). A combination of the two can provide extremely rich and fruitful results" (66).

12. Russell also defines the core of narrative as its event line, declaring that she will "refer to only the temporally ordered sequences as 'narrative' because the Event-line of the Mombasan narrative discourses is carried almost entirely by such sequences of clauses" (Russell 1981:141). With this statement, Russell justifies her choice to define narrative narrowly by suggesting that it is in the nature of Kiswahili narrative to eschew extraneous evaluative or orientative clauses.

13. As Russell (1981:144) notes, tense as well as sequencing is a necessary consideration in judgments about causality.

14. "The prefix -KA- may occur in the Indicative Mood, also in the Subjunctive. Wherever it occurs, it expresses an action or state which follows another action. Therefore its time implication is consecutive to the time expressed in the preceding verb" (Ashton 1944:133).

15. According to Ashton (1944:37), "the -ME- tense . . . [expresses] the completion of an action and/or the resultant state. Though it corresponds to many tense forms in English, the underlying concept is constant." Examples include *Amefika* (He has arrived); *Amechoka* (He is tired).

16. The coda is sometimes formulaic in Kiswahili stories. Maw (1992: 12) recounts how a speaker ends a long tale with the following phrase: "Kama ni mbaya, utanipa mwenyewe" (If it's no good [sc. the story], you must tell me one yourself [sc. a better]).

17. For discussions of reported speech in Kiswahili, see Maw 1969; Russell 1981.

18. The phrase "personal experience stories" has been used by many scholars to refer to narratives about oneself that people routinely produce in casual English-language conversation. According to Bauman (1986:33–34), some version of personal experience as the basis of a narrated story is a typical referent in the work of some of the leading analysts. In part, this is to distinguish between narratives of real events that the narrator participated in, which are generally the stuff of conversational storytelling, and other genres of narration, namely, fictional stories. Bauman makes the important point that "personal experience" may be a misnomer, as the stories are often about other people and at times do not recount things that really happened. His point is well taken:

> If we are to develop our understanding of those stories we have labeled personal experience narratives, thereby implicating the relationship between narrative and event and the management of point of view, then it is crucial that we set about investigating those dimensions of relationship directly, bolstering our social and linguistic insights with literary ones, to-

ward a deeper and more nuanced comprehension of the forms and functions of this powerful expressive vehicle (1986:35).

Chapter Four

1. *Edda* is the period that a woman remains secluded in her home after the death of her husband (four months and ten days) or upon divorce (three months or three menstrual periods). The reason cited for this command from the Koran is to determine if the woman is pregnant. Other reasons cited by informants are to show respect for the dead man or to avoid gossip about the reasons behind a divorce. During *edda,* a woman is not supposed to leave the house unnecessarily. If she goes out, she must cover herself completely. In the past, women wore gloves and socks outside. A woman observing *edda* should not decorate herself *(jipamba),* including plucking her eyebrows or using henna, makeup, perfume, or fragrant soap. Women should have no contact with men outside the immediate family during *edda.* There are class differences in the degree to which a woman can comply with *edda* restrictions, as poorer women, or those with no servants, may be forced to leave the house. In recent years, many Swahili women go out during *edda* after divorce.

2. There is a wide range of discussions of gender and Islamic law; see, e.g., Beck and Keddie 1978; Dwyer 1978b, 1982, 1990; Hatem 1986, 1987; Hay and Wright 1984; Kandiyoti 1991; Mernissi 1975; E. Moore 1994; Shaheed 1994; Starr 1990, 1992.

3. How speakers produce the terms routinely associated with a discourse is instrumental to the outcome of a dispute, but it might also effect broader change (see also Wagner-Pacifici 1994:4). Noting Merry's description of disputants who learn legal language and then use it against the power of the state, Mertz (1992a:440) argues that "Merry's account elegantly illustrates the connection between creative uses of language and struggles over legal power, showing us the larger social structure at stake in seemingly mundane, face-to-face legal encounters."

4. In a note about the history of the term *haqq,* Geertz (1983) gives a nod to the possibility that it developed first in reference to actual rules and then became linked to ideas of justice and truth. The definition of *haki* provided in the standard Kiswahili dictionary also lists these three senses (Johnson and Madan 1939:124).

5. Schools of Islamic law vary with respect to whether payment for medical treatment is due to a wife. Although under Hanafi law it is not an actionable claim, kadhis sometimes allow it, because it reflects the spirit of laws mandating maintenance.

6. A man can return to his wife and rescind the divorce within three months of issuing a revocable divorce. If the divorce is irrevocable, he cannot return to her until she has first been married to someone else.

7. In polygamous marriages, a wife cannot be forced to live under the same roof as another wife. Also, women sometimes live apart from their

husbands in order to care for aging parents; however, the husband must agree.

8. In examining Muslim doctrine, Ahmed (1992) directs attention to Islam's "Ethical voice" as a means of counteracting the "Establishment voice," which emphasizes strict applications of law that have historically oppressed women (see also Mernissi 1991). Ahmed argues that ethical principles are embedded in the Islamic thought and religious teachings of many Muslim communities. Activist scholars, primarily Muslim feminists, have found that separating the discourses of law and ethics constitutes an important strategy for transforming relations of power.

9. One can guard against possession by a *jini* by wearing an amulet that contains writings from the Koran, drinking a special preparation, or going through a curing ceremony. *Majini* can also be appeased with gifts and other kinds of recognition and attention.

10. Liquid medicines are prepared by writing Koranic sayings on paper, placing the paper in water so that the ink bleeds off, and prescribing certain dosages to be given to the patient or to someone whom the patient would like to influence.

11. Legal discourse offers speakers specific terms (such as "rights"), ways of conceptualizing problems, and forms of argumentation. Moreover, legal discourse includes distinct genres (e.g., opening arguments, testimony).

12. Philips (1994b:62) argues that her approach "will counter the image of the agents of nation-states as constantly pushing for more coherence and uniformity with an image of state domination that involves the active proliferation of ideological diversity as well."

Philips's assertion (1994b) that postcolonial legal systems are characterized by multiple ideologies has been addressed in other terms by those who examine legal pluralism with attention to the imposition of bureaucracy or the erosion of customary law and courts (see, e.g., Abel 1973; Burman and Harrell-Bond 1979; Hooker 1975; Merry 1988; Moore 1986, 1989; Snyder 1981).

13. Symbolic beating has been interpreted as hitting in places where there will be no lasting marks or long-term pain (such as buttocks or thighs) or hitting with a harmless object (such as a pillow, feather, or palm leaf).

14. On pronouncing the first or second divorce *(talaka)*, a man should proceed to the Kadhi's Court with those who witnessed the divorce, in order to register it and obtain two copies of the divorce certificate, one of which is given to the woman. For the next three months, the woman must maintain *edda.* If the husband does not return to her in that period of time, and thereby revoke the divorce, it becomes an official divorce, and she is free to marry again. If he returns to her after that time, they need to remarry officially. An irrevocable divorce ensues on the pronouncement of three *talaka*s, through a kadhi's decree of divorce, or if a woman has bought herself out of a marriage through a special kind of divorce. Kadhis do not permit men to pronounce three *talaka*s at once.

15. One young wife violated this understanding by leaving the matri-

monial home to search for her father-in-law, asking his whereabouts from neighbors. When she finally located him at a teashop with his friends, she beckoned him and, within earshot of the others, began to complain about his son. Both father and son condemned her for exposing the family's turmoil. Her behavior occasioned a letter written by her husband to her parents, who lived in another town, complaining that she had yet to learn how to behave as a married woman. The parents were asked to instruct their daughter to seek out her own elders nearby (her sister and the sister's husband) if she needed assistance.

16. The opposite is true as well. There are a number of cases of parents instigating conflict in the marriage of a son or daughter in order to arrange a more advantageous match.

17. Analyzing marital disputes among Jordanian Muslims, Antoun makes the point that consanguineal ties are strategically played against conjugal ties (1990:37). His analysis counters the assumption of scholars that, for Muslims, patrilineal demands influence marital disputing. He also refutes the assumption that the deployment of Islamic law in a dispute tends to favor consanguineal ties over conjugal interests, a point that also applies to the Swahili example (see also Caplan 1995:218–19). Another observation of his is also relevant: "Islamic law . . . can work to support the wife in her demand for divorce against the interests of both the conjugal and consanguine unit" (53).

18. Subchiefs and assistant registrars hold civil service positions, which at the time of my research were occupied by respected Swahili Muslims.

19. A former kadhi well known for practicing spiritual medicine insisted that he never mixed his efforts to alter spiritual health with the work of the court. He kept the two separate by seeing clients for spiritual medicine only at his house. An assistant registrar from an area outside of Malindi was not so conscientious. He was known to hear the disputes of couples and then, after counseling them on Islamic law, adopt them as clients for spiritual medicine. Several well-known Malindi elders were skilled in preparing medicines as well as in wielding the discourses of Islamic law and Swahili ethics when mediating disputes.

20. Lowy makes the observation, almost as an aside, that in contrast to men, Ghanaian women tend to go "straight" to state courts, the least moral disputing option (see also Lazarus-Black 1991; Nader 1990). He speculates that "the difference may reflect a bias against women who are in conflict with [male elders]" (1978:203). By failing to pursue this point, he leaves the implication that for women, preserving a good name is of less interest than winning their claims in a context with a less local, patriarchal bias. However, two other factors might motivate women's behavior. First, the bias that women experience in the *afiesem* may include silencing in addition to unfair outcomes. Thus, by going to court, women seek a forum where they can express their claims and gain an audience. Second, women are implicated differently than men in estimations of the morality of speaking in a particular

site. Women may achieve or lose their good name by actions other than choice of disputing forum (e.g., by making a legal claim).

21. Philips (1994b) comments on the gendering of Tongan courts by pointing out that sometimes the fact that men occupy roles as legal personnel is taken for granted and other times it must be explicitly stated why women cannot serve as judges. With reference to the gendering of law at the level of the state, she claims that "what law is and does is quite varied in Tonga, and the genderedness of the Tongan state in the legal realm is not an implicit, seamless web, but consists as well of flashes, of displays of explicit stances on gender that themselves are not necessarily coherent" (84–85).

22. Typologies of commonly occurring disputes are useful for comparative purposes and provide a sense of the range of problems in a society. They establish a semblance of order in ethnographies that are largely about the disorder of conflict. Yet that order can be deceptive. Neat typologies fail to reflect the interconnection of kinds of marital conflict in any given dispute. Moreover, typologies risk missing the way in which "what a dispute is about" is situationally negotiated, contingent, and evolving, no less for the analyst than for the parties involved. Another criticism of typologies of marital conflict stems from the problem of identifying marriage itself as a pancultural institution, given the variety of forms that it takes and the range of its social functions. Collier (1988) describes marital problems, and indeed the marital relation itself, as differing significantly in class and classless societies. Recognizing the cultural specificity of marital disputing, Nader (1990) argues that the content and form of such disputes are linked directly to the kinds of resources available in a community and their patterns of distribution.

23. My discussion of conflict over support attends to class in a limited way. It points out the complexity of formulating one set of requirements with which to measure support. It is difficult to develop a model of what causes conflict in the Malindi community without a significant body of data on class-related phenomena, including employment patterns, a regional economic analysis, and analyses of individual household economies. Such investigations are beyond the scope of this study.

24. In many contexts, including coastal Kenya, marital disputes involve different issues depending on the age of the parties involved and—an often related factor—the length of the marriage. According to Nader (1990), in their early years Zapotec marriages tend to be bombastic, and the turmoil involves adultery, jealousy, commitment, control, and abandonment. As couples mature together, issues of property become the central stakes of marital conflict. As Nader suggests, a mature wife's thoughts about her future, including problems over securing money for her old age and inheritance for her children, become most central in her estimations of problems worthy of dispute.

25. Informants point out that thirty Kenyan shillings per day is an absolute minimum on which to run a household with several children and that

the members of many households certainly expect a standard of living that demands more support. At that time this was about fifty cents.

26. The prices of most basic subsistence goods were, at the time, set by the Kenyan government. Prices for oil, flour, rice, etc., were raised and lowered periodically. Waswahili awaited the announcements of changes with some dread.

27. About a third of Shella families own their homes, and some derive income from rent. Although this provides some security in a tight housing market, these families are vulnerable to unexpected expenses. Those who fish or work in the tourist industry go through difficult times depending on the weather and the season.

28. Women with limited schooling or restrictions on their mobility do piecework sewing in their homes. These and other economic strategies, such as lending schemes or selling cooked food, flavored ice pops, or flowers to neighbors or local stores, provide a safety net of cash when a husband fails to make a maintenance payment.

29. Most women expect additional, comparatively large amounts for children's clothing once a year for the Idd-ul-Fitr celebration at the end of Ramadhan. To clothe a little girl properly for three days of Idd festivities, a mother of even modest means might wish to spend five hundred Kenyan shillings or more. Many families also purchase new clothing for the celebration of Maulidi (the Prophet's birthday) about six months after Idd-ul-Fitr, although this expense is a less customary requirement.

30. The discourse around this type of conflict is revealing. Often, it is women who want big weddings and funerals for reasons associated with status. Men privately complain about the cost of housing and feeding guests, yet they admit to enjoying the festivities. Publicly, some men adopt the discourse of reformist Islam, arguing that the large celebrations contravene Islamic principles.

31. The two Kiswahili words most commonly used for "love" have several meanings. *Mapenzi* refers to the kind of love felt by spouses who have been together for a long time. Such love is rarely present at the time of a wedding but grows through the couple's good-faith coexistence. Ideally, one should feel the enduring and supportive bonds of *mapenzi* toward anyone who is *ndugu*—the set of extended family members, often including distant relatives who for reasons of proximity or emotional connection are important in one's daily emotional life (cf. Willis 1993:98). *Mapenzi* is a tame version of love when contrasted to *mahaba,* which is the intense passion associated with falling in love. Feelings of *mahaba* are rarely acted on, as they invariably lead one to the danger of extramarital sex. When a Swahili wife requests material evidence of her husband's love, it is *mapenzi* rather than *mahaba* to which she refers. To speak of *mahaba* would invoke a baser passion that couples should hide from those around them (see also Fuglesang 1994:158).

32. Even the few women who admitted to me that they knew that Is-

lamic law does not require their labor in the home insisted that they chose to do household work in order to contribute to the marriage.

33. The kadhis claim that planning a family in order to be able to provide adequately for children is appropriate under Islamic law. They admit that this might require the use of birth control. According to a popular pamphlet on law prepared by M. K. Mazrui, Islam permits the use of various kinds of temporary birth control *(kuzuia kwa muda)* but does not permit methods that are permanent *(kuzuia kabisa kabisa).*

34. Most legal interpretations recognize that men should divide the nights spent with a wife equally among all wives, although they are not required to engage in sex each time they spend the night with a wife. Some schools recognize that women are entitled to engage in sex with their husband at a minimum of once every four months (see, e.g., Haeri 1989:47).

35. In the past, consummation of the marriage was achieved by the man's using his finger wrapped in cloth. This allowed for a clear demonstration of the new bride's virginity.

36. Foods that prepare a bridegroom for sexual tasks include milk, meat, and savory snacks. These are served to all male guests as well and are thought to enhance the sexual performance of everyone in the postwedding celebration. By contrast, female wedding guests are served sweets. The only rationale given is that women like sweets more than men do.

37. The inability to bear children can also cause great difficulties for a married couple. The likely causes, impotence and infertility, are not uncommon for several reasons, including marriage between cousins who, at least initially, find sex difficult and marriages between young women and much older men who experience sexual problems. Of course, a man can marry another wife in order to produce children. An infertile woman certainly risks divorce, although there are many examples of such women who remain married, agreeing that the husband obtain children through a second wife or through fosterage. Rarely does the discourse of spiritual problems or even that of medical problems turn into one of rights to impregnation.

38. Much conflict over sex occurs when a couple disagrees about the appropriateness of the amount or type of sexual activity. For example, women complain of men's excessive demands for sexual intercourse and requests for oral or anal intercourse. To address these problems, people sometimes turn to practitioners skilled in making medicines to relieve excessive desires or to foster desires that are more appropriate (see also Mernissi 1991).

39. The following circumstances are considered good reasons for taking an additional wife: the first wife is unable to engage in sex; the first wife is unable to bear children; or the man is compelled to live far away from the first wife.

40. When a woman requests divorce from a husband who is unwilling to sever their ties, she can try to persuade him by offering to "forgive" payment of the *mahari* and the maintenance during *edda*. This type of divorce

is irrevocable, meaning that a husband cannot take his wife back until after she has married another man. In note 229 to the Holy Koran, Farsy (1969: 54) protests this arrangement, calling it a sin yet recognizing that couples do it. At a mosque lecture, a Muslim preacher counseled those attending that if a woman has done no wrong, she must be given her bridewealth on divorce. If she wants out because of another man or some other wrongdoing, the husband can keep her bridewealth or make her pay him the amount, if he has already paid. Thus, the coastal religious elite holds divergent views.

41. Several years after divorcing Sauda, Jamal was dividing his time between two wives. He had fathered eight children with five different wives, most of them short-term.

42. A learned man who specializes in preparing Swahili medicines, including remedies to relieve or counteract excessive jealousy, expressed his conviction that "jealousy is the seed of divorce" (wivu ni mbegu na talaka).

43. Men who provide equivalent financial support for each wife can still be accused of failing to devote comparable emotional attention to each. In common parlance, this means that a man must "love" each wife to the same degree. The assessment of this claim is notoriously problematic, since "love," or emotional commitment, is an intangible. In commenting on the section about polygamy in Bakari's nineteenth-century ethnography of Swahili culture, Winifred Allen suggests that polygamy poses few problems (Bakari 1981:278 n. 42). She argues that the law permitting multiple marriages by men is very clear and accepted, by women as well as men. She rejects modern apologists of Islam who say that the Koran's provision for a man to have four wives *if he can treat them equally* must be treated as ironic and, in actuality, constitutes an endorsement of monogamy.

44. One popular story concerns a Mombasa man with three wives. Each wife works outside the home. The remarkable thing in the eyes of the observers is that they all live in the same house. With four salaries coming in, they can hire someone to cook, clean, and care for the children. Those who narrate the story acknowledge that this arrangement is very rare.

45. Husbands have the authority to refuse to allow their wives to travel. If a wife perceives the travel to be necessary (for example, on the occasion of illness or death in the family), she might be tempted to disobey her husband. I witnessed an argument in which a wife requested her husband's permission to travel to see her family, and he refused. He was uncertain about how the household would be managed without her, as no one could cook for him and the children. She was angry when he lectured her that it was his right to refuse permission, citing a story from the Prophet Mohammed's life *(hadith)*. In the story, the Prophet refused to allow one of his wives to travel to see her dying father. The wife disobeyed him. When she reached her father's bedside and told him the circumstances of her travel, he reprimanded her for disobeying her husband and sent her home immediately. Such stories, when told to justify expectations about behavior, invoke Islamic legal tenets.

Chapter Five

1. This division of space by gender resembles the division described by Boddy (1989) for Sudanese women. The Swahili spatial configuration does not imply the same deep connection with enclosure and wholeness noted by Boddy.

2. Ibn Battuta offers the earliest evidence of institutionalized Muslim law on the coast with his description of Islamic courts in fourteenth-century Mogadishu, the present-day capital of Somalia. In this early period, foreign and local traders transcended ethnic and regional differences by relying on principles of Islamic law to conduct business (Nurse and Spear 1985).

3. In 1596, the sultan of Malindi was ordered to report all civil and criminal cases to the resident Portuguese captain. Coastal residents, fearful of the Inquisition in other parts of the Portuguese empire, endured interference in their judicial activities but continued their worship as Muslims relatively unhindered (Pouwels 1987:39).

4. The sultans of Zanzibar included (from Pouwels 1987:104):
Said b. Sultan (1806–56)
Majid b. Said (1856–70)
Barghash b. Said (1870–88)
Khalifa b. Said (1888–90)
Ali b. Said (1890–93)
Hamid b. Thuwain (1893–96)
Hamud b. Muhammad (1896–1902)
Ali b. Hamud (1902–11)
Khalifa b. Harub (1911–60)

5. Religious freedom was a constant source of tension, as the Busaidi periodically tried to promote a reformist version of Islam (Ibadi) among the Sunni Muslims. For example, Barghash, the "reformer" sultan (1870–88), made a concerted effort at religious reform through Ibadi tenets but encountered much resistance (see Pouwels 1987:203). In general, the sultanate had little interest in promoting religion, which it carefully separated from the business of a secular state.

6. Resentment of the Busaidis grew; especially disliked were the district governors who amassed wealth at the expense of townspeople. *Maliwali* from the Banu Salim b. Khalfan al-Busaidi clan in Malindi lent money to landowners and then foreclosed on unpaid loans to obtain property (Pouwels 1987:110). Pouwels (1987:111) describes how the power of individual district governors grew: "Armed with the rights of intervention in local quarrels and the power of imprisonment and seizure of property, [*maliwali*] often succeeded in enriching themselves and in playing off local clans against each other." The indigenous population was forced to deal with systems of patronage established and controlled by the increasingly bold *maliwali*.

7. Before Busaidi rule, kadhis were tied to foreign regimes (e.g., the

Omanis) or were considered foreign elements in the community (e.g., the Mazruis); however, the mid-nineteenth-century kadhis were learned Waswahili.

8. In a speech announcing the establishment of the East Africa Protectorate, Sir Arthur Hardinge, appointed to govern the region, guaranteed that "all cases and law suits between natives will continue to be decided according to the *sheria*" (Mungeam 1978:68).

9. The eleven *liwali*'s courts were Vanga, Gasi, Mombasa, Takaungu, Malindi, Mambrui, Lamu, Siu, Faza-Itembe, Mkunumbi, and Hindi. Salim (1973:82) provides a more detailed discussion of these early years of the colonial political and legal systems.

10. During the colonial period, *maliwali* and *mudir* were, for the most part, ethnically Arabs, and many had ties to the Busaidi sultanate. The promotion of Arabs rather than indigenous Africans or Waswahili was in keeping with the colonial governor's plan to institute indirect rule through the most "developed" members of the population. By the early twentieth century, twelve *maliwali* and six *mudir* governed coastal life.

Salim (1973:75–80) describes Sir Arthur Hardinge's plan to favor Arabs in the colonial administration. An 1896 letter from Hardinge to Salisbury indicates the racial and cultural bias underlying his plan for Native Administration (Mungeam 1978:81):

> We cannot ourselves "colonize," in the true sense of the word, the tropical coast belt of East Africa, and if instead of utilizing we extirpate the Arab and the Mohammedan, with his conceptions of law and order, of education, even if it be not very high and progressive, and of a morality which if not ours, is yet superior to that of the savage, there is nothing that we can put in his place. This is one of my reasons for deprecating the reckless crusading attitude towards him, his religion, and his customs, which finds favour in some circles at home.

Arabs took full advantage of the opportunities afforded them and "lorded it over" the non-Arab population (Salim 1973:87). Hardinge's plan began to fall apart when his administration ended. Subsequently, the ruling powers focused attention on governing through members of Kenya's larger and more prominent ethnic groups, particularly those who entered missionary schools.

11. The Chief Kadhis of Kenya include the following:

Sh. Sayyid Abdul-Rahman b. Ahmed 1895–1924? (a.k.a. Mwinyi Abudi)

Sh. Sulaiman b. Ali Al-Mazrui 1924?–37

Sh. Al-Amin b. Ali Abdallah

b. Nafi Al-Mazrui 1937–47

Sh. Seyyid Ali b. Said Ahmad Badawy

Jamalil-Lail 1947–early 1950s

Sh. Muhammad Kassim Al-Mazrui early 1950s–1968

Sh. Abdallah Swaleh Al-Farsy 1968–81

Sh. Mohammed Nassor Nahdy 1982–present

Bakari (1995:170) lists the first Chief Kadhi's name as Shariff Abdulrahman Saggaf, which appears to be a variation on the name above. Some Chief Kadhis loomed larger than life by virtue of their piety and philanthropy, their activities as educators, and their numerous writings on Islam. Sh. Al-Amin b. Ali Mazrui was especially prolific, and his publications continue to enjoy wide distribution.

12. Pouwels (1987:176) describes the creation of the Waqf Commission in 1906 to oversee Muslim charities as one of the first ordinances applying Muslim law in Kenya. The commission entailed a range of reforms that diverged from standard legal practice at the time (see Pouwels 1987: 177).

13. Text of a letter from "A Tax Payer" to the editor of the *Daily Standard,* October 1, 1928 (Attorney General Deposit 4:50, Kenyan National Archives):

> You might remember that in the year 1922 a movement was afoot to retrench Government servants whose service, if retrenched would be an economy.
>
> The Committee did the best it could but now I would like to impress upon the mind of Government and of your readers that there are at present Government Servants who are in the service for over 20 years but who are also overpaid.
>
> These are, the Mudirs, Khadis, and of course Liwalis. These three posts are absolutely a waste of public money, and could be replaced by the eager young clerks who are now on their way to join Government Service. I believe I shall be supported in this by the Education Department which is responsible for the future welfare of its pupils.

14. Text of a letter from Chief Justice J. W. Barth to the Governor, Nairobi, June 18, 1928 (Attorney General Deposit 4:50, Kenyan National Archives):

> When recently at Mombasa I was approached by Mr. Morrison an advocate practising there who I think has closer touch with native opinion at the Coast than most other Europeans whether officials or not. He has asked me if I would represent to Your Excellency the hardships caused and the feeling engendered by the abolition of Kathi's posts. I think there is a great danger of those who do not know the functions of a Kathi thinking that a Kathi is just a native Magistrate who has certain judicial functions. He is more than that and enters very largely into any important step of a Mohamedan's life. He is in fact a necessary officer to a Mohamedan population and his usefulness cannot be judged by the number of cases tried by him. He must or should be a competent lawyer to deal with complex matters of inheritance, marriage and divorce. I doubt of more than a very limited number of Mudirs are capable of performing a Kathi's duties.
>
> The duplication of Kathi's and Mudirs might be obviated if the Courts Ordinance were amended to give a Kathi ordinary second class civil powers in addition to the powers he already has.

15. Most cases from early in the century involved maintenance claims, although many women managed on their own (or tried to) rather than pursue court actions. Strobel (1979:93) explains women's avoidance of the courts: "Women's absence from public roles inhibited them from fully exercising their personal rights. Since no females judged cases, legal decisions affecting women were in the hands of male makadhi. Although these men often granted women their legal rights and were not necessarily ogres, they came from the stratum of society that was most likely to believe in female weakness, inability to make decisions, and lack of virtue."

Strobel's discussion (1979) of gender and religious sect suggests that women may have been ignoring the authority of the kadhis as representatives of establishment Islam. Women had already joined the Quaddiriyya (Islamic brotherhoods), which allowed them more participation in Islamic practices that reflected local interests.

16. Anderson (1955:109) paints a harsh portrait of the Islamic courts with respect to gender relations: "Stipulations in favour of a wife inserted in marriage contracts are always regarded as null and void; the principal of 'equality' in marriage is apparently applied according to the texts by all Qadis, questions of religion, family, trade and character all being taken into account; and no dissolution of marriage is ever granted for cruelty, however extreme." Anderson retrieves the image of the kadhis by pointing out that they would allow dissolution if two arbiters decided that the marriage should end.

17. The Kadhi's Courts Act was one of several changes in the administration of justice in the postcolonial Kenyan state. Others include the Magistrate's Courts Act (No. 17 of 1967) and the Judicature Act (No. 16 of 1967). All of these have undergone subsequent amendments.

18. Some Chief Kadhis (such as the three Mazrui Chief Kadhis of the mid-twentieth century) were members of the elite, Arab *ulama* class, while others (such as Mwinyi Abudi, the first Chief Kadhi) were considered indigenous elders. Distrust of kadhis at the end of the nineteenth century led townspeople to enter the debate over who would be named the first Chief Kadhi to ensure that the British would not appoint a *sharifu* or *ulama*, those learned but orthodox "foreigners" who were thought of as untrustworthy, exploitative, and sometimes ignorant of local practice (Pouwels 1987:162). The deliberations lasted over one year. Community members petitioned the British government to require candidates to submit to an examination. The petitioners relied on their belief that the *ulama* and the Mazruis would refuse to submit out of pride and would thereby leave the position open to a scholar with stronger community ties (Salim 1973:82). Indeed, this occurred, and Mwinyi Abudi, a venerated scholar from Siu but not a *sharifu* or Arab *ulama*, assumed the post of Chief Kadhi in 1902. The Mazruis gained control of the post in the 1930s.

19. As described in Farsy's pamphlets, some practices and beliefs, though permitted, are not to be considered part of Islam proper, such as

dhikiri (a prayer ritual), ceremonies that venerate local "saints," burning incense while praying, and large celebrations for the Prophet's birthday (Maulidi), among others.

20. Saidi Musa (Farsy's Tanzanian student and publisher) informs readers in the fourth edition of Farsy's *Bidda* (Part 1) that the first printing sold out in four months and the third in one month, despite protests against publication of the volume. Musa also claims that some of Farsy's speeches were disrupted by those who opposed him and that his life was threatened (Farsy 1981). Farsy's firm stand against *bidhaa,* as evidenced in the following poem from the abovementioned handbook (Farsy 1977:xiii), led to confrontation with some Swahili people:

When Holy people say:	And attest
That this thing:	Is not done
What's written by God:	Can't be wiped away
Let's wipe it away:	We'll see (what happens).
Wali wakisema:	Na kusaliki
Kuwa jambo hili:	Halifaniki
Andikalo Mola:	Halifutiki
Hebu lifuteni:	Nasi tuone.

Farsy's poem hints of dire consequences if Muslims ignore God's word, such as by engaging in local practices that might be *bidhaa.*

21. In the postcolonial period, those of the elite classes (i.e., Mazruis and shariffs) face some discrimination in their attempts to become kadhis. The prominent positions that they held under the British led to resentment that has yet to fade. One Malindi shariff has applied several times for the post of kadhi, with no success. In the 1990s, however, as the Chief Kadhi approaches retirement, it is possible that his successor will be of the elite class.

22. The Kadhi's Courts are open each weekday from 8:00 A.M. until about 4:30 or 5:00 P.M.. The one-hour lunch break begins at 1:00.

23. There are Kadhi's Courts in nine locations, each serving a town or city and the surrounding area: Mombasa, Malindi, Nairobi, Lamu, Isiolo, Wajir, Garissa, and Kisumu. There has been some discussion of establishing more courts in up-country areas (e.g., Machakos and western Kenya) to handle cases for the growing Muslim population. The Mombasa court, where both the Mombasa kadhi and the Chief Kadhi hear cases, serves as the main court.

24. The position of court clerk has been accorded respect in the past. In her life history, Shamsa Muhashamy writes: "As far back as I remember, my father had his work; he was a clerk in the court. It was hard in those days to find a good person. He was one who was called; that is, he was one of Mombasa's intelligent men" (quoted in Mirza and Strobel 1989:95). Clerks are still respected, but they are, for the most part, younger men (and some young women) rather than elders. In smaller courts, they are quite

influential, and, as they mature, the men can be regarded as community elders.

25. Applicants submit to a written examination that tests their knowledge of Islamic law and their fluency in English. Subjective qualifications like personal integrity and leadership ability are evaluated in consultations among government and community leaders, including former kadhis. Kadhi's Court records are kept in English, as mandated by the Kenyan government. Until the early 1970s, they were written in Kiswahili, sometimes using Arabic script. Kadhis take handwritten notes in English on most cases; thus, they need translation skills as well as English literacy. Rather than serving as a badge of honor, youth and Western education are sometimes associated with abandoning Swahili values and disinterest in the concerns of the local population (see Fuglesang 1994).

In the postcolonial period, there have been problems filling vacancies for the position of kadhi. Highly qualified persons prefer to teach at Islamic institutes, often sponsored by wealthy Middle Eastern governments or private organizations, where they can command higher salaries than they would as Kenyan civil servants. Also, the skills required to be a kadhi are obtained only after years of study; thus, there are few qualified candidates. Factional differences make it particularly hard to appoint a Chief Kadhi.

26. In 1986, a kadhi of Digo ethnicity was appointed. The Digo are one of the nine Mijikenda peoples. Willis (1993:197) makes the point that, among the Mijikenda Muslims, Digo have been most effective in maintaining non-Swahili identity.

27. A Swahili Kenyan raised in Lamu, Sheikh Nahdy is a conciliatory figure who has staved off conflict over *bidhaa* and other controversial issues by approaching them rather equivocally. Nahdy refuses to condemn local practices and, during most of his tenure, has been less outspoken than previous Chief Kadhis. As he approaches retirement, he has become stern in denouncing Muslims who challenge his decisions or authority. He has also reacted harshly to government attempts to weaken his office or the position of Islam. He takes his responsibilities as the international representative of Kenyan Muslims quite seriously and has traveled to Iran, Iraq, Egypt, and the United Arab Emirates to meet with other Muslim religious leaders.

28. The clerks described by Yngvesson (1993) have the official role of conducting show-cause hearings, in which they create initial legal documents and have the power to decide the disposition of claims.

29. The Malindi Kadhi's Court clerk during the time of this research wielded considerable power. He was about forty, a career civil servant from a respected Swahili family in Malindi. Most disputants carefully followed his counsel, as he had a reputation for efficiency. People sought him out for advice at his house, on the street, or at the mosque. Many invoked kin connections with him in an effort to capture his attention and sway his perspective. His unceremonious manner in the office both encouraged people to bring problems to court and, because women in particular found him

approachable, gave him the reputation of teetering on the edge of violating their *heshima*. He laughed off rumors of impropriety and emphasized his commitment to making the Kadhi's Court part of the modern judiciary, where everyone has a right to be heard. Secular education had convinced him of the importance of institutional rationality. Although a practicing Muslim, he routinely framed disputes through Swahili ethics or, more rarely, state law, and thus he clashed repeatedly with the kadhis.

30. A circular distributed to Kadhi's Court assistant registrars is typical of the attempts to limit their jurisdiction and control the procedures they employ (Circular 1 of 1986). Designed to stem a rising tide of marriages performed improperly or illegally, the directive insists that assistant registrars ascertain that each party is of marriageable age and wants to marry. The directive rescinds permission for assistant registrars to conduct marriages when the woman has no guardian or if she is not present. In such circumstances, the parties must proceed to the kadhi.

31. Rosen (1989:310), writing of Moroccan courts, states: "Indeed it can be argued that unlike many complex legal systems that propel investigation and decision-making up to the higher reaches of the legal order, in Morocco the process of adjudication continually pushes matters down and away from the *qadi*—down to the level where local custom and circumstance can become most significant."

32. The most serious public disagreements between kadhis and local elders concern decisions about the timing of holy day (Idd) observances. Even though the Kenyan government authorizes the Chief Kadhi to announce the start of the two main holidays based on the sighting of the new moon in Kenya, some *ulama* insist on celebrating on the same days as Muslims in Saudi Arabia. Other *ulama* object to the procedures used in the sighting: "One of the sheiks in Mamburui [*sic*] said the moon must be sighted in Mombasa or Lamu and news conveyed to the Malindi Kadhi by the Chief Kadhi. They argue that the sighting can only be accepted if reported by a responsible person or the Chief Kadhi. . . . 'We cannot accept the news of the sighting from someone of questionable faith,' said one imam" (*Daily Nation*, June 10, 1986, p. 5). One kadhi denounced the Mambrui *ulama*, historically renegade religious elders, for deliberately ignoring the Chief Kadhi's authority as set out in the Kenyan constitution. In the kadhi's opinion, they could be sued in secular court for failing to obey an official order, although he admitted that this would accomplish little. This example demonstrates the complexity of overlapping authority that, ironically, leads an official Muslim leader to turn to the secular state to resolve a religious conflict.

33. The notable decrease in the number of cases filed in 1982 is attributable to the attempted coup in August of that year. In the political unrest that followed, government offices functioned only minimally, and citizens were restricted in their movements.

34. An early 1987 article in the Kenyan *Daily Nation* reported the following statistics for the Malindi Kadhi's Court: for 1986, 110 divorces and

97 marriages; for 1985, 109 divorces and 98 marriages. These statistics reflect the number of individuals who registered their marriages or divorces. Marriages and divorces often go unreported for a variety of reasons, including the desire to keep them secret, unfamiliarity with the court process, and neglect. After an outcry over the article, there was speculation that the disparity was even higher for other coastal areas and that the records were being systematically altered. Coastal residents disapproved of national exposure of the much misunderstood Muslim divorce rate, and non-Swahili Kenyans (especially Christians) were shocked to have confirmed their anecdotal impression that Muslims divorce on a whim.

35. Cases that were pending at the conclusion of this research are also classified as "no resolution."

36. This woman brought a case against her husband for neglect. When they came to court, he alleged that she had committed adultery and then left home. It is one of the few cases in which it appears that a wife is using the court strategically to avoid being formally accused of a serious offense.

37. The Kadhi's Court attempts to find the man through a process server. If that fails, it posts, at the front of the courthouse, a notice to appear. If he does not appear within one month after the date of posting, the court hears the case in his absence.

38. According to agreements reached in Kadhi's Court cases, thirty Kenyan shillings ($1.85 in 1986) is a standard amount paid to a woman per day to maintain the household. A former kadhi said that the amount had been three shillings per day in the 1960s. The amount for clothing in 1985–86 was 100 to 150 KS a month.

39. In 1985–86, the monthly amount for child support varied widely, from 150 KS to much larger sums.

40. If a man does not pay, the woman can return to court and file a notice to show cause. If his failure to pay continues, the kadhi arranges for him to bring the payments to court. If he still fails to pay, the court can attach his salary or take his property, although this is rarely done.

41. One case involving a woman from a town near Malindi demonstrates how such a settlement can come about. This woman had taken her husband to court for back maintenance and won a judgment against him. He was forced to sell their house, which she then purchased with the help of her own family. Her husband did not, however, use this money to pay the maintenance debt. The woman returned to court to sue for the money and divorce. The kadhi and clerk suggested that she obtain a conditional divorce by forgiving the debt, as the man indicated that he had no money. Seeking to avoid a long and acrimonious case by encouraging such a settlement is a typical strategy of court personnel.

42. For further details on the legal history of children's issues, see Anderson 1955; Mwangi 1995:258.

43. In the early 1980s, Swahili women flooded the lower courts with custody cases brought with the assistance of Children's Officers, who were

mostly female. The senior resident magistrate at the time issued a directive suggesting that the Kadhi's Courts make divorce more difficult in order to reduce the caseload in the civil courts. The kadhis became furious at the attempt to regulate their operation and have been defending the right for Muslims to divorce ever since. In an interesting twist, the only female Swahili magistrate was granted permission by her superiors to refuse to handle any claims involving custody that concerned illegitimate births.

44. The kadhis themselves foster connections with the secular government when they request the police to enforce Kadhi's Court decisions by seizing property, removing children from abusive homes, or forcing witnesses to appear in court. Although kadhis often threaten disputants that the government can be called in, they rely on these officials only sporadically. They are cautious in decisions to involve the police, as Muslims become greatly offended at the intrusion of the secular state in community or family matters.

45. *Hussein bin M'Nasar v. Abdullah bin Ahmed* (1937) 17 K.L.R. 95, as cited in Morris 1964:15 n. 59.

46. *Masood bin Said v. Said bin Salim bin Mohamed Ghulum* (1947) 14 E.A.C.A. 32 and *Baraka binti Said Bahmishi v. Salim bin Abed Busawadi* (1942) 20 K.L.R. 34.

47. The orthodox screening of witnesses (*tazkiya* or *ta'dil*) is the questioning of witnesses by the judge prior to their giving testimony. The judge assesses whether the moral character of a witness warrants allowing him or her to give evidence in open court.

48. The justification—from both written sources and informants—for the disparity in the weighing of testimony is that women are both forgetful and uncertain about events in the world. If one woman should experience forgetfulness or confusion, a second woman will be able to remind her and thus corroborate her testimony—or not, as the case may be. According to Schacht (1964:198), the testimony of women is not admitted in accusations of moral offenses. For example, in accusations of *zina* (sexual intercourse between unmarried persons), evidence must come from four male witnesses. The principle that women are not effective witnesses has been the target of law reform in other Muslim societies (Beck and Keddie 1978; cf. Dwyer 1978a:26).

49. Similarly to men, women speak for themselves in court. An exception to this is that the permission of the father or a male guardian is required for a woman to be eligible to marry. If a woman has reason not to ask a relative to represent her, the kadhi can become her guardian in order to grant permission.

50. Minors are incarcerated in several kinds of facilities, including Approved Schools—tightly controlled, single-sex residential schools.

51. The revered former kadhi Gosso Ibrahim long served in Garissa and other areas of northeastern Kenya that are populated by non-Swahili people (Somalis, Boranis, etc.). He related the story of a Somali woman who

was jailed in the late 1960s for refusing to return to her husband. She cited a reason that Gosso said women occasionally offer: she simply did not want her husband anymore. Gosso explained that he asked the woman a series of questions: Does he provide maintenance? Does he beat you? Does he insult you? Does he insult your parents? When the answers indicated proper behavior by the husband, Gosso told her to go outside for ten minutes and contemplate two possibilities: returning to her husband or going to jail. Gosso knew that, like other wives to whom he had given this choice, this woman did not believe that he would actually send her to jail. She returned after ten minutes and announced, "I still won't return to my husband." Her sentence of three months in jail was cut short when she agreed to return to her husband.

52. Although the examples related to me suggest that both men and women have been jailed, none of the women in these stories were of Swahili ethnicity. Although it may be the case that Swahili women need less coercion, it is also possible that ethnic prejudice makes jailing women of other ethnic groups (e.g., Somali or Giriama) less problematic for kadhis in terms of *he-shima*.

53. Most Muslim advocates are ethnically South Asian and have been trained through secular higher education.

54. If a case was originally decided by the Chief Kadhi, two other kadhis sit as assessors. The Chief Kadhi is the assessor in all other instances.

55. For example, one appeal challenges the jurisdiction of the Kadhi's Courts over matters of valuation in inheritance (High Court App. 9 of 1974; Kadhi's Court [Malindi] 10 of 1973). The lower-court decision was affirmed; however, the appeal demonstrates that Kadhi's Court jurisdiction is open to challenge.

56. High Court App. 28 of 1983; Kadhi's Court [Mombasa] 121 of 1980; High Court App. 37 of 1979; Kadhi's Court [Mombasa] 36 of 1979. An earlier Court of Appeal case, *Ayoob v. Ayoob* (1968) E.A. 72, held Muslim marriage to be far inferior to that of English marriage. A couple married under both systems is not considered divorced if the divorce is carried out through pronouncement *(talak)* alone.

57. In High Court App. 28 of 1983, the High Court overturned the Kadhi's Court decision granting a divorced wife her claim to furniture: "the divorced wife becomes entitled to immediate payment of the whole of the unpaid dower . . . if marriage has been consummated. She can take utensils and comb but she is not entitled to 'furniture' under any provision of Muslim law." The kadhi with whom I discussed this case pointed out that the "Islamic law" quoted by a secular judge in this decision and by advocates in the appellate memorandum was taken from a legal text used by another Muslim sect and therefore not relevant to coastal legal practice. Similarly, in High Court App. 37 of 1979; Kadhi's Court [Mombasa] 36 of 1979, the kadhi writing the appellate decision overturned on the grounds that under

Islamic law "misunderstanding" is not reason enough to grant a divorce to a woman but, rather, "mistreatment" must be proved. This opinion corrected the original judgment to conform to the practice in the Swahili courts. The other opinion, written by a secular judge, invoked Islamic principles not normally followed in Kadhi's Courts. Failing to realize that Islamic law varies by sect and by customary practice, the judge cited Islamic law that was irrelevant to coastal legal practice.

58. High Court App. 50 of 1984; Kadhi's Court [Mombasa] 23 of 1984.

59. There are several types of oaths under Islamic law (e.g., continence vow, self-redemption oath). *Lian* is an imprecation pronounced by a husband in order to disavow a child. According to the source consulted by the kadhis (Nawawi 1914:360), a husband pronounces *lian* by making the following statement four times: "God is my witness that I am sincere in accusing this my wife of the crime of fornication." After that, he indicates his intention to disavow the child resulting from his wife's adultery. He need not produce proof of the adulterous act. The couple is immediately divorced and forbidden from marrying again. The disavowal can take place any time during the pregnancy or soon after the birth (Nawawi 1914:361).

60. Early versions contained provisions outlawing polygamy and demanding that fathers support their children even if born out of wedlock. Although President Jomo Kenyatta intended to improve women's status through these reforms, more recent proposals seek to reconcile the law with actual practice. Thus, proposals eliminate criminal penalties for bigamy, citing the high number of violators (*Daily Nation,* May 1988). Those advocating such versions profess concern for preserving religious freedom as it concerns personal law. Few Kenyans, Muslim or non-Muslim, take the proposed Marriage and Divorce Act seriously (although several letters on file at the Malindi Kadhi's Court were written by Muslims to kadhis and other religious authorities in protest of it). Believing its passage to be highly unlikely, coastal Muslims dismiss the act, but they resent its repeated considerations in Parliament as improper attempts to regulate their lives in ways contrary to Muslim law. Some comment wryly that members of Parliament would never agree to an act that would force them to pay support for children born of their own casual unions.

61. Charles Njonjo, the notorious attorney general who served under Kenyatta, is credited with spearheading efforts to modernize the Kenyan judiciary and with achieving many of his goals, particularly professionalization.

62. Even with a will, Muslims are only permitted to devolve one-third of their estate to persons or institutions other than those who would inherit under Islamic law in the event of intestate succession.

63. The act never came into widespread use among Muslims, given the considerable opposition. Moreover, customary legal practice in Kenya received increased legitimacy through the widely publicized decision in a case

involving rights to bury the body of a prominent Nairobi attorney (see Cohen and Odhiambo 1992; Ojwang and Mugambi 1989; Stamp 1991).

64. One case involving a very different threat to religious freedom was
mentioned to me by the Chief Kadhi and several others. In the early 1980s,
a man married a Christian woman who had converted to Islam for the purpose of marrying under Islamic law. They worked together and shared some
expenses, including the purchase of land. They divorced, and she reverted
to Christianity. When he filed a case against her in Kadhi's Court to obtain
some of the joint property, she was so convinced that the kadhi would rule
against her, a Christian, that she asked a Catholic bishop to urge the kadhi
to put aside any biases in rendering a decision. The kadhi decided in her
favor, and the bishop publicly thanked him for his fairness. Some members
of the Islamic community were angry that any suspicion would be raised;
others were angry because the man should have known better than to try
to keep property to which the wife had contributed.

65. Even less charitably, some men allege that the kadhis simply like
women or that a kadhi may want to free a particular woman from a troubled
marriage in order to marry or seduce her. Though these stories are widespread, they concern only *some* court personnel. No formal charges of mis-
conduct have been filed, although some individuals have been reprimanded
in a variety of ways. There are also as many stories about elders potentially
exploiting clients as about court personnel.

66. Mather and Yngvesson (1980) employ the categories of expansion
and narrowing to describe processes associated with the transformation of
disputes. When third parties become conscious of their role in implementing
social change, expansion need not be the primary form of social change.
Rather, a series of cases of narrowing decided in particular, perhaps innovative, ways can produce significant change as well, especially if cases of this
type have not previously been heard. Thus, the third party produces "innovative" decisions simply because they are new to that forum.

Chapter Six

1. Hayden (1987) emphasizes the cultural specificity of linguistic phenomena and challenges attempts to universalize Atkinson and Drew's conclusions (1979) about turn-taking in British courts.

2. According to Schiffrin (1990:241), "a participation framework is
comprised of a set of positions which individuals within perceptual range
of an utterance may take in relation to what is said." Irvine (1996:135) offers
the helpful suggestion that it is "more useful to retain a quite simple set of
primary participant roles (Speaker, Addressee, and third parties present and
absent), while deriving the more subtle types (sponsor, Ghost writer, etc.)
from a notion of intersecting frames and dialogic relations."

3. The initial narratives told in Kadhi's Court differ from those told
later in the case or mediation in several ways that have an impact on the

tasks at hand. First, at the moment when the initial narratives are produced, little else has been articulated in court that requires a direct response. Of course, this is not the case if the parties have been to the court previously, and most cases involve a history of prior accusations and justifications in other contexts (i.e., ones without the presence of the kadhi or clerk). When in court, disputants are motivated to defend against anticipated attacks (Atkinson and Drew 1979). Thus, justification, even prior to accusation, is an important strategy in initial accounts. However, this is not to say that disputants calculate to produce speech that directly addresses these tasks. Depending on the kadhi's question, the prior interaction, and disputants' understandings of the situation, the tasks required are often ambiguous, yet the initial narratives can and do address a range of tasks. Moreover, initial narratives of trouble present evidence not only of the events of the dispute (and the speaker's evaluation of them) but also of what the speaker thinks presents a "good case" (Goldman 1986:231).

4. Wolfson bases this conclusion on her analysis of the conversational historical present (CHP), a performance feature whereby speakers of English narrate in the present tense when they are telling a story about something that occurred in the past. Wolfson explains that speakers tend not to produce CHP if they are uncomfortable with their interlocuters, and more specifically if, because of power differentials, they are uncertain as to how listeners will evaluate their remarks.

5. Wolfson identifies an important link between power relations among speakers and their tendencies toward narrative performance, but there are at least two reasons that Wolfson's analysis diverges from my study of narrative in Kadhi's Court. One is that Wolfson's findings are based on narratives elicited specifically for her study. Although telling a story, even in an interview, is a culturally salient act (see Linde 1993), and the narrators may have been engaged in functions associated with conversational storytelling (e.g., engaging or impressing the listener), they did not need to perform other linguistic tasks, such as proving a point or mitigating responsibility, as do the disputants who narrate in Kadhi's Courts. In part, variations in the production of performance features reflect the functions that narrators are expected to address or intend for their narrations to accomplish. A second limitation of Wolfson's study is its cultural specificity. Studies by Russell and Maw suggest that narration itself plays a particular role in Swahili social life— one that might contrast with narrative in Britain, the site of Wolfson's study.

6. Pomerantz (1978) demonstrates that, in ordinary conversation, the allocation of responsibility occurs in an ordered fashion. Ordering is different in the courtroom, where the question-and-answer organization leads witnesses to justify their behaviors in anticipation of a blaming statement.

7. Kiswahili metanarrative evaluation is much more common in personal or conversational narratives than in folktales and other conventionalized genres of fictional stories.

8. There are no examples of sound effects (ideophones) in any of the

narratives analyzed specifically for this study, although a few occurred during other parts of mediations and cases.

9. This example demonstrates the difficulty posed by translating evaluatives. Preserving utterance length while capturing evaluative meaning presents a challenge (see, e.g., Tedlock 1971).

10. According to Russell (1981:221), vowel lengthening can also show a continuative aspect, as in her example *akenda:,* which she interprets as meaning to go for a long time or way.

11. Russell (1981:223) makes two important points about raised pitch in Swahili narratives. First, it is almost always associated with dialogue. Second, variations in pitch in dialogue "[help] to mark off the speech of one character from that of another."

12. In addition to evaluation through phonology and lexical items, speakers can also embed evaluation within a narrative through variations in syntax. As in other kinds of evaluation, non-neutral usages, that is, ones that are not generally produced and are thus "marked," are evaluative in that they draw attention to the semantic content of the narration.

13. Idd, or Iddi, refers to the two major Muslim holidays. The first day of the three-day observance is also the first day of the Muslim month.

14. Exclamations, which include *yoo, ee, ha,* or *a,* can be produced by listeners as well as narrators (Russell 1981:223). Russell (1981:230) points out that *kumbe* in the sentence-initial position functions as a sentence adverbial as well as lending evaluative force with respect to the utterance that follows. Her claim that "it seems to denote the speaker's assessment of the information which follows it as astonishing, unexpected, disgraceful, etc." is valid for the term's use, though rare, in Kadhi's Court accounts.

15. A high-level tonic is "high level on the first accented syllable of the tonic part followed by high level on all succeeding syllables" (Maw and Kelly 1975:8).

16. For Maw (1992:42), the unusual high-level tonic incorporates "the feeling of tension followed by release—physical as well as psychological. The idea of being 'on a high' and then 'coming down to earth' is realised acoustically in the use of this intonation." Maw's point is well taken that the glottal stop constitutes a physical tension in the vocal apparatus that is sustained through the pause and then released with the final words of the sentence. Yet her other claims about acoustic iconicity are unconvincing without a consideration of Swahili cultural understandings about height and grounding as they relate to tension and resolution, as well as about the relation between rising tones and either height or tension. Her argument relies on a notion of suspense as being elevated, a metaphorical link that strikes me as less salient in Kiswahili than in English. Moreover, the assumption that the listener waits in anticipation for the narrator to come down from the high level tonic and pronounce a resolution misrepresents how the dramatic pause generally operates in Kiswahili. Only rarely is the listener surprised by what is revealed after the pause; most narrators have already given

clues to the ultimate point. Interlocutors sometimes join with the speaker to pronounce the word together, thus taking advantage of the pause to gain or share the floor, if only momentarily.

17. Bauman and Briggs (1990) offer an important review of scholarship on iconicity (see also Feld 1982; Parmentier 1985).

18. Herzfeld (1988) makes this point with reference to belief: "if we accept that the presence or otherwise of belief is something on which an anthropologist is poorly equipped to pronounce (Needham 1972), the question of conviction is irrelevant" (320). Anthropologists must resign themselves to dealing with representations of beliefs, feelings, and sentiment rather than gaining access to the presence of convictions in the minds of those observed. It is, of course, possible to identify effects on the listener that result from the production of linguistic forms, a project that requires a contextualized processual analysis rather than assumptions about what a particular form is capable of conveying.

19. Berk-Seligson (1990) describes the virtually universal connection between passive verbs and distancing of the subject from an action. William O'Barr has suggested that passives, which are common in Kiswahili conversation, contribute to mitigation and blame avoidance (personal communication).

20. Goldman (1986:229) notes that the organization of power in court, although not overtly sexist, certainly belies the official ideology that disputing contexts are egalitarian:

> Not only is dispute talk an extremely structured activity, it is also conducted within a framework of egalitarian ideals. These purport to equalise sexual imbalances extant in other behavioural domains. It is less the use of a confrontational rhetoric based on overt sexism than the accepted participant-role structure which, through procedural biases, acts to mitigate the outcome effectiveness of women's arguments. This 'powerlessness' is not a quality of the mooted claims—that is, as lacking credibility or convincingness (cf. O'Barr 1983)—but a reflection or assessment of their impact for outcome construction, choice and realisation.

21. Goldman (1986) does suggest that this disparity in speech can happen procedurally, as men are asked first if they want to divorce. He also mentions that it is difficult for men to divorce because of the expense. Yet it is not clear whether these understandings about the gendered role of law are widespread or routinely enacted.

Chapter Seven

1. Goffman's interest in the positions of conversational participants emerged out of his suspicion that the categories "speaker" and "hearer" were too simplistic to be useful analytic tools. These categories lacked the complexity to reflect the changes in "footing"—reframings of the conversation event—that occur in most conversations (Goffman 1981:128).

2. As Schiffrin (1990:242) notes: "the animator produces talk, the author creates talk, the figure is portrayed through talk, and the principal is responsible for talk." Goodwin (1990:233) lists several other roles, thus providing a more complex typology: principal, emitter, animator, figure, strategist, and author (see also Goffman 1981; Irvine 1996).

3. Schiffrin (1990:249–50) points out that four aspects of storytelling are integral to how the shifts are accomplished: selective interpretation, deictic shifts, evaluation, and contextualization.

4. The narrator's movement between the narrated event and the narrative event creates "involvement" or enhances listeners' participation (Tannen 1989; see also Goodwin 1984; Goodwin 1990). A number of narrative devices "like the more extended metanarrational statements, have the effect of bridging the gap between the narrated event and the storytelling event by reaching out phatically to the audience, giving identificational and participatory immediacy to the story" (Bauman and Briggs 1990:69). Similarly, Schiffrin (1990:252) argues that aspects of narration that are instrumental in refiguring participation frameworks (e.g., deictic shifts, evaluatives) "all help transform the person who listens to a story into an audience that vicariously participates in the narrator's experience."

5. Goffman (1981:140) claims that although podium occasions of binding talk, such as court trials, auctions, briefing sessions, and course lectures, "can often support participants who are fully in the audience role, they also necessarily support another class of hearers, ones who are more committed by what is said and have more right to be heard than ordinarily occurs in platform entertainments."

6. Although in the following passage Schiffrin is discussing stories told in conversation, her points are relevant to disputing contexts:

> Stories can be used to support a speaker's claim during argument because they lead the listener toward a sympathetic alignment with the position being argued. Another way of saying this is that stories create a testimony for the position—a testimony which invites the listener to join in an interactional allegiance and endorse the speaker's position. Thus, what a story can create is a *widened base of support* for the position. . . . In other words, stories delegate much of the supportive work in an argument—including responsibility for truth and sincerity—to different parts of the self, and to the audience (1994:253).

7. The two families were related before Ahmed and Amina married, in part through other marriages. For example, Ahmed's sister is the wife of Amina's brother. Amina's father is Ahmed's uncle as well as his father-in-law. Over the years, a number of problems created tension among family members, and thus the families had few resources to deal with Ahmed and Amina's problems.

8. A confusing interchange follows Ahmed's last remark. The kadhi tries to determine why the couple has come to court. Ahmed responds by explaining that he had come several times to ask whether Amina had re-

quested to speak to the kadhi. He reports that the clerk told him each time to be patient and wait for her to either come to court or return home. Ahmed became frustrated and decided to summon Amina to court himself by writing an official-looking letter requesting her appearance. The kadhi reprimands Ahmed by suggesting that he has only confused the matter. Ahmed's assumptions about his own legal authority are reflected not only by his attempt to call Amina to court but also in the linguistic forms that he produces.

9. Since negatives are marked forms in narration (generally, events that *occur* are narrated), narration of events that do not occur reveals the narrator's expectations, another dimension of the story (Russell 1981:236).

10. "Mama" is commonly used as a term of reference and address for Waswahili women. In this usage, it is respectful. Subsequently, in Text 7.4, line 1, the kadhi refers to her as "Ma Amina," thus producing a similarly respectful variation of "Mama."

11. As Silverstein (1979) notes, poetic language can operate to (1) make a certain event look like a ritual and (2) give it authority by virtue of commenting on the canons of talking.

12. Amina's mention of a specific time in line 58 suggests that she begins her narration of real events at that point. This topic is quickly cut off as she reports Ahmed's speech.

13. In his analysis of power in family discourse, Watts (1991) offers a nuanced consideration of the concept of "floor" in conversation analysis. He argues against the tendency to conflate "floor" with a turn at talk: "Being on the floor means participating in the 'what's going on', and participation itself is also part of the 'what's going on'" (44). Thus, anyone who is participating in the "what's going on" is on the floor, even though not everyone on the floor takes a turn nor are all turns enacted on the floor (45).

14. Bauman and Briggs (1990:70) note the many ways that people have discussed the overt and implicit signals through which hearers participate. Duranti (1994:165) makes a similar point:

> When we examine how judging is done in real life, or at least, in our case, in Samoan discourse, we find that people usually do not make explicit the performative verbs that would qualify their assertions as different types of claims about the world. In other words, speakers do not qualify their judgments as blamings, accusations, or praises. On the contrary, they leave the force of their utterances to be figured out and, more often, to be coconstructed by others. It is the context that carries the illocutionary force of an utterance, and it is the other participants in the interaction, with their responses, assessments, counteraccusations, and affective stances, who produce the stuff out of which an interpretation of speech is made possible, for them first, and for us, later.

15. For discussions of this strategy in other contexts, see, e.g., Dingwall 1988; Sarat and Felstiner 1986. For contrasting approaches, such as disentangling, see, e.g., Goldman 1983; Watson-Gegeo and White 1990.

16. The kadhi goes so far as to offer several hypotheticals that present

reasons why someone might stay late at a wake and thus constitute excuses for behavior similar to Amina's.

17. Ochs et al. (1992) describe how co-narrators reframe accounts. Reframings are often responses to interlocutors' comments, and sometimes the theory of cause and effect advanced to explain the inciting incident differs from the narrator's original proposition.

18. Questions by disputants are more common in mediations than in cases, where the range of linguistic interaction is narrow (see also Dingwall 1988).

19. According to Labov (1972:385), in narrative "[o]vert questions that are not embedded in the dramatic action, but asked directly of the listener, have a direct evaluative function." Thus, they reveal the speaker's evaluation of a particular report of events or an assessment.

20. The term *bwana* has different regional meanings in Kenya. Among coastal Swahili people, it is generally a term of familiarity used among intimates. It is used rarely in reference to women. Terms of address that imply inequality include *Sheikh* and *mzee* (elder), both of which are used instead of *bwana* by women to address kadhis. There are no examples of *bwana* produced by a woman in court, which might be construed as "uppity" or at least violating the *heshima* between women and male authority figures.

21. Holmes's division (1982) of invariant and canonical tags is relevant for typologizing Kiswahili tags. Dubois and Crouch (1975) make essentially the same distinction, labeling the two types "formal" and "informal." Invariant tags in English include "right" and "okay." Canonical tags are syntactically complex structures like "isn't it" and "shouldn't it."

These are the major types of tags in Kiswahili:

INVARIANT TAGS

(1) *Kweli.* This tag appears frequently in the casual speech of Swahili men and women. Its use resembles that of "right" or "really" in English.

Atafika	*kesho*	*kweli?*
(She + fut. + arrive	tomorrow	truly?)
"She will arrive tomorrow truly?"		

Depending on the intonation of the main clause and of the tag, this construction can reflect different degrees of certainty on the part of the speaker and thus can be more or less of a hedged declaration.

(2) *Eh.* This invariant tag is similar to one identified by Holmes (1982) in English spoken by New Zealand adolescents.

Siwezi	*kumtupa*	*kabisa, eh?*
(I + neg. + able	inf. + dir. ob. + abandon	entirely eh?)
"I'm not able to abandon her entirely, eh (am I)?"		

This tag serves a primarily affective function.

CANONICAL TAGS

(1) *Siyo/Sindiyo*. *Siyo* is glossed in Swahili grammar books as "is it not so?"

Tutakwenda   *siyo?*
(We + fut. + go   it + neg. + is + dem.)
"We are going is it not so?"

The rather bulky translation is somewhat misleading, as *siyo* is an informal, frequently used tag. The English gloss of "is it not so" can be blamed on British colonial grammarians. A bilingual English/Swahili speaker would likely offer the gloss "We are going, is it?" A related tag is *si ndiyo*.

(2) *Ushaona/Ushasikia*, etc. This tag is perhaps the most complex in form and usage. The literal translations of the several variations include *ushaona* (you have already seen), *ushasikia* (you have already heard), and *ushafahamu* (you have already understood). Variations in tense allow for *waona* (you see). In deciding whether one of these utterances is a tag question or a discourse marker, intonation must be considered:

Sasa bwanako   *si*   *mtu*   *mbaya,*   *ushaona?*
(Now man + your   neg. + be   person   bad   you + "have already
                                                         tense" + see?)
"Now your husband isn't a bad person have you already seen?"

Since rising intonation in Swahili is associated with questioning in a manner similar to English, the example above illustrates a tag question usage.

22. Holmes's analysis (1982) of the affective and modal functions of tag questions is an exception that influenced my approach to tags (Hirsch 1987, 1990). According to Holmes, the polarity of the main clause and the tag, as well as the intonation of each, determines the degree to which a tag functions either modally or affectively. Modal tags express a speaker's orientation to the contents of an utterance (i.e., the speaker's degree of certainty about the information being asserted). Tags that do not hedge propositions out of uncertainty express affective meaning.

23. In data consisting of radio and television interviews, classroom discussions, and casual conversations, Holmes finds nearly ten times as many affective tags as modals. Affective tags facilitate or prod conversation. In an analysis of gender differences in tags, Holmes (1984) finds little difference in the total number of tags produced by men as opposed to women. Her analysis of tag function, however, reveals that women use more affective tags. In addition, men are twice as likely to use modal rather than affective tags. Holmes's finding that women produce more affective tags is consistent with the claims of a number of researchers who have established women's role as facilitators of conversation (see, e.g., Edelsky 1979; Fishman 1978).

24. My finding of gender difference contrasts with studies of English speakers that emphasize women's prominent role in facilitating interaction

(see, e.g., Fishman 1978; Linde 1993). Arguing that women try to facilitate interpersonal relations while narrating, Linde (1993:79) implies that they want to preserve the event-world relationships through non-narrative appeals that evaluate the narrative and request responses. Noting that her finding reflects scholarly arguments linking women to relational approaches, Linde backs away from this interpretation by providing a counterexample from Goodwin (1990) and calling for more research. From a somewhat different perspective, the telling of the narrative itself constitutes emphasis on relationships among people. This point draws on Conley and O'Barr's distinction (1990) between rule-oriented and relationship-oriented accounts told by disputants in small-claims courts. My findings that Swahili women tend to narrate corresponds to their claim that women in small-claims courts tell accounts that emphasize the relationships in their lives. Yet it is also the case that, even if women have a commitment to privileging relationships, only some of them are able to be sustained in interaction.

Chapter Eight

1. The rules of evidence in many contexts, including Kenya, are intended to limit such reports of speech, disallowing them as evidentiary facts. There are fewer restrictions on reporting such speech when the substance of a dispute is directly related to an instance of speech, such as in claims about verbal contracts, promises, or threats.

2. According to Russell (1981:241), "[i]t looks very much as though a relatively high proportion of dialogue is a property of the generic structure of Mombasa fictional narrative." She argues that the percentage of clauses as dialogue is higher in fictional as opposed to personal narratives. She attributes this to the fact that the fictional narratives are more likely to be performed.

3. Philips's typology (1986:161) of reported speech includes quoted speech (reported speech "framed as what another person actually said"); reports of substance ("classic indirect speech in which direct or quoted speech can be inferred"); and topic naming (either a subject-verb combination when the verb is a lexicalized speech act or the same combination with a more complex description of the speech act).

4. Many scholars recognize that reported speech is constructed speech. According to Coulmas (1986:54), "the claim that part of what one says is an exact repetition of what somebody else said must be distinguished from the stylistic possibility of saying something in such a way as if somebody else said it. The various ways of reporting speech must be understood as stylistic possibilities rather than in terms of truth functions relating an utterance to another."

5. Based on an analysis of two instances of escalating verbal aggression, one from Tonga and one from the United States, Philips (1995:1) finds
strikingly similar self-representations by the young women of blameless vic-

timhood in their discourse structurings of their experiences. Both women portray themselves as passive and fearful. At the same time, the different cultural contextualizations of the acts of aggression in the two accounts give the women's stories very different meanings. This finding of both commonalities and differences across cultures in women's representations of verbal aggression invites consideration of the extent to which we as women do and do not share common problems in a global context.

6. According to Philips (1995), there are several possible explanations for the cross-cultural appearance of the strategy of creating blameless victims: (1) The asymmetries between the blameless victim and the blameworthy aggressor may result from the fact that accounts of escalating conflict are told sequentially, thus separating and contrasting the two roles (which is an artifact of language); (2) Western notions of victims' requiring blameless status may have, through processes of imperialism and colonization, migrated to many contexts; and (3) the position of women cross-culturally may lead us to present ourselves as blameless victims as a universal strategy.

7. According to Besnier (1990:306), rhetorical questions reported as the reaction of a speaker at the time are a means of commenting on the behavior of others and, at the same time, establishing quite subtly one's own credibility.

8. Goodwin (1982) claims that idealized minimal sequences are primarily associated with the future plans of a speaker. That is, speakers rehearse what they will say in "reporting" to interlocutors. The reconstructions are similar, although in the past, and provide very explicit examples of the way in which past events are reconstructed through reported speech.

9. In Islam, taking an oath is a very serious speech act that puts anyone who is lying in grave mortal danger.

Chapter Nine

1. Philips (1992) posits a useful distinction between explicit and implicit dimensions of language ideology, which she develops with reference to theories of ideology emerging from Marx's approach to the concept. She is most interested in those scholars who follow Bakhtin, Voloshinov, and others in drawing a closer connection between embedded and overt forms of ideology, effectively linking ideology to practice.

2. Ideologies of language, which provide evidence of how speakers conceptualize the language they produce, are embedded in and enacted through the speech of Kadhi's Court participants as well as expressed overtly through statements they make about what language does and how it operates (Hanks 1989; Philips 1992, 1994a). This distinction is premised on the difference between talk about practice and practice itself. Philips notes the correspondence between the division as she conceptualizes it and Hanks's concepts (1989) of "metalanguage," which is talk about talk, and "metalingual function." Philips argues (1994a:2 n. 1):

I use the distinction between explicit and implicit bad language ideology in a manner similar to the development of such a distinction in Marxist discussions of ideology (Philips 1992). It is related to the distinction between talk about practice and practice (Philips 1991) prompted by Bourdieu's (1972) most influential discussion of practice and to Silverstein's (1976) distinction between metapragmatics and pragmatics. In a similar vein, Hanks has proposed we distinguish between "metalanguage, or talk that is directly focused on talk, and metalingual function, which is the more general capacity of verbal signs to incorporate meaning components (even backgrounded ones) that signal how the sign is to be interpreted" (Hanks 1989: 107; see also Silverstein 1992).

3. "Diego uses a number of metapragmatic resources, including the portrayal of the setting, the formal characteristics of the quoted speech, and the thinking-speaking frame, in contextualizing his speech as conforming to the counseling and obonobu modes of speaking rather than the anger/jealousy mode" (Briggs 1988b:459).

4. In his analysis of discourse in a Samoan meeting, Duranti (1994: 111–12) describes how explicit though conventional statements about talk are used to rearrange the discourse context in order to move to more formal or less formal discourse in terms of the application of linguistic rules. The resulting discourse contrasts with that heard in more ceremonial segments of the meeting.

5. Matoesian (1993:44) goes on to say that "as a consequence, the original complainant gets inveigled or finessed, as it were, into responding to the complaint about complaining, and thus abandoning pursuit of the prior complainable."

6. Her silence is understandable, as it is not up to her, as a woman, to dictate her desire to be divorced. In the end, it is the prerogative of a man to pronounce divorce. Whether she wants Shaaban or not is somewhat beside the point.

7. The Kiswahili versions are "Sisi hatupendi mambo marefu, pendo mambo mafupi" and "Hakuna maneno mengi hapa. Nataka kumaliza kila mtu enda zake."

8. By uttering the Arabic exclamation "Mashallah," the kadhi effectively praises the achievement of the hypothetical husband in keeping his improper activities covered up. Russell (1981) glosses the expression as "very much"; however, its use is generally to guard against the bad effects of openly praising a person or event, thus exposing them. Such a usage reinforces the notion that the utterance of words has performative force in Swahili social relations. I am grateful to Mary Porter for reminding me of this important aspect of linguistic usage.

9. In some situations of extreme conflict, disputants search for the source of the "words" among potential candidates for arranging witchcraft. If devils are behind all bad actions, then simply participating in a bad act means listening to those who delight in action contrary to God's will. A

Swahili *mwalimu* (learned person) claimed that inviting devils implies that one becomes united with evil spirits. He gave the following example: one person verbally abuses another person, and the abused neglects to make a defense. At the moment of the embarrassing and disabling situation of being abused, devils enter the abused. The individual will begin to think that s/he should have said something or should have fought back. The person's reasoning sometimes escalates into obsessive thinking that prolongs the problem, encouraging further aggressive behavior. The person might become consumed with arranging for revenge. Evil spirits torment people by provoking further evil thoughts. If one gives in to those thoughts or becomes obsessed by them, one invites devils. Those whose words invite evil spirits are not always responsible for their predicament. In some instances, trouble brought through words is thought to be caused by witchcraft or magic commissioned by someone else. A woman under the influence of witchcraft—perhaps done by a jealous co-wife or a neighbor—is, then, the conduit for a message but is not responsible for the message conveyed or its effects.

10. "Dawa ya moto ni maji."
11. "Wacha maneno ya upuzi" and "Usiseme haya hapa."

References

Abdulaziz, Mohamed. 1979. *Muyaka: Nineteenth Century Swahili Popular Poetry.* Nairobi: Kenya Literature Bureau.

Abel, Richard. 1973. "A Comparative Theory of Dispute Institutions in Society." *Law and Society Review* 8:217.

Abrams, Kathryn. 1994. "The Narrative and the Normative in Legal Scholarship." In *Representing Women: Law, Literature, and Feminism,* edited by S. Heinzelman and Z. Wiseman, 44–57. Durham, N.C.: Duke University Press.

Abu-Lughod, Lila. 1986. *Veiled Sentiments: Honor and Poetry in a Bedouin Society.* Berkeley and Los Angeles: University of California Press.

———. 1990. "The Romance of Resistance: Tracing Transformations of Power through Bedouin Women." *American Ethnologist* 17 (1): 41–55.

———. 1991. "Writing against Culture." In *Recapturing Anthropology: Working in the Present,* edited by R. Fox. Santa Fe, N.M.: School of American Research Press.

Adelsward, V., K. Aronsson, and P. Linell. 1988. "Discourse of Blame: Courtroom Construction of Social Identity from the Perspective of the Defendant." *Semiotica* 71:34.

Ahmed, Leila. 1992. *Women and Gender in Islam: Historical Roots of a Modern Debate.* New Haven and London: Yale University Press.

Alcoff, Linda. 1988. "Cultural Feminism versus Poststructuralism: The Identity Crisis in Feminist Theory." *Signs: Journal of Women in Culture and Society* 13:405–36.

Allen, James de Vere. 1973. "Town and Country in Swahili Culture." In *Final Report of the International Symposium Organized by the German Cameroun Commission for U.N.E.S.C.O.,* 298–316.

———. 1993. *Swahili Origins: Swahili Culture and the Shungwaya Phenomenon.* Athens: Ohio University Press.

Anderson, J. N .D. 1955. *Islamic Law in Africa.* London: Frank Cass and Co.

———. 1976. *Law Reform in the Muslim World.* London: Athlone Press.

Antoun, Richard. 1990. "Litigant Strategies in an Islamic Court in Jordan." In *Law and Islam in the Middle East,* edited by D. Dwyer, 35–60. New York: Bergin and Garvey.

Appadurai, Arjun. 1991. "Global Ethnoscapes." In *Recapturing Anthropology: Working in the Present,* edited by R. Fox. Santa Fe, N.M.: School of American Research Press.

Arens, W. 1975. "The Waswahili: The Social History of an Ethnic Group." *Africa* 45 (4): 426–38.

Ashton, E. O. 1944. *Swahili Grammar.* London: Longman.

Atkinson, J. Maxwell, and Paul Drew. 1979. *Order in Court: The Organization of Verbal Interaction in Judicial Settings.* Atlantic Highlands, N.J.: Humanities Press.

Bakari, Mohamed. 1995. "The New 'Ulama in Kenya." In *Islam in Kenya,* edited by M. Bakari and S. Yahya, 168–93. Nairobi: Mewa Publications.

Bakari, Mohamed, and Saad S. Yahya, eds. 1995. *Islam in Kenya: Proceedings of the National Seminar on Contemporary Islam in Kenya.* Nairobi: Mewa Publications.

Bakari, Mtoro bin Mwinyi. 1981. *The Customs of the Swahili People.* Berkeley and Los Angeles: University of California Press.

Barrett, Michele. 1992. "Words and Things: Materialism and Method in Contemporary Feminist Analysis." In *Destabilizing Theory: Contemporary Feminist Debates,* edited by M. Barrett and A. Phillips, 201–19. Stanford, Calif.: Stanford University Press.

Bauman, Richard. 1986. *Story, Performance, and Event: Contextual Studies of Oral Narrative.* Cambridge: Cambridge University Press.

Bauman, Richard, and Charles L. Briggs. 1990. "Poetics and Performance as Critical Perspectives on Language and Social Life." *Annual Review of Anthropology* 19:59–88.

Beck, Lois, and Nikki Keddie, eds. 1978. *Women in the Muslim World.* Cambridge: Harvard University Press.

Bennett, Lance, and Martha Feldman. 1981. *Reconstructing Reality in the Courtroom: Justice and Judgment in American Culture.* New Brunswick, N.J.: Rutgers University Press.

Berg, F. J. 1968. "The Swahili Community of Mombasa, 1500–1900." *Journal of African History* 9 (1): 35–56.

Bergman, Jeanne. 1996. "A Willingness to Remember: The Persistence of Duruma Culture and Collective Memory." Ph.D. diss., University of California, Berkeley.

Berk-Seligson, Susan. 1990. *The Bilingual Courtroom: Court Interpreters in the Judicial Process.* Chicago: University of Chicago Press.

Besnier, Niko. 1990. "Conflict Management, Gossip, and Affective Meaning on Nukulaelae." In *Disentangling: Conflict Discourse in Pacific Societies,* edited by K. Watson-Gegeo and G. White, 290–334. Stanford, Calif.: Stanford University Press.

———. 1992. "Reported Speech and Affect on Nukulaelae Atoll." In *Responsibility and Evidence in Oral Discourse*, edited by J. Hill and J. Irvine, 161–81. Cambridge: Cambridge University Press.

Bloch, Maurice. 1975. *Political Language and Oratory in Traditional Society*. New York: Academic Press.

Boddy, Janice. 1989. *Wombs and Alien Spirits: Women, Men, and the Zar Cult in Northern Sudan*. Madison: University of Wisconsin Press.

Bohannan, Paul. 1957. *Justice and Judgment among the Tiv*. London: Oxford University Press.

Borker, Ruth. 1980. "Anthropology: Social and Cultural Perspectives." In *Women and Language in Literature and Society*, edited by S. McConnell-Ginet, R. Borker, and N. Furman, 26–44. New York: Praeger.

Bourdieu, Pierre. 1972. *Outline of a Theory of Practice*. Cambridge: Cambridge University Press.

Brenneis, Donald. 1988. "Language and Disputing." *Annual Review of Anthropology* 17:221–37.

Brenneis, Donald, and Fred Myers, eds. 1984. *Dangerous Words: Language and Politics in the Pacific*. New York: New York University Press.

Briggs, Charles. 1986. *Learning How to Ask: A Sociolinguistic Appraisal of the Role of the Interview in Social Science Research*. Cambridge: Cambridge University Press.

———. 1988a. *Competence in Performance: The Creativity of Tradition in Mexicano Verbal Art*. Philadelphia: University of Pennsylvania Press.

———. 1988b. "Disorderly Dialogues in Ritual Impositions of Order: The Role of Metapragmatics in Warao Dispute Mediation." *Anthropological Linguistics*, special issue, "Narrative Resources for the Creation and Mediation of Conflict," 30 (3–4): 448–91.

———. 1992a. "Generic versus Metapragmatic Dimensions of Warao Narratives: Who Regiments Performance?" In *Reflexive Language: Reported Speech and Metapragmatics*, edited by J. Lucy, 179–212. Cambridge: Cambridge University Press.

———. 1992b. "Linguistic Ideologies and the Naturalization of Power in Warao Discourse." *Pragmatics* 2 (3): 387–404.

Brown, Beverly. 1987. "Gender and Islamic Law in Kenya." Paper presented at the American Anthropological Association Annual Meeting, Philadelphia.

Brown, Penelope. 1993. "Gender, Politeness, and Confrontation in Tenejapa." In *Gender and Conversational Interaction*, edited by D. Tannen, 144–62. New York: Oxford University Press.

Bumiller, Kristin. 1991. "Fallen Angels: The Representation of Violence against Women in Legal Culture." In *At the Boundaries of the Law: Feminism and Legal Theory*, edited by M. Fineman and N. Thomadsen, 95–112. New York: Routledge.

Burman, Sandra, and Barbara Harrell-Bond, eds. 1979. *The Imposition of Law*. New York: Academic Press.

Butler, Judith. 1993. *Bodies That Matter: On the Discursive Limits of "Sex."* New York and London: Routledge.

Cameron, Deborah. 1985. *Feminism and Linguistic Theory*. London: Macmillan.

Cameron, Deborah, Elizabeth Frazer, Penelope Harvey, M. B. H. Rampton, and Kay Richardson, eds. 1992. *Researching Language: Issues of Power and Method*. London and New York: Routledge.

Caplan, Patricia Ann. 1975. *Choice and Constraint in a Swahili Community: Property, Hierarchy, and Cognatic Descent on the East African Coast*. London and New York: Oxford University Press.

————. 1976. "Boys' Circumcision and Girls' Puberty Rites among the Swahili of Mafia Island." *Paideuma* 28:29–43.

————. 1989. "Perceptions of Gender Stratification." *Africa* 59 (2): 196–208.

————. 1995. " 'Law' and 'Custom': Marital Disputes on Northern Mafia Island, Tanzania." In *Understanding Disputes: The Politics of Argument*, edited by P. Caplan, 203–22. Oxford Providence: Berg.

Chanock, Martin. 1985. *Law, Custom, and Social Order: The Colonial Experience in Malawi and Zambia*. Cambridge: Cambridge University Press.

Chow, Rey. 1991. "Violence in the Other Country: China as Crisis, Spectacle, and Woman." In *Third World Women and the Politics of Feminism*, edited by C. Mohanty, A. Russo, and L. Torres, 81–100. Bloomington: Indiana University Press.

Coates, Jennifer, and Deborah Cameron, eds. 1988. *Women in Their Speech Communities: New Perspectives on Language and Sex*. London: Longman.

Cobb, Sara. 1994. "Stabilizing Violence: Structural Complexity and Moral Transparency in Penalty Phase Narratives." Paper presented at the Law and Society Association Annual Meeting, Phoenix, June.

Cohen, David, and E. Atieno Odhiambo. 1992. *Burying S.M.: The Politics of Knowledge and the Sociology of Power in Africa*. Athens: Ohio University Press.

Collier, Jane. 1973. *Law and Social Change in Zinacantan*. Stanford, Calif.: Stanford University Press.

————. 1988. *Marriage and Inequality in Classless Societies*. Stanford, Calif.: Stanford University Press.

Comaroff, Jean, and John Comaroff. 1991. *Of Revelation and Revolution: Christianity, Colonialism, and Consciousness in South Africa*. Chicago: University of Chicago Press.

Comaroff, John, and Simon Roberts. 1981. *Rules and Processes: The Cultural Logic of Disputes in an African Context*. Chicago: University of Chicago Press.

Commission on the Law of Marriage and Divorce (Kenya). 1968. *Report of the Commission on the Law of Marriage and Divorce.* Nairobi: Government of Kenya.

Commission on the Law of Succession (Kenya). 1968. *Report of the Commission on the Law of Succession.* Nairobi: Government of Kenya.

Conley, John M., and William M. O'Barr. 1990. *Rules versus Relationships: The Ethnography of Legal Discourse.* Chicago: University of Chicago Press.

Constantin, François. 1987. "Condition Swahili et Identité Politique." *Africa* 57 (2): 219–33.

———. 1989. "Social Stratification on the Swahili Coast: From Race to Class?" *Africa* 59 (2): 145–60.

———. 1993. "Leadership, Muslim Identities, and East African Politics: Tradition, Bureaucratization, and Communication." In *Muslim Identity and Social Change in Sub-Saharan Africa,* edited by L. Brenner, 36–58. Bloomington and Indianapolis: Indiana University Press.

Coombe, Rosemary. 1991. "Contesting the Self: Negotiating Subjectivities in Nineteenth-Century Ontario Defamation Trials." In *Studies in Law, Politics, and Society* 11:3–40. Greenwich, Conn.: JAI Press.

Cooper, Frederick. 1977. *Plantation Slavery on the East Coast of Africa.* New Haven, Conn.: Yale University Press.

———. 1980. *From Slaves to Squatters: Plantation Labor and Agriculture in Zanzibar and Coastal Kenya, 1890–1925.* New Haven, Conn.: Yale University Press.

———. 1987. *On the African Waterfront: Urban Disorder and the Transition of Work in Colonial Mombasa.* New Haven and London: Yale University Press.

Cooper, Frederick, and Ann Stoler. 1989. "Tensions of Empire: Colonial Control and Visions of Rule." *American Ethnologist* 16 (4): 609–21.

Coulmas, Florian. 1986. "Nobody Dies in Shangri-La: Direct and Indirect Speech across Languages." In *Georgetown University Roundtable on Languages and Linguistics 1985,* edited by D. Tannen and J. Alatis. Washington, D.C.: Georgetown University Press.

Curtin, Patricia Romero. 1984. "Lamu Weddings as an Example of Social and Economic Change." *Cahiers d'Études Africaines* 24:131–55.

Danet, Brenda. 1980. "Language in the Legal Process." *Law and Society Review* 14:445–564.

———. 1985. "Legal Discourse." In *Handbook of Discourse Analysis,* vol. 3, *Discourse and Dialogue,* edited by T. van Dijk, 273–91. London: Academic Press.

de Lauretis, Teresa. 1990. "Eccentric Subjects: Feminist Theory and Historical Consciousness." *Feminist Studies* 16:115–50.

di Leonardo, Micaela, ed. 1991. *Gender at the Crossroads of Knowledge: Feminist Anthropology in the Postmodern Era.* Berkeley and Los Angeles: University of California Press.

Dingwall, Robert. 1988. "Empowerment or Enforcement? Some Questions about Power and Control in Divorce Mediation." In *Divorce Mediation and the Legal Process,* edited by R. Dingwall and J. Eekelar, 150–67. Oxford: Clarendon Press.

Dingwall, Robert, and John Eekelar, eds. 1988. *Divorce Mediation and the Legal Process.* Oxford: Clarendon Press.

Dirks, Nicholas, Geoff Eley, and Sherry Ortner, eds. 1994. *Culture/Power/History: A Reader in Social Theory.* Princeton, N.J.: Princeton University Press.

Dubois, Betty L., and Isabel Crouch. 1975. "The Question of Tag Questions in Women's Speech: They Don't Use More of Them, Do They?" *Language in Society* 4:289–94.

Duranti, Alessandro. 1994. *From Grammar to Politics: Linguistic Anthropology in a Western Samoan Village.* Berkeley and Los Angeles: University of California Press.

Duranti, Alessandro, and Charles Goodwin, eds. 1992. *Rethinking Context: Language as an Interactive Phenomenon.* Cambridge: Cambridge University Press.

Dwyer, Daisy Hilse. 1978a. "Bridging the Gap between the Sexes in Moroccan Judicial Practice." In *Sexual Stratification: A Cross-Cultural Perspective,* edited by A. Schlegel, 41–66. New York: Columbia University Press.

———. 1978b. *Images and Self-Images: Male and Female in Morocco.* New York: Columbia University Press.

———. 1982. "Outside the Courts: Extra-legal Strategies for Subordination of Women." In *African Women and the Law: Historical Perspectives,* edited by J. Hay and M. Wright, 90–109. Boston: Papers on Africa.

———, ed. 1990. *Law and Islam in the Middle East.* New York: Bergin and Garvey.

Eastman, Carol. 1971. "Who Are the Waswahili?" *Africa* 41 (3): 228–36.

———. 1984a. "An Ethnography of Swahili Expressive Culture." *Research in African Literatures* 15 (3): 313–34.

———. 1984b. "Wangwana and Wanawake." *Journal of Multilingual and Multicultural Development* 5 (2): 97–112.

———. 1988. "Women, Slaves, and Foreigners: African Cultural Influences and Group Processes in the Formation of Northern Swahili Coastal Society." *International Journal of African Historical Studies* 21 (1): 1–20.

Edelsky, Carole R. 1979. "Question Intonation and Sex Roles." *Language in Society* 8:15–32.

El-Zein, Abdul Hamid. 1974. *The Sacred Meadows: A Structural Analysis of Religious Symbolism in an East African Town.* Studies in African Literature. Evanston, Ill.: Northwestern University Press.

Enloe, Cynthia. 1993. *The Morning After: Sexual Politics at the End of the Cold War.* Berkeley and Los Angeles: University of California Press.

Epstein, A. L. 1967. "The Case Method in the Field of Law." In *The Craft of Social Anthropology*, edited by A. L. Epstein, 205–30. London: Tavistock.

Ewick, Patricia, and Susan Silbey. 1995. "Subversive Stories and Hegemonic Tales: Toward a Sociology of Narrative." *Law and Society Review* 29 (2): 197–226.

Fallers, Lloyd. 1969. *Law without Precedent: Legal Ideas in Action in the Courts of Colonial Busoga*. Chicago: Aldine.

Farsy, Sheikh Abdallah Swaleh. 1965. *Ndoa-Talaka na Maamrisho Yake*. Zanzibar: Mulla Karimjee Mulla Mohamedbhai.

———. 1969. *Quarani Takatifu*. Nairobi: The Islamic Foundation.

———. 1977. *Bidda*. Part 1. Moshi: Sheikh Saidi Musa.

———. 1981. *Bid-a*. Part 2. Moshi: Sheikh Saidi Musa.

Feld, Stephen. 1982. *Sound and Sentiment: Birds, Weeping, Poetics, and Song in Kaluli Expression*. Philadelphia: University of Pennsylvania Press.

Felstiner, William, Richard Abel, and Austin Sarat. 1980. "The Emergence and Transformation of Disputes: Naming, Blaming, Claiming." *Law and Society Review* 15 (3): 631–54.

Ferguson, Kathy E. 1984. *The Feminist Case against Bureaucracy*. Philadelphia: Temple University Press.

———. 1993. *The Man Question: Visions of Subjectivity in Feminist Theory*. New York: Routledge.

Fineman, Martha, and Roxanne Mykitiuk, eds. 1994. *The Public Nature of Private Violence: The Discovery of Domestic Abuse*. New York: Routledge.

Fisher, Sue. 1984. "Institutional Authority and the Structure of Discourse." *Discourse Processes* 7:201–24.

———. 1995. *Nursing Wounds: Nurse Practitioners, Doctors, Women Patients, and the Negotiation of Meaning*. New Brunswick, N.J.: Rutgers University Press.

Fisher, Sue, and Kathy Davis, eds. 1993. *Negotiating at the Margins: The Gendered Discourses of Power and Resistance*. New Brunswick, N.J.: Rutgers University Press.

Fishman, Pamela. 1978. "Interaction: The Work Women Do." *Social Problems* 25:133–35.

Foster, Deborah D. 1984. *Structure and Performance of Swahili Oral Narrative*. Ph.D. diss., University of Wisconsin.

Foucault, Michel. 1979. *Discipline and Punish: The Birth of the Prison*. New York: Vintage Books.

———. 1980. *Power/Knowledge: Selected Interviews and Other Writings, 1972–1977*. New York: Pantheon Books.

———. 1983. "The Subject and Power." In *Michel Foucault: Beyond Structuralism and Hermeneutics*, 2d ed., edited by H. L. Dreyfuss and P. Rabinow, 208–26. Chicago: University of Chicago Press.

Freeman-Grenville, G. S. P. 1988. *The Swahili Coast, Second to Nineteenth Centuries*. London: Variorum.

Fuglesang, Minou. 1994. *Veils and Videos: Female Youth Culture on the Kenyan Coast*. Stockholm: Stockholm Studies in Social Anthropology.

Gal, Susan. 1991. "Between Speech and Silence: The Problematics of Research on Language and Gender." In *Gender at the Crossroads of Knowledge: Feminist Anthropology in the Postmodern Era*, edited by M. di Leonardo, 175–203. Berkeley and Los Angeles: University of California Press.

Geertz, Clifford. 1983. *Local Knowledge: Further Essays in Interpretive Anthropology*. New York: Basic Books.

Giles, Linda. 1987. "Possession Cults on the Swahili Coast: A Reexamination of Theories of Marginality." *Africa* 57 (2): 235–57.

Glassman, Jonathon. 1991. "The Bondsman's New Clothes: The Contradictory Consciousness of Slave Resistance on the Swahili Coast." *Journal of African History* 32:277–312.

———. 1995. *Feasts and Riot: Revelry, Rebellion, and Popular Consciousness on the Swahili Coast, 1856–1888*. Portsmouth, N.H.: Heinemann.

Goffman, Erving. 1961. *Asylums: Essays on the Social Situation of Mental Patients and Other Inmates*. Garden City, N.Y.: Anchor.

———. 1981. *Forms of Talk*. Philadelphia: University of Pennsylvania Press.

Goldman, Laurence. 1983. *Talk Never Dies: The Language of Huli Disputes*. London: Tavistock.

———. 1986. "The Presentational Style of Women in Huli Disputes." *Papers in New Guinea Linguistics* 24:213–89.

Goodwin, Charles. 1981. *Conversational Organization: Interaction between Speakers and Hearers*. New York: Academic Press.

———. 1984. "Notes on Story Structure and the Organization of Participation." In *Structures of Social Action*, edited by J. M. Atkinson and J. Heritage, 225–46. Cambridge: Cambridge University Press.

———. 1986. "Audience Diversity, Participation, and Interpretation." *Text* 6 (3): 283–316.

Goodwin, Marjorie H. 1982. " 'Instigating': Storytelling as Social Process." *American Ethnologist* 9:799–819.

———. 1990. *He-Said-She-Said: Talk as Social Organization among Black Children*. Bloomington: Indiana University Press.

Greenhouse, Carol. 1986. *Praying for Justice: Faith, Order, and Community in an American Town*. Ithaca, N.Y.: Cornell University Press.

Grima, Benedicte. 1992. *The Performance of Emotion among Paxtun Women*. Austin: University of Texas Press.

Grimshaw, Allen, ed. 1990. *Conflict Talk: Sociolinguistic Investigations of Arguments in Conversations*. Cambridge: Cambridge University Press.

Gulich, Elisabeth, and Uta M. Quasthoff. 1985. "Narrative Analysis." In *Handbook of Discourse Analysis*, vol. 2, *Dimensions of Discourse*, edited by T. van Dijk, 169–98. London: Academic Press.

Gulliver, Philip H. 1977. "On Mediators." In *Social Anthropology and Law*, edited by I. Hamnet, 15–52. London: Academic Press.

Haeri, Shahla. 1989. *Law of Desire: Temporary Marriage in Shi'i Iran*. Syracuse, N.Y.: Syracuse University Press.

Halliday, M. A. K., and R. Hasan. 1976. *Cohesion in English*. London: Longman.

Hanks, William. 1989. "Texts and Textuality." *Annual Review of Anthropology* 18:95–127.

Hatem, Mervyn. 1986. "The Enduring Alliance of Nationalism and Patriarchy in Muslim Personal Status Laws: The Case of Modern Egypt." *Feminist Issues* 6 (1): 19–41.

———. 1987. "Class and Patriarchy as Competing Paradigms for the Study of Middle Eastern Women." *Comparative Studies in Society and History* 29:811–18.

Haviland, John. 1988. " 'We Want to Borrow Your Mouth': Tzotzil Marital Squabbles." *Anthropological Linguistics* 30 (3–4): 395–447.

Hay, Jean, and Marcia Wright, eds. 1984. *African Women and the Law: Historical Perspectives*. Boston: Boston University.

Hayden, Robert. 1987. "Turn-Taking, Overlap, and the Task at Hand: Ordering Speaking Turns in Legal Settings." *American Ethnologist* 14 (2): 251–70.

Herzfeld, Michael. 1988. "Embarrassment as Pride: Narrative Resourcefulness and Strategies of Normativity among Cretan Animal-Thieves." *Anthropological Linguistics* 30 (3–4): 319–44.

Hickmann, Maya. 1992. "The Boundaries of Reported Speech in Narrative Discourse: Some Developmental Aspects." In *Reflexive Language: Reported Speech and Metapragmatics*, edited by J. Lucy, 63–90. Cambridge: Cambridge University Press.

Hill, Jane H., and Judith T. Irvine, eds. 1992. *Responsibility and Evidence in Oral Discourse*. Cambridge: Cambridge University Press.

Hill, Jane H., and Ofelia Zepeda. 1992. "Mrs. Patricio's Trouble: The Distribution of Responsibility in an Account of Personal Experience." In *Responsibility and Evidence in Oral Discourse*, edited by J. Hill and J. Irvine, 197–225. Cambridge: Cambridge University Press.

Hinton, Leanne, Johanna Nichols, and John J. Ohala, eds. 1994. *Sound Symbolism*. Cambridge: Cambridge University Press.

Hirsch, Susan F. 1987. "Same Form, Different Function: Tag Questions in Swahili Legal Disputes." Paper presented at the Symposium on Language and Gender: A Cross-Linguistic, Cross-Cultural Perspective, University of Utah, April.

———. 1990. "Gender and Disputing: Insurgent Voices in Coastal Kenyan Muslim Courts." Ph.D. diss., Duke University.

———. 1993. "Challenging Power through Discourse: Cases of Seditious Speech from Kenya." Paper presented at the Law and Society Association Annual Meeting, Chicago, May.

————. 1994. "Kadhi's Courts as Complex Sites of Resistance: The State, Islam, and Gender in Postcolonial Kenya." In *Contested States: Law, Hegemony, and Resistance,* edited by M. Lazarus-Black and S. Hirsch, 207–30. New York: Routledge.

Hirsch, Susan F., and Mindie Lazarus-Black. 1994. "Performance and Paradox: Exploring Law's Role in Hegemony and Resistance." In *Contested States: Law, Hegemony, and Resistance,* edited by M. Lazarus-Black and S. Hirsch, 1–31. New York: Routledge.

Holmes, Janet. 1982. "The Functions of Tag Questions." *English Language Research Journal* 3:40–65.

————. 1984. "Hedging Your Bets and Sitting on the Fence: Some Evidence for Hedges as Support Structures." *Te Reo* 27:47–52.

Hooker, M. B. 1975. *Legal Pluralism: An Introduction to Colonial and Neo-colonial Laws.* Oxford: Clarendon.

Horton, Mark. 1987. "The Swahili Corridor." *Scientific American* 257: 86–93.

Hymes, Dell. 1981. *"In Vain I Tried to Tell You": Essays in Native American Ethnopoetics.* Philadelphia: University of Pennsylvania Press.

Irvine, Judith T. 1992. "Insult and Responsibility: Verbal Abuse in a Wolof Village." In *Responsibility and Evidence in Oral Discourse,* edited by J. Hill and J. Irvine, 105–34. Cambridge: Cambridge University Press.

————. 1996. "Shadow Conversations: The Indeterminacy of Participant Roles." In *Natural Histories of Discourse,* edited by M. Silverstein and G. Urban, 131–59. Chicago and London: University of Chicago Press.

Jackson, Tudor. 1970. *The Law of Kenya: An Introduction.* Nairobi: Kenya Literature Bureau.

Jefferson, Gail. 1978. "Sequential Aspects of Storytelling in Conversation." In *Studies in the Organization of Conversational Interaction,* edited by J. Schenkein, 219–48. New York: Academic Press.

Johnson, Frederick, and A. Madan. 1939. *A Standard Swahili-English Dictionary.* Oxford: Oxford University Press.

Just, Peter. 1992. "History, Power, Ideology, and Culture: Current Directions in the Anthropology of Law." *Law and Society Review* 26 (2): 373–412.

Kandiyoti, Deniz, ed. 1991. *Women, Islam, and the State.* Philadelphia: Temple University Press.

Kedar, Leah. 1987. *Power through Discourse.* Norwood, N.J.: Ablex.

Keenan, Elinor. 1974. "Norm Makers, Norm Breakers: Uses of Speech by Men and Women in a Malagasy Community." In *Explorations in the Ethnography of Speaking,* 2d ed., edited by R. Bauman and J. Sherzer, 125–43. Cambridge: Cambridge University Press.

Khalid, Abdallah. 1977. *The Liberation of Swahili from European Appropriation: A Handbook for African Nation-Building.* Nairobi: East African Literature Bureau.

Kindy, Hyder. 1972. *Life and Politics in Mombasa*. Nairobi: East African Literature Bureau.

King, Noel Q. 1981. Preface to *The Customs of the Swahili People,* by M. Bakari. Berkeley and Los Angeles: University of California Press.

Kirkman, James. 1964. *Men and Monuments of the East African Coast.* London: Lutterworth Press.

Kitching, Gavin. 1980. *Class and Economic Change in Kenya: The Making of an African Petite-Bourgeoisie.* New Haven, Conn.: Yale University Press.

Knappert, Jan. 1967. *Traditional Swahili Poetry: An Investigation into the Concepts of East African Islam as Reflected in the Utenzi Literature.* Leiden, Netherlands: E. J. Brill.

———. 1970. "Social and Moral Concepts in Swahili Islamic Literature." *Africa* 11:125–36.

———. 1979. *Four Centuries of Swahili Verse: A Literary History and Anthology.* London: Heinemann.

Kratz, Corinne. 1994. *Affecting Performance: Meaning, Movement, and Experience in Okiek Women's Initiation.* Washington, D.C.: Smithsonian Institution Press.

Kramarae, Cheris. 1982. "Gender: How She Speaks." In *Attitudes towards Language Variation,* edited by E. B. Ryan and H. Giles. London: Edward Arnold.

Kramarae, Cheris, Marjorie Schulz, and William M. O'Barr, eds. 1984. *Language and Power.* Beverly Hills, Calif.: Sage.

Kulick, Don. 1992. "Anger, Gender, Language Shift, and the Politics of Revelation in a Papua New Guinean Village." *Pragmatics* 2 (3): 281–96.

Labov, William. 1972. "The Transformation of Experience in Narrative Syntax." In *Language in the Inner City,* edited by W. Labov, 354–96. Philadelphia: University of Pennsylvania Press.

Labov, William, and J. Waletzky. 1967. "Narrative Analysis." In *Essays on the Verbal and Visual Arts,* edited by J. Helm, 12–44. Seattle: University of Washington Press.

Lakoff, Robin. 1975. *Language and Woman's Place.* New York: Harper and Row.

Landberg, Pamela W. 1986. "Widows and Divorced Women in Swahili Society." In *Widows in African Societies,* edited by B. Potash, 107–38. Stanford, Calif.: Stanford University Press.

Lazarus-Black, Mindie. 1991. "Why Women Take Men to Magistrate's Court: Caribbean Kinship Ideology and Law." *Ethnology* 30 (2): 119–33.

———. 1994. *Legitimate Acts and Illegal Encounters: A History and Ethnography of Life and Law in Antigua and Barbuda.* Washington, D.C.: Smithsonian Institution Press.

Lazarus-Black, Mindie, and Susan F. Hirsch, eds. 1994. *Contested States: Law, Hegemony, and Resistance.* New York: Routledge.

Le Cour Grandmaison, Colette. 1989. "Rich Cousins, Poor Cousins: Hidden Stratification among the Omani Arabs in Eastern Africa." *Africa* 59 (2): 176–84.

Le Guennec-Coppens, Françoise. 1983. *Les Femmes Voilées de Lamu, Kenya. Variations Culturelles et Dynamiques Sociales.* Paris: Editions Recherche sur les Civilisations.

———. 1989. "Social and Cultural Integration: A Case Study of the East African Hadramis." *Africa* 59 (2): 185–95.

Levi, Judith. 1982. *Linguistics, Language, and Law.* Bloomington: Indiana University Linguistics Club.

———. 1990. "The Study of Language in the Legal Process." In *Language in the Judicial Process,* edited by J. Levi and A. Walker, 3–38. New York: Plenum Press.

———. 1994. "Language and Law: A Bibliographic Guide to Social Science Research in the U.S.A." *Teaching Resource Bulletin* (American Bar Association) 4.

Levi, Judith, and Anne Grafam Walker. 1990. *Language in the Judicial Process.* New York: Plenum Press.

Levinson, Stephen. 1983. *Pragmatics.* Cambridge: Cambridge University Press.

Lewis, I. M. 1966. "Spirit Possession and Deprivation Cults." *Man* 1:307–29.

Lienhardt, Peter. 1959. "The Mosque College of Lamu and Its Social Background." *Tanganyika Notes and Records,* no. 53:228–42.

Linde, Charlotte. 1993. *Life Stories: The Creation of Coherence.* New York and Oxford: Oxford University Press.

Lowy, Michael J. 1978. "A Good Name Is Worth More Than Money: Strategies of Court Use in Urban Ghana." In *The Disputing Process: Law in Ten Societies,* edited by L. Nader and H. Todd, 181–208. New York: Columbia University Press.

Lucy, John A., ed. 1992. *Reflexive Language: Reported Speech and Metapragmatics.* Cambridge: Cambridge University Press.

Macleod, Arlene. 1991. *Accommodating Protest: Working Women, the New Veiling, and Change in Cairo.* New York: Columbia University Press.

Mahoney, Maureen, and Barbara Yngvesson. 1992. "The Construction of Subjectivity and the Paradox of Resistance: Reintegrating Feminist Anthropology and Psychology." *Signs: Journal of Women in Culture and Society* 18 (1): 44–73.

Makhlouf, Carla. 1979. *Changing Veils: Women and Modernization in North Yemen.* Austin: University of Texas Press.

Marcus, Isabel. 1994. "Reframing 'Domestic Violence': Terrorism in the Home." In *The Public Nature of Private Violence: The Discovery of Domestic Abuse,* edited by M. Fineman and R. Mykitiuk, 11–35. New York: Routledge.

Markova, Ivana, and Klaus Foppa, eds. 1991. *Asymmetries in Dialogue.* Hertfordshire, England: Harvester Wheatsheaf.

Martin, B. G. 1971. "Notes on Some Members of the Learned Classes of Zanzibar and East Africa in the Nineteenth Century." *African Historical Studies* 4 (3): 525–45.

Martin, Esmond Bradley. 1973. *The History of Malindi: A Geographical Analysis of an East African Coastal Town.* Nairobi: East African Literature Bureau.

———. 1975. *Malindi: The Historic Town on Kenya's Coast.* Nairobi: Kenya Marketing and Book Publishing.

Mather, Lynn, and Barbara Yngvesson. 1980. "Language, Audience, and the Transformation of Disputes." *Law and Society Review* 15 (3): 775–821.

Matoesian, Gregory M. 1993. *Reproducing Rape: Domination through Talk in the Courtroom.* Chicago: University of Chicago Press.

Maw, Joan. 1969. *Sentences in Swahili: A Study of Their Internal Relationships.* London: School of Oriental and African Studies.

———. 1974. *Swahili Style.* London: School of Oriental and African Studies.

———. 1992. *Narrative in Swahili: Sentence Structure, Intonation, and the Storyteller.* London: School of Oriental and African Studies.

Maw, Joan, and John Kelly. 1975. *Intonation in Swahili.* London: School of Oriental and African Studies.

Maw, Joan, and Yahya Ali Omar. 1985. "The Language of Social Control." In *Swahili Language and Society: Papers from the Workshop Held at the School of Oriental and African Studies in April 1982,* edited by J. Maw and D. Parkin. Vienna: Afro-Pub.

Maw, Joan, and David Parkin, eds. 1985. *Swahili Language and Society: Papers from the Workshop Held at the School of Oriental and African Studies in April 1982.* Vienna: Afro-Pub.

Mazrui, Alamin M., and Ibrahim Noor Shariff. 1994. *The Swahili: Idiom and Identity of an African People.* Trenton, N.J.: Africa World Press.

Mbaabu, Ireri. 1985. *Utamaduni wa Waswahili.* Nairobi: Kenya Marketing and Book Publishing.

Mernissi, Fatima. 1975. *Beyond the Veil: Male-Female Dynamics in a Modern Muslim Society.* Cambridge: Schenkman.

———. 1991. *The Veil and the Male Elite: A Feminist Interpretation of Women's Rights in Islam.* Reading, Mass.: Addison-Wesley Publishing Company.

Merry, Sally Engle. 1988. "Legal Pluralism." *Law and Society Review* 22 (5): 869–96.

———. 1990. *Getting Justice and Getting Even: Legal Consciousness among Working-Class Americans.* Chicago: University of Chicago Press.

Mertz, Elizabeth. 1985. "Beyond Symbolic Anthropology: Introducing Semiotic Mediation." In *Semiotic Mediation: Sociocultural and Psychological Perspectives,* edited by E. Mertz and R. Parmentier, 1–18. New
York: Academic Press.
———. 1992a. "Language, Law, and Social Meanings, Linguistic/Anthro-
pological Contributions to the Study of Law." Review of *Getting Justice
and Getting Even,* by Sally Engle Merry; and *Rules versus Relationships,*
by John Conley and William M. O'Barr. *Law and Society Review* 26
(2): 413–45.
———. 1992b. "Learning What to Ask: Metapragmatic Factors and Meth-
odological Reification." In *Reflexive Language: Reported Speech and
Metapragmatics,* edited by J. Lucy, 159–74. Cambridge: Cambridge
University Press.
———. 1994. "Legal Language: Pragmatics, Poetics, and Social Power."
Annual Review of Anthropology 23:435–55.
Mertz, Elizabeth, and Richard Parmentier, eds. 1985. *Semiotic Mediation:
Sociocultural and Psychological Perspectives.* New York: Academic
Press.
Mey, Jacob L. 1993. *Pragmatics: An Introduction.* Oxford and Cambridge:
Blackwell.
Middleton, John. 1992. *The World of the Swahili: An African Mercantile
Civilization.* New Haven, Conn.: Yale University Press.
Migot-Adholla, Shem, Katama Mkangi, and J. Mbindayo. 1982. *Study of
Tourism in Kenya: With Emphasis on the Attitudes of Residents of the
Kenyan Coast.* Nairobi: Institute for Development Studies.
Minow, Martha, Michael Ryan, and Austin Sarat, eds. 1992. *Narrative, Vio-
lence, and the Law: The Essays of Robert Cover.* Ann Arbor, Mich.:
University of Michigan Press.
Mirza, Sarah, and Margaret Strobel, eds. 1989. *Three Swahili Women: Life
Histories from Mombasa, Kenya.* Bloomington: Indiana University
Press.
Moerman, Michael. 1988. *Talking Culture: Ethnography and Conversation
Analysis.* Philadelphia: University of Pennsylvania Press.
Mohanty, Chandra. 1991. "Under Western Eyes: Feminist Scholarship and
Colonial Discourses." In *Third World Women and the Politics of Femi-
nism,* edited by C. Mohanty, A. Russo, and L. Torres, 51–80. Blooming-
ton: Indiana University Press.
Moore, Erin. 1994. "Law's Patriarchy in India." In *Contested States: Law,
Hegemony, and Resistance,* edited by M. Lazarus-Black and S. Hirsch,
89–117. New York: Routledge.
Moore, Henrietta. 1994. *A Passion for Difference: Essays in Anthropology
and Gender.* Bloomington and Indianapolis: Indiana University
Press.
Moore, Sally Falk. 1978. *Law as Process: An Anthropological Approach.*
London: Routledge and Kegan Paul.

―――. 1986. *Social Facts and Fabrications: Customary Law on Kilimanjaro, 1880–1980.* Cambridge: Cambridge University Press.

―――. 1989. "History and Redefinition of Custom on Kilimanjaro." In *History and Power in the Study of Law: New Directions in Legal Anthropology,* edited by J. Starr and J. Collier, 277–301. Ithaca, N.Y.: Cornell University Press.

Morris, Henry F. 1968. *Evidence in East Africa.* London: Sweet and Maxwell.

Mungeam, G. H. 1978. *Kenya, Selected Historical Documents, 1884–1923.* Nairobi: East African Publishing House.

Murphy, William. 1990. "Creating the Appearance of Consensus in Mende Political Discourse." *American Anthropologist* 92 (1): 24–41.

Mutunga, Willie. 1994. "Witchcraft Accusations and the State in Kenya." Paper delivered at the African Studies Association Annual Meeting, Toronto.

Mutungi, Onesmus. 1977. *The Legal Aspects of Witchcraft in East Africa.* Nairobi: East African Literature Bureau.

Mwangi, Kuria. 1995. "The Application and Development of Sharia in Kenya: 1895–1990." In *Islam in Kenya,* edited by M. Bakari and S. Yahya, 252–59. Nairobi: Mewa Publications.

Nader, Laura. 1969. *Law in Culture and Society.* Chicago: Aldine.

―――. 1990. *Harmony Ideology: Justice and Control in a Zapotec Mountain Village.* Stanford, Calif.: Stanford University Press.

Nader, Laura, and Harry Todd, eds. 1978. *The Disputing Process: Law in Ten Societies.* New York: Columbia University Press.

Nader, Laura, and Barbara Yngvesson. 1973. "On Studying the Ethnography of Law and Its Consequences." In *Handbook of Social and Cultural Anthropology,* edited by J. Honigman, 883–921. Chicago: Rand McNally.

Nasir, S. A. A. 1972. *Al-Inkishafi: The Soul's Awakening.* Nairobi: Oxford University Press.

Nawawi, Mahiudin abu Zakaria Yahya Ibn Sharifen. 1914. *Minhaj et Talibin: A Manual of Muhammadan Law According to the School of Shafii.* Translated from the French by L. W. C. Van den Bargby and E. C. Howard. London: W. Thacker.

Nicholls, C. S. 1971. *The Swahili Coast.* New York: Africana Publishing.

Nimtz, August H. 1980. *Islam and Politics in East Africa: The Sufi Order in Tanzania.* Minneapolis: University of Minnesota Press.

Nurse, David, and Thomas Spear. 1985. *The Swahili: Reconstructing the History and Language of an African Society, 800–1500.* Philadelphia: University of Pennsylvania Press.

O'Barr, William M. 1982. *Linguistic Evidence: Language, Power, and Strategy in the Courtroom.* New York: Academic Press.

O'Barr, William M., and Bowman T. Atkins. 1980. " 'Women's Language' or 'Powerless Language'?" In *Women and Language in Literature and*

Society, edited by S. McConnell-Ginet, R. Borker, and N. Furman, 93–110. New York: Praeger.

Ochs, Elinor. 1979. "Transcription as Theory." In *Developmental Pragmatics*, edited by E. Ochs and B. Schieffelin, 43–72. New York: Academic Press.

———. 1992. "Indexing Gender." In *Rethinking Context: Language as an Interactive Phenomenon*, edited by A. Duranti and C. Goodwin, 335–58. Cambridge: Cambridge University Press.

Ochs, Elinor, C. Taylor, D. Rudolph, and R. Smith. 1992. "Story-Telling as a Theory-Building Activity." *Discourse Processes* 15 (1): 37–72.

Ojwang, J. B., and J. N. K. Mugambi, eds. 1989. *The S.M. Otieno Case: Death and Burial in Modern Kenya*. Nairobi: Nairobi University Press.

Paine, Robert, ed. 1978. *Politically Speaking: Cross-Cultural Studies of Rhetoric*. Philadelphia: Institute for the Study of Human Issues.

Papanek, Hanna. 1973. "Purdah: Separate Worlds and Symbolic Shelter." *Comparative Studies in Society and History* 15:283–325.

Parkin, David. 1972. *Palms, Wine, and Witnesses: Public Spirit and Private Gain in an African Farming Community*. London: Intertext Books.

———. 1985. "Entitling Evil: Muslims and Non-Muslims in Coastal Kenya." In *The Anthropology of Evil*, edited by D. Parkin, 224–43. London: Basil Blackwell.

———. 1989. "Swahili Mijikenda: Facing Both Ways in Kenya." *Africa* 59 (2): 161–75.

Parmentier, Richard. 1985. "Diagrammatic Icons and Historical Processes in Belau." *American Anthropologist* 87:840–52.

———. 1992. "The Political Function of Reported Speech: A Belaun Example." In *Reflexive Language: Reported Speech and Metapragmatics*, edited by J. Lucy, 261–86. Cambridge: Cambridge University Press.

Peake, Robert. 1989. "Swahili Stratification and Tourism in Malindi Old Town, Kenya." *Africa* 59 (2): 209–20.

Personal Narratives Group. 1989. *Interpreting Women's Lives: Feminist Theory and Personal Narratives*. Bloomington: Indiana University Press.

Philips, Susan. 1984. "The Social Organization of Questions and Answers in Courtroom Discourse: A Study of Changes of Plea in an Arizona Court." *Text* 4 (1): 225–48.

———. 1986. "Reported Speech as Evidence in an American Trial." In *Georgetown University Roundtable on Languages and Linguistics 1985*, edited by D. Tannen and J. Alatis, 154–70. Washington, D.C.: Georgetown University Press.

———. 1987. "On the Use of WH Questions in American Courtroom Discourse: A Study of the Relation between Language Form and Language Function." In *Power through Discourse*, edited by L. Kedar, 83–112. Norwood, N.J.: Ablex.

————. 1992. "A Marx-Influenced Approach to Ideology and Language: Comments." *Pragmatics* 2 (3): 377–85.

————. 1994a. "Bad Language in Tonga." Paper presented at School of American Research Conference on Language Ideologies, Santa Fe, April.

————. 1994b. "Local Legal Hegemony in the Tongan Magistrate's Courts; How Sisters Fare Better than Wives." In *Contested States: Law, Hegemony, and Resistance,* edited by M. Lazarus- Black and S. Hirsch, 59–88. New York: Routledge.

————. 1995. "Escalation of Verbal Aggression in a Tongan Narrative and an OJ Simpson Narrative: Constructing Blameless Victims." Paper presented at the Law and Society Association Annual Meeting, Toronto, June.

Polanyi, Livia. 1985. "Conversational Storytelling." In *Handbook of Discourse Analysis,* vol. 3, *Discourse and Dialogue,* edited by T. van Dijk, 183–201. London: Academic Press.

————. 1989. *Telling the American Story: A Structural and Cultural Analysis of Conversational Storytelling.* Cambridge, Mass.: MIT Press.

Pomerantz, Anita. 1978. "Attributions of Responsibility: Blamings." *Sociology* 12:115–21.

Porter, Mary. 1992a. "Swahili Identities in Postcolonial Kenya: Gender Representations in Educational Discourses." Paper presented at the American Ethnological Society Annual Meeting, Memphis, April.

————. 1992b. "Swahili Identity in Post-Colonial Kenya: The Reproduction of Gender in Educational Discourses." Ph.D. diss., University of Washington, Seattle.

————. 1995. "Talking at the Margins: Kenyan Discourses on Homosexuality." In *Beyond the Lavendar Lexicon: Authenticity, Imagination, and Appropriation in Lesbian and Gay Languages,* edited by W. Leap, 133–54. New York: Gordon and Breach.

Pouwels, Randall Lee. 1979. "Islam and Islamic Leadership in the Coastal Communities of Eastern Africa, 1700–1914." Ph.D. diss., University of California at Los Angeles.

————. 1987. *The Horn and the Crescent: Cultural Change and Traditional Islam on the East African Coast, 800–1900.* Cambridge: Cambridge University Press.

Prins, A. H. J. 1961. *The Swahili-Speaking Peoples of Zanzibar and the East African Coast.* London: International African Institute.

Quinn, Naomi. 1996. "Women Theorizing Gender: The Case of Cultural Anthropology." Typescript.

Roberts, Simon. 1979. *Order and Dispute: An Introduction to Legal Anthropology.* Harmondsworth, England: Penguin.

Romero, Patricia. 1988. "Mama Hadija: A Life History as Example of Family History." In *Life Histories of African Women,* edited by P. Romero, 140–58. London and Atlantic Highlands, N.J.: The Ashfield Press.

Rosaldo, Renato. 1989. *Culture and Truth: The Remaking of Social Analysis.* Boston: Beacon Press.

Rosen, Lawrence. 1984. *Bargaining for Reality: The Construction of Social Relations in a Muslim Community.* Chicago: University of Chicago Press.

———. 1989. "Islamic 'Case Law' and the Logic of Consequence." In *History and Power in the Study of Law: New Directions in Legal Anthropology,* edited by J. Starr and J. Collier, 302–19. Ithaca, N.Y.: Cornell University Press.

Ruete, Emily. 1886. *Memoirs of an Arabian Princess.* 2d ed. New York: D. Appleton and Co.

Russell, Joan. 1981. *Communicative Competence in a Minority Group: A Sociolinguistic Study of the Swahili-Speaking Community in the Old Town, Mombasa.* Leiden, Netherlands: E. J. Brill.

———. 1985. "Women's Narration: Performance and the Marking of Verbal Aspect." In *Swahili Language and Society: Papers from the Workshop Held at the School of Oriental and African Studies in April 1982,* edited by J. Maw and D. Parkin, 89–106. Vienna: Afro-Pub.

Salim, Ahmed. 1973. *Swahili-Speaking Peoples of Kenya's Coast, 1895–1965.* Nairobi: East African Publishing House.

———. 1985. "The Illusive Mswahili—Some Reflections on His Identity and Culture." In *Swahili Language and Society: Papers from the Workshop Held at the School of Oriental and African Studies in April 1982,* edited by J. Maw and D. Parkin. Vienna: Afro-Pub.

Sarat, Austin. 1993. "Speaking of Death: Narratives of Violence in Capital Trials." *Law and Society Review* 27 (1): 19–58.

Sarat, Austin, and William Felstiner. 1986. "Law and Strategy in the Divorce Lawyer's Office." *Law and Society Review* 20:93–134.

Schacht, Joseph. 1964. *An Introduction to Islamic Law.* Oxford: Clarendon Press.

Schiffrin, Deborah. 1990. "The Management of a Co-operative Self in Argument: The Role of Opinions and Stories." In *Conflict Talk: Sociolinguistic Investigations of Arguments in Conversations,* edited by A. Grimshaw, 241–59. Cambridge: Cambridge University Press.

———. 1994. *Approaches to Discourse.* Oxford and Cambridge: Blackwell.

Scott, James. 1990. *Domination and the Arts of Resistance: Hidden Transcripts.* New Haven, Conn.: Yale University Press.

Shaheed, Farida. 1994. "Controlled or Autonomous: Identity and the Experience of the Network, Women Living under Muslim Laws." *Signs: Journal of Women in Culture and Society* 19 (4): 997–1019.

Shariff, Ibrahim Noor. 1973. "Waswahili and Their Language: Some Misconceptions." *Kiswahili* 43 (2): 67–75.

Shee, Ali M. 1984. *Hishima ya Mwanamke Katika Dini na Mila.* N.p., n.d.

Shepherd, Gill. 1987. "Rank, Gender, and Homosexuality: Mombasa as a Key to Understanding Sexual Options." In *The Cultural Construction of Sexuality,* edited by P. Caplan, 240–70. London and New York: Tavistock.

Sherzer, Joel. 1987. "A Discourse-Centered Approach to Language and Culture." *American Anthropologist* 89:295–310.

Shuman, Amy. 1986. *Storytelling Rights: The Uses of Oral and Written Texts by Urban Adolescents.* Cambridge: Cambridge University Press.

Silverstein, Michael. 1976. "Shifters, Linguistic Categories, and Cultural Description." In *Meaning in Anthropology,* edited by K. Basso and H. Selby, 11–55. Albuquerque: University of New Mexico Press.

———. 1979. "Language Structure and Linguistic Ideology." In *The Elements: A Parasession on Linguistic Units and Levels,* edited by P. Clyne, W. Hanks, and C. Hofbauer, 193–247. Chicago: Chicago Linguistics Society.

———. 1985. "Language and the Culture of Gender: At the Intersection of Structure, Usage, and Ideology." In *Semiotic Mediation: Sociocultural and Psychological Perspectives,* edited by E. Mertz and R. Parmentier, 219–59. New York: Academic Press.

———. 1992a. "Metapragmatic Discourse and Metapragmatic Function." In *Reflexive Language: Reported Speech and Metapragmatics,* edited by J. Lucy, 33–58. Cambridge: Cambridge University Press.

———. 1992b. "The Uses and Utility of Ideology: Some Reflections." *Pragmatics* 2 (3): 311–23.

Silverstein, Michael, and Greg Urban, eds. 1996. *Natural Histories of Discourse.* Chicago and London: University of Chicago Press.

Snyder, Francis. 1981. "Colonialism and Legal Form: The Creation of Customary Law in Senegal." *Journal of Legal Pluralism and Unofficial Law* 9:49–90.

Spear, Thomas. 1978. *The Kaya Complex: A History of the Mijikenda Peoples of the Kenya Coast to 1900.* Nairobi: Kenya Literature Bureau.

Stamp, Patricia. 1991. "Burying Otieno: The Politics of Gender and Ethnicity in Kenya." *Signs: Journal of Women in Culture and Society* 16 (4): 808–45.

Starr, June. 1990. "The Role of Turkish Secular Law in Changing the Lives of Rural Muslim Women, 1950–1970." *Law and Society Review* 23 (3): 497–523.

———. 1992. *Law as Metaphor: From Islamic Courts to the Palace of Justice.* Albany: SUNY Press.

Starr, June, and Jane Collier, eds. 1989. *History and Power in the Study of Law: New Directions in Legal Anthropology.* Ithaca, N.Y.: Cornell University Press.

Steedly, Mary Margaret. 1993. *Hanging without a Rope: Narrative Experience in Colonial and Postcolonial Karoland.* Princeton, N.J.: Princeton University Press.

Stigand, C. H. 1913. *The Land of Zinj.* London: Constable.

Strathern, Marilyn. 1987. "An Awkward Relationship: The Case of Feminism and Anthropology." *Signs: Journal of Women in Culture and Society* 12 (2): 275–92.

Strobel, Margaret. 1975. "Women's Wedding Celebrations in Mombasa, Kenya." *African Studies Review* 18 (3): 35–45.

———. 1979. *Muslim Women in Mombasa, 1890–1975.* New Haven, Conn.: Yale University Press.

Swartz, Marc J. 1979. "Religious Courts, Community, and Ethnicity among the Swahili of Mombasa: An Historical Study of Social Boundaries." *Africa* 49 (1): 29–40.

———. 1982. "The Isolation of Men and the Happiness of Women: Sources and Uses of Power in Swahili Marital Relationships." *Journal of Anthropological Research* 38:26–44.

———. 1983. "Culture and Implicit Power: Maneuvers and Understandings in Swahili Nuclear Family Relationships." In *Political Anthropology,* vol. 2, edited by M. Aronhoff, 19–38. New Brunswick, N.J.: Transaction Books.

———. 1991. *The Way the World Is: Cultural Processes and Social Relations among the Mombasa Swahili.* Berkeley and Los Angeles: University of California Press.

Swartz, Marc, and Yahya A. Omar. 1985. "Relationship Terms and Cultural Conformity among the Swahili of Mombasa." In *Swahili Language and Society: Papers from the Workshop Held at the School of Oriental and African Studies in April 1982,* edited by J. Maw and D. Parkin, 229–46. Vienna: Afro-Pub.

Tannen, Deborah. 1989. *Talking Voices: Repetition, Dialogue, and Imagery in Conversational Discourse.* Cambridge: Cambridge University Press.

Tanner, R. E. S. 1962. "Relationships between the Sexes in a Coastal Islamic Society." *African Studies* 21 (2): 70–82.

———. 1964. "Cousin Marriage in the Afro-Arab Community of Mombasa, Kenya." *Africa* 34 (2): 127–38.

Tedlock, Dennis. 1971. "On the Translation of Style in Oral Narrative." *Journal of American Folklore* 84 (331): 114–33.

Tiersma, Peter. 1993. "Linguistic Issues in the Law." *Language* 69 (1): 113–37.

Trimingham, J. Spencer. 1964. *Islam in East Africa.* Oxford: Clarendon Press.

Tsing, Anna L. 1990. "Gender and Performance in Meratus Dispute Settlement." In *Power and Difference,* edited by J. Atkinson and J. Errington, 95–126. Stanford, Calif.: Stanford University Press.

Urban, Greg. 1991. *A Discourse-Centered Approach to Culture: Native South American Myths and Rituals.* Austin: University of Texas Press.

Vincent, Joan. 1990. *Anthropology and Politics: Visions, Traditions, and Trends.* Tucson: University of Arizona Press.

Wagner-Pacifici, Robin. 1994. *Discourse and Destruction: The City of Philadelphia versus MOVE.* Chicago: University of Chicago Press.

Watson-Gegeo, Karen Ann, and Geoffrey White, eds. 1990. *Disentangling: Conflict Discourse in Pacific Societies*. Stanford, Calif.: Stanford University Press.

Watts, Richard J. 1991. *Power in Family Discourse*. Berlin and New York: Mouton de Gruyter.

Werner, Alice, and William Hichens, trans. 1934. *Mwana Kupona, ca. 1836–ca. 1860. Advice upon Wifely Duty*. Medstead, Hampshire, England: Azania Press.

White, Lucie. 1991. "Subordination, Rhetorical Survival Skills, and Sunday Shoes: Notes on the Hearing of Mrs. G." In *At the Boundaries of the Law: Feminism and Legal Theory*, edited by M. Fineman and N. Thomadsen, 40–58. New York: Routledge.

Williams, Patricia. 1991. *The Alchemy of Race and Rights*. Cambridge: Harvard University Press.

Willis, Justin. 1993. *Mombasa, the Swahili, and the Making of the Mijikenda*. Oxford: Clarendon Press.

Wolf, Margery. 1992. *A Thrice-Told Tale: Feminism, Postmodernism, and Ethnographic Responsibility*. Stanford, Calif.: Stanford University Press.

Wolfson, Nessa. 1978. "A Feature of Performed Narrative: The Conversational Historical Present." *Language in Society* 7 (2): 215–37.

Woolard, Kathryn A. 1992. "Language Ideology: Issues and Approaches." *Pragmatics* 2 (3): 235–49.

Woolard, Kathryn, and Bambi Schieffelin. 1994. "Language Ideology." *Annual Review of Anthropology* 23:55–82.

Yngvesson, Barbara. 1988. "Making Law at the Doorway: The Clerk, the Court, and the Construction of Community in a New England Town." *Law and Society Review* 22 (3): 409–48.

———. 1993. *Virtuous Citizens, Disruptive Subjects: Order and Complaint in a New England Court*. New York: Routledge.

Index